THE LAW OF
EQUITABLE REMEDIES

Other books in *Essentials of Canadian Law* Series

ESSENTIALS OF
CANADIAN LAW

THE LAW OF EQUITABLE REMEDIES

JEFFREY BERRYMAN

Professor of Law
Faculty of Law
University of Windsor

IRWIN
LAW

A Quicklaw Company

Published in 2000 by
Irwin Law
Suite 930, Box 235
One First Canadian Place
Toronto, Ontario
M5X 1C8

ISBN: 1-55221-042-1

Canadian Cataloguing in Publication Data

Berryman, Jeffrey Bruce
   The law of equitable remedies

(Essentials of Canadian law)
Includes bibliographical references and index.
ISBN 1-55221-042-1

1. Equitable Remedies – Canada.   I. Title.   II. Series.

KE1309.B47 2000   347.71'077   C99-933050-0
KF1249.B47 2000

Printed and bound in Canada.

1   2   3   4   5   04   03   02   01   00

SUMMARY
TABLE OF CONTENTS

DETAILED TABLE OF CONTENTS

CHAPTER 3:
INTERLOCUTORY INJUNCTIONS: SPECIFIC AREAS   39

CHAPTER 14:
SPECIFIC PERFORMANCE: CONTRACTS OF PERSONAL SERVICE *271*

CHAPTER 15:
ENFORCEMENT OF CONTRACTS BY INJUNCTIONS *285*

To Hazel and David (deceased)

FOREWORD

Jeff Berryman has written an excellent text that will be of very great value to Judges, Lawyers and Students. This book is extremely well organized and written with commendable clarity. It provided an instructive and interesting weekend of reading for me.

There can be no doubt that we are very much part of a global economy. More and more Canadians are transacting internationally. The importance of interim injunctions in commercial matters is recognized in this book. What must be established is set out clearly and in logical order. Similarly the relatively recent arrival of *Mareva* injunctions is well set out. They have an obvious significance to all those doing business in other countries. Their history and the requirements which applicants must satisfy are carefully reviewed. Similarly *Anton Piller* injunctions and their importance in relation to documents are carefully considered.

Injunctive relief will be sought with ever increasing frequency as Canadians extend their international business activities. This text with its scholarly historical review is presented with an excellent mixture of academic learning and orderly pragmatism. It will be an invaluable resource for all members of the profession.

I have stressed the chapters dealing with injunctions because they are so very important and topical. Yet there are other aspect of equitable relief such as specific performance that are set out with the same orderly clarity that makes this book such a delight to read. It will be a cherished addition to every legal library.

The Honourable Peter Cory, Q.C.

PREFACE

The path taken by Canada with respect to the development of equity and equitable remedies has been quite different from that trod by other Commonwealth common law jurisdictions, most notably the United Kingdom, Australia, and New Zealand. In those countries one will find an active scholarship on the role of equity, and in most law schools a compulsory course can be found with the word "equity" in the title. In Canada, however, there are few modern texts devoted to the understanding of equity itself, although many are written on aspects of equity's progeny, and it is more than likely that a law student will graduate without being exposed to any systematic study of the law of equity or even equitable remedies. This is not to suggest that this state of affairs is necessarily bad, but simply to record an observation.

This book has been written to provide a quick reference to the law that governs the granting of equitable remedies in common law Canada, and will form a companion to Jamie Cassels' book on common law remedies. It is written to assist law students in their legal studies as well as practitioners who require immediate guidance on an area of remedial law that is becoming increasingly important.

In the following chapters, after a brief history of equity, the law relating to specific equitable remedies is detailed starting with interlocutory injunctions. This type of injunction is one of the most frequently sought equitable remedies. Available practically at any time of the day they are the law's para-medics — a quick response to expanding court dockets, complex multi-party litigation, and a remedy of choice giving recognition to new substantive and procedural rights. Chapters 7 to 9 cover permanent injunctions. Chapters 10 to 14 are devoted to the other main coercive remedy, specific performance. In this area Canadian courts have chartered a new course, no longer keeping specific performance as the presumptive remedy in real property contracts. The change wrought in the availability of specific relief for contracts of realty may herald changes in the availability of specific relief in other areas where traditionally it has not played an active role. Chapter 15 deals with the enforcement of contracts by injunctions. An interesting aspect of equitable relief is that it is sanctioned by the use of contempt of court powers — these are outlined in chapter 16 on enforcement. Chapters 17 and 18 look at equitable damages and equitable compensation respectively. The latter remedy has become extremely topical in Canada. Some have argued that it is creating an equitable tort regime. Finally, chapter 19 deals with rectification. Left out of this book is the issue of rescission although it is touched upon in chapter 11. Rescission is inextricably linked to substantive doctrines of contract and the distinction between common law and equitable rescission is seldom drawn. Accounting for profits, tracing, equitable receivers and remedial constructive trusts have also been omitted. Most of these remedies are peculiar to particular areas of substantive law and would make this book less manageable.

I have tried to state the law, as I understand it, as of January 2000. However, equitable remedies is not an area which remains static. While there is little in the way of statutory changes, the evolution of equitable doctrine through cases has been quite rapid over the last three decades. Developments in other countries that share a common law tradition also shape this important subject. Where appropriate, I have included cases and new theoretical perspectives from these countries.

A number of people have made this book possible, In particular my colleagues, George Stewart, William Bogart, Brian Etherington, Lakshman Marasinghe, Raymond Brown, Michael Tilbury of Melbourne University, and Robyn Carroll of the University of Western Australia, have provided their thoughts and critique on ideas developed in this book. Hiroshi Kawanishi, Aaron Atkinson and Rosa Lupo, all student researchers supported by the Ontario Law Foundation, have assisted me on various aspects of this book. A special thanks is owed to Jamie Cassels who reviewed my manuscript and to Jo Roberts for editing it. The completion of the book would not have been possible without William Kaplan's invitation and support to contribute to Irwin Law's Essentials of Canadian Law series, and to Jeffrey Miller for attending to all the technical matters which accompany publication. I must also thank my wife, Carol McDermott, for her endless support and patience while writing this book. Finally, I wish to thank the Honourable Peter Cory for providing a foreword.

CHAPTER 1

HISTORICAL OVERVIEW

A. A BRIEF HISTORY OF EQUITY

This overview begins with a brief history of equity, and concludes with some observations on the state of equity jurisprudence in Canada.

Most legal systems present a paradox. The very *raison d tre* of a legal system is to provide a just ordering and moral guidance to the citizenry. Such a goal places a premium on universality and certainty — a citizen needs to rest secure in his knowledge of the application of laws and legal principles before undertaking activities or entering into adjudication. The paradox is that slavish attention to rules and principles can itself perpetuate an injustice. As any human rights lawyer will attest, nothing is more unjust than the application of a principle of equality in disparate situations. It was against a background of extreme common law rigidity and the need to ameliorate its consequences that the principle of equity developed.[1]

Prior to its transformation between 1700 and 1800, the common law had grown inflexible in both procedure and substantive law. The former was controlled by a writ system which demanded that litigants frame their disputes within a known class of actions; the latter, by a

---

1   The picture of equity presented here follows an Aristotelian approach: see, *Nicomachean Ethics* rev. ed., trans. H. Rackham (Cambridge, Harvard University Press, 1968) Book V, c. 10.

monopolistic concern with the protection of real property and the prevention of civil unrest. Contractual actions, for example, were not
enforced because a promise had been made or consideration had
passed, but rather because the primary means of contracting was
through the creation of a penal bond, the breach of which gave rise to
an action for debt on the bond. The common law also developed a
bifurcated model of adjudication, in which fact-finding lay with the
jury and annunciation of law with the judge.

Confronted with an unyielding common law, and dissatisfied with
its outcomes, litigants would occasionally petition the monarch, and
later the king in council, for a dispensation from the "king's justice".
The frequency of these petitions caused the monarch to pass them on
to his or her chancellor for resolution. Chancellors were drawn from
ecclesiastical circles and, naturally, their reference points were rooted
in canon law and the practices of the ecclesiastical courts. This emerging jurisprudence was marked by its concern for the conscience of the
individual, in the knowledge that the violation of a promise made
before God threatened the promisor's soul. The chancellor, as the sole
arbiter of fact and law, did not distinguish between the two, and hence
his decision making was pragmatic, robust, and highly contextualized.

Contemporary populist notions of equity as a principle which soft-
ened the common law into greater fairness are indeed supported by historical antecedents. The notion that the chancellor could hear a petition
and grant a dispensation from the rigours of the common law finds its
modern equivalent in the notion that equity is only available after proof
that the common law is deficient or inadequate. The concern for the
protection of a person's conscience imbues the modern concern with
the protection of fiduciary duties, confidential information, and the
coercive enforcement of contracts by specific performance.

The common law judges did not sit idly by while the chancellor
continued dispensing justice. These inroads undermined not only the
supremacy of the common law, but also the pecuniary self-interest pursued by both judges and court officials in having litigants brought
before the common law courts. In the political transformation of
England in the seventeenth century the power of the chancellor, as an
executive arm of the King, was placed under scrutiny. The common
law courts, whose judges had aligned themselves with the cause of Parliament during the Civil War, saw to it that equity would have a much
diminished role in the future. Chancery courts also became victims of
their own success. The recognition given to parol (oral) contracts and
to the "use," or trust — perhaps equity's greatest contribution to contemporary jurisprudence — meant that more litigants sought assistance.

The highly particularized and idiosyncratic justice of early equitable principles gave way to the establishment of procedural and substantive rules and doctrines.

During the eighteenth and early nineteenth centuries England experience both unprecedented population growth and the emergence of a commercial class. As a result, land and varying divisions of real property took on increasing importance. Equity jurisprudence became preoccupied with property disputes, particularly concerning trusts and the recognition that equity gave to equitable title. The new theories of *laissez-faire* economics and social Darwinism carried over into law. The earlier values of equity were not consistent with these new philosophies. (Even at this stage there were relatively few equity judges, and the ability of one chancellor to exert a profound influence on equity jurisprudence was still very real. Lords Nottingham (1673–82), Hardwicke (1736–56), and Eldon (1801–27) are credited most with schematizing equity.[2]) At the same time, the common law courts had transformed their own procedures and substantive law. New forms of property and capital developed out of dealings with shares, goods, services, labour and manufacturing, and found a receptive place in the common law courts.

At the close of the nineteenth century equity jurisprudence appeared even more ossified than the common law had ever been, and less relevant. The description of the chancery court immortalised by Charles Dickens in *Bleak House* was most apt. The Judicature Acts of 1873–75 that fused common law and chancery courts brought about a procedural rationalization in which the substantive content of two great doctrinal areas could be administered in each other's respective court. But by then the populist notion of equity "taking the pinch out of the common law shoe" was truly emasculated.

B. THE RECEPTION OF EQUITY INTO CANADA

The introduction of equity jurisdiction into Canada varies from province to province. For example, in Nova Scotia chancery practice was introduced as part of the prerogative powers of the lieutenant-governor

---

2   Writing in 1818, Lord Chancellor Eldon could state, "[I]t is not the duty of a Judge in equity to vary rules, or to say that rules are not to be considered as fully settled here as in a court of law"; and "The doctrines of this Court ought to be as well settled and made as uniform almost as those of the common law": see *Davis v. Duke of Marlborough* (1819), 2 Swan. 108, 36 E.R. 555 at 569 (Ch.); and *Gee v. Pritchard* (1818), 2 Swan. 402, 36 E.R. 670 at 674 (Ch.).

whereas in Ontario it required the passage of legislation. The experience of Ontario is given have as a representative sample of the often chequered history of chancery practice in Canada.

There was no great demand for equity jurisdiction in Upper Canada prior to its legislative creation in 1837. Where equity's intervention was warranted common law courts did what they could, or the Executive Council would intervene by passing private legislation. Within the Province there was a distinct hostility to the creation of a chancery court. The practicing bar, experienced in common law, saw no need; the legislature believed the expense was not justified; and the public held a general suspicion about a chancery court that, based on English experience, was known for long delays and increased litigation costs. However, by 1837 the growth in the Province's population and the demand this created for a more sophisticated legal system gave sufficient impetus to create a distinct chancery court.

Unfortunately, once in operation the court began to emulate the worst practices of its English counterpart, and leaders in the legal profession were quickly calling for reform or abolition. Throughout the next two decades many reforms were suggested, and some enacted. However, by 1873 the idea that there should be a fusion of law and equity had taken hold. In that year legislation was enacted which made it possible for a case initiated in one court to be resolved in the other, as long as the matter fell within the second court's jurisdiction. Each court, however, retained its own procedure. This transition stage to full fusion enabled both courts to become familiar with each other's jurisdiction and methods. In 1881 the final step was taken. One court, although still retaining distinct divisions, could now exercise both substantive jurisdictions, and provided one unified procedure to handle all civil disputes. Finally, in 1913 legislation dismantled the divisional structure and created one common court.

A hallmark of Canadian experiences on the development of equity is that the creation of a separate and distinct chancery court came late and was relatively short-lived. As such, at no time did a strong independent chancery bar develop. For example, writing in 1847, *The Globe* newspaper noted that there were only "two or three distinguished chancery lawyers" practicing in Ontario.[3] Although Canadian developments largely followed similar reforms in the United Kingdom, New York was also an influence — by 1881, New York had thirty years of experience in successfully fusing common law and chancery courts

---

3   *The Globe* (6 October 1847).

in one unified court structure. Without a strong chancery bar,[4] and because lawyers in Canada have not maintained a bifurcated bar between barristers or solicitors,[5] Canadian Courts have tended to eschew debates about the nature of fusion and have created a distinctive equity jurisprudence.

C. MODERN EQUITABLE JURISDICTION

Most equity writers commence a section under this title by distinguishing between the exclusive or original jurisdiction of equity, and an ancillary jurisdiction supportive of common law rights. In the former is placed the law of trusts, a fiduciary's obligation, and the protection of confidences. In the latter are the remedies of specific performance, injunction, rescission and rectification. There is nothing functionally wrong with this classification but I would suggest that it does not give a true picture of modern equity practice in Canada.

Canadian equity has been shaped by five specific developments.

1) Perhaps the first, although not necessarily an obvious one, has been the development of restitution and the fact that it is doctrinally based on the notion of unjust enrichment. In Canada, this happened at an early stage. It is normally traced to the Supreme Court of Canada's decision in *Deglman* v. *Guaranty Trust Co. of Canada*.[6] The Canadian doctrine of unjust enrichment asks three questions:

   • Has there been an enrichment by the defendant?
   • Has it been at the expense of the plaintiff resulting in a corresponding impoverishment?
   • Is there any juristic justification for the transfer?

---

4   The significance of this fact should not be under-estimated. As a comparison, one should note the development of equity in Australia, which is doctrinally better articulated than in Canada. Much of this doctrinal development and writing comes out of New South Wales, which only legislated concurrent jurisdictions in common law and equity as late as 1972.

5   As part of fusion in 1881 the Law Society of Upper Canada assumed jurisdiction over barristers (a term used for those lawyers who practiced in the common law courts), counsel (a term used for those lawyers who practiced in the chancery court), attorneys (a term used for those engaged in conveyancing and drafting documents), and solicitors (a term used in chancery courts to describe those lawyers engaged in drafting trusts and contracts), and admitted lawyers as both barristers and solicitors.

6   [1954] S.C.R. 725.

As a result, Canadian jurisprudence has been forced to review the notion of a person acting in "good conscience" earlier than many other jurisdictions. The third question (is there any juristic reason that explains the transfer) gives a court-wide latitude to bring various forms of conduct within the rubric of unjust enrichment. The notion of "conscience" is no longer a protection of an individual or subjective conscience; rather, it is an expression of normative behaviour expected of a party in a particular relationship that is amenable to legal scrutiny. But in Canada we have become used to seeing the expression of conscience in ever-expanding fields as courts have extended the notion of fiduciary, the protection of confidences, and the requisite level of care expected of professionals. In a book on equitable remedies it is not necessary to delve further into the extension of substantive equitable rights through the rubric of unjust enrichment (restitution), apart from noting that Canada has had a comparatively longer history of being willing to undertake such extension, and that as a necessary corollary, remedial adaptation has been a consistent feature of our law.

Building a jurisprudence around unjust enrichment has also tender to focus concern on substantive outcome. Again, this can be contrasted with both Australia and the United Kingdom where emergent restitutionary trends tend to focus on unconscionable conduct, and are thus dominated by a concern with procedural unfairness.

2) As mentioned earlier, Canadians have tended to avoid debates about the fusion of law and equity. There is no clarion call against the fusion fallacy, as found in other jurisdictions,[7] and few passionate champions of doctrinal purity. We have been willing to mix equitable and common law remedies, and to review case outcomes informed by the remedial goal being pursued rather than be tied to a remedy that was historically awarded based on the particular cause of action commenced.

3) Much recent remedial development, such as the remedies for breach of fiduciary duty and growth in demand for interlocutory relief, respond to profound social changes: in particular, the process of capital accretion, the transformation from manufacturing to a service and knowledge economy, and increased technological sophistication,

---

7   The fusion fallacy refers to the argument that the fusion of equity and common law was only of procedure and not substantive doctrine. See discussion at Chapter 1, section D. "Jurisdiction." For its most eloquent argumentation, see the work of R. P. Meagher, W.M.C. Gummow & J.R.F. Lehane, *Equity, Doctrines and Remedies*, 3d. ed. (Sydney: Butterworths, 1992).

demand new legal responses. We are entering an era in which the main capital assets of a business are the particular systems and processes of manufacturing rather than the machines themselves. Thus, for example, a car manufacturer still has an assembly plant to produce a physical product. However, its main wealth lies in intangibles, such as its systems of product design, that take a model from concept to market in months rather than years; its management systems, ensuring just-in-time delivery of parts to reduce inventory; its creative advertising to generate demand; and its product financing schemes for customers. These assets are amorphous and ephemeral. It is only a collection of legal rights and remedies that give them value. Many of these assets are held by knowledge workers who now have the capacity to take their skills away with them rather than being required to bring simple physical and manual dexterity to the factory floor. The remedies needed to protect these new assets are quite different from those developed alongside the traditional manufacturing economies of the past.

Another function of a service economy is the increasing importance of leisure as a part of well-being. We have not emerged into the leisure society often envisaged in the 1960s, when our greatest fear was not knowing what we would do with all our leisure time. Nevertheless, we do see leisure, be it sport, home entertainment, dining, or travel, as a significant part of our "lifestyle". A third of our disposable income goes to these pursuits and to the increasingly complex structures that support them. Consider the contractual arrangements in professional sports: the player contracts that keep a star player bound to a team, or a sponsor to a player; the legal arrangements of a team in a league; the rights to broadcast an event; and the endorsements of products and sponsors. Such contracts were almost unheard of when the Judicature Acts were passed, and the legal remedies needed to support them are very different from those envisaged in an earlier time. Much of this development has called upon equity for assistance.

In the fall of 1998 pressure on Asian economies led to a massive stock market fall, the repercussions of which reverberated around the world. The causes of this collapse were manyfold, but one underlying fact made it all possible — the rapid transfer of money from one jurisdiction to another made possible by technology. This new globalization of our economic, legal, and political systems calls into question the continued relevance of the nation state which is either powerless or reluctant to control such movement. Again, the legal structures that support this new world filter down to our more mundane domestic legal systems; for example, in orders to restrain the removal or transfer of assets and to determine the appropriate forum for litigation.

4) At the turning of the century, Canada has emerged as a multicultural society with a plurality of political, religious, and cultural values, and a commensurately complex statutory regime supporting competing visions of a virtuous life. Added to this milieu has been the enactment of the *Canadian Charter of Rights and Freedoms*,[8] necessitating the rapid creation of an interpretive jurisprudence by the Supreme Court of Canada. Increasingly, Canadians find resolution of social issues in the law. The fashioning and declaring of rights between individuals, and between government and individuals, has challenged the courts. While much of the statutory material provides clear guidance of these rights, it is often left for the courts to fashion remedies from a general exhortation to do what is "just and convenient". Again, the traditional remedies of injunction and declaration have been used in this field.

5) Canada is a federal, bilingual, and bijural country. A federal country experiences different tension than unitary states around *stare decisis*, rules of civil procedure and jurisdiction. Canada's vast geographical size has also shaped our beliefs about the value of land and the practices we adopt for its transfer. Another significant influence is the common border we share with the United States of America, a country that generates an enormously influential jurisprudence and acts as a stimulus of intellectual ideas.

The above is not to suggest that doctrine no longer plays a part in modern Canadian equity. Indeed, now more than ever there appears to be a need for doctrinal structure to provide guidance after a period of unprecedented growth.[9] However, equity's development in Canada will probably continue to reflect its early history rather than be bound by rigid doctrinal precedents received from afar. In the text that follows, the intent is both to articulate the applicable principles and to identify the underlying features which influence, or should influence, a court in determining the availability of an equitable remedy.

---

8   Part 1 of the *Constitution Act, 1982*, being Schedule B to the *Canada Act 1982* (U.K.), 1982, c. 11.

9   See the call made by Madame Justice B.M. McLachlin, "The Place of Equity and Equitable Doctrines in the Contemporary Common Law World: A Canadian Perspective" in D. Waters, ed., *Equity, Fiduciaries and Trusts 1993* (Scarborough, Ont: Carswell, 1993) 37.

D. THE RELATIONSHIP BETWEEN RIGHTS AND REMEDIES, AND COMMON LAW AND EQUITABLE REMEDIES

There are two axis in the remedial matrix; the relationship between substantive right and remedy, and that between common law and equitable remedies.

1) The Relationship between Rights and Remedies

On this axis, debate centres on three approaches:

a) A monistic view of remedies as being inseparable from rights, which sees remedies as having the sole goal of maximizing the right.

b) A clear differentation between right and remedy, particularly with respect to function. Rights should be morally aspiring, certain, and principled, while remedies are pragmatic and discretionary. The rules setting out rights and remedies have quite distinct structures, justifications, and goals.

c) An acknowledgment of the differences in structures, justifications, and goals, with a recognition of a high level of integration between the two. Under this approach an adjudicator is often seen as moving backyard and forward along the axis, in fashioning both a right and a remedy, informed by studying the other respective end of the pole.[10]

One illustration of the difference among these three approaches is the treatment of remedies for trespass to real property. Under the first approach, the protection of property from trespass would best be attained, and thereby maximized, by grant of an injunction. Such a remedy enforces the principle that the only way to acquire a right of transgression is by consensual agreement, irrespective of any competing interest the trespasser may have. Under the second approach, a remedy of damages may be favoured simply based on difficulties with enforcing an injunction. Under the third approach, an injunction may be varied, to balance the fear that confining a property owner to damages may give the trespasser a private right of expropriation against the social utility of the trespasser's conduct. An adjudicator may thus move

---

10 See the discussion by K. Cooper-Stephenson, "Principle and Pragmatism in the Law of Remedies" in J. Berryman ed. *Remedies: Issues and Perspectives* (Scarborough, Ont.: Carswell, 1991) 1.

towards fashioning a suspended injunction (where the injunction is granted but its enforcement suspended for a period of time) or a compensatory injunction (the injunction is granted but the property holder pays compensation to the trespasser) as an appropriate response.

I tend towards the latter two approaches. It would seem contradictory in a text about "equitable" remedies not to see them as having distinctive structures, justifications and goals. This is particularly so where equity carries overtones of its historical role as ameliorating the common law; and (even without these echoes) where traditionally the law has spoken of an "ancillary" role for equitable remedies. The extent to which equitable remedies inform and shape substantive rights, i.e. the differentation between the second and third approaches, does not have to be resolved here. This is a text about possibilities: it assumes proof of a substantive right and suggests when, and which, equitable remedies may arise.

2) The Relationship between Common Law and Equitable Remedies

The question here becomes whether the traditional hierarchy, that accorded common law damages as of right and equitable remedies as within the court's discretion, is still relevant. While much academic writing suggests that the law of remedies has entered a stage of non-hierarchical integration, it is difficult to discern an explicit acceptance of this in judicial opinions. While I am somewhat drawn intellectually to the former, this text is written accepting the latter. Much discussion centres on where and how the applicable discretionary threshold is drawn. Underlying the academic writing is the desire for remedial flexibility, in the simple belief that maybe the plaintiff does actually know what she wants. It is up to the defendant to refute the plaintiff's remedy of choice. But for judges, who traditionally conceive their role as the top of an adjudicative apex, it is difficult to escape from the position that the "discretion", in that equitable remedies are said to be discretionary, is for the judge alone to exercise.

FURTHER READINGS

BERRYMAN, J., ed., *Remedies: Issues and Perspectives* (Scarborough, Ont.: Carswell, 1991)

BROWN, E., "Equitable Jurisdiction and the Court of Chancery in Upper Canada" (1983) 21 Osgoode Hall Law Journal, 275

Law of Remedies: Principles and Proofs, [1995] Spec. Lect. L.S.U.C.

PARKINSON, P., ed., *The Principles of Equity* (Sydney: The Law Book Company, 1996)

PERELL, P.M., *The Fusion of Law and Equity* (Markham, Ont.: Butterworths, 1990)

SHARPE, R.J., *Injunctions and Specific Performance*, looseleaf (Aurora, Ont.: Canada Law Book, 1998)

TILBURY, M., *Civil Remedies* (Sydney: Butterworths, 1990)

WATERS, D.W.M., ed., *Equity, Fiduciaries and Trusts* (Agincourt, Ont.: Carswell, 1993)

CHAPTER 2

INTERLOCUTORY INJUNCTIONS: GENERAL PRINCIPLES

A. INTRODUCTION

There are three distinct stages in any civil proceeding:

- the period leading up to the trial,
- the actual trial resulting in a judgment, and
- the executing of the judgment.

The interlocutory phase refers to any part of the period prior to judgment. Interlocutory proceedings can focus on the matter in dispute or simply support some ancillary aspect of the claim.

An injunction is an order granted by a court of competent jurisdiction that instructs a (legal) person to do, or refrain from doing, a particular thing. Thus, an interlocutory injunction is simply an injunction granted during any proceeding prior to judgment. It is one of the most potent weapons in the court's remedial arsenal. Open any case report, and the odds are high that an interlocutory injunction application will be reported. Because the orders are available prior to any proceeding being launched they are unique in the law of remedies. But this extraordinary characteristic also underlies the potential for abuse, where the injunction becomes an unwarranted intrusion in a person's affairs. Courts have insisted on particular safeguards being followed in granting interlocutory injunctions and in their execution. Some of these safeguards vary depending on the cause of action filed to support the request for the order.

An interlocutory injunction can literally be sought at any time. Where the circumstances warrant, it can be granted without notice first being served on the defendant and without proceedings having been started. These characteristics make the interlocutory injunction an essential tool in litigation management. In fact, much of the attraction of the remedy is the ability to get a preliminary trial of the disputed merits, which may assist in settlement discussions or avoid costly court delays in hearing cases.

An interlocutory injunction is also an important public law remedy: for example, a government agency may seek the remedy to enforce public rights. It is also utilised by individuals as a remedy against governmental (in)action by public agencies, particularly against a background of a traditional reluctance in law to award damages in such circumstances.

In many disputes an interlocutory injunction can quickly shift the focus from what is originally cast as a private and mono-centric dispute into a public and poly-centric one. For example, an interlocutory injunction granted to prevent a nuisance generated by the construction of a building may well lead to the total cessation of work, with immediate consequential repercussions for all those associated with the project. These secondary parties will not be party to the dispute but may bear the initial brunt of the remedy. In some areas where there is a high element of public interest in the outcome, legislatures have stepped in to provide guidance, or to remove entirely the courts' jurisdiction to grant interlocutory orders.

Unlike a damages judgment, where the successful plaintiff must seek further judicial remedies for enforcement and where the court thus plays a rather passive role, an interlocutory injunction is immediately binding on the party to whom it is addressed and invites proceedings for contempt if the order is disobeyed. While such proceedings are still initiated by a successful plaintiff there is an immediacy between the potential contempt and the contempt proceedings that is lacking in the process of rendering a defendant a judgment debtor. For this reason, and because non-observance is an immediate challenge to judicial authority, courts have paid greater attention to the administration of injunctions.

From this quick introduction it can readily be seen that interlocutory injunctions present myriad issues that must be analyzed.

B. THE FUNCTION OF INTERLOCUTORY INJUNCTIONS

An injunction granted prior to a proper trial of the merits cannot have as its primary function the settlement of the dispute. The rationale for interlocutory injunctions lies elsewhere, in the effective management of the dispute by both the parties and the court. Originally, it was argued that the primary function was the maintenance of the status quo. Unfortunately, defining what the status quo was, and from whose vantage-point, proved to be an illusory goal. For example, take the enforcement of a restraint of trade clause. Is the status quo, normally defined as the last point of time when the parties were in harmony, when the defendant left the plaintiff's employment; when he started a business; or when the defendant's activities began to impinge on the plaintiff's actual revenues? Should the injunction force the closure of the defendant's business, or merely prevent further solicitation of new clients or work? Further, new situations called for much more than preservation of the status quo, however defined. For example, the *Mareva* injunction, a restraint on the removal of assets by a defendant from the court's jurisdiction, went further than merely freezing future activities of the defendant. Rather, it required affirmative acts of compliance over matters totally outside the area of dispute, simply to ensure the effectiveness of judgment once, and if, awarded.

The contemporary justification for interlocutory relief lies in the need to fashion an order that ensures effective relief can be rendered at the final trial. This goes beyond a forensic identification of the status quo and seeks to identify existing and potential risks that both parties will experience while waiting for trial, as well as risks in the conduct of the trial and the enforcement of judgment. While all litigation entails some form of delay and hence further loss to one or both litigants, it is only the risk of irreparable harm that supports the need for preliminary intervention by a court.

C. TERMINOLOGY

The definition of an interlocutory injunction has already been given in the introduction. The term "interlocutory" will be used in this book, although it is common for rules of civil procedure to refer to "interim" injunctions as well. An interim injunction is normally one that has been granted for a specified period. The plaintiff must return to the court at the end of this period to seek the injunction's continuance. A fixed period of time is designated

- to ensure that the litigants will return to court to report on the success or otherwise of the court's order,
- to allow the defendant time to file a response,
- to permit cross examination on the plaintiff's affidavit evidence

An interlocutory injunction is normally enforceable until trial or some other determination of the action. A motion for an interlocutory injunction will usually be made with notice to the other side; however, in special circumstances it can be made *ex parte* (without notice to the other side). An interlocutory injunction application can also be heard *in camera*, where the public is excluded from the hearing, to preserve confidentiality.

D. JURISDICTION

The ability of Canadian common law courts to grant injunctions derives from two sources.

1) "Just and Convenient" Equitable Relief

Found in most of the common law provinces is a statute that carries forward the fusion of law and equity from the old Judicature Acts into their modern idiom,[1] that a court has the power to award interlocutory relief wherever it is "just and convenient" to do so. For a time there was a body of opinion that fusion only meant procedural fusion, and that to determine whether equitable relief could be granted post-Judicature Acts one had to find an existing precedent within the old chancery courts pre-Judicature Acts. This opinion has given way to the view that, even accepting the premise of procedural fusion only, the passage of time and judicial development since the Acts supports both substantive fusion and a recognition that new rights created over the last 100 years merit similar developments in the law of remedies.[2]

2) The Inherent Jurisdiction of a Superior Court

The second source of jurisdiction derives from the peculiar notion that superior court of record exercises an inherent jurisdiction. It is because

---

1 See Alberta, *Judicature Act*, R.S.A. 1980, c. J-1, ss. 4, 5; British Columbia, *Law and Equity Act*, R.S.B.C. 1996, c. 253, ss. 4, 5; Manitoba, *The Court of Queen's Bench Act*, S.M. 1988-89, c. 4, ss. 32, 33(3); Nova Scotia, *Judicature Act,* R.S.N.S. 1989, c. 240, s. 41; Ontario, *Courts of Justice Act*, R.S.O. 1990, c. C.43, s. 96; and Prince Edward Island, *Supreme Court Act*, R.S.P.E.I. 1988, c. S-10, s. 29.

2 See *United Scientific Holdings Ltd.* v. *Burnley Borough Council*, [1978] A.C. 904 (H.L.); *LeMesurier* v. *Andrus* (1986), 54 O.R. (2d) 1 (C.A.), leave to appeal to S.C.C. refused, [1986]; 2 S.C.R. v.; and *Canson Enterprises Ltd.* v. *Boughton & Co.*, [1991] 3 S.C.R. 534.

our superior courts can trace their lineage through antiquity to the earliest English courts that they carry this designation. Inherent jurisdiction operates in two ways.

a) The first way ensures that there will always be a court to vindicate a legal right where one is found to exist. This power will more commonly be found in provincial Superior Courts, or courts of general jurisdiction.

b) A second way concerns the inherent jurisdiction held by superior courts to control their own procedures, of which the granting of interlocutory injunctions is but one manifestation.

A statutory court, that is, the Federal Court, will have its inherent jurisdiction in the first sense of the term proscribed by its empowering statute, but will, nevertheless, retain broad inherent jurisdiction, as used in the second sense of the term, to control its own procedures, including the issuing of injunctions.[3] In contrast, inferior courts are confined in both senses of the term, to the jurisdiction found in their empowering statute and the remedial powers provided therein. Thus, for example, there is no power in Ontario's Small Claims Court to issue an interlocutory injunction.[4]

The jurisdiction to grant an interlocutory injunction is given in aid of a substantive legal claim — it is not available simply when the applicant believes that a wrong has been suffered and that it would be "just and convenient" to have an order. The plaintiff must show that an interlocutory injunction is necessary to protect an existing recognized "legal" right, one that is justiciable. However, as we shall soon see, in section E.1., "Accessibility Thresholds," the claim that a justiciable legal right exists is flexible, particularly in light of the fact that at the interlocutory stage the level of proof the plaintiff needs to demonstrate such a claim can vary significantly.

---

3   In *Canada (Human Rights Commission)* v. *Canadian Liberty Net*, [1998] 1 S.C.R. 626 [*Canadian Liberty Net*], a majority of the Supreme Court held that the Federal Court had the power within its inherent jurisdiction to grant an interlocutory injunction enforcing a human rights commission's finding that the applicant was guilty of a discriminatory practice, and requiring it to desist its activities pending a hearing of a human rights tribunal. The granting of the interlocutory injunction was consistent with a fair and liberal interpretation of the Court's statutory authority to exercise control over the exercise of power by federal administrative decision makers. The result of the majority opens the door to concurrent jurisdiction between the Federal Court and provincial superior courts. The dissenting minority would have strictly construed the Federal Court's inherent jurisdiction, to minimize the possible overlap with provincial superior courts.

4   *Moore* v. *Canadian Newspapers Co.* (1989), 69 O.R. (2d) 262 (Div. Ct.).

A second aspect of jurisdiction asks whether a plaintiff must have a justiciable substantive claim within the court's jurisdiction before being granted an interlocutory injunction. As the following discussion will show, both the House of Lords and the Supreme Court of Canada have recently addressed this issue, although apparently coming to contrary results. The Supreme Court of Canada appears to have adopted a liberal attitude to a court's jurisdiction and whether the plaintiff's substantive claim must come before the same court that has granted the interlocutory relief. The English House of Lords, however, has vacillated on this point, concerning the granting of a *Mareva* injunction.[5]

In *Siskina (Cargo Owners)* v. *Distos Compania Naviera S.A.*, *The Siskina*,[6] the House of Lords ruled that a Mareva injunction would only be awarded where the plaintiff's substantive cause of action was justiciable within the court's own jurisdiction. In that case the plaintiff had sought an injunction to restrain the removal of insurance proceeds from the United Kingdom in a shipping dispute in which the cause of action was only justiciable in a foreign court.

However, in *Channel Tunnel Group Ltd.* v. *Balfour Beatty Construction Ltd.*,[7] the House of Lords reconsidered its position in *The Siskina*. In this case the defendant was employed by the plaintiff to construct the English Channel tunnel. The contract contained a compulsory arbitration process to resolve disputes using arbitrators located in Brussels. A dispute arose and the defendant proposed to withdraw its services. Such a proposal was in clear contravention of the construction contract and the process agreed upon to resolve disputes. The plaintiff brought an action in the United Kingdom, where the defendant was resident, to prevent the withdrawal of services and to enforce the dispute resolution mechanism in the contract. The defendant sought a stay of proceedings. The House of Lords resolved the appeal in affirming the defendant's stay of proceedings. Much of this part of the dispute centred on the interpretation of the relevant *Arbitration Act*[8] provisions.

However, the court also considered the broader issue of its jurisdiction to grant the plaintiff an injunction based on the power to grant an injunction where it is "just and convenient to do so." The defendant maintained in argument that a court did not have power to grant an injunction pursuant to that court's inherent jurisdiction in any case which the parties

---

5   See *Mareva Compania Naviera S.A.* v. *International Bulkcarriers S.A.*, *The Mareva* (1975) [1980], 1 All E.R. 213n (C.A.), and discussion below.
6   (1977), [1979] A.C. 210 (H.L.).
7   [1993] A.C. 334 (H.L.).
8   *Arbitration Act 1975* (U.K.), 1975, c. 3.

had agreed was subject to foreign arbitration, particularly where the court had issued a stay in favour of preserving that arbitration process.

The House of Lords did not accept the defendant's contentions. Lord Browne-Wilkinson, with whom all but Lord Mustill concurred on this point, interpreted *The Siskina* as having two requirements: One, that the defendant was amenable to service, either personally or subject to the rules of service outside the court's jurisdiction; and two, that the plaintiff required interlocutory relief in support of a cause of action recognized in English law. However, the claim, while recognized in English law, did not require that the final order on the substantive cause of action come from an English court. An English court had jurisdiction to grant interim relief, even where a final order could only come from some other court or arbitral body. Lord Mustill hesitated from adopting Lord Browne-Wilkinson's approach on this issue. Rather, he confined himself to the situation concerning arbitration and the need for ancillary relief. However, from his remarks it would appear that the only occasion when the principles in *The Siskina* would limit the ability of a court to grant interlocutory relief would be where both parties were foreign and had not chosen England as the seat of the arbitration. Any purported ousting of jurisdiction would be ineffective. Once the court has been asked to rule, it would appear from Lord Mustill's tenor that the court has jurisdiction. However, jurisdiction and exercise of discretion must be distinguished and on the latter point Lord Mustill would not have granted the plaintiff the injunction.

In *Mercedes-Benz A.G. v. Leiduck*,[9] the Privy Council reaffirmed the restrictive approach taken in *The Siskina*. There the plaintiff was again seeking a *Mareva* injunction, to restrain the removal of assets from Hong Kong. Neither plaintiff nor defendant was a resident of Hong Kong, and the substantive cause of action, based on a breach of contract, was justiciable in Monaco where litigation had been commenced. The only connection to Hong Kong was the fact that the defendant had another company incorporated there and the evidence suggested that the defendant may have applied some of the allegedly misappropriated funds from the disputed contract to his Hong Kong company. The plaintiff, fearing that the defendant might also transfer his funds out of Hong Kong into a safer haven, brought an action before the Hong Kong courts solely for a *Mareva* injunction. A majority of the Privy Council accepted Lord Mustill's contention that "[t]he court has no power to make orders against persons outside its territorial jurisdiction unless

---

9   [1995] 3 W.L.R. 718.

authorised by statute" and that there was "no inherent extra-territorial jurisdiction."[10] The court relied upon the particular wording of the Hong Kong code of civil procedure, which was identical to the United Kingdom code. The Privy Council could not find a statutory power to support a *Mareva* injunction standing alone, where it was not ancillary to a justiciable cause of action within the court's own jurisdiction.

A dissenting opinion was given by Lord Nicholls. He prefaced his remarks with the observation that it would appear unjust if a person operating internationally could so easily defeat the judicial process. Lord Nicholls referred by analogy to the *Channel Tunnel* case. If two parties resident in Hong Kong agreed their dispute would be resolved in another jurisdiction, the Hong Kong court would, nevertheless, have jurisdiction to restrain the removal of assets from Hong Kong pending the outcome of the dispute in the other jurisdiction. But for the contractual provision, the plaintiff could have continued with its action before the Hong Kong court. Does the result differ where the defendant does not reside within the Hong Kong court's jurisdiction? Lord Nicholls differs with the majority in saying that it does not make a difference because the pursuit of a *Mareva* injunction can stand alone; thus, it falls within the relevant civil code provisions regarding service of foreigners. In what capacity can a *Mareva* injunction stand alone? The *Mareva* injunction is granted in support of a prospective foreign judgment, not merely as ancillary to a cause of action. Nor should the prospective nature of the relief bar its grant. As Lord Nicholls points out, there are other examples, such as *quia timet* injunctions, which have prospective effect. Similarly, the issuing of a *Mareva* injunction may only be effective in some circumstances in advance of the point at which it could legally be said that the cause of action accrued. Finally, we are apt to give far greater attention to the notion of a cause of action. This is a lawyer's term for the type of facts that give rise to a cause of action. The causes of action are never closed and already "extends very widely, into areas where identification of the underlying 'right' may be elusive."[11]

By Order in Council the English legislature has now effectively reversed the decision in *Mercedes-Benz A.G.* v. *Leiduck* by allowing the High Court to grant interim orders in aid of an action commenced, or about to be commenced, in a foreign country.[12]

---

10   *Ibid.* at 725.

11   *Ibid.* at 738.

12   See Order in Council, The Civil Jurisdiction and Judgments Act 1982 (Interim Relief) Order 1997 (S.I. 1997 No. 302) and the decision in *Credit Suisse Fides Trust S.A.* v. *Cuoghi* [1997] 3 All ER 724.

The Supreme Court of Canada has recently addressed jurisdictional issues and interlocutory relief in the context of a labour dispute. In *Brotherhood of Maintenance of Way Employees Canadian Pacific System Federation* v. *Canadian Pacific Ltd.*[13] the Supreme Court had to determine whether the British Columbia Supreme Court had jurisdiction to award an interlocutory injunction preventing the immediate implementation of a new work schedule imposed by Canadian Pacific Ltd. while the union was grieving the issue before an arbitrator. Under the *Canada Labour Code*[14] there was no interim relief which either the arbitrator, before whom the grievance was heard, or the federal Labour Relations Board could award to prevent the implementation of the new scheduling pending the arbitrator's decision. Two distinct questions were raised before the Supreme Court. The first dealt with whether a court had jurisdiction to award relief where there was a purportedly exclusive code of remedies in the applicable legislation. On this issue the Supreme Court reiterated its earlier line of authority, indicating deference, but not servility, to an administrative regime by saying that where the *Canada Labour Code* provided "no adequate alternative remedy" the court had a jurisdiction to grant relief.[15] The second question clearly raised the issue whether the British Columbia court had jurisdiction to grant interlocutory injunctions in circumstances where there was no cause of action to which the injunction was ancillary. On this issue, the Supreme Court took the position that a court has jurisdiction "to grant an injunction where there is a justiciable right, wherever that right may fall to be determined."[16] The Supreme Court reiterated this position, assuming that it was the approach adopted by the House of Lords following the *Channel Tunnel* decision.

The Canadian position gives a wide jurisdiction to a court to grant interlocutory relief, without the need for it to be ancillary to a substantive cause of action justiciable in the court's own jurisdiction. This position would now appear to be at odds with that practiced by courts in the United Kingdom. In Canada there must still be a justiciable issue, but this will go to whether the plaintiff has attained the requisite threshold to support this form of equitable relief. Jurisdiction must also be kept distinct from the exercise of discretion to grant an injunction. Concerns about extra-territorial reach, service, and enforcement go to discretion, not jurisdiction.

---

13   [1996] 2 S.C.R. 495 [*Brotherhood*]. See also *Canadian Liberty Net*, above note 3.
14   R.S.C. 1985, c. L-2.
15   *Brotherhood*, above note 13 at 499.
16   *Ibid.* at 505.

E. THE TEST FOR INTERLOCUTORY INJUNCTIONS

1) Accessibility Thresholds

Before an interlocutory injunction can be granted, the plaintiff must prove that she has a legal cause of action supporting the demand for injunctive relief. An immediate dilemma for the court becomes apparent: What level of proof of a claim is required, and how can that be accurately assessed prior to a full-blown trial of the merits? A legal cause of action requires two essential components — an infringed legal right, and factual evidence pointing to that infringement. Accessibility thresholds describe the minimum level of proof of both components that a plaintiff must demonstrate before the case can move to an examination of the discretionary merits.

Underlying accessibility is concern about the appropriateness of giving a remedy prior to proper merit adjudication, but this is balanced against judicial timeliness, measured in further losses or transgressions of the plaintiff's rights. These issues bring into play competing claims of irreparable harm by the litigants depending on whether or not the injunction is granted. The court also has institutional concerns with respect to credibility if it makes a wrong decision at an interlocutory stage, and with perceptions about case management where interlocutory proceedings take precedence over other trials.

Most judgments in common law countries tend to confuse accessibility thresholds and claims to irreparable harm. Often what results is a checklist of factors with little in the way of guidance to their use. The issues should be kept distinct. Varying accessibility thresholds leads to uncertainty in application for similarly situated claims, resulting in otherwise meritorious plaintiffs failing to secure relief. A high threshold will also encourage litigants to treat interlocutory proceedings as an effective preliminary trial, when the conditions traditionally thought necessary to make that effective, such as examination of witnesses, legal argument, and contemplative judicial time, are not present. It is also difficult to see how adoption of varying standards filters its way through to what the plaintiff must demonstrate at the interlocutory stage. Does a strong *prima facie* case require more affidavit evidence than a "serious question to be tried"?

The classical model for interlocutory injunctions required a plaintiff to demonstrate a *"prima facie"* case.[17] *Prima facie,* in this context,

---

17   *Challender* v. *Royle* (1887), 36 Ch. D. 425.

means that the plaintiff has provided sufficient affidavit evidence coupled with a valid substantive claim to prove his case such that he would
win at trial. This finding could only be disturbed if further evidence
came to light that detracted from the probative value of the evidence
provided at the interlocutory hearing, or provided additional pertinent
facts. This standard was significantly altered by the House of Lords in
American Cyanamid Co. v. *Ethicon Ltd.*[18] The appellant, American Cyanamid, was the registered proprietor of a patent for absorbable sutures
that disintegrated once they had served their purpose and were then
absorbed into the body. The respondent, Ethicon, also marketed
sutures made from animal tissue called catgut. At the time the appellant introduced its patented product in 1970, the respondent was the
dominant supplier of catgut sutures in the United Kingdom. By 1973,
the appellant had succeeded in capturing fifteen percent of the suture
market. Concerned at this inroad into the suture market, the respondent launched its own absorbable suture. The appellant immediately
alleged that the respondent's suture infringed its patent and launched
an interlocutory injunction action to restrain the respondent from marketing absorbable sutures in the United Kingdom. In the trial court,
after a three day hearing, an interlocutory injunction was granted. This
was subsequently reversed in the Court of Appeal after an eight day
hearing. Both lower courts felt constrained by authority to apply a
prima facie test as the appropriate threshold model.

The House of Lords reversed the Court of Appeal and restored the
trial judge's decision. In coming to that decision, the court effectively
lowered the threshold to requiring the court to be "satisfied that the
claim is not frivolous or vexatious," that "there is a serious question to
be tried," and that the plaintiff has a "real prospect of succeeding."[19]
The rationale for doing this was based on the unreliability of making
determinations on conflicting affidavit evidence of substantive claims
without benefit of detailed argument and in a climate of judicial haste.
The threshold articulated was to be applied generally across all spheres
of law (although this has not been the outcome in the United Kingdom) and applied to both the factual issues of infringement as well as
the legal claim that such a right existed.

In Canada, *American Cyanamid* met with a mixed reception. While
it was generally followed, other competing threshold tests survived. In
Yule Inc. v. *Atlantic Pizza Delight Franchise (1968) Ltd.*,[20] a decision that

---

18   [1975] A.C. 396 (H.L.).

19   *Ibid.* at 406–08.

20   (1977), 17 O.R. (2d) 505 (Div. Ct.) [*Yule*].

has been repeatedly cited in Canada, three differing tests were posited. In addition to the *American Cyanamid* test are the classical model and "multi-factor" tests. The classical model (also called the "multi-requisite" test) requires a strong *prima facie* threshold. The "multi-factor" test also utilizes a strong *prima facie* standard, but does not characterize it as an initial threshold; it is merely one of six factors to be considered in exercising the discretion to grant interlocutory relief.[21]

The tendency has been for a lack of consistency in determining an appropriate threshold. Higher standards have been required by some courts in particular causes of actions — for example, the enforcement of restraint of trade clauses has normally been drawn at the higher *prima facie* or strong *prima facie* threshold tests, as have requests for *Mareva* and *Anton Piller* injunctions. Further Canadian developments will now have to be viewed in light of the Supreme Court of Canada's decision in *RJR-MacDonald Inc.* v. *Canada (A.G.)*.[22]

In *RJR-MacDonald*, the Supreme Court considered the applicable test for interlocutory relief sought by a plaintiff who wished to restrain the implementation of the federal government's restrictions on tobacco advertising, pending a challenge to the constitutionality of the legislation. The Supreme Court accepted the *American Cyanamid* standard, indicating that it was quite undesirable for a trial judge to engage in a "prolonged examination of the merits."[23] The adoption of this threshold was justified considering the complex nature of assessing constitutional rights. The Supreme Court's application of the *American Cyanamid* test (formulated in an intellectual property dispute), in a constitutional setting, coupled with its tacit endorsement of Sharpe's[24]

---

21   The other five factors are:
- if the plaintiff's action doesn't succeed at trial can the plaintiff pay damages?
- is the order necessary to maintain the status quo?
- will the plaintiff suffer irreparable harm without the injunction?
- the balance of convenience, and
- does the defendant's interest merit equal consideration to that of the plaintiff?

22   [1994] 1 S.C.R. 311 [*RJR-MacDonald*].

23   *Ibid.* at 338.

24   The Supreme Court reference to R.J. Sharpe, *Injunctions and Specific Performance*, was to the 2d ed. (Aurora, Ont.: Canada Law Book, 1992): "The *American Cyanamid* standard is now generally accepted by the Canadian courts, subject to the occasional reversion to a stricter standard": at 2-13. In the looseleaf ed. (1998) the text has been revised to read: "While *Cyanamid* has generally been followed in Canada and England, in several instances judges have balked at the prospect of ignoring or minimizing the strength of the plaintiff's case. There has also been a subtle tendency to elevate the standard to be met by the plaintiff on the merits": at § 2.280.

statement of the Canadian position, suggests a high level of acceptance of a low threshold test across all areas.

The threshold test of "serious issue to be tried" requires the plaintiff to raise an issue either of fact or law requiring resolution. Crossing this low threshold simply allows the plaintiff to move to the discretionary phase of the interlocutory proceedings and to the need to show why the injunction is necessary. As part of this inquiry the court may ultimately return to the plaintiff's substantive merits but the threshold requirement should rarely be used to prevent the plaintiff from being granted interlocutory relief.

2) Irreparable Harm

Having crossed the accessibility threshold the plaintiff moves to the discretionary phase of the interlocutory injunction proceedings. In this phase the plaintiff is required to demonstrate that without the interlocutory injunction she will suffer irreparable harm. The notion of irreparable harm both incorporates and substitutes for the traditional discretionary barrier to equitable remedies; namely, proof that common law remedies are inadequate. In one sense, because there is no equivalent or competing common law remedy at the interlocutory stage (the closest may be in the area of self-help remedies such as replevin), the common law remedy must be *ipso facto* inadequate. In another sense, the very harm complained of at the interlocutory phase may be capable of actual quantification, and therefore the common law remedy will *ultimately* be available and adequate, yet an interlocutory injunction may still be granted.

Irreparable harm as a concept means a harm that is incapable of being remedied by any other means at the time of trial. It is the plaintiff's exposure to this particular type of harm that justifies the interlocutory intervention. As suggested above, this is the critical phase of the interlocutory proceedings, because it goes to the very heart of the issue in fashioning what is necessary to ensure that effective relief is awarded at the trial of the merits. Despite the centrality of this issue few courts have ever developed a systematic way of reviewing claims of irreparable harm. Often what happens is that the issue of irreparable harm quickly becomes subsumed into an assessment of the merits.

Irreparable harm requires an assessment of a number of issues.

- How is the harm irreparable?
- How much harm is irreparable?
- Who will suffer the irreparable harm?

Determining how harm is irreparable requires an assessment of how the law would normally compensate for the particular harm raised: if the common law remedy of damages is adequate, then equitable intervention is unjustified.

In the area of public law, where damages do not play a significant remedial role, does an evaluation of irreparable harm have to be measured against the availability and adequacy of other public law remedies? Yet adequacy is measured in degrees. Does the test require serious or minor inadequacy? In other cases the inadequacy may not stem from difficulties in identification and quantification but in the financial ability of the defendant to pay. Does this count? Yet another problem is whether irreparable harm suffered by third parties, who may or may not be party to the dispute, should be evaluated. In the area of public law often the claim of irreparable harm will be to the public interest. How is this claim to be evaluated?

In *RJR-MacDonald*, the Supreme Court gave its approach to irreparable harm in the following terms:

> "Irreparable" refers to the nature of the harm suffered rather than its magnitude. It is harm which either cannot be quantified in monetary terms or which cannot be cured, usually because one party cannot collect damages from the other.[25]

The Court also clearly indicated that at this stage it is the applicant's irreparable harm alone that is the sole focus. It should be recalled that the Supreme Court was addressing interlocutory injunctions in a constitutional context where it freely admitted that the claim of irreparable harm, given the relatively undeveloped jurisprudence on the availability of *Charter* damages, was quickly established. Focusing upon the "nature of the harm" and conceiving it in terms of difficulties with monetary quantification is consistent with most other court decisions. Magnitude is unimportant at this stage, but this is not significant because it will immediately return at the next stage — consideration of the balance of convenience.

The types of harm that have been found to constitute irreparable harm defy any rational classification. The case reports do not always distinguish between whether it is the nature of the harm that is regarded as irreparable, or whether the plaintiff failed to demonstrate that she would in fact suffer the harm claimed, and thereby failed to

---

25   *RJR-MacDonald*, above note 22 at 341.

meet the evidential burden. In order to give some overview, what follows is a non-exhaustive list of the types of injuries that courts have readily found as constituting irreparable harm.

a) Harm that has traditionally defied quantification; for example, harm to reputation, career enhancement, or which threatens to harm a person's career.[26]

b) Harm to the viability of a business, including goodwill, market share, or a person's livelihood.[27]

c) Claims in support of a restraint of trade clause.[28]

d) Claims based on some intellectual property infringement, patent, copyright, passing off,[29] protection of confidentiality, or fiduciary relationship.[30]

e) Claims where the quantification of damages is known but where they are unlikely to be recovered.[31]

f) Claims dealing with the infringement of some natural resource or with the quiet enjoyment of land.[32]

g) Claims that raise an infringement of the public interest as constituting irreparable harm.[33]

3) Balance of (In)convenience

A plaintiff who has crossed the accessibility threshold and shown a risk of irreparable harm has largely proved his case. However, the grant of an

---

26   See *Mott-Trille* v. *Steed* (1996), 27 O.R. (3d) 486 (Gen. Div.); *Kernaghan* v. *Softball Saskatchewan* (1987), 42 D.L.R. (4th) 364 (Sask. Q.B.): *T.(S.)* v. *Stubbs* (1998), 38 O.R. (3d) 788 (Gen. Div.); and *Elguindi* v. *Canada (Minister of Health)* (1996), [1997] 2 F.C. 247.

27   See *R.L. Crain Inc.* v. *Hendry* (1988), 48 D.L.R. (4th) 228 (Sask. Q.B.); *Yule*, above note 19; *Daishowa Inc.* v. *Friends of the Lubicon* (1996), 27 O.R. (3d) 215 (Div. Ct.), leave to appeal to S.C.C. refused, [1996] S.C.C.A. No. 528; and *Kun Shoulder Rest Inc.* v. *Joseph Kun Violin and Bow Maker Inc.* (1997), 72 C.P.R. (3d) 373 (F.C.T.D.).

28   See *Tradeland Agencies Ltd.* v. *MacKinnon* (1979), 5 Sask. R. 438 (Q.B.).

29   See *General Mills Canada Ltd.* v. *Maple Leaf Mills Ltd.* (1980), 52 C.P.R. (2d) 218 (Ont. H.C.); and *Source Perrier (Societe Anonyme)* v. *Canada Dry Ltd.* (1982), 36 O.R. (2d) 695 (H.C.).

30   See *Drabinsky* v. *KPMG* (1998), 41 O.R. (3d) 565 (Gen. Div.).

31   *Mareva* injunctions: see *David Hunt Farms Ltd.* v. *Canada (Minister of Agriculture)*, [1994] 2 F.C. 625 (C.A.).

32   See *MacMillan Bloedel Ltd.* v. *Mullin*, [1985] 3 W.W.R. 577 (B.C.C.A.), leave to appeal to S.C.C. refused [1985] 5 W.W.R. lxiv; and *Bolton* v. *Forest Pest Management Institute* (1985), 21 D.L.R. (4th) 242 (B.C.C.A.).

33   See *RJR-MacDonald*, above note 22.

interlocutory injunction is obviously going to impact upon the defendant's rights, with the real possibility of the incursion of irreparable harm by the defendant. In *American Cyanamid*, Lord Diplock observed:

> the plaintiff's need for ... protection must be weighed against the corresponding need of the defendant to be protected against injury resulting from his having been prevented from exercising his own legal rights for which he could not be adequately compensated under the plaintiff's undertaking in damages if the uncertainty were resolved in the defendant's favour at the trial. The court must weigh one need against the other and determine where "the balance of convenience" lies.
>
> It would be unwise to attempt even to list all the various matters which may need to be taken into consideration in deciding where the balance lies, let alone to suggest the relative weight to be attached to them. These will vary from case to case.[34]

The issues discussed under the previous heading are equally applicable here, but there are also some particular issues that weigh in the defendant's favour.

a) Delay

An unexplained delay by a plaintiff after she becomes aware of a possible infringement of rights can impact in two ways. The delay may constitute evidence that the harm suffered by the plaintiff is not considered serious and thus not irreparable. Or, in the period of delay the defendant may have significantly changed its position, thus increasing the likelihood of incurring irreparable harm. In *American Cyanamid*, the House of Lords distinguished between the situation where a defendant was merely required to postpone commencement of a marketing opportunity, and the situation where a defendant would be required to stop actual production and selling of a product line.

b) Undertaking

A plaintiff is normally required to give an undertaking in damages so that if the plaintiff is unsuccessful in its suit the defendant has immediate recourse after proof of loss to recover. Even if the potential harm to the defendant is quantifiable in damages, and thus not irreparable, courts have insisted upon a real and meaningful undertaking given by

---

34 Above note 18 at 406, 408. This passage was specifically endorsed in *RJR-MacDonald*. See also *Manitoba (A.G.) v. Metropolitan Stores (MTS) Ltd.*, [1987] 1 S.C.R. 110.

the plaintiff. Although impecuniosity of the plaintiff and the inability to give a meaningful undertaking is not an absolute barrier to the granting of an interlocutory injunction, it has been described as a potent factor.[35]

Once a court is confronted with competing claims of irreparable harm it is required to undertake a true balancing of convenience. At this stage courts readily move towards finding comparative disadvantage to both parties, which justifies moving to merit adjudication to tip the balance. This was an approach reluctantly endorsed in *American Cyanamid*, although, in the context of constitutional litigation, it is not an approach that the Supreme Court found favour with in *RJR-Mac-Donald*. Despite the Supreme Court's exhortations that the magnitude of irreparable harm should not be considered when initially reviewing the plaintiff's claim for interlocutory relief, it inevitably creeps back in under the guise of balance of convenience. Courts conceive of comparative irreparable harm as a type of arithmetic product, of probability of success multiplied by risk of harm. Whoever will experience the most, wins the case.

It is difficult to withstand the allure of merit adjudication to tip the balance. The nature of legal practice constantly entails assessment of risk and determinations on the probabilities of outcomes. Naturally, these traits are brought to the motions' court. But focusing on merit adjudication, even if it is inevitable, tends to subsume at least two other tasks that could be undertaken, and which would better ensure attainment of the goal of interlocutory injunctions; that is, to ensure effective relief at the date of trial.

The first task that could be undertaken by a court is to subject the respective claims of irreparable harm to heightened scrutiny. Does the evidence actually address the claims of irreparable harm, or is it primarily aimed at showing the strength of the plaintiff's allegations of infringement?

The second task would be to consider what alternative type of order could be fashioned to meet the competing claims. On occasion courts have refused to grant an interlocutory injunction after extracting from the defendant an undertaking to keep proper records of

---

35   See *Allen v. Jambo Holdings Ltd.*, [1980] 1 W.L.R. 1252 (C.A.); and *Cambridge Credit Corp. Ltd. (Receiver Appointed) v. Surfers Paradise Forests Ltd.*, [1977] Qd. R. 261 (S.C.) [*Cambridge Credit*].

account, so that the plaintiff's losses can be more readily quantified if she wins the case,[36] or to undertake some other restorative work.[37]

Other possible solutions would be for the court to insist upon an expedited hearing process of the merits, or to require the parties to negotiate an interlocutory order tailored to their particular needs.[38]

One area where preliminary merit adjudication seems unavoidable is where the interlocutory injunction application will be determinative of the issues between the parties. This exception was recognized in *N.W.L. Ltd.* v. *Woods, The Nawala,*[39] a case dealing with picketing and the rights of a trade union to "black" the plaintiff's ship from any port in the United Kingdom. In declining to grant an injunction the court recognized that the parties would never return to court to try the merits, and that any such action would be futile in a labour context and go only to exacerbate labour relations. In this context it was appropriate to tip the balance of convenience based on an appreciation of the likely outcome if the matter had gone to trial. In addition to the labour field, this exception has been applied in numerous cases. For example, it has been applied where the facts were not in dispute,[40] where the sole issue was a question of law,[41] where the issue was a question of reasonableness of a restrictive covenant,[42] where there was little dispute on the facts and the sole issue is a question of law,[43] where the injunction was sought to inhibit free speech,[44] and where the injunction was needed to enforce an intellectual property right.[45]

Once the court has determined that the balance of convenience lies with the plaintiff the interlocutory injunction should be granted.

---

36   See *Cemasco Management Ltd.* v. *Analysis Film Releasing Corp.* (1979), 24 O.R. (2d) 389 (H.C.).

37   See *Kamloops (City of)* v. *Southern Sand & Gravel Co.* (1987), 43 D.L.R. (4th) 369 (B.C.S.C.) (order requiring the defendant to cover excavated site with topsoil and reseed).

38   See N. Campbell, "The Interlocutory Injunction in Canada: Reading Smoke Signals" (1995) Spec. Lect. L.S.U.C. 211.

39   [1979] 1 W.L.R. 1294 (H.L.).

40   See *Dialadex Communications Inc.* v. *Crammond* (1987), 57 O.R. (2d) 746 (H.C.).

41   See *R.* v. *Secretary of State for Transport, ex parte Factortame Ltd. (No.2),* [1991] 1 A.C. 658 (H.L.); and *Ontario Federation of Anglers & Hunters* v. *Ontario (Ministry of Natural Resources)* (1999), 43 O.R. (3d) 760 (Sup. Ct.).

42   See *Cantol Ltd.* v. *Brodi Chemicals Ltd.* (1978), 23 O.R. (2d) 36 (H.C.).

43   See *C-Cure Chemical Co. Ltd.* v. *Olympia & York Developments Ltd.* (1983), 71 C.P.R. (2d) 153, leave to appeal to C.A. refused (1983), 33 C.P.C. 192n.

44   See *Canada Metal Co.* v. *Canadian Broadcasting Corp.* (1975), 7 O.R. (2d) 261 (Div. Ct.).

45   See *Smith, Kline & French Canada Ltd.* v. *Novopharm Ltd.* (1983), 72 C.P.R. (2d) 197 (Ont. H.C.).

4) Alternative Tests for Interlocutory Injunctions[46]

Although both the classical and *American Cyanamid* models dominate discourse on the appropriate tests for interlocutory injunctions in Anglo-Canadian law, there are other competing models.

John Leubsdorf has proffered a model for determining the standard for interlocutory relief based on the concept of integrating both the accessibility threshold and irreparable harm.[47] Leubsdorf starts by illustrating the dilemma a court faces between the risk that one party will suffer irreparable harm and the further risk that the court will be proved to have acted erroneously in making its decision. Confronted with this dilemma, the court should evaluate on whom the greatest risk of irreparable loss exists. Where risk is borne exclusively by the applicant, the injunction should be granted. Although there is still a risk that this decision will ultimately be proven to have been erroneous, the harm caused the defendant can readily be compensaated at trial. The converse applies if the risk of irreparable harm falls exclusively on the defendant, in which case the injunction should be denied. Of course, these are not hard cases. Where both sides raise the spectre of incurring irreparable losses, Leubsdorf suggests the court should first "appraise the likelihood that various views of the facts and the law will prevail at trial" and, second, "assess the probable loss of rights to each party if [the court] acts on a view of the merits that proves to be erroneous."[48] A combination of these two factors will identify the party who is likely to suffer more irreparable harm. Leubsdorf admits that his model incorporates the same features as the *American Cyanamid* approach, but, rather than sequentially ordering them, he attempts to demonstrate their interrelationship, the sum of which gives a measure of irreparable harm.[49]

Richard Posner, both as judge[50] and as academic,[51] has in typical Posnerian fashion rendered Leubsdorf's approach into a formula. The

---

46   I have canvassed the arguments raised in this section more fully in J. Berryman, "Interlocutory Injunctions and Accessibility Thresholds: Or Once More Round the Mulberry Bush" (1989) 5 I.P.J. 137.

47   See J. Leubsdorf, "The Standard for Preliminary Injunctions" (1978) 91 Harv. L. Rev. 525.

48   *Ibid.* at 541.

49   Tacit support in the United Kingdom for Leubsdorf's model can be found in *Films Rover International Ltd.* v. *Cannon Film Sales Ltd.* (1986), [1987] 1 W.L.R. 670 (Ch.).

50   See *American Hospital Supply Corp.* v. *Hospital Products Ltd.*, 780 F.2d 589 (7th Cir. 1985).

51   See R.A. Posner, *Economic Analysis of Law*, 5th ed. (New York: Aspen Law & Business, 1998).

injunction should be granted "if but only if $P(Hp) > (1 - P)Hd$ where P is the probability that the plaintiff will prevail in the full trial on the merits (and therefore $1 - P$ is the probability that the defendant will prevail), Hp is the irreparable harm that the plaintiff will suffer if a preliminary injunction is not granted to maintain the status quo pending the trial, and Hd is the irreparable harm the defendant will suffer if the preliminary injunction is granted."[52]

R.G. Hammond (now a judge of the New Zealand High Court) challenges Leubsdorf's model on the issue that to require a judge to measure the likelihood that she is wrong in her assessment of the plaintiff's claim of infringed legal rights would require a Herculean effort of self-criticism, and is extremely subjective. Hammond offers his own alternative of a "variable threshold" model.[53] In his model, the appropriate accessibility threshold should be determined only after discerning what is the real nature of the dispute and what type of threshold is appropriate for that kind of dispute. Thus, a strong *prima facie* test may be appropriate where the issue involves defamation and the public interest of free speech, while a lower good arguable case threshold may be appropriate where the issue is one of public safety.[54] Unfortunately, Hammond's model is open to criticism where the choice of threshold is equally left to the subjective whim of the judge. The burden on the plaintiff would seem appreciable where the plaintiff could not readily tell in advance what threshold test he would be expected to meet. The plaintiff could also be drawn into a preliminary trial to determine the appropriate threshold level.

The apparent difference between Leubsdorf's model and that adopted in *American Cyanamid* is that in the former the judge is required to determine the probability of judgment error, and factor that into the calculation of who will suffer the most irreparable loss. In the latter case, the judge is to assume judicial error and then to determine the extent of irreparable harm as a consequence. However, determining the probability of judicial error seems very close to determining the strength of the applicant's case. The risk of error increases as the allegedly infringed legal right appears more marginal, either as a matter

---

52   *Ibid.* at § 21.4.

53   See R.G. Hammond, "Interlocutory Injunctions: Time for a New Model?" (1980) 30 U.T.L.J. 240.

54   Support for Hammond's approach can be found in *Yule*, above note 20; and in *Beecham Group* v. *Bristol Laboratories Pty. Ltd.* (1968), 118 C.L.R. 618 (Austl. H.C.), although *Beecham* was rejected in *Australian Coarse Grain Pool Pty. Ltd.* v. *Barley Marketing Board of Queensland* (1982), 46 A.L.R. 398 (Austl. H.C.).

of substantive law or for lack of a complete evidential base. In this sense, Leubsdorf's model fails at the same point that *American Cyanamid* does: when both parties can demonstrate aspects of irreparable loss, it requires the court to return to an analysis of the merits of the applicant's case. It is for this reason that I have argued that less attention should be paid to determining the appropriate accessibility threshold and more attention focused on the respective parties' claims of irreparable loss. Varying thresholds can only act to deter otherwise meritorious claimants, whereas focusing and enriching our analysis of irreparable harm returns us to the underlying rationale for interlocutory relief, namely, to fashion an order that ensures effective relief can be rendered at the final trial. While returning to the strength of the substantive merits may be inevitable, it is important to realize that much can be done before this point is reached.

F. UNDERTAKINGS

As indicated earlier, an undertaking in damages will normally be required from a plaintiff when seeking an interlocutory injunction unless the court orders otherwise. If a plaintiff either fails at trial, or abandons the claim, the defendant is entitled to recover all damages flowing from the wrongfully obtained interlocutory injunction "unless there are special circumstances to the contrary." Such damages can include full solicitor and client costs necessary to defend the litigation, particularly where the defendant has had to defend against the plaintiff's serious allegations maintained over a long period.[55] (A municipality that was unsuccessful in enforcing its zoning bylaw where the defendant had found a loophole in the relevant legislation was nevertheless shielded from any claim under its undertaking, as it fell within a special circumstances exemption.)[56]

The undertaking is given on behalf of the plaintiff and is owed to the court. It does not create any contractual relationship with the defendant and thus cannot be used to support either a suit or counterclaim. Where the plaintiff is either the Crown or other public authority, they have not normally been required to give an undertaking unless

---

55   See *Church of Jesus Christ of Latter Day Saints v. King* (1998), 41 O.R. (3d) 389 (C.A.).

56   See *Ontario (A.G.) v. Yeotes* (1982), 35 O.R. (2d) 248 (H.C.), appeal allowed on merits (1981), 31 O.R. (2d) 589 (C.A.), leave to appeal to S.C.C. refused (1981), 37 N.R. 356n.

they are suing to enforce their own proprietary rights.[57] The undertaking must be real and meaningful. While an impecunious plaintiff will not be denied an interlocutory injunction because her undertaking is worthless, impecuniosity is a "potent factor" to be taken into account when deciding to grant an interlocutory injunction.[58] But the court may dispense with the need for an undertaking where the plaintiff's case is compelling and she does not have the financial capacity to give an undertaking.[59] It is possible for the defendant to ask that the plaintiff fortify his undertaking by posting a bond or some other form of security. The onus lies on the defendant to establish that fortification is necessary, and is met when the defendant can show "a likelihood of a significant loss arising as a result of the injunction and a sound basis for belief that the undertaking will be insufficient."[60] It is also possible for the court to seek an undertaking from the defendant to keep proper records, so that the plaintiff will be able to prove and quantify his loss, in return for denying the plaintiff his injunction application.[61]

G. *EX PARTE* APPLICATIONS

Where it is either not feasible to serve the defendant in a timely fashion, or where the plaintiff requires the element of surprise to protect its position, an interlocutory injunction can be made *ex parte* (without notice). Such an order will only be granted in the most extraordinary circumstances and should only be given for such period of time as is necessary to protect the plaintiff's position and to afford time to serve proper notice. Rule 40.02(1) of Ontario's *Rules of Civil Procedure*[62] states that an injunction ordered without notice cannot be granted for a period longer than ten days. In rare situations the order can be granted even before an action has been commenced. In these circumstances the court will require an additional undertaking from the plaintiff to file pleadings. Because the defendant is not present, courts have

---

57   See *Hoffmann-La Roche & Co. (A.G.)* v. *Secretary of State for Trade and Industry* (1974), [1975] A.C. 295 (H.L.).

58   See *Cambridge Credit*, above note 35.

59   See *Delta (Corporation of)* v. *Nationwide Auctions Inc.* (1979), 100 D.L.R. (3d) 272 (B.C.S.C.).

60   *Supreme Court Practice 1995 (U.K.)*, O. 29 s. 3 (*The White Book*), cited with approval in *McCaffery Group Inc.* v. *Bradlee* (1997), 204 A.R. 334 at 338 (Q.B.).

61   See *Kraus Group Inc.* v. *McCarroll*, [1995] 9 W.W.R. 633 (Man. Q.B.).

62   R.R.O. 1990, Reg. 194, r. 40.02(1).

insisted upon strict compliance with a plaintiff's lawyer's duty to the court to make full and frank disclosure of all material facts, even those which are adverse to the plaintiff's position. Full and frank disclosure requires that:

1) Material facts must be fully disclosed — that is, — those which are material for the judge to know when dealing with the application as made. Materiality is for the court to determine, not the plaintiff's legal advisers.
2) The applicant must make proper inquires before the application is made. This is an objective test and covers facts that the applicant could have known if reasonable steps had been taken over such inquires.
3) The extent of these inquires must depend on all the circumstances of the case including
   (a) the nature of the applicant's case,
   (b) the probable effect on the defendant if the order is granted, and
   (c) the degree of legitimate urgency at the time of making inquires.
4) If material non-disclosure is proven then the court should ensure that the applicant is deprived of any advantage she may have derived from the wrongfully obtained injunction. However, whether the fact not disclosed is of sufficient materiality to justify or require immediate discharge of the order, without examination of the merits, depends on the importance of the facts to the issues which were to be decided by the judge on the application. The innocence of the applicant in either not perceiving the relevance of the non-disclosed fact or not being aware of the fact itself, is an important but not decisive consideration.
5) Not every omission to disclose will automatically result in the discharge of the injunction. Ultimately it is a question of how the court should exercise its discretion.[63]

Failure to abide by the duty to make full and frank disclosure will be taken seriously by the court. In addition to the discharge of the injunction it may also lead to an adverse award for solicitor and client costs, and ultimately an award of punitive damages at the trial of the merits.[64]

---

63   These factors were taken from *Brink's-MAT Ltd.* v. *Elcombe*, [1988] 1 W.L.R. 1350 (C.A.), as approved in *Pulse Microsystems Ltd.* v. *SafeSoft Systems Inc.* (1996), 134 D.L.R. (4th) 701 (Man. C.A.). See also *United States of America* v. *Friedland* [1996] O.J. No. 4399 (Nov. 5th 1996) (Ont. Gen. Div.).

64   See the award of aggravated damages in *Columbia Picture Industries Inc.* v. *Robinson* (1986) [1987] Ch. 38 (Ch.), but which should be more accurately regarded as punitive damages.

An applicant can also request that a motion for an interlocutory injunction be heard *in camera*. Under the respective provincial rules of civil procedure (for example, in Ontario see section 135 of the *Courts of Justice Act*[65]) a court may order that the public be excluded from a hearing where there is a possibility of serious harm or injustice to any person. Courts have stressed the paramount importance of ensuring the openness of court proceedings to the public and will only exercise the power to exclude where it is "necessary to protect social values of superordinate importance."[66] Speculation on the adverse impact that public awareness may have on an applicant's business is not of sufficient importance to justify exclusion of the public.[67]

In addition to authorizing an *in camera* proceeding, a court can also allow a plaintiff to use John or Jane Doe as an alias. The court can also seal the record, preventing access other than to counsel of record, in the following situations:

- where public disclosure would threaten the safety of a witness,
- to protect a child,
- to protect a secret process, or
- where the administration of justice would be rendered impracticable by the presence of the public.[68]

H. JOHN AND JANE DOE ORDERS

In some situations a plaintiff will not know the names of all the potential defendants who are impinging on his or her rights — common examples are an interlocutory injunction used to prevent protesters picketing a plaintiff's business or trespassing, or where the plaintiff's intellectual property rights are being violated by unknown street or market vendors. In these types of situations the courts have condoned the use of a John and Jane Doe order. Two distinct questions arise:

- Can an injunction be made against a person who is unknown?
- Can an injunction be effective against a person not a party to the litigation?

Both these questions are answered in the affirmative.

---

65   Above note 1.

66   *Canadian Newspapers Co.* v. *Canada (A.G.)* (1985), 49 O.R. (2d) 557 at 576 (C.A.).

67   See *McCreadie* v. *Rivard* (1995), 43 C.P.C. (3d) 209 (Ont. Gen. Div.).

68   See *John Doe* v. *Canadian Broadcasting Corp.* (1993), [1994] 2 W.W.R. 666 (B.C.S.C.), aff'd (1993), [1994] 2 W.W.R. 679 (B.C.C.A.) [*John Doe*].

With respect to the second question, the Supreme Court of Canada has held that a non-party to a suit is nevertheless bound to obey an order where their actions fall within the scope of the order. In *Mac-Millan Bloedel Ltd.* v. *Simpson*,[69] MacMillian Bloedel had successfully obtained a series of interlocutory injunctions aimed at preventing pro-testers from blocking the logging operations in British Columbia. The orders had named several defendants by name, followed by a general description — "John Doe, Jane Doe and Persons Unknown." The defen-dant fell into this category and appealed the decision to grant the injunction. The first ground of appeal concerned whether the court had jurisdiction to grant an injunction against the public in a civil matter, preventing conduct that properly fell within the criminal law and was amenable to criminal prosecution by the attorney general. At the time of these actions the attorney general had taken the decision not to lodge criminal charges against the protesters, preferring to leave it to the given property owners through the civil courts. The Supreme Court held that the individual property owner had standing to sue where his own prop-erty right was being interfered with, or where the plaintiff experienced special damage as a result of an interference to a public right.

With respect to a suit against unidentified persons, the Supreme Court noted the paradox presented by existing authorities: only a person named in a suit was bound by it, but every citizen had the obligation to obey a court order on pain of being charged with contempt of court. The resolution of this paradox required the dominance of the latter proposi-tion if the rule of law meant anything. Protection was given to unnamed parties in a requirement that they be made aware of the order and the consequences of disobeying it, and be afforded an opportunity to comply before its enforcement. In addition, the order should be clear and circum-scribed to cover only what is necessary to protect the plaintiff's rights.

With respect to the first question (can an order be made against unnamed parties?) the Supreme Court did not have to deal with this matter, based on its findings that even an unnamed person must com-ply with a court order. The court observed that this was an issue of pleadings, which had not been litigated, although it opined that no authority had been given to suggest that the use of such appellations would invalidate an order.

Because our courts rarely deal with hypothetical issues and are dependent upon a *lis*, or suit, a John and Jane Doe action is a legal fic-tion that entitles the plaintiff to seek relief against unknown persons by

---

69   [1996] 2 S.C.R. 1048.

making them a party. As long as the court is assured that a cause of action exists, a plaintiff should not be deprived of appropriate relief simply because the defendant has been able to obscure her identity. The import issue is to ensure that the defendant, once known, has an opportunity to challenge the injunction. This has been the position taken by the Federal Court of Appeal with respect to injunctions that have been used in actions for copyright and trademark infringement against some known and named defendants as well as unknown street vendors and market stall operators. In *Montres Rolex S.A.* v. *Balshin*,[70] the Federal Court of Appeal indicated that a John and Jane Doe order should not be granted where the plaintiff has failed to take reasonable steps to name the putative defendant and that caution should be exercised.[71] In addition, a John and Jane Doe order would not be issued against prospective defendants once the plaintiff had proven it held copyright in a trial of the merits against other John and Jane Doe defendants. Against prospective defendants the plaintiff would have to initiate a new action.

I. APPELLATE REVIEW

Because the granting of an interlocutory injunction is a discretionary matter appellate courts have limited the role of review. It is not sufficient to overrule the trial judge simply because the appellate court would have exercised the judge's discretion differently. The trial judge's assessment can only be set aside if one of the following circumstances exists:

- it demonstrates a misunderstanding of the law or of the evidence before the court;
- a wrong inference has been drawn, which later evidence has shown to be in error;
- there has been a change of circumstances after the order that would have justified the trial judge varying the initial order; or
- the trial judge's order is so aberrant that no reasonable judge could have reached the decision.

After satisfying any of the above, an appellate court is entitled to exercise its own discretion as if the matter was *de novo*.[72]

---

70 (1992), [1993] 1 F.C. 236 (C.A.).
71 John and Jane Doe has also been authorized by a court as the style of cause where the court has agreed to keep the identity of a litigant hidden from the public: see *John Doe*, above note 68.
72 See *Hadmor Productions Ltd.* v. *Hamilton* (1982), [1983] 1 A.C. 191 (H.L.).

FURTHER READINGS

BEAN, D.M.A., *Injunctions* 7th ed. (London: F.T. Law & Tax, 1997)

CAMPBELL, N., "The Interlocutory Injunction in Canada: Reading Smoke Signals", [1995] Spec. Lect. L.S.U.C. 211

CRERAR, D.A., "'The Death of the Irreparable Injury Rule' in Canada" (1998) 36 Alta. Rev. 957

MEEHAN E. & J.H. CURRIE, *Injunctions* (Scarborough, Ont.: Carswell, 1996)

PERELL, P.M., "The Interlocutory Injunction and Irreparable Harm" (1989) 68 Can. Bar Rev. 538

SHERIDAN, L.A., *Injunctions in General* (Chichester, U.K.: B. Rose, 1994)

STOCKWOOD, D., *Injunctions: A Practical Handbook* (Agincourt, Ont.: Carswell, 1985)

CHAPTER 3

INTERLOCUTORY INJUNCTIONS: SPECIFIC AREAS

This chapter covers particular specific areas where interlocutory injunctions have been applied. The chapter is not intended to be an exhaustive digest of all areas but examines the more commonly awarded interlocutory injunctions, and the special rules, or adaptations to the general principles detailed in the previous chapter, which exist.

A. MANDATORY INTERLOCUTORY INJUNCTIONS

It is necessary to add a further refinement to our injunction taxonomy. Most injunctions are normally classified as being "prohibitive," in that they seek to enjoin the defendant from continuing a particular course of action — in the case of interlocutory orders, down to the point of judgment. The other type of injunction, the "mandatory" injunction, can be broken down into two sub-classifications: The first, "restorative mandatory injunctions," requires the defendant to repair the consequences of her own wrongful act. The second type requires the defendant to continue performing some positive obligation that may be derived from a contractual or statutory undertaking.

In the past, it was commonly said that a prohibitive injunction was more easily obtained than a mandatory injunction. Furthermore, the latter would not be granted in an interlocutory application unless there was a "high degree of assurance that at the trial it will appear that the injunction was rightly granted."[1] This was because an order enjoining an activity was seen as being less complicated than an order for affirmative action — it involved less cost to the defendant, fewer problems with court supervision, and was easier to formulate into an effective order. Of course, an order to enjoin an activity can prove just as costly as an order to continue performance. Similarly, many affirmative obligations can be expressed in negative form and thus lead to enforcement through the back door. This realization has given way to the current position, where the court will look more at the nature of the dispute, and the particular risks of injustice to the parties, than at the fact that the requested order has been framed in prohibitive rather than mandatory language.[2]

In addition to the general principles, a court will consider the following factors before ordering an interlocutory injunction requiring the defendant to take positive steps in compliance:

1) Will the order cause the defendant a greater waste of resources, either time or money, than merely being delayed in commencing something he would otherwise be entitled to do?

2) Will the granting of the relief make it unlikely that the plaintiff will return to bring the matter on for trial? In other words, is the plaintiff getting complete relief at the interlocutory stage, making the proceeding determinative of the dispute?[3]

3) Can the order be expressed with sufficient clarity so that the defendant, and any subsequent court, knows what was expected of the defendant to be in compliance?

4) Are there any other "due process" concerns about the use of coercive and intrusive power to achieve the particular end without the protection of a full trial?

5) Has the defendant increased the impugned activities after being informed of the plaintiff's request for judicial assistance?

---

1   *Shepheard Homes Ltd.* v. *Sandham* (1970), [1971] Ch. 340 at 351 Megarry J.

2   See *Films Rover International Ltd.* v. *Cannon Film Sales Ltd.*, [1987] 1 W.L.R. 670 (Ch); and *Businessworld Computers Pty. Ltd.* v. *Australian Telecommunications Commission* (1988), 82 A.L.R. 499 (F.C. Austl.).

3   See *2261324 Manitoba Ltd.* v. *Domo Gasoline Corp.* (1995), [1996] 3 W.W.R. 708 (Man. Q.B.), aff'd (1996), 110 Man. R. (2d) 158 (C.A.); and *Olynick* v. *Kelvington Credit Union Ltd.* (1991), 91 Sask. R. 156 (C.A.).

The appropriate threshold test for interlocutory mandatory injunctions is not settled. Some courts have adopted the *American Cyanamid* model,[4] other have insisted upon a higher standard.[5] It is still rare for the court to order a mandatory interlocutory injunction.[6]

B. ENFORCEMENT OF RESTRAINT OF TRADE COVENANTS

It is common to find in employment contracts, and contracts for the sale of a business, a restraint of trade clause purporting to prevent an employee or vendor from starting up in opposition to an employer or purchaser following termination or purchase. These clauses normally restrict the promisor (covenantor) in a defined geographical area and for a certain period of time. The clauses are the subject of much judicial scrutiny to determine their reasonableness both between the parties and in the wider public interest.[7] Because the temporal nature of the clause is often most important, a plaintiff is drawn to interlocutory enforcement of the covenant. Courts have recognized that the interlocutory hearing will often be determinative of the dispute between the parties, and that the enforcement of the clause will turn on the legal assessment of the reasonableness of the clause alone. The interpretation of the reasonableness of restraint of trade clauses has turned more on past precedent and a visceral reaction to what is reasonable, rather than on a detailed contextual analysis of the appropriate level of market protection. Courts have been tempted to make a definitive ruling at the interlocutory stage and have therefore insisted upon a high threshold level.[8] However, this is not a universal practice and other courts have readily turned to a balance of convenience analysis after applying a low threshold test.[9] Some courts, particularly in the United Kingdom,

---

4   See *Peerless (Guardian ad litem of)* v. *British Columbia School Sports* (1998), 157 D.L.R. (4th) 345 (B.C.C.A.); and *Hart Leasing and Holdings Ltd.* v. *St. John's (City of)* (1992), 101 Nfld. & P.E.I.R. 131 (Nfld. C.A.).

5   See *Manos, Foods International Inc.* v. *Coca-Cola Ltd.* (1997), 74 C.P.R. (3d) 2 (Ont. Gen. Div.).

6   See *Parker* v. *Camden London Borough Council* (1985), [1986] Ch. 162 (C.A.).

7   See **Elsley Estate** v. *J.G. Collins Insurance Agencies Ltd.*, [1978] 2 S.C.R. 916; *Stephens* v. *Gulf Oil Canada Ltd.* (1976), 11 O.R. (2d) 129 (C.A.), leave to appeal to S.C.C. refused [1976], 1 S.C.R. xi; and *Doerner* v. *Bliss & Laughlin Industries Inc.*, [1980] 2 S.C.R. 865.

8   See, for example, *Cantol Ltd.* v. *Brodi Chemicals Ltd.* (1978), 23 O.R. (2d) 36 (H.C.).

9   See *Steel Art Co.* v. *Hrivnak* (1979), 27 O.R. (2d) 136 (H.C.).

have suggested that when the plaintiff brings an action where the restraint of trade clause has already been in effect for much of its stipulated period, then a full trial of the merits may be justified at the interlocutory stage. If reasonableness of the restraint of trade clause is not contested, irreparable harm has been assumed.[10] Some courts have suggested that if the restraint clause is reasonable, and there is a clear breach, the issues of irreparable harm and inconvenience can be downplayed. The burden of proving that no harm will be caused then lies on the party seeking to escape the enforcement of the covenant.[11]

C. INTERLOCUTORY INJUNCTIONS PROTECTING INTELLECTUAL PROPERTY AND PREVENTING BREACHES OF CONFIDENCE

Where there is an infringement of a registered trademark or copyright, or a plaintiff is bringing a passing-off action (that is, where one party represents that their business, wares or services are those of another), the accepted threshold test is now the *American Cyanamid* model. However, if the interlocutory proceedings are likely to be determinative of the substantive dispute, courts have been willing to accord more weight to the strength of the plaintiff's case.[12] Care must also be taken here in that many of the intellectual property disputes may start as *Anton Piller* orders, where a higher threshold has traditionally been insisted upon.

In patent infringement cases the majority of courts now favour the *American Cyanamid* test.[13] However, under the *Patent Act*[14] there is a screening process to determine validity before a patent is issued. The question often before the court concerns the reliance that can be placed on this process. A practice adopted by some courts suggests that if a court has previously upheld the patent in other litigation, then an injunction

---

10   See *Apotex Fermentation Inc.* v. *Novopharm Ltd.*, [1994] 7 W.W.R. 420 (Man. C.A.).

11   See *Bank of Montreal* v. *James Main Holdings Ltd.* (1982), 28 C.P.C. 157 (Ont. Div. Ct.); and *Miller* v. *Toews* (1990), [1991] 2 W.W.R. 604 (Man. C.A.).

12   See *Syntex Inc.* v. *Novopharm Ltd.* (1991), 126 N.R. 114 (Fed. C.A.), leave to appeal to S.C.C. refused [1991] 3 S.C.R. xi (trademark infringement); and *Upjohn Co.* v. *Apotex Inc.* (1993), 68 F.T.R. 262 (T.D.) (copyright infringement).

13   See *Cutter Ltd.* v. *Baxter Travenol Laboratories of Canada Ltd.* (1980), 47 C.P.R. (2d) 53 (F. C.A.), leave to appeal to S.C.C. refused (1980), 33 N.R. 266n; *Turbo Resources Ltd.* v. *Petro Canada Inc.*, [1989] 2 F.C. 451 (C.A.); and *Signalisation de Montréal Inc.* v. *Services de Béton Universels Ltée* (1992), [1993] 1 F.C. 341 (C.A.).

14   R.S.C. 1985, c. P-4.

will be granted in the matter before the court on the same patent. Where the defendant has provided little evidence to dispute the validity of the plaintiff's patent, again, an injunction will be granted. However, where the defendant has introduced strong evidence disputing the validity of the plaintiff's patent the injunction will be denied, although the defendant may be ordered to keep an account; thus enabling the plaintiff to prove damages more easily should she be successful at trial.[15]

Even where information does not fall within the classic actions for the protection of intellectual property (i.e., copyright, trademark, and patent rights) a trade secret or other confidential information may be protected pursuant to an action for breach of confidence. Where information having a quality of confidence has been conveyed to another person (i.e., information that is neither public property nor public knowledge), and the information has been communicated in a fashion to make clear to the other person that it was communicated in confidence, and that other person has misused or used the information in an unauthorized manner, then an action for breach of confidence exists.[16]

Confidential information can be divided essentially into two categories.

1) One category involves the privacy interest a person has in keeping from the public personal details of their life or other family matters. In this category, keeping confidential information away from the public domain is at the heart of the dispute, and can only be protected through a breach of confidence action. A common remedy is an interlocutory injunction to prevent public disclosure prior to a substantive cause of action being proved.

2) The second category of confidential information involves commercial and trade secrets, such as customer lists or a secret manufacturing process. Again, an interlocutory injunction will be useful to prevent misuse of this type of information, although the risk to the applicant is not with respect to a privacy interest but is simply to prevent commercial exploitation to the financial detriment of the applicant.

In the first category, the form of action resembles the action to prevent publication of defamatory material. The courts have demonstrated

---

15   See *Teledyne Industries Inc.* v. *Lido Industrial Products Ltd.* (1978), 19 O.R. (2d) 740 (C.A.).

16   See *LAC Minerals Ltd.* v. *International Corona Resources Ltd.*, [1989] 2 S.C.R. 574; *Cadbury Schweppes Inc.* v. *FBI Foods Ltd.*, [1999] 1 S.C.R. 142; and R.D. Manes & M.P. Silver, *The Law of Confidential Communications in Canada* (Toronto: Butterworths, 1996) at P.91 ff.

a willingness to grant an injunction to prevent the disclosure unless there is a compelling public interest argument to support publication.[17] While courts are sensitive to the fact that an interlocutory injunction is tantamount to a prior restraint on public disclosure (usually by the media), this must be balanced against the privacy interest of the individual. Thus, injunctions have been granted to prevent the publication of details of sexual practices communicated between friends, unless they were of a type which had a "grossly immoral tendency;"[18] to protect the identity of a person who has had a penile implant;[19] to prevent the breach of a fiduciary duty owed to a plaintiff;[20] to prevent the publication of confidential hospital records identifying doctors who had contracted HIV/AIDS yet who were still practicing in the hospital;[21] and to protect solicitor-client documents from being disclosed on a local television show.[22]

With respect to the second category of confidential information, courts have been willing to grant interlocutory relief on the same basis as applied in other forms of intellectual property. The appropriate threshold test would appear to be either the *American Cyanamid* model or the *prima facie* case,[23] before moving onto an assessment of irreparable harm and balance of convenience. Where the information has been placed into the public domain an injunction will be refused.

---

17 See *Lion Laboratories Ltd.* v. *Evans* (1984), [1985] Q.B. 526 (C.A.).

18 See *Stephens* v. *Avery*, [1988] Ch. 449.

19 See *T.(S.)* v. *Stubbs* (1998), 38 O.R. (3d) 788 (Gen. Div.), but compare with *B.(A.)* v. *Stubbs* (1999) 44 O.R. (3d) 391. In *T.(S.)*, the plaintiff introduced psychiatric evidence that suggested that the disclosure of his identity would be very traumatic and damaging. Similar evidence was not called in *B.(A.)*.

20 See *Drabinsky* v. *KPMG* (1998), 41 O.R. (3d) 565 (Gen. Div.). The court also held that in the circumstances of a fiduciary relationship the plaintiff does not have to find either irreparable harm or balance of convenience. A fiduciary duty of loyalty and good faith is enough.

21 See *X* v. *Y*, [1988] 2 All E.R. 648 (Q.B.).

22 See *Amherst (Town of)* v. *Canadian Broadcasting Corp.* (1993), 126 N.S.R. (2d) 221 (S.C.T.D.), interlocutory proceedings, final injunction upheld (1994), 133 N.S.R. (2d) 277 (S.C.A.D.).

23 See *B.W. International Inc.* v. *Thomson Canada Ltd.* (1996), 137 D.L.R. (4th) 398 (Ont. Gen. Div.). On either test plaintiff could not demonstrate that an investment report that it sold to subscribers was confidential when it came into the hands of *The Globe & Mail* newspaper. See also *Danik Industries Ltd.* v. *Just Rite Bumpers & Accessories Ltd.* (1993), 48 C.P.R. (3d) 20 (B.C.S.C.), aff'd (1993), 81 B.C.L.R. (2d) 91 (C.A.). The plaintiff successfully sought an interlocutory injunction against the defendant from building bicycle car-racks that it had designed. Damages could not adequately reflect the loss of goodwill or disruption in the marketplace the plaintiff had acquired. Further, the balance of convenience lay with the plaintiff as this was its sole product, whereas the defendant had built the bike racks to use up surplus metal-manufacturing capacity.

D. INTERLOCUTORY INJUNCTIONS AND LABOUR DISPUTES

The most effective weapon labour has in a dispute is the withdrawal of services in strike action, often leading to primary picketing (against the employer) and secondary picketing (against other companies owned by the employer or having dealings with the employer). The repercussions for the employer include a disruption to her business, often trespass and obstruction to her business premises, and interference with arrangements between the employer and other third parties. For an employer, an interlocutory injunction aimed at preventing any one, or all, of these practices seems a most expeditious remedy. For a court, the area is a political minefield. The injunction action will rarely deal with the primary issue of conflict between the employer and employees. If the injunction is granted, it will effectively deal a damaging blow to the employees' bargaining position, and can escalate the conflict — particularly where there is the prospect that the injunction will be disobeyed, or where other employees withdraw services in sympathy with the strikers. However, a court cannot lightly ignore a plaintiff's request for intervention, particularly where the labour dispute has resulted in violent confrontations and damage to property.

Owing to the politically charged atmosphere surrounding labour disputes, most legislatures have enacted legislation circumscribing the courts' power to grant interlocutory injunctions. Often this legislation leaves the matter within the exclusive jurisdiction of a specialist labour tribunal, although the Supreme Court of Canada has held that the courts retain a residual power to intervene where the legislation provides no adequate alternative remedy.[24] The legislative provisions differ widely between provinces. For example, in British Columbia a court may only grant an injunction where there is either "immediate danger of serious injury to an individual" or "actual obstruction or physical damage to property."[25] In all other cases, the Labour Relations Board has exclusive jurisdiction to issue orders relating to picketing, striking,

---

24 See *St. Anne Nackawic Pulp & Paper Co.* v. *C.P.U., Local 219,* [1986] 1 S.C.R. 704 at 727; and *Brotherhood of Maintenance of Way Employees Canadian Pacific System Federation* v. *Canadian Pacific Ltd.,* [1996] 2 S.C.R. 495.
25 *Labour Relations Code,* R.S.B.C. 1996, c. 244, s. 137(2).

or locking out. In Ontario, the court may only grant an injunction concerning a labour dispute[26] when:

> reasonable efforts to obtain police assistance, protection and action to prevent or remove any alleged danger of damage to property, injury to persons, obstruction of or interference with lawful entry or exit from the premises in question or breach of the peace have been unsuccessful.[27]

If the court has jurisdiction, the legislation also changes the way the motion is to be heard by the court. In particular, affidavit evidence must exclude hearsay evidence — but there is a right to cross examination at the hearing of any deponent, there is an immediate right to appeal to the Court of Appeal, and only in the rarest of cases can the motion be heard *ex parte*. However, where the defendant's activities fall outside the definition of a 'labour dispute', the court retains its normal jurisdiction to award an injunction, for example, to prevent a trespass or nuisance.

Where courts have granted interlocutory injunctions preventing picketing and similar actions, they have insisted upon a high threshold test and judicial restraint. This is consistent with the exception acknowledged in *N.W.L. Ltd.* v. *Woods, The Nawala*.[28]

E. INTERLOCUTORY INJUNCTIONS TO RESTRAIN DEFAMATION AND INJURIOUS FALSEHOOD

Courts have been extremely cautious when granting interlocutory injunctions to prevent the publication of defamatory material. The application of the traditional test — that a plaintiff is likely to suffer irreparable harm that is not readily compensable by way of damages —

---

26   A "labour dispute" is defined in the *Act* as meaning a dispute over conditions of employment with the employer. Thus, secondary picketing (picketing against other employers or suppliers with a hope to bring pressure on the employer with whom the employees are engaged in a labour dispute) has not normally been regarded as a labour dispute within the purview of s.102. See, for example, *Hersees of Woodstock Ltd.* v. *Goldstein*, [1963] 2 O.R. 81 (C.A.); and *Darrigo's Grape Juice Ltd.* v. *Masterson*, [1971] 3 O.R. 772 (H.C.). Where the employees described their picketing as a political protest, they also fell outside the definition of a labour dispute; see *Ontario (A.G.)* v. *Ontario Teachers' Federation* (1997) 36 O.R. (3d) 367 (Gen. Div.).

27   *Courts of Justice Act*, R.S.O. 1990, c. C.43, s. 102(3).

28   [1979] 1 W.L.R. 1294 (H.L.). See also *R.J.R.-MacDonald Inc.* v. *Canada (A.G.)* [1994] 1 SCR 311 at 338, and *Fletcher Challenge Canada Ltd.* v. *Local 1092* (1998) 155 DLR (4th) 638 (BCCA).

would tend to favour the plaintiff. However, courts have weighed a plaintiff's individual interest against the wider public interest of freedom of speech and freedom of the press. Considerable weight is accorded the latter interests and it is only in the clearest of cases, where the defendant admits the falsity of the defamatory comments, or where it would be impossible for him to succeed on a plea of justification, that an injunction will be granted. If the defendant intends to defend the publication by raising justification, or some other defence such as qualified privilege or fair comment, the court will not issue an injunction unless the defence is clearly without merit or the defendant is acting with malice.[29]

In *Canada (Human Rights Commission)* v. *Canadian Liberty Net*,[30] the defendant was operating a voice mail system which promoted anti-Semitic and racist comments. After an investigation, the Canadian Human Rights Commission believed such activities were a violation of the *Canadian Human Rights Act*[31] and requested the Human Rights Tribunal be impaneled to make a final determination. In the interim, the Commission sought an interlocutory injunction from the Federal Court to restrain the defendant from continuing its voice mail system pending the Tribunal's determination. Neither the Commission nor the Tribunal had power to give interim orders and thus the Commission requested the relief from the Federal Court in reliance of its inherent jurisdiction. In the course of its judgment the Supreme Court indicated that in matters of pure speech the *American Cyanamid* test was inappropriate. In particular, the application of the irreparable harm and balance of convenience criteria were viewed as "grievously undermining"[32] the right of freedom of expression as enshrined in section 2(b) of the *Charter*.[33] Both criteria made it practically impossible for the person making the expression ever to satisfy the test because his particular interest in speech is unlikely ever to have a "tangible or measurable interest other than the expression itself."[34] In contrast, the other party will almost always have some interest to benefit from the suppression of speech. The Supreme Court declined to rule on what would be an appropriate

---

29   See *Canada Metal Co.* v. *Canadian Broadcasting Corp.* (1975), 7 O.R. (2d) 261 (Div. Ct.); and *John Doe* v. *Canadian Broadcasting Corp.* (1993), [1994] 2 W.W.R. 663 (B.C.S.C.), original *ex parte* order set aside (1993), [1994] 2 W.W.R. 666 (B.C.S.C.), aff'd (1993), [1994] 2 W.W.R. 679 (B.C.C.A.).

30   [1998] 1 S.C.R. 626 [*Canadian Liberty Net*].

31   R.S.C. 1985, c. H-6.

32   *Canadian Liberty Net*, above note 30 at 665.

33   *Canadian Charter of Rights and Freedoms*, Part 1 of the *Constitution Act, 1982*, being Schedule B to the *Canada Act 1982* (U.K.), 1982, c. 11 [*Charter*].

34   *Canadian Liberty Net*, above note 30 at 665 [*emphasis omitted*].

threshold test since the issue was moot by the time it came before the court. However, it did comment favourably upon the approach adopted in *Champagne* v. *Collège d'enseignement général & professionnel de Jonquiere*[35] to the effect that prior restraint of allegedly defamatory material will only be justified in the "rarest and clearest of cases."[36]

An allied tort to defamation in the business world is the tort of injurious falsehood or trade libel. Such an action is actionable in tort, and often as a breach of the *Competition Act*[37] relating to false advertising. To be actionable, the plaintiff must establish that the offending statements were false and made with the intent to cause injury without lawful justification, and that the plaintiff has occasioned actual economic loss as a result of the statements. In these circumstances courts have readily granted an interlocutory injunction applying an *American Cyanamid* approach. The loss of goodwill and market share will almost invariably justify the conclusion that the balance of convenience lies with the plaintiff, resulting in the granting of an interlocutory injunction.[38]

F. INTERLOCUTORY INJUNCTIONS AND CONSTITUTIONAL LITIGATION

Interlocutory injunctions hold particular appeal to litigants seeking to impugn governmental action on constitutional grounds. Generally, the traditional public law remedies of declarations and *certiorari* have not been available on an interlocutory basis although some provincial legislation allows for interim orders on a judicial review application (see discussion below). Litigants have also been emboldened by the advent of the *Charter* and its open remedial prescription to fashion a remedy "as the court considers appropriate and just in the circumstances."[39]

The two leading cases in this area, both from the Supreme Court of Canada, are *Manitoba (A.G.)* v. *Metropolitan Stores (MTS) Ltd.*[40] and *RJR-MacDonald Inc.* v. *Canada (A.G.)*.[41] In *Metropolitan Stores*, a union had applied to the Manitoba Labour Board to have a first contract imposed on an employer pursuant to the relevant legislation. The employer

---

35   [1997] R.J.Q. 2395 (Que. C.A.) [*Champagne*].

36   *Canadian Liberty Net*, above note 30 at 668, citing *Champagne*, above note 35 at 2402.

37   R.S.C. 1985, c. C-34, ss. 36, 52.

38   *Mead Johnson Canada* v. *Ross Pediatrics* (1996), 31 O.R. (3d) 237 (Gen. Div.).

39   *Charter*, above note 33, s. 24(1).

40   [1987] 1 S.C.R. 110 [*Metropolitan Stores*].

41   [1994] 1 S.C.R. 311 [*RJR-MacDonald*].

wished to challenge the constitutionality of the statutory power of the Labour Board to impose a first contract, on the grounds that it violated sections 2(b) & (d), and 7 of the *Charter*, and sought to stay proceedings before the Labour Board pending a resolution of the constitutional challenge. The trial court had refused the stay. The Court of Appeal had granted the stay. The Supreme Court reversed the Court of Appeal.

In *RJR-MacDonald*, the applicant sought an interlocutory stay against the enforcement of the *Tobacco Products Control Regulations*,[42] which had placed controls on tobacco advertising. The applicant had successfully challenged the constitutionality of the legislation in the Quebec Superior Court, which had held the legislation *ultra vires*. In the Court of Appeal the legislation was upheld as being valid. The applicant intended to appeal the constitutional issue to the Supreme Court, and in the interim sought a stay against any attempt to enforce the regulations. The applicant failed to win the stay, although on the substantive merits of the constitutional issue, the applicant was ultimately successful in having the regulations struck down.[43]

A plaintiff raising a *Charter* challenge will likely be bringing an action against a public authority, law enforcement agency, administrative board, public official or the minister responsible for the impugned legislation. The plaintiff will be seeking either a stay in proceedings or injunction: If an order is granted the court may temporarily suspend the legislation against all parties, or it may order an exemption, according relief to the plaintiff before the court, but remaining in effect against all others. Regardless of these different possibilities, the Supreme Court has stated that the applicable test for granting relief will remain the same, subject always to the admonition that every case "turns on its own facts".

1) The Applicable Test in Constitutional Litigation

a) The applicable test is one adapted from private law with necessary modifications to take account of the poly-centric public interest issue always present in constitutional litigation. The Supreme Court reaffirmed the *American Cyanamid* approach and the serious question to be tried threshold. This approach is adopted because at the interlocutory stage a court is not in a position to undertake a detailed analysis of the complex factual and legal issues engaged in

---

42   S.O.R./89-21.
43   See *RJR-MacDonald Inc. v. Canada (A.G.)*, [1995] 3 S.C.R. 199.

constitutional litigation, particularly if the claim requires scrutiny pursuant to section 1 of the *Charter*. In addition, the court is concerned to ensure that the attorney general has been notified of the constitutional challenge and has time to complete pleadings. In accepting this threshold, the Supreme Court rejected a more conservative approach, which had suggested that there should be a presumption of constitutional validity — particularly where as in *RJR-MacDonald*, a lower appellate court, had upheld the validity of the impugned legislation. The Supreme Court stated that such a presumption would be inconsistent with the development of *Charter* rights, which requires every court to review an alleged *Charter* infringement carefully. The threshold is crossed when the court is satisfied that the constitutional challenge raises a serious issue to be tried. The prior decision of lower courts, if the matter is on appeal, or of another court where a similar issue has been argued, are not determinative of whether the case raises a serious issue to be tried.

The Supreme Court recognized two exceptions to the serious issue to be tried threshold; the first is that more detailed analysis of the merits will be justified if the interlocutory application is likely to be determinative of the action. This will occur when the right that the applicant is seeking to protect can only be exercised immediately, or where the result will "impose such hardship on one party as to remove any potential benefit from proceeding to trial."[44] Examples of this exception include where the applicant is seeking to restrain picketing,[45] or where a leader of a national political party is seeking to participate in a televised party leaders' debate,[46] or where one party is seeking to prevent another from having an abortion.[47] The Court said that the circumstances in which this exception will apply are rare.

The second exception arises where the constitutional challenge presents a simple question of law alone. An example given by the court of

---

44   *RJR-MacDonald*, above note 41 at 338.

45   See *Ontario (A.G.)* v. *Dieleman* (1994), 20 O.R. 229 (Gen. Div.), where the attorney general sought interlocutory injunctions against pro-life advocates to prevent picketing outside hospitals, abortion clinics, and the homes of doctors who performed abortions. The effect of coming within the exception resulted in the court applying a higher *prima facie* case threshold. The court then moved onto a full *Charter* analysis of the conflicting rights including a section 1 analysis. The eventual order was constructed to balance the right of picketing, and the freedom of expression it entailed, against the rights of privacy of women using abortion services, so as to impair the right to freedom of expression as little as possible.

46   See *Trieger* v. *Canadian Broadcasting Corp.* (1988), 66 O.R. (2d) 273 (H.C.).

47   See *Tremblay* v. *Daigle*, [1989] 2 S.C.R. 530.

this exception is if the government proceeded to pass legislation imposing a state religion. Such an action would violate section 2(a), could not be saved under section 1 and, therefore, could be struck down immediately. Again, cases within this exception will be extremely rare.

b) The second part of the *American Cyanamid* test requires the applicant to show irreparable harm. The Supreme Court narrowly defined irreparable harm to be either a harm which cannot be quantified in monetary terms or which cannot be cured. Because there are no monetary remedies concerning *Charter* litigation, the assessment of irreparable harm presents more difficulties. Until such time as there are a developed jurisprudence in this area the Supreme Court suggested that an applicant will quickly meet this test, even where his damages are theoretically easily quantifiable.

c) The third part of the test is balance of (in)convenience. In constitutional litigation this becomes the dominant factor because it brings into play important public interest factors. Within the constitutional setting public interest is multi-layered: these layers include the following:

- Claims of latent or background public interest. (There is a general public interest in having all legislation enforced. But there is also a public interest in having the *Charter* enforced as a document of fundamental rights.)
- The specific public interest objectives behind the impugned legislation. (Against this can be contrasted the general public interest, as represented by the applicant, of a competing vision to the specific objectives being pursued in the legislation. This type of material is often the subject of a section 1 analysis.)
- The specific public interest claims of the applicant distinguishing her from other similarly situated parties.
- The public interest present in remedial impact. (Is the court being asked for a suspension, impacting upon many people, or an exemption, confined to a limited class of applicants?)

Even after breaking down the competing claims based on public interest, courts must then devise ways to create a scale upon which to evaluate the balance. Unlike private litigation, where arguably the parties' claims of irreparable harm can be measured against the impact that the injunction will have on *economic self-interest*, there is no similar scale in constitutional litigation.[48]

---

48 See J. Cassels, "An Inconvenient Balance: The Injunction as a Charter Remedy" in J. Berryman, ed., *Remedies: Issues and Perspectives* (Scarborough, Ont.: Carswell, 1991) 271, particularly at 267ff.

The Supreme Court has not broken up the public interest elements as suggested in the preceding paragraph, although it has clearly recognized that all four levels of the public interest are legitimate when considering the balance of convenience. The Court has provided the following direction on how the competing claims are to be evaluated:

1) An applicant who alleges public interest harm must "convince the court of the public interest benefits which will flow from the granting of the relief sought."[49] A private applicant is presumed to be acting out of self-interest and cannot simply make the claim that the impugned government action does not represent the public interest.

2) A public authority is entitled to a lower burden than is a private applicant when establishing that irreparable harm will result. As long as the public authority is charged with the duty of promoting or protecting the public interest and it is acting pursuant to the impugned legislation then it does not have to demonstrate actual irreparable harm to the public interest.

3) The court should refrain from ascertaining whether actual harm will result should the administrative authority be restrained from acting. To do so would require a court to evaluate the effectiveness of government action, a task outside the purview of *Charter* scrutiny.

4) The extent of the order's impact on the public at large can influence the balance of convenience. If the order will only impact upon a discrete and limited number of applicants, or can be limited so as to minimize the affect on the public, then it can be more readily granted.

5) Maintenance of the status quo is of limited value in tipping the balance because a principle function of the *Charter* is to provide individuals with a means to challenge the existing order.

Applying the above test, in *Metropolitan Stores*[50] the constitutional challenge raised a serious issue to be tried. The employer claimed irreparable harm in that it would be forced to accept a first contract; one that, without the power of the Labour Board acting under the authority of the impugned legislation, the union may not have been able to negotiate at the bargaining table. Against this, the union raised the public interest that its survival would be compromised if it could not take the legislative advantage of seeking the Labour Board's authority to impose a first contract after negotiations had proved unsuccessful. In addition, the trial judge had correctly taken into consideration the public interest

---

49   *RJR-MacDonald*, above note 41 at 344–45.
50   Above note 40.

repercussions on other similarly situated bargaining agents if the power of the Labour Board to impose a first contract were to be suspended for the two to three years it would take to resolve the constitutional challenge. The trial judge had correctly evaluated these considerations in deciding to deny the stay of proceedings. The Supreme Court was of the opinion that the Court of Appeal had exceeded its powers of appellate review in overturning the exercise of the trial judge's discretion.

In *RJR-MacDonald*, the constitutionality of the tobacco regulations raised a serious constitutional issue concerning restrictions on freedom of speech through advertising. The applicant was able to demonstrate irreparable harm in that it would incur expense in making changes to its packaging to comply with the impugned regulations. Although this harm was readily quantifiable in monetary terms and would not constitute irreparable harm in a private suit, the difficulty in bringing suit against the Crown for compensation if the plaintiff was successful in its *Charter* challenge justified a finding of irreparable harm. Turning to the balance of convenience, the loss to the applicant was purely financial. Although the imposition of the expenditure to comply with the regulations would involve economic hardship for the applicant, it was easily of a size to absorb those expenditures. The regulations were imposed to protect public health and the applicant conceded that health warnings on tobacco products did have an effect on public awareness of the health concerns of smoking. The applicant could not show any public interest in the continuation of the current packaging requirements, rather than the new requirements. The balance of convenience lay with the respondent and therefore no stay was justified.

2) Evaluating the Public Interest — A Case Example: *Hogan v. Newfoundland (Attorney General)*

The decision of the Newfoundland Court of Appeal in *Hogan v. Newfoundland (A.G.)*[51] highlights the difficulty of evaluating the public interest in constitutional cases. The appellants, adherents of the Roman Catholic faith, had sought an interlocutory injunction to suspend the creation of an integrated education system, pending a hearing of their case to determine the constitutionality of recent amendments. These amendments had abrogated their rights respecting denominational schools as found in the terms of Union between Newfoundland and Canada. Before the chambers judge, an injunction had been denied

---

51   (1998), 163 D.L.R. (4th) 672 (Nfld. C.A.).

mainly on the grounds that in the judge's opinion the applicant's case had little chance of success on the merits. This finding had been used to tip the balance of convenience in the defendant's favour.

The Appeal Court criticized the chambers judge for using his view of the merits to determine where the balance of convenience lay. In doing so, he had misapplied the Supreme Court of Canada's direction on when it was justified to turn to merit adjudication to determine the balance of convenience. This case neither fell within the recognized exceptions nor presented a situation where the balance between the litigants was even. Turning to an evaluation of the public interest and where the balance of convenience lay, the applicants had argued that the right to denominational schools was one of long standing. If the injunction was denied it would be impossible to re-establish denominational schools should it ultimately be determined that the legislation creating an integrated school system was unconstitutional. In this sense, by proceeding ahead the government was in effect doing an "end run" around the constitutional issue. By allowing the government to continue with implementing the system now, regardless of the result of the litigation, the court would be impotent to restore the applicants to their current position if they subsequently won on the merits.

In the Court of Appeal, this argument, based on the public interest of seeing constitutional rights of minorities upheld, would have been persuasive had its underlying premise, (namely, the impossibility of re-establishing denominational schools), stood up to scrutiny. The evidence before the court did not support this premise. While the affidavit evidence did suggest it was highly unlikely that denominational schools would be re-established, it was not an impossibility. On the other side of the balance of convenience was the public interest expressed in the legislation establishing the integrated school system. In the Court's opinion, irreparable harm to the public interest must be assumed if the implementation of legislation were restrained. The applicant argued that the only element of harm to the government, if restrained from implementing the legislation pending the final hearing, would be the additional cost of continuing the denominational school system a further year. This interest should not be used to outweigh "long-cherished and entrenched constitutional rights."[52] While these were valid factors in determining where the balance lay, it was also necessary to place them in context. The school system was due to open in one month, students had been advised which school they were

---

52   *Ibid.* at 699.

attending, teacher allocations had been made, and school board elections had all taken place. The granting of an injunction at this juncture threatened to turn the educational system into chaos.

The Court expressed some disquiet over the tactics used by the attorney general, that may have delayed applicants in the commencement of litigation so as to use the start up or the school year as a factor in the government's favour. Nevertheless, the balance of convenience lay with the attorney general and the injunction was denied.

In *Hogan*, it is interesting to observe how the balance of convenience is struck. The court sees very real and immediate chaos in the education system if the injunction is granted, but is somewhat dismissive of the real loss of denominational education if the applicants' substantive claim is upheld. The suggestion that it is not an impossibility to re-establish denominational education if successful, and at the same time accepting that in practical terms it is unlikely to happen, seems something less than a level playing field when balancing these rights. The conflict in *Hogan* is between the constitutional protection of minority education rights and the legislative desire to create a more streamlined and economically efficient non-denominational school system. The legislature is not asserting any particular constitutional right other than the right to legislate. If the constitution is to have any teeth a special value must attach to constitutional rights even in interlocutory applications. The case also stresses the importance of expeditious litigation in bringing forward an interlocutory application.

It is doubtful whether courts will ever be able to create a better scale on which to evaluate public interest claims beyond the criteria listed above. However, in finding a balance it is important to remember the underlying values of the *Charter* in providing protection for minorities. Interlocutory injunction litigation should not become servant to simple majoritarian scales of convenience. One price we all pay, with the advent of a *Charter*, is the possibility of delay in governmental action while courts ensure constitutional compliance when requested by a litigant. The return is to have laws which reflect the plurality of values which make up Canada and which instill a greater respect for the rule of law.

G. INTERLOCUTORY INJUNCTIONS PENDING AN APPEAL OF UNSUCCESSFUL INTER-LOCUTORY INJUNCTION APPLICATION

Although a judge may have declined to grant an interlocutory injunction, it is perfectly consistent to grant an injunction for the very limited purpose of enabling the unsuccessful applicant to appeal the initial decision. Such an interlocutory injunction may be ordered to maintain the status quo pending an appeal and to ensure that the appellant's appeal rights are not rendered worthless.[53] The converse situation, where an injunction has been granted but the defendant wishes to appeal, is subject to the rights of the appellant to request a stay pending appeal under the respective rules of civil procedure.[54]

H. INTERLOCUTORY INJUNCTIONS TO ENFORCE MUNICIPAL B-LAWS

Municipalities have been held to have standing in their own right to bring an interlocutory injunction application to enforce their bylaws. This right is often conferred by statute.[55] In considering whether an interlocutory injunction should be granted, courts have usually referred to the *American Cyanamid* test as endorsed by the Supreme Court in *RJR-MacDonald*. There is no authoritative statement that a higher standard than good arguable case is required, although in most situations the municipality has proved a *prima facie* case that its bylaw is being infringed.[56] The test is easier to meet where the defendant has already been convicted of not complying with the bylaw, although a prior conviction is not vital to the granting of an interlocutory injunc-

---

53   See *Erinford Properties Ltd.* v. *Cheshire County Council*, [1974] 1 Ch. 261; *Chartered Bank* v. *Daklouche*, [1980] 1 W.L.R. 107 (C.A.); and the interim order of Sharpe J. in *United States of America* v. *Friedland*, [1996] O.J. No. 4399 (Gen. Div.).

54   In Ontario, see rule 63.01 of the *Rules of Civil Procedure*, R.R.O. 1990, Reg. 194; and *Courts of Justice Act*, above note 27 s. 19(1)(b).

55   In Ontario, see *Municipal Act*, R.S.O. 1990, c. M.45, s. 328.

56   See *Metropolitan Toronto (Municipality of)* v. *N.B. Theatrical Agencies Inc.* (1984), 44 O.R. (2d) 574 (H.C.) ("substantial issue") [*N.B. Theatrical Agencies*]; and *Regina (City of)* v. *Cunningham*, [1994] 7 W.W.R. 90 (Sask. Q.B.), citing *American Cyanamid* but requiring a "strong *prima facie*" case.

tion.[57] More attention is paid to the second and third elements of the *American Cyanamid* test.

A municipality does not have to show irreparable harm in the same way that a private litigant would. It is sufficient proof of irreparable harm for the municipality to simply want its bylaw enforced, particularly where the bylaw is being "flagrantly violated".[58] The irreparable harm is to the municipality's residents who have a legitimate expectation that bylaws will be enforced.[59] However, some courts have insisted that a municipality should not be treated differently and should provide actual evidence of irreparable harm.[60]

With respect to the balance of convenience, courts have experienced much more difficulty in weighing the respective claims. Often defendants will assert that compliance with the bylaw will force them to close their business. Some courts have dismissed this claim as being irrelevant in some cases[61] — others have considered it of vital concern.[62] Much would appear to turn on the merits of the defendant's claim that she is complying with the bylaw, or that she has legitimate grounds for challenging its validity. Where the defendant is simply playing for time and has continued to flout the bylaw, the injunction has been granted.

I. INTERLOCUTORY INJUNCTIONS TO PREVENT HARASSMENT

An important function of injunctions is to restrain one person from molesting, harassing or annoying another. Often these injunctions arise in the context of domestic relationships that have failed. In most provinces, legislation has conferred upon a court the power to make a non-molestation order[63] where there is evidence to justify a belief that the enjoined party will harass, or has threatened to harass, the plaintiff.

---

57   See *Burlington (City of)* v. *Video Matic 24 Hr. Movie Rentals Inc.* (1994), 34 C.P.C. (3d) 54 (Ont. Gen. Div.) [*Video Matic*] (relying upon the lower "good arguable case" threshold).

58   *N.B. Theatrical Agencies*, above note 56 at 580.

59   See *Markham (Town of)* v. *Eastown Plaza Ltd.* (1992), 11 M.P.L.R. (2d) 134 (Ont. Gen. Div.).

60   See *Fort Erie (Town of)* v. *Frenchman's Creek Estate Inc.* (1994), 23 M.P.L.R. (2d) 73 (Ont. Gen. Div.).

61   See *N.B. Theatrical Agencies*, above note 56.

62   See *Video Matic*, above note 57.

63   In Ontario, see *Family Law Act*, R.S.O. 1990, c. F.3, s. 46.

The order is not granted simply to prevent conduct that may embarrass the plaintiff. It must be conduct that raises anxiety or irritation to a substantial degree.[64] It is also possible for a court to grant exclusive possession of the matrimonial home to one spouse regardless of the ownership rights between the spouses.[65]

Outside domestic relationships it is also possible to gain an interlocutory injunction enjoining one party from harassing another based on an action of private nuisance. In *Pateman* v. *Ross*,[66] the court granted an interlocutory injunction enjoining the defendant from harassing the plaintiff and his new spouse. The defendant had previously been romantically involved with the plaintiff and had not been willing to accept his termination of the relationship. She had persisted in telephoning and mailing letters to the plaintiff over a considerable period of time. In *McKerron* v. *Marshall*,[67] the defendant had started a personal crusade to have the plaintiff terminated from her position as a teacher. As part of this campaign the defendant had written letters alleging that the plaintiff was emotionally abusing her students, had surreptitiously taped conversations with the plaintiff's students, and had affixed signs to the plaintiff's car. The court issued an injunction requiring the defendant to stay away from where the plaintiff was employed, but did not prevent the defendant from advancing a complaint about the plaintiff to the College of Teachers.[68]

---

64   See *Sniderman* v. *Sniderman* (1981), 25 R.F.L. (2d) 319 (Ont. H.C.).

65   In Ontario, see *Family Law Act*, above note 63, s. 24. Subsection (2) provides for interim orders, while subsection (3) provides a non-exclusive list of criteria that includes the best interests of the children affected, financial position of both spouses, and any violence committed by one spouse against the other spouse or children.

66   (1988), 68 Man. R. (2d) 181 (Q.B.).

67   (1998), 69 O.T.C. 393 (Gen. Div.).

68   Another way to prevent harassment is section 810 of the *Criminal Code*, R.S.C. 1985, c. C-46, which allows a court to require from an individual a recognizance (otherwise known as a "peace bond") where grounds exist which leads the court to believe that he will cause injury to, or damage the property of, another person.

FURTHER READINGS

CASSELS, J., "An Inconvenient Balance: The Injunction as a Charter Remedy" in J. Berryman, ed., *Remedies: Issues and Perspectives* (Scarborough, Ont.: Carswell, 1991) 271

GORA, C., HARLAND, C. & KENT C., "New Rules & Flexible Tools: An Inquiry Into the Framework for the Award of Interlocutory Injunctions in Intellectual Property Matters at the Federal Court of Canada" (1997), 76 Can. Bar Rev. 396

SHERIDAN L.A., *Injunctions in Particular Cases* (Chichester, U.K.: B. Rose, 1994)

CHAPTER 4

INTERLOCUTORY INJUNCTIONS RESTRAINING DISPOSITION OF ASSETS PENDING TRIAL: *MAREVA* INJUNCTIONS

A. INTRODUCTION

Courts have jealously guarded the granting of interlocutory injunctions, as an extraordinary form of relief. Nowhere is this more evident then when a plaintiff seeks an order to restrain the disposition of assets pending trial. A strong current throughout Anglo-Canadian law has been the position that a person's assets are sacrosanct until she is declared a judgment debtor. This position could be maintained where the ability of a person to deal with her assets was measured in days. However, today, the computerization and globalization of the financial sector means that monetary assets can be transferred instantaneously. In addition, it is now possible for a person to reside in one country, yet hold most of his assets in other countries. One legal response to the technological advancement of financial services has been the *Mareva* injunction, which seeks to restrain the removal or dissipation of assets away from the court's jurisdiction pending a trial of the merits. This form of remedy is obviously attractive to plaintiffs who not only gain preliminary protection of their final judgment if successful, but can also significantly disrupt the defendant's activities and thus gain further leverage in any settlement negotiations. Realizing this potential for abuse, courts have exhibited a particularly cautious approach to the development of *Mareva* injunctions.

B. HISTORICAL DEVELOPMENT

Prior to the development of the *Mareva* injunction, the law had developed several approaches to the preservation of assets pending trial. Many of these approaches survive today.

1) Where a plaintiff asserts a proprietary claim over a specific asset, the ownership of which is in dispute, interlocutory injunctions are readily granted. The respective codes of civil procedure provide for an order concerning the interim preservation of property.
2) Where the plaintiff is asserting a proprietary claim to trace into specific property, or that the property is held on a constructive trust, the court will grant an interlocutory injunction.
3) Where a plaintiff is seeking a remedy of specific performance the court will grant an injunction, or the plaintiff will be able to register a *lis pendens* preventing the sale of the property to a third party.
4) Where a defendant has fraudulently conveyed property to a third party so as to defeat her creditors, an interlocutory injunction can be granted to restrain any further dealings on the property while the impugned transaction is being litigated. However, for such a remedy to be available the plaintiff must be a creditor and establish an intent to defraud on the part of the defendant.
5) The court can grant a *quia timet* injunction, although as we will see below there are special rules with respect to granting this type of injunction that make it practically ineffective in this area.

The above actions do not accommodate a broad restraint on removal or dissipation of assets that are not the subject of the dispute, or where the plaintiff is not adjudged a creditor. In addition, the claims will normally require notice and cannot be made on an *ex parte* basis.

In 1975 the *Mareva* injunction was born, taking its name from *Mareva Compania Naviera S.A.* v. *International Bulkcarriers S.A., The Mareva.*[1] The plaintiff, a shipowner, was making a claim for hire under a time charterparty. The defendant, a foreign corporation, had subchartered the ship to the President of India. The sub-charterer paid freight into the defendant's bank account in the United Kingdom. The defendant defaulted on one of the payments of the time charter and the plaintiff commenced an action against it for breach. However, the plaintiff was concerned that the defendant's assets in the United Kingdom would disappear once an action was launched and sought an

---

1   (1975), [1980] 1 All E.R. 213n (C.A.).

injunction, which was granted to restrain the removal or disposal of the assets outside the court's jurisdiction. At the time, the Court of Appeal said little to establish the parameters of the jurisdiction.

The most significant legal impediment to the *Mareva* jurisdiction had been the principles taken from *Lister & Co.* v. *Stubbs*,[2] and it was on these principles that the trial judge in *Mareva* had thought that such an injunction was unavailable. Two principles emerge from *Lister* v. *Stubbs*: one, that execution cannot be obtained prior to judgment; and two, that judgment cannot be obtained before trial. These principles support a general hesitancy by courts towards granting interlocutory relief, but also manifest a particular concern with undue interference in the defendant's business as well as the adverse impact such an injunction may have on the rights of the defendant's other creditors.

Following the *Mareva* decision this type of order became a daily occurrence in English courts, particularly in the field of shipping contracts, and soon received the imprimatur of the House of Lords.[3]

Soon after its creation, Canadian courts also adopted the *Mareva* injunction jurisdiction. The Supreme Court finally gave its approval in *Aetna Financial Services Ltd.* v. *Feigelman*.[4] In that case Aetna was a federally incorporated company with a head office in Montreal and offices in Toronto and Manitoba. Aetna's business was factoring clients' accounts. Pre-Vue Co. was one of its customers. Aetna also held a debenture over Pre-Vue and had in fact exercised a power of appointing a receiver pursuant to the debenture. Pre-Vue was challenging the exercise by Aetna of appointing a receiver, claiming that it had acted precipitously. At the commencement of that litigation Aetna had taken the business decision to consolidate its business operations in either Montreal or Toronto and had taken steps to close its Manitoba office. Pre-Vue commenced interlocutory proceedings seeking to restrain Aetna from transferring its assets away from Manitoba. In the trial court a *Mareva* injunction was granted. The Manitoba Court of Appeal affirmed the trial judgment, although modified the amount covered by the injunction. The Supreme Court upheld the appeal on point of law but reversed the trial judgment holding that, while the *Mareva* injunction had a role to play in Canada, the facts before the court did not justify such an order in this case.

---

2   (1890), 45 Ch. D. 1 (C.A.).

3   See *Siskina (Cargo Owners)* v. *Distos Compania Naviera S.A.*, *The Siskina* (1977), [1979] A.C. 210 (H.L.).

4   [1985] 1 S.C.R. 2 [*Aetna*].

Several points emerge from *Aetna* and are discussed below; however, the overarching theme of the Supreme Court's decision concerns the relationship between the two *Lister* v. *Stubbs* principles and the *Mareva* jurisdiction. On this, the court expressed the view that the *Mareva* jurisdiction should be viewed as a closely controlled exception to the former principles and that care should be exercised so that the jurisdiction does not become a form of "litigious blackmail."[5]

Since its birth, the development of the *Mareva* injunction has been dramatic. In the United Kingdom the jurisdictional base has been legislated and a detailed practice direction has been issued governing the exercise of the jurisdiction.[6] The injunction has been granted

- against domestic and foreign defendants shifting assets outside the court's jurisdiction or disposing of them within national boundaries,
- against a defendant shifting assets extra-territorially, and
- in aid of the criminal law.

Canada has adopted most of these developments, although with less vigour.

C. JURISDICTION

Jurisdictional issues arise in three contexts:

- the jurisdictional basis of the court to award the injunction;
- whether the applicant's substantive cause of action must be justiciable within the court's jurisdiction for a *Mareva* injunction to be granted; and
- the notion of jurisdiction as it applies to the impugned actions of the defendant in removing assets from the court's jurisdiction.

With respect to jurisdictional basis the United Kingdom has specifically legislated the *Mareva* jurisdiction in section 37(3) of the *Supreme Court Act*,[7] which confirms judge-made developments in this area. In *Aetna*, the Supreme Court if Canada affirmed that the jurisdiction to grant a *Mareva* injunction lay within the broad power contained within the respective provincial Courts of Justice Acts, which gives a court a general power to award interlocutory injunctions wherever it is "just and convenient" to do so.

---

5   *Ibid.* at 37.
6   See [1994] 4 All E.R. 52.
7   1981 (U.K.), c. 54. See also Civil Procedure Rules (UK) rule 25.1.19, 'Freezing injunction,' and Chancery Practice Directory, 25 CPO-003.

With respect to the second jurisdictional issue (whether the applicant's cause of action must be justiciable within the court's actual jurisdiction), we saw in chapter 2 that the United Kingdom courts have vacillated on this very issue concerning *Mareva* injunctions. The conservative approach, first voiced in *The Siskina*[8] and subsequently reaffirmed by the Privy Council in *Mercedes-Benz A.G.* v. *Leiduck*,[9] requires that the applicant have an actual cause of action justiciable within the court's jurisdiction. The liberal approach, formulated in *Channel Tunnel Group Ltd.* v. *Balfour Beatty Construction Ltd.*[10] and followed in the dissenting judgment of Lord Nicholls in *Mercedes-Benz*, simply requires a justiciable issue which would be recognized by the domestic court from whom the *Mareva* injunction is being sought. This approach does not require the substantive cause of action to be heard by a court within that same jurisdiction. The injunction is given to support the prospective granting of a judgment from a competent court in either a domestic or foreign jurisdiction. The *Civil Jurisdiction and Judgments Act*[11] has compounded the issue. This was enacted to comply with the *European Judgment Convention* 1968,[12] which obliges contracting states to pass legislation allowing the interlocutory court orders of another contracting state to be held enforceable. The *Civil Jurisdiction and Judgments Act* has led to the spectre of plaintiffs commencing an action in another contracting state and coming to the United Kingdom simply to seek the advantage of a common law *Mareva* injunction.[13] Canada does not have similar legislation, a fact which has been commented upon in at least one Canadian court.[14]

---

8   Above note 3.

9   [1995] 3 W.L.R. 718 (P.C.) [*Mercedes-Benz*]. The United Kingdom has now passed by Order in Council the Civil Jurisdiction and Judgments Act 1982 (Interim Relief) Order 1997 (S,I, 1997 No. 302) which confers upon the High Court the power to grant an interim protection measure in aid of an action commenced, or about to be commenced, in a foreign country. The effect of the order is to reverse the position taken in *Mercedes-Benz*.

10   [1993] A.C. 334 (H.L.) [*Channel Tunnell*].

11   1982 (U.K.), c. 27.

12   *Convention on Jurisdiction and the Enforcement of Judgments in Civils and Commercial Matters*, Brussels, 27 September 1968.

13   See, for example, *Republic of Haiti* v. *Duvalier* (1989), [1990] 1 Q.B. 202 [*Republic of Haiti*] (C.A.), where the plaintiff commenced its action in France, but sought a world wide *Mareva* injunction from the United Kingdom primarily to assist in gaining disclosure of the whereabouts of the defendant's assets.

14   See *Baur* v. *Nelvana Ltd.*, [1991] O.J. No. 2364 (Gen. Div.) [Commercial List], Farley J. [*Baur*].

As discussed in chapter 2 the position in Canada is not entirely clear. The Supreme Court in *Brotherhood of Maintenance of Way Employees Canadian Pacific System Federation* v. *Canadian Pacific Ltd.* followed the *Channel Tunnel* approach and held that a court had jurisdiction "to grant an injunction where there is a justiciable right, wherever that right may fall to be determined."[15] In that case the right fell within the jurisdiction of the federal Labour Relations Board. The interlocutory injunction could only be granted by the British Columbia court because the Board did not have a legislative power to grant similar relief. The liberal approach appears to be consistent with the direction the Supreme Court has recently been taking, to revise the rules on conflict of laws to give more generous rules for the recognition and enforcement of foreign judgments. In particular, the Supreme Court has encouraged the notion of full faith and credit being given to other courts' judgments and to rely upon a "real and substantial connection" test to determine in which state the action should be brought.[16] If greater recognition is to be accorded the substantive judgments of foreign courts it seems consistent that prospective interlocutory orders should be available to ensure effective enforcement of those same judgments. On the other hand, the conservative approach would be more consistent with the tenor of the exceptional nature of the relief as recognized in *Aetna*.

The liberal approach is preferable. There is no public interest being served in allowing litigants to evade judgments given by competent courts of another jurisdiction merely because they operate internationally. When, and if, the plaintiff has got his judgment from a foreign court, or other arbitral body, and is seeking its reciprocal enforcement within a Canadian jurisdiction, granting a *Mareva* injunction is simply the interlocutory recognition of a latent right. The defendant is not penalized by allowing the court to consider the plaintiff's request — the plaintiff will have to meet the same test for interlocutory relief as if the cause of action arose within the court's jurisdiction. In fact, the defendant will still have the opportunity to object to the reciprocal enforcement of the plaintiff's judgment after it is obtained in a foreign court.

With respect to the third aspect of jurisdiction, the *raison d'être* of the *Mareva* injunction is to prevent the removal of assets away from the jurisdiction of the court. The initial *Mareva* cases presented clear cases where the threat was the removal of assets outside the territorial

---

15   [1996] 2 S.C.R. 495 at 505.
16   See *Morguard Investments Ltd.* v. *DeSavoye*, [1990] 3 S.C.R. 1077; *Amchem Products Inc.* v. *British Columbia (Workers' Compensation Board)*, [1993] 1 S.C.R. 897; and *Hunt* v. *T & N Plc.*, [1993] 4 S.C.R. 289.

boundaries of the United Kingdom. In Canada, assets can be moved from one province to another (unless the sum claimed is small, and the cost of pursuing the defendant to another province would be great); and from a common law province to civil law Quebec as well as outside national boundaries. Jurisdiction in a federal state takes on a number of dimensions. In *Aetna* the Supreme Court noted that all provinces, including Quebec, provided for the reciprocal enforcement of judgments obtained in another province. In addition, the court noted that corporations could be incorporated both provincially and federally and that in the latter case the business can be considered as "residing" throughout Canada. Against this backdrop the Court considered "removal from the jurisdiction" to mean outside Canada — transfers within Canada did not constitute "removal." The plaintiff was left to rely upon reciprocal enforcement legislation after judgment was obtained in Manitoba. The Supreme Court did not state this as an absolute rule and indicated, without further elucidation, that for other purposes jurisdiction could be defined to within provincial boundaries.

Subsequent Canadian cases have interpreted *Aetna* as elevating the federal jurisdictional questions as being an important but not definitive factor. In one case[17] Southin J. held that a *Mareva* injunction should be granted preventing the defendant from transferring assets from British Columbia to Alberta. As she indicated, to expect the plaintiff to incur the cost of chasing a corporate defendant across Canada for judgment of a claim for $100,000 of which $65,000 was in British Columbia would be, "if not prohibitory, certainly inhibitory."[18] The enforcement difficulties justified the injunction.

The *Mareva* injunction has also been granted preventing the dissipation of assets within the court's jurisdiction.[19]

D. ACCESSIBILITY THRESHOLD

Contrary to the position practiced in the United Kingdom, where courts have accepted the *American Cyanamid* serious question to be tried threshold, Canadian courts have generally expressed a preference for either a *prima facie* or strong *prime facie* threshold. However, there is recent evidence to suggest that British Columbian courts now favour the *American*

---

17 See *Gateway Village Investments Ltd.* v. *Sybra Food Services Ltd.* (1987), 12 B.C.L.R. (2d) 234 (S.C.).

18 *Ibid.* at 242.

19 See *Liberty National Bank & Trust Co.* v. *Atkin* (1981), 31 O.R. (2d) 715 (H.C.).

Cyanamid position.[20] The Supreme Court in *Aetna* did not express a definitive position in this regard, although it cited with approval the position of the Ontario Court of Appeal in *Chitel* v. *Rothbart*,[21] which adopted the *prima facie* standard. However, the Ontario Court of Appeal has recently insisted upon a strong *prima facie* standard.[22] There is a distinction between good arguable case and *prima facie* case. In the former, the court must simply be satisfied that the plaintiff has a cause of action that is neither frivolous nor vexatious. In the latter, the plaintiff must show through affidavit evidence that all the elements of the case have been established to justify final judgment, and the probative value of the evidence must be upheld at trial. How a difference between *prima facie* and strong *prima facie* translates into operational effect or in the way counsel prepares the motion is unclear. To the cynic the difference may be nothing more than the level to which counsel can shout and remonstrate on the evils of the defendant, particularly on an *ex parte* motion.

Some courts have suggested that the appropriate accessibility threshold will be influenced by the strength of the applicant's case with respect to the other matters which have to be proved and, in particular, the likelihood that the defendant is attempting to evade judgment.

If jurisdictional issues do not require the substantive cause of action to be justiciable within the domestic court, it is still a requirement that some justiciable issue exists in a competent forum. In *Channel Tunnel*,[23] the justiciable issue had to be one which would have been recognized within the jurisprudence of the domestic court. Thus, it would appear that a novel cause of action which is part of a foreign court's legal system would not necessarily support a *Mareva* injunction in a Canadian court unless Canadian jurisprudence would accord equal recognition to the alleged legal infringement in the foreign court.

Perhaps the outer extremes of the threshold issue are tested in the context of *Mareva* injunctions in aid of the criminal law. In these cases the injunction is being sought to ensure that the Crown will recover a fine if imposed, or to recover the profits of a crime as authorized by statute once a conviction has been entered. It is not immediately apparent how a civil accessibility threshold should be interpreted. The court cannot readily evaluate the attorney general's discretion to prosecute. In

---

20   See *Silver Standard Resources Inc.* v. *Joint Stock Co. Geolog* (1998), 168 D.L.R. (4th) 309 (B.C.C.A.).

21   (1982), 141 D.L.R. (3d) 268 (C.A.).

22   See *R.* v. *Consolidated Fastfrate Transport Inc.* (1995), 24 O.R. (3d) 564 (C.A.) [*Consolidated Fastfrate*].

23   Above note 10.

these circumstances, should the court view the likely conviction of the defendant through the lens of a civil court and require only a balance of convenience, or should it require the applicant to prove on a criminal standard that the defendant will be convicted beyond all reasonable doubt? In *R. v. Consolidated Fastfrate Transport Inc.*, the Ontario Court of Appeal insisted upon a "strong *prima facie* case ... that the accused person will likely be convicted of the offence."[24] This appears to be a halfway point between civil interlocutory and criminal burdens.

E. DISSIPATION OF ASSETS

An important part of the applicant's case is the need to establish a real risk that the defendant will dissipate his assets prior to judgment. There are two distinct issues involved:

* Must the applicant show an "intent" to evade judgment, or merely the potential "effect" of doing so?
* What type of evidence will a court require to demonstrate a risk of dissipation?

On the first issue, of intent or effect, a starting point for most Canadian courts has been the judgment of McKinnon J. in *Chitel* v. *Rothbart*,[25] and endorsed in *Aetna*. The primary focus of the test is to determine whether the defendant has been dealing with her assets in a "manner clearly distinct from his usual or ordinary course of business or living."[26] This test tends to eschew differences between intent and effect although other commentators have suggested that it requires some evidence of improper motive or intention on the part of the defendant.[27] Certainly the Federal Court of Appeal holds this position.[28]

---

24   Above note 22 at 579, Galligan J.A. The injunction was denied on the basis that the Crown could not show an improper purpose for the transfer of assets out of the court's jurisdiction.

25   (1982), 39 O.R. (2d) 513 (C.A.).

26   *Ibid.* at 532–33.

27   See M.A. Springman, G.R. Stewart & M.J. MacNaughton, *Fraudulent Conveyances and Preferences*, looseleaf (Scarborough, Ont.: Carswell, 1994) at s. 2-13; and D.M. McAllister, *Mareva Injunctions*, 2d ed. (Scarborough, Ont.: Carswell, 1987) at 97.

28   See *Marine Atlantic Inc.* v. *Blyth* (1993), 113 D.L.R. (4th) 501 (C.A.). The Court indicated that evidence about financial difficulties was insufficient to justify an order — there had to be a genuine risk of removal and a threat to arrange assets so as to defeat adversaries.

The "effect only" position has gathered momentum in recent times. In *Mooney v. Orr*,[29] the plaintiff brought an action against the defendant to discharge a *Mareva* injunction. The plaintiff was known as an international deal-maker who had structured his deals to "minimize income tax, to protect wealth from various forms of attack (creditors, spouses and other family members), and to ensure income."[30] The defendant had brought an action against the plaintiff on a counterclaim. The defendant was aware of how the plaintiff had structured his affairs before entering into a business relationship that had soured. The defendant, during the course of the original proceedings, had sought a *Mareva* injunction and an order to disclose the whereabouts of the plaintiff's assets offshore. The defendant could not show that the plaintiff had removed assets from Canada or that the plaintiff had done anything to make his assets less exigible since entering into the business deal with the defendant. The lack of evidence demonstrating that the plaintiff was doing anything to render the court process impotent was not seen as a barrier to the granting of the injunction. Huddart J. allowed the injunction to continue, at least until full disclosure had been given by the plaintiff, at which stage the plaintiff could again seek its discharge. For Huddart J. the guiding principle was to fashion an order that showed to the world that the court was not impotent "in the face of those who choose to order their affairs so as to keep all their options for themselves."[31]

The Ontario Court of Appeal has divided on this issue. In *Consolidated Fastfrate*, Galligan and Houlden JJ. adopted the position that if the defendant's purpose in removing assets was to avoid judgment then the injunction should be granted. However, if the purpose was legitimate, albeit that it had the effect of avoiding judgment, the injunction should not be granted. Clearly, motive is important. Weiler J. was equally emphatic in stating that an improper motive requirement was not required. In her opinion, the key issue was the extent to which the defendant's dealings were outside the ordinary course of business. When considering this issue it was appropriate to look at the following:

---

29 (1994), [1995] 3 W.W.R. 116 (B.C.S.C.) [*Mooney*]. After the defendant filed a satisfactory affidavit disclosing his assets, the injunction was dissolved: (1994), 1 B.C.L.R. (3d) 150 (S.C.). See also *Gudaitis v. Abacus Systems Inc.* (1995), 35 C.P.C. (3d) 266 (B.C.S.C.).

30 *Mooney*, above note 29 at 133.

31 *Ibid.* Huddart J.'s expansionist approach in *Mooney* has now been endorsed by the British Columbia Court of Appeal in *Silver Standard Resources Inc. v. Joint Stock Co Geolog* [1997] 7 WWR 289 at 300.

- the size of the judgment which would be obtained against the defendant;
- the effect it would have on the defendant's financial position;
- the timing of the asset removal;
- whether the payment was of a business debt or not;
- the ability to trace assets through any business reorganization; and
- the possibility of reciprocal enforcement of judgment in the jurisdiction the assets are being transferred to.

Proof of intent has not been a mandatory requirement in the United Kingdom, where intent, real risk, and "effect without reasonable excuse" are all accepted.[32] To require proof of intent would seem unduly restrictive. Proof of intent to evade, like fraud, entails proof of a defendant's state of mind. The likelihood that this could be established at an interlocutory proceeding before discoveries are completed is remote. Effect focuses on objectively verifiable evidence, which may then justify an inference that the defendant is attempting to evade judgment. The checklist approach of Weiler J. is more concrete than attempting to determine individual motive and intent.

With respect to the type of evidence needed to prove risk of dissipation, in addition to the checklist of factors provided by Weiler J., can be added the suggestions of Mustill J.:

> It is not enough for the plaintiff to assert a risk that the assets will be dissipated. He must demonstrate this by solid evidence. This evidence may take a number of different forms. It may consist of direct evidence that the defendant has previously acted in a way which shows that his probity is not to be relied on. Or the plaintiff may show what type of company the defendant is (where it is incorporated, what are its corporate structures and assets, and so on) so as to raise an inference that the company is not to be relied on. Or, again, the plaintiff may be able to found his case on the fact that inquiries about the characteristics of the defendant have led to a blank wall. Precisely what form the evidence may take will depend on the particular circumstances of the case. But the evidence must always be there.[33]

When presenting the application for the injunction it is incumbent upon the plaintiff to make full and frank disclosure of all matters in her knowledge that are material. Failure to disclose can result in the injunc-

---

32   See *Ghoth v. Ghoth*, [1992] 2 All E.R. 920 (C.A.).

33   *Ninemia Maritime Corp. v. Trave Schiffahrtsgesellschaft mbH & Co KG, The Niedersachsen*, [1984] 1 All E.R. 398 (Q.B.) at 406, aff'd [1983] 1 W.L.R. 1412 (C.A.).

tion being set aside.[34] While it was once a requirement that the plaintiff also provide some evidence that the defendant had assets within the court's jurisdiction, this is no longer required where the court is prepared to give a *Mareva* injunction covering assets outside the court's jurisdiction. However, a plaintiff is still required to give particulars of the sum claimed, and thus the amount that the injunction will cover.

F. IMPACT ON THIRD PARTIES

A *Mareva* injunction is an *in personam* remedy which is addressed to the person and does not attach directly to his assets. At one time Lord Denning M.R. suggested that the order acted *in rem* and would bind third parties even without they having notice of the order.[35] This suggestion has been rejected by most commentators and other judges for the sound reason that if the interlocutory order had such an effect it would make it extremely difficult for third parties to act within the parameters of the order. It would also appear to adversely impact upon the rights of third parties and other creditors who would have no knowledge that such an order had been granted.[36]

Since the *Mareva* injunction proscribes the defendant's ability to deal with his assets it does not operate to effect the rights of other third parties over the same assets. Thus, it has been said that the intent of the *Mareva* injunction is not to rewrite the laws of insolvency[37] and the plaintiff will not gain any priority ahead of other creditors of the defendant simply because he has moved for a *Mareva* injunction. Similarly, a secured creditor can request that the order be amended so that she will be able to exercise her security rights over a particular asset. A defendant will also be permitted to meet *bona fide* expenses from money subject to the order even if the meeting of these claims will exhaust the assets available to met the plaintiff's claim. It is for the defendant to establish that the expenses are *bona fide*.

A *Mareva* injunction is normally addressed to the defendant in person, and to his agents and servants. The order can also be addressed to other specific third parties who may be holding assets of the defendant.

---

34 See *Third Chandris Shipping Corp.* v. *Unimarine S.A.*, [1979] Q.B. 645 (C.A.), which was endorsed in *Aetna*, above note 4.

35 See *Z Ltd.* v. *A-Z and AA-LL*, [1982] Q.B. 558 (C.A.).

36 See *Derby & Co.* v. *Weldon (Nos. 3 & 4)* (1989) [1990] Ch. 65 (C.A.) [*Derby*].

37 See *Aetna*, above note 4 at 26, citing Goff J. in *Iraqi Ministry of Defence* v. *Arcepey Shipping Co. S.A.* (1980), [1981] Q.B. 65 at 71.

All parties are bound by the order once they have notice of it and will be in contempt of court if they then fail to comply. The obligation upon the third party is to do what they reasonably can to prevent the dissipation of the assets by the defendant. The order cannot bind the assets of a third party who is not a party to the litigation. However, if the money is owed by the third party to the defendant then the court can order that the funds be paid into court or a frozen bank account in a bank that has notice of the order.

The impact of a *Mareva* injunction on third parties is of particular concern to banks and other financial institutions who may be put to expense to comply with the injunction and who need precise instructions to ensure compliance. The English Court of Appeal dealt with these issues in *Z Ltd.* v. *A-Z and AA-LL*,[38] a case involving a massive fraud scheme in which the defendants had defrauded the plaintiffs of $2,000,000. The funds had been paid into several bank accounts and used to acquire other fixed assets. The plaintiffs had been successful in gaining a *Mareva* injunction and the action only continued at the request of the five clearing banks who wished elucidation of their responsibilities under the *Mareva* injunction. Lord Denning M.R. made the following points:[39]

1) If third parties are put to expense, or incur any other liability, as a result of complying with the order, they are entitled to complete indemnification by the plaintiff. A court can request a specific undertaking from the plaintiff to this effect.
2) The plaintiff should be as specific as possible to the bank or third party concerning the claim, so that they can identify what assets are covered by the injunction and to what extent.
3) If the plaintiff cannot give sufficient detail of the precise nature of the defendant's assets held by the third party, he can request the third party to undertake a search and the cost of such search will be recoverable against the plaintiff.
4) The plaintiff should give the names of the third parties to whom notice of the injunction is to be given so that they can be included in the order, although other names can be added subsequently.
5) It is appropriate to stipulate the amount of the plaintiff's claim in any order addressed to the defendant in person, as any third parties covered by the order may not necessarily know the value of the

---

38   Above note 35.
39   *Ibid.* at 575–77.

defendant's assets. However, it may be more appropriate to stipulate that all the assets held by the third party are covered by the order.

6) If the defendant is entitled to draw upon the account held by the third party to meet "normal living expenses" an amount should be stipulated. A third party should not be expected to determine the veracity of the defendant's expenditures.

7) An order can be made affective over a joint account if the court so orders, although the court must have good reason for believing that the assets in the account are the assets of the defendant.[40]

8) The court should ensure an early return date when granting the *Mareva* injunction so that both the defendant and third party can be given the earliest possible opportunity of being heard if they wish to challenge the order or parts of it.

9) A plaintiff will be expected to give an undertaking in damages when seeking the order.

G. DISCOVERY AND OTHER ORDERS IN AID OF IDENTIFYING THE LOCATION AND AMOUNT OF ASSETS

A plaintiff may believe that the defendant has assets but is unaware of their location or amount. An important ancillary part of the *Mareva* injunction is the ability of the court to order discovery in aid of the injunction. The discovery should only go as far as to identify the location and amount of the assets. It is important that this discovery process does not infringe the defendant's rights to raise objections to discovery, nor unnecessarily seek to gather information not germane to the success of the *Mareva* order.

On rare occasions a court can order that a receiver be appointed as part of the *Mareva* injunction.[41] In addition, an *Anton Piller* injunction can also be granted with a *Mareva* injunction, (as discussed in chapter 5.)

Courts in the United Kingdom have also resurrected the writ of *ne exeat regno* to restrain a person from leaving the jurisdiction of the court, the defendant must surrender her passport until security has

---

40 See *S.C.F. Finance Co.* v. *Masri*, [1985] 1 W.L.R. 876 (C.A.).

41 See *Walter E. Heller Financial Corp.* v. *American General Supply of Canada (1969) Ltd.* (1986), 56 O.R. (2d) 257 (C.A.); and *Carter (Receiver of)* v. *Carter* (1988), 29 C.P.C. (2d) 150 (Ont. H.C.). See also *Ontario Courts of Justice Act*, R.S.O. 1990, c. C.43 s. 101.

been given for the plaintiff's claim.[42] There would appear to be no reported decision in Canada exercizing a similar jurisdiction.

H. EXTRA-TERRITORIALITY

The issues of extra-territoriality and jurisdiction overlap and have a number of permutations. We saw under jurisdiction that it is still an open question whether the plaintiff's substantive cause of action must be justiciable within the court to support a *Mareva* injunction, although this will normally be the case. Where the plaintiff's cause of action is not justiciable within the court's jurisdiction but the defendant is, and has assets within the court's jurisdiction, the Privy Council has held that a court lacks jurisdiction to grant a *Mareva* injunction.[43] At least one Ontario court has come to the same conclusion with respect to *Mareva* injunctions.[44]

Where the plaintiff's cause of action arises in the court's jurisdiction and the defendant is amenable to the same jurisdiction, a court can award a *Mareva* injunction restraining the defendant from dealing with assets both within the court's jurisdiction and assets held extra-territorially. Because the injunction operates *in personam* the defendant can be held in contempt of court for failing to deal with her assets held overseas as the court instructs. The court can order the defendant to disclose the amount and whereabouts of the assets held overseas, and it can prevent the transfer of those assets from one jurisdiction to another. The latter is a particular problem where the defendant may be tempted to move assets from one jurisdiction, which has a reciprocal enforcement of judgment regime, into another country which does not make similar accommodations for Canadian judgments. In *Mooney*,[45] Huddart J. gave a non-exhaustive list of the factors, taken from current authorities that were influential in determining the exercise of the judicial discretion to grant a *Mareva* injunction having extra-territorial effect. These factors were:

1) the nature of the transaction (local, national, international) giving rise to the cause of action;

---

42   See *Bayer A.G.* v. *Winter*, [1986] 1 W.L.R. 497 (C.A.); and *Allied Arab Bank Ltd.* v. *Hajjar* (1987) [1988] Q.B. 787.

43   See *Mercedes-Benz*, above note 9. But note that pursuant to the United Kingdom *Civil Jurisdiction and Judgments Act* 1982 (U.K.), c. 27, a court in the United Kingdom can grant a *Mareva* injunction to enforce an interlocutory order granted by a court in a signatory state: see *Republic of Haiti*, above note 13.

44   See *Baur*, above note 14.

45   Above note 29.

2) the risks inherent in that transaction;
3) the residency of the defendant;
4) enforcement rights for judgment creditors in the jurisdiction where
    the defendant's assets are located;
5) the amount of the claim; and
6) the history of the defendant's conduct.[46]

The Canadian judgments have not commented upon the more critical issues, such as the impact on third parties, and the extent to which the framing of the order may amount to an excessive jurisdictional reach such that it offends accepted norms of international law of conflicts. These issues have bedevilled the United Kingdom courts and have been the subject of strident academic criticism.[47]

Third parties have been subject to *Mareva* injunctions where they have notice of the order and the injunction is cast in sufficient terms to define what the third party must do to comply. However, a third party outside the court's jurisdiction cannot be made subject to the order because this would amount to an excessive claim of extra-territoriality, and thus violate the principles of comity amongst national courts. The situation of a third party who has offices in many jurisdictions, particularly banks, raises special concerns. The third party could potentially be in breach of the order for actions taken by its subsidiary, branch, or even principal office in another jurisdiction in which the assets of the defendant lie. To meet this concern the United Kingdom courts have created what is known as the *Babanaft* proviso as amended by the comments in *Derby & Co. Ltd.* v. *Weldon (Nos. 3 & 4)*.[48] This proviso purports to protect third parties from potential contempt proceedings

---

46 *Ibid.* at 130.
47 See R. Crawford, "The Extra-Territorial Effect of *Mareva* Injunctions — The Sleeping Giant in Fairyland" (1990), 18 Austl. Bus. L. Rev.
48 Above note 36. The proviso, *ibid.* at 84, reads:

    Provided that, in so far as this order purports to have extra territorial effect, no person shall be affected thereby or concerned with the terms thereof until it shall be declared enforceable or be enforced by a foreign court and then it shall only affect them to the extent of such declaration or enforcement unless they are: (a) a person to whom this order is addressed or an officer of or agent appointed by a power of attorney of such a person or (b) persons who are subject to the jurisdiction of this court and (i) have been given written notice of this order at their residence or place of business within the jurisdiction, and (ii) are able to prevent acts or omissions outside the jurisdiction of this court which assist in the breach of the terms of this order.

    Now the UK Chancery Practice Direction 25-CPO-004, 'Freezing Injunction Order to restrain assets worldwide.'

by immunizing them if they come within the exceptions outlined in the proviso. Unfortunately, the proviso is also subject to criticism.[49]

The fact that a worldwide *Mareva* still acts *in personam* has been given as the main reason why the order does not amount to an excessive assumption of extra-territorial jurisdiction,[50] in violation of principles of international law.

I. *MAREVA* INJUNCTIONS IN AID OF THE CRIMINAL LAW

Section 462.33 of the *Criminal Code*[51] makes provision for the attorney general to apply for an *ex parte* order of restraint over property. To gain the order the attorney general must prove reasonable grounds exist for believing that the property is subject to forfeiture. Forfeiture is the actual taking of the proceeds of crime by the state, and is provided under section 462.37, in the case of conviction, and section 462.38, where the person has absconded.

Mareva injunctions have been used to supplement the criminal law to insure that if a fine is imposed, there are assets upon which the Crown may execute its judgment. In *Consolidated Fastfrate*,[52] the Crown sought a Mareva injunction against the defendant who at that time had been charged with offences under the *Competition Act*,[53] although a verdict had not been entered. The defendant had also begun to wind up its business and return to the United States. Fearing that if the defendant was convicted there would be no way that the Crown could ensure a substantial fine was paid, it brought these civil proceedings for the injunction. The injunction was denied on the basis that the Crown had provided no evidence that the defendant was by its actions attempting

---

49   See A. Malek & C. Lewis, "Worldwide *Mareva* Injunctions: The Position of International Banks" [1990] Lloyds Mar. & Com. L.Q. 88. The authors suggest that because an international bank operates across frontiers, a bank may be compelled to comply with the order to give instructions to its foreign branch. This in turn could be a violation of a local law of the foreign branch, or be in breach of contract when a defendant draws a cheque on the account that is then wrongfully dishonoured. See also Justice A. Rogers, "The Extra-Territorial Reach of the *Mareva* Injunction" [1991] Lloyds & Com. L.Q. 231.

50   See *Babanaft International Co. S.A. v. Bassatne* (1989), [1990] Ch. 13 at 25, Kerr L.J.; and *Derby*, note 36 at 83, Lord Donaldson M.R.

51   R.S.C. 1985, c. C-46.

52   Above note 22.

53   R.S.C. 1985, c. C-34.

to evade judgment. Galligan J.A. indicated that before the Crown could be successful in gaining a *Mareva* injunction in aid of the criminal law it would have to satisfy:

1) demonstrate that the accused had assets within the court's jurisdiction,
2) demonstrate a strong *prima facie* case that the accused person is likely to be convicted of the offence and that the fine will equal or exceed the value of the assets to be attached,
3) demonstrate that the accused is dissipating or removing the assets for the improper purpose of making them unavailable to pay the fine, and
4) give an undertaking respecting damages.[54]

In Australia, a *Mareva* injunction has also been given to the commissioner of taxation where the commissioner has issued an additional taxation assessment and where the defendant was in the process of liquidating its assets and transferring the money out of the court's jurisdiction.[55] In Canada, provisions in the *Income Tax Act*[56] allow the minister to make an ex parte application to the court to collect assessed taxes where there are reasonable grounds to believe that delay would jeopardize collection. In addition, where a taxpayer is fleeing Canada without paying her taxes the minister may demand immediate payment and commence seizure of goods and chattels by way of summary execution.[57]

FURTHER READINGS

BERRYMAN, J., "*Mareva* Injunctions: Canadian and Australian Comparisons" in R. Carroll, ed., *Civil Remedies: Issues and Developments* (Sydney: Federation Press, 1996) c. 7

BLACK V. & BABIN E., "*Mareva* Injunctions in Canada: Territorial Aspects" (1997) 28 C.B.L.J. 430

GEE, S., *Mareva Injunctions and Anton Piller Relief*, 4th ed. (London: Sweet & Maxwell, 1998)

HOYLE, M.S.W., *The Mareva Injunction and Related Orders*, 3rd ed. (London: Lloyd's of London Press, 1997)

---

54 *Consolidated Fastfrate*, above note 22 at 579.
55 See *Deputy Commissioner of Taxation v. Sharp* (1988), 82 A.C.T.R. 1 (S.C.).
56 B.S.C. 1985 (5th Supp), c. 1, s. 225.2(2).
57 *Ibid.* s. 226.

KUNC, F., "*Mareva* Injunctions" in P. Parkinson, ed., *The Principles of Equity* (Sydney: LBC Information Services, 1996) c. 20

MICHELL, P., "The *Mareva* Injunction in Aid of Foreign Proceedings" (1996) 34 Osgoode Hall L.J. 741

SADINSKY, S., "Interlocutory Injunctions and Procedures: The *Mareva* Injunction" in J. Berryman, ed., *Remedies: Issues and Perspectives* (Scarborough, Ont.: Carswell, 1991) 175

INTERLOCUTORY INJUNCTIONS TO SEIZE PROPERTY OR DOCUMENTS: *ANTON PILLER* INJUNCTIONS

A. INTRODUCTION

The *Anton Piller* injunction has been termed a "civil search warrant." It allows the plaintiff to take documents or property into custody where she is able to show that there is a real risk of the defendant destroying them before the plaintiff's substantive cause of action comes to trial. The order is available *ex parte* and surprise is an important element to ensure the effectiveness of the order. Because the order has the potential to be a significant intrusion into the defendant's affairs, courts have created special procedural safeguards to accommodate the interest of both litigants. The order has been particularly effective in dealing with intellectual property infringement, although it is not confined to that area.

B. JURISDICTION

Anton Piller injunctions can be divided into two categories.

1) Injunction to Dispose of the Issues

In the first category are cases where the injunction will dispose of the issues in dispute between the parties. The plaintiff is seeking the order to recover property in which he has a proprietary interest, such as confidential papers, or, to ensure the withdrawal from sale of commodities that infringe the plaintiff's trademark, patent or copyright. In this category, the property, be it a document or infringing article, is the subject matter of the dispute.

Cases can be disposed at this stage either because of the nature of the target subjects or the type of market in which they operate. With respect to intellectual property, the market is often highly volatile and the infringing goods will often only have an ephemeral value. Timing is a decisive factor for the plaintiff and he will want to use an *Anton Piller* order to rid the market of infringing articles for as long as the market holds. Once the market has collapsed the plaintiff will see little value in proceeding to a substantive trial of the merits of his cause of action.

In respect to target subject, *Anton Piller* orders have been directed at defendants either engaged in manufacturing operations illicitly reproducing intellectual property, or at retailers who form the lower echelons in pyramidal marketing of illicit material. Again, timing is decisive. Again, the plaintiff will not wish to proceed to trial of the merits; in any case, the target subject defendants are unlikely to have the resources to contest the plaintiff's action.

2) Injunction to Preserve Evidence

The second category of *Anton Piller* injunctions concerns the preservation of evidence necessary to further a substantive cause of action. Two features distinguish this category from the first:

- the plaintiff may have no proprietary interest in the property (usually documents) which is not the subject matter of the dispute.
- the importance of the documents to the plaintiff is their evidentiary value to prove a substantive cause of action. Mere recovery alone will not compensate for the plaintiff's injury.

In Canada, for both categories the jurisdictional base for *Anton Piller* injunctions has been found in three areas. In all the common law provinces as well as the Federal Court rules there are provisions relating to the interim inspection and preservation of property. These rules have primarily been created to give the plaintiff an opportunity to either inspect premises or ensure property is retained in safe custody before judgment is rendered. While these rules encompass many aspects of the *Anton Piller* jurisdiction, they do not encompass all. It is difficult to include documents within the notion of "property" as envisaged in the rules; documents have their own process of disclosure through the discovery process. Some courts have also insisted that pleadings be closed before moving pursuant to these rules, in which case the advantage of an *ex parte* interlocutory process would be lost.

Finally, it would be difficult to authorize interrogatories under the rules. These have become an important part of an *Anton Piller* injunction to identify the names of suppliers of infringing articles and the location of the property in dispute.

A second jurisdictional base, and the approach formerly followed in the United Kingdom, is as a function of the court's inherent jurisdiction to control its own procedures. *Anton Piller* injunctions often appear to mirror pre-trial discovery, a matter that has always lain within the court's discretion to control. The United Kingdom has now created a statutory jurisdictional base for *Anton Piller* injunctions found in the Civil Procedure Act 1997 s.7. The Act renames the injunction a 'Search Order'.[1]

A third jurisdictional base is in the general "just and convenient" power of a court to order an injunction.

C. ACCESSIBILITY THRESHOLD

The plaintiff must establish a strong *prima facie* case against the defendant.[2] Some courts have gone further and suggested that the plaintiff must show an "extremely" strong *prima facie* case.[3] Pitching the accessibility threshold at this level has been justified on the basis of the extraordinary nature of the remedy and the potential for abuse of the defendant's rights. However, this high threshold level does create an anomaly with other interlocutory injunctions, inviting the spectre of otherwise meritorious plaintiffs being thwarted in their effort to get the injunction, or parties using this form of relief to seek a preliminary trial of the merits. The justification for lowering the threshold level in *American Cyanamid*[4] — namely, wishing to abstain from expressing opinions on the merits based on unchallenged evidence — seems equally applicable in the case of *Anton Piller* injunctions. The real concern for courts is how to protect the plaintiff's and defendant's legitimate interests from unlawful or unnecessary interference. This can be achieved by a careful scrutiny of the other grounds necessary to justify

---

1   See Civil Procedure Rules UK 25.1.21 and Chancery Practice Direction 25 CPD – 005 'Search Order – Order to preserve evidence and property'.

2   See *Piller (Anton) K.G. v. Manufacturing Processes Ltd. [Anton Piller]*, [1976] Ch. 55 (C.A.); and *Nintendo of America Inc. v. Coinex Video Games Inc.* (1982), [1983] 2 F.C. 189 (C.A.) [*Nintendo*].

3   See *Rank Film Distributors Ltd. v. Video Information Centre* (1981), [1982] A.C. 380 (H.L.) [*Rank Film*].

4   *America Cynamid Co. v. Ethicon Ltd.*, [1975] A.C. 396 (H.L.).

the injunction and the attendant procedural safeguards developed by the courts concerning the order's execution. Threshold levels are a particularly blunt and arbitrary way to achieve this goal.

D. ELEMENTS OF THE INJUNCTION

Unlike many other injunctions the issue of proof of irreparable harm plays little if any role in the decision to grant an *Anton Piller* order. Its minimized role stems from the fact that when first created *Anton Piller* orders were seen primarily as preserving evidence and thus acted as an extension to the discovery process. However, as the order quickly expanded it became an important weapon in seizing infringing material to prevent the further incursion of a wrong where there was a real risk that the material would be destroyed if notice of proceedings was given. In this category, the *Anton Piller* order takes on true remedial aspects. Yet a further outgrowth of the *Anton Piller* order has been the ability to couple it with a *Mareva* injunction and thus secure a form of seizure of assets to secure eventual judgment. As Mullan has stated, under this scenario the order "clearly become[s] a pre-trial remedy."[5] However, even in the latter two categories the preservation of evidence is still an important function being served by the order and may by itself justify the courts' involvement.

In substitution of irreparable harm courts have insisted that, in addition to a strong *prima facie* case, a plaintiff must establish that the damage resulting from the defendant's infringement, either actual or potential, is very serious to the plaintiff.[6] The plaintiff can establish seriousness either by demonstrating the degree of disruption such activity will cause to her business (i.e., loss of goodwill if the defendant continues selling inferior-quality goods which violate her intellectual property rights), or, by a monetary quantification of damages (i.e., the likely loss of sales should the defendant continue selling infringing material) which, in the plaintiff's particular circumstances, is seen as being "serious." Where all that is at stake is the need to preserve evidence, rather than prevent further wrong, Mullan has suggested that the court should also ask how the loss of the evidence will effect the chances of the plaintiff to prove her case.

---

5   D.J. Mullan, "*Anton Piller* Orders: Life at the Extremity of the Courts' in J. Berryman, ed., *Remedies: Issues and Perspectives* (Scarborough, Ont.: Carswell, 1991) 189 at 198.

6   This element, and the need to provide clear proof that the defendant will destroy the property if notice is given, were established by Ormrod L.J. in *Anton Piller*, above note 2.

Additionally, the plaintiff must provide clear evidence that the defendant holds in his possession incriminating documents or property and that there is a real possibility he may destroy such material if notice were given of any proceedings. When considering this element courts have been persuaded by looking at the character of the defendant, and the usual practices of pirates of copyright.[7] Nevertheless, there is a considerable burden on the plaintiff to provide concrete evidence that there is a real risk of destruction of the material subject to the order should notice be given. This evidence may arise during the course of proceedings already commenced against the defendant, as in *E.M.I. Ltd. v. Pandit,*[8] or as part of an undercover investigation organized by the plaintiff, as in *Nintendo of America Inc. v. Coinex Video Games Inc.*[9]

In *E.M.I.*, incidentally the first reported *Anton Piller* case, the plaintiff had gained an interlocutory injunction against the defendant for infringement of copyright. Part of the initial order required the defendant to furnish the plaintiff with an affidavit, detailing the defendant's suppliers of infringing material and to whom the defendant had passed on the infringing material. After receipt of the affidavit the plaintiff commenced the present proceedings, seeking an *Anton Piller* order to recover any documents in the defendant's possession which would assist in identifying suppliers and customers of the defendant. In bringing forward this order the plaintiff was now able to show that the defendant's original affidavit had contained "a pack of lies," had been supported by forged letters as exhibits, and that the defendant had engaged in an "expensive, extensive, and quite deliberate course of dealing in infringement of the plaintiffs' copyright."[10] Under these circumstances the court readily granted the plaintiff's request for a further *ex parte* order to seize documents from the defendant's premises.

In *Nintendo*, the plaintiff brought an action against the defendant for infringement of copyright held over two video arcade games, Donkey Kong and Donkey Kong Junior. In seeking an *Anton Piller* order, the plaintiff provided affidavit evidence of its private investigator to the effect that the defendant was willing to sell the investigator a pirate version of the plaintiff's games. In addition, the plaintiff established by affidavits that the defendants operated on a cash basis and had behaved in

---

7   See *Lock International Plc. v. Beswick*, [1989] 1 W.L.R. 1268; and *Busby v. Thorn EMI Video Programmes Ltd.*, [1984] 1 N.Z.L.R. 461 (C.A.).

8   [1975] 1 W.L.R. 302 (Ch.) [*E.M.I.*].

9   Above note 2.

10   *E.M.I.*, above note 8 at 304.

an "extremely evasive and secretive manner," that the corporate defendants were "vehicles of convenience" able to disband and relocate on a moment's notice, and that the defendants had changed their corporate name a number of times.[11] Taken together, these affidavits justified the conclusion by the court that the plaintiff had demonstrated a real possibility that infringing material may be destroyed if notice was given without an *Anton Piller* order.

Because the plaintiff wants the element of surprise, *Anton Piller* injunction applications will usually be made *ex parte* and heard *in camera*. The potentially draconian effect of the order has lead courts to require a high level of disclosure on the part of the plaintiff. The plaintiff must make full and frank disclosure of all matters that may have a bearing on the court's consideration of the application, including matters that may be adverse to the plaintiff's case. A failure to do so can result in the order being set aside, an adjustment being made to costs, or even the imposition of punitive damages.[12]

The plaintiff will have to give the usual undertaking in damages, but will also have to give an undertaking concerning matters of how the order is executed. These are dealt with in the next section.

E. PROCEDURAL SAFEGUARDS

The courts have imposed numerous procedural safeguards on the execution of *Anton Piller* injunctions, perhaps more than on any other form of interlocutory injunction. These requirements attest to the uniqueness of the order, and the fact that it appears to operate like a civil search warrant, without any of the process requirements which form part of the public law relating to search warrants.

---

11   *Nintendo*, above note 2 at 195.

12   See *Pulse Microsystems Ltd.* v. *SafeSoft Systems Inc.* (1996), 134 D.L.R. (4th) 701 (Man. C.A.); and *Columbia Picture Industries Inc.* v. *Robinson* (1986), [1987] Ch. 38. In Ontario there is the suggestion that failure to make full and frank disclosure must result in setting aside the order. See *US of A.* v. *Friedland* [1996] O.J. No. 4399, and *Computer Security Products Ltd.* v. *Forbes* [1999] O.J. No. 4573 (Ont. Superior Ct.). In other jurisdictions the court maintains its discretion either to set aside, or, to continue the order where there is sufficient evidence to support the injunction once all the facts are known. See *Adobe Systems Inc.* v. *KLJ Computers* [1999] 3 F.C. 621.

1) Form of Order

The aim of the order is the location and preservation of documents and property. The order should specify in detail exactly what property is covered, or which documents (or the nature of their subject matter) the defendant is required to provide and for which the plaintiff is entitled to search. The plaintiff is not entitled to undertake a "fishing expedition" through the defendant's premises or documents in the vain hope of discovering some incriminating evidence. Nor is the plaintiff entitled to gain information that may give him a commercial advantage by having access to a rival's records.

In the Federal Court, *Anton Piller* injunctions have been given out against known and unknown parties under the guise of John and Jane Doe orders. These injunctions have been used against street and market vendors of pirated intellectual property. The plaintiff has been able to establish that certain vendors are dealing in illicit goods and wishes to do a sweep of an area to seize the infringing property from all dealers. The Federal Court has been prepared to grant such a broad-ranging injunction, as long as there is an opportunity for a defendant to later challenge the plaintiff's assertion to entitlement to the order.[13]

2) Search

Although the injunction has been described as a civil search warrant, it does not actually authorize the plaintiff to make forcible entry. The order requires the defendant to allow the plaintiff entry to inspect and to take into custody infringing documents or property. Failure to comply exposes the defendant to possible contempt of court proceedings.[14] Although this distinction between conferring actual powers of entry and requiring entry on pain of contempt is subtle, it is nevertheless important. The defendant can always refuse entry, and that decision must be respected. The only recourse for the plaintiff is to commence contempt proceedings.

Under a practice direction issued in the United Kingdom[15] an independent supervising solicitor familiar with the operation of *Anton Piller* orders must accompany the plaintiff's solicitor. If the defendant wishes to challenge the granting of the injunction, she must allow the super-

---

13   See *Fila Canada Inc.* v. *Doe*, [1996] 3 F.C. 493 (T.D.).
14   See *Anton Piller*, above note 2.
15   See Chanery Practice Direction 25-CPO-005.

vising solicitor entry to the premises before seeking to either rescind or vary the order before the court.

3) Service

As a condition of granting the injunction the plaintiff is normally required to give an undertaking that upon arrival at the defendant's premises he will explain the purpose of the order and the consequences of non-compliance. The plaintiff must afford the defendant time to consider her response including contacting her solicitor.[16] The order may also specify how many people may enter the premises, and the day and hours that it can be executed. A record should be made of any material removed, and the defendant furnished with a copy. Where property or documents are removed the United Kingdom practice requires that these be placed in the hands of the plaintiff's solicitor.

In Canada a similar order can be made, although it is not a mandatory requirement that the property or documents be placed in the plaintiff's solicitor's control. There is no requirement in Canada to have an independent supervising solicitor appointed or, indeed, to have a solicitor serve the order on the defendant. For intellectual property infringement, it is common in Canada to use the services of articling students and private investigators when undertaking a sweep of street vendors.

4) Interrogatories

An important part of both *Mareva* and *Anton Piller* injunctions is the attachment of interrogatories in aid of the injunction. These interrogatories are often used to elicit the location of assets, property and documents. On other occasions they may request from the defendant the names of suppliers, manufacturers and other retailers dealing in illicit manufacturing and distribution. The answers to these interrogatories can assist the plaintiff in the execution of the injunction, but may expose the defendant to criminal prosecution if the answers constitute incriminating statements. A difficulty has arisen in striking a balance between what is needed to ensure the effectiveness of the order while acknowledging the defendant's traditional common law protection accorded the defendant against being forced to make self-incriminating statements.

---

16   See *Grenzservice Speditions Ges.m.b.H* v. *Jans* (1995), 129 D.L.R. (4th) 733 (B.C.S.C.).

In the United Kingdom the House of Lords, in *Rank Film Distributors Ltd.* v. *Video Information Centre*,[17] found in the common law a protection against self-incrimination for a defendant subject to an *Anton Piller* order. The defendant could not be required to answer interrogatories that would have revealed the name of suppliers, receivers, and producers of illicit films in breach of the plaintiff's copyright. This protection against self-incrimination would not be granted where the risk of subsequent criminal prosecution was low and would result in only a minimal criminal penalty.

Rank Film dramatically curtailed the utility of the *Anton Piller* order. However, subsequent legislative changes abrogated the impact of the decision inasmuch as it applied to intellectual property infringements and passing-off actions.[18] In all other disputes, the decision represents the position of the common law privilege in the United Kingdom, although it is now possible that the court may require that a term be inserted into the order which purports to abrogate *Rank Film*.[19]

In *Sociedade Nacional de Combustiveis de Angola U.E.E.* v. *Lundqvist*,[20] the United Kingdom Court of Appeal had to determine the extent to which the common law privilege covered a defendant who through both *Anton Piller* and *Mareva* injunctions was required to disclose details and whereabouts of assets. The defendant had allegedly defrauded the plaintiff by making secret profits on the sale of the plaintiff's oil. The *Mareva* and *Anton Piller* orders required the defendant to furnish documents, refrain from disposing of assets both in the United Kingdom and worldwide, and disclose the whereabouts of all other assets.

The Court of Appeal indicated that in order to raise the privilege, the defendant was required to show "grounds to apprehend danger to the witness, and those grounds must be reasonable, rather than fanciful."[21] In this case that test was met. The disclosure of the value of the defendant's assets could provide evidence to prove a case of conspiracy to defraud, and therefore should not be disclosed. However, the court went on to hold that the location of assets could be ordered. This evidence was regarded as innocuous and did not raise reasonable grounds

---

17   Above note 3.

18   See *Supreme Court Act 1981* (U.K.), 1981, c. 54, s. 72.

19   See *A.T. & T. Istel Ltd.* v. *Tully* (1992), [1993] A.C. 45 (H.L.).

20   (1990), [1991] 2 Q.B. 310 (C.A.) [*Sociedade Nacional*].

21   *Ibid.* at 324. The test that Lord Wilberforce applied in *Rank Film*, above note 3, is somewhat wider. In that case the privilege could be raised where the disclosure "may set in train a process which may lead to incrimination or may lead to the discovery of real evidence of an incriminating character.": *ibid.* at 443.

to apprehend danger to the defendant. In addition, such disclosure would aid the plaintiff in enforcing the *Mareva* injunction in other jurisdictions. The court found that the disclosure of evidence of asset location was subject to part of the plaintiff's undertakings given in return for the original *Mareva* order. These undertakings — requiring leave of the court before commencing any proceedings in a foreign court, and, not to use any information disclosed pursuant to the order in any proceedings, domestic or foreign, without leave — were seen to give the defendant sufficient protection. Similar undertakings given in *Rank Film* were seen as being insufficient protection and of dubious validity.

In the end, the order (which required the defendant to disclose the location, but not the amount, of assets outside the court's jurisdiction) gave the plaintiff most of what it sought in the orginal injunction application. But the judgment of Browne-Wilkinson V.C. indicates just how precarious a position the plaintiff was in. As he points out, the decision of the court "makes it clear that a properly formulated claim to privilege against incrimination can be put forward."[22] Browne-Wilkinson V.C. went on to call for legislative intervention similar to what had been done following the *Rank Film* decision.

The issue of self-incrimination in either *Mareva* or *Anton Piller* orders has not been dealt with by Canadian courts.[23] The issue in Canada is made complex largely because both federal and provincial *Evidence Acts* have been enacted which provide for a statutory privilege against self-incrimination. In essence, all these Acts compel the witness to answer questions, but provide a protection against the use of such answers in any subsequent prosecution. The Acts are not without problems, and, arguably, do not apply to either *Anton Piller* or *Mareva* defendants. The Acts contemplate a "witness" who is "testifying" in a "proceeding," and at the time of service of the injunctive order the *Mareva* or *Anton Piller* defendant does not appear to satisfy any of these conditions. The Acts have led David Paciocco[24] to conclude that Canadian courts should decline to follow *Rank Film*, and that the *Anton Piller* defen-

---

22   *Sociedade Nacional*, above note 20 at 338.

23   In *Chin-Can Communication Corp.* v. *Chinese Video Centre Ltd.* (1983), 70 C.P.R. (2d) 184 (F.C.T.D.), Addy J. alluded to possible self-incrimination problems in a copyright infringement case, particularly in light of new *Charter* provisions. However, he did not feel that it was necessary, in light of his findings in other parts of the case, to deal with the matter.

24   The provisions and their application are fully discussed in D.M. Paciocco, "*Anton Piller* Orders: Facing the Threat of the Privilege Against Self-Incrimination" (1984),34 U.T.L.J. 26; and J. Berryman, "*Anton Piller* Injunctions: An Update" (1985) 2 I.P.J. 49.

dant should be compelled to answer without any privilege being conferred. Paciocco's argument is fourfold, and can be summarized as follows:

1) To follow *Rank Film* would seriously impair the *Anton Piller* order. Why follow a decision that has itself been abrogated in the United Kingdom?
2) The trend in Canadian jurisprudence is to curtail exclusionary rules, based on principles against self-incrimination.
3) First, the underlying rationale for the privilege is not served by an extension to *Anton Piller* defendants. That rationale is to encourage truthfulness and candour in the witness box. Since the *Anton Piller* defendant will always have something to lose, even if the answers are not incriminatory, the rule does not encourage candid information. Second, arguments supporting the privilege have more weight when it is the Crown that is pursuing the investigation. Where it is a civil action and the Crown is a mere bystander, the balance is tipped in favour of allowing the plaintiff's action.
4) The plaintiff could proceed to trial and compel the defendant to answer the same questions that the defendant has failed to respond to in the original *Anton Piller* order.

Paciocco was writing on the *Anton Piller* order and not the *Mareva* injunction. However, the same arguments would appear to be valid save that, in a *Mareva* fact pattern, the Crown may not be a mere bystander and the prospect of a criminal prosecution may be more real.

The preferable solution is to compel the defendant to answer the interrogatories or produce the document, but confer a privilege against subsequent use of the documents or answers in any subsequent prosecution. Interestingly, this has been the solution favoured by the New Zealand Court of Appeal in *Busby v. Thorn EMI Video Programmes Ltd.*[25] In that case the majority saw the privilege as being the creature of common law and within the court's inherent jurisdiction to "prevent abuse of process by the avoidance of unfairness."[26] In addition, since the administration of justice in New Zealand took place in a unified court system, and the laws of evidence were largely "lawyers' law," the majority saw no impediment to advancing such a privilege. The minority judgment saw the majority's approach as more appropriate for the legislature and not one within judicial competence.

---

25 Above note 7.
26 *Ibid.* at 471.

F. EXTRA-TERRITORIAL APPLICATION AND *ANTON PILLER* ORDERS

An *Anton Piller* order acts *in personam*. Thus, it is quite possible to have an order requiring the defendant to allow the plaintiff entry to premises owned by the defendant in another jurisdiction and to take custody of documents and property subject to the order. Where the defendant is amenable to the court's jurisdiction then the order can be enforced through contempt powers and other consequences of non-compliance. This raises the spectre of the plaintiff being authorised to travel to another jurisdiction and require the defendant to permit entry so that documents or property can be seized. This prospect has alarmed some who suggest that such an order would be an infringement of a foreign country's sovereignty and an excess of jurisdiction in international law.[27]

The issue of extra-territoriality has arisen in at least three reported decisions before English courts. In *Protector Alarms Ltd.* v. *Maxim Alarms Ltd.*,[28] the plaintiff sought an order to enter premises situated in Scotland as well as England. The defendant's principal place of business was Scotland although it had other offices situated in England. Goulding J. declined to grant the injunction in as far as it applied to the offices located in Scotland. In his opinion the preferable approach was for the plaintiff to seek the order from a Scottish court. If the order was unattainable there, either because it would not be granted by a Scottish court or did not form part of the law of Scotland, then this was further reason not to exercise a jurisdiction from afar by acceding to the plaintiff's request.

In *Cook Industries Inc.* v. *Galliher*,[29] the plaintiff sought inspection of a flat located in Paris. The plaintiff had successfully obtained judgment in these proceedings before a United States court against the second defendant, Sarlie, for fraud and manipulation of shares. The plaintiff alleged that Sarlie had entered into an arrangement with the first defendant, Galliher, whereby Sarlie had the use of Galliher's apartment in Paris to store property. Galliher held the lease of the Paris apartment although the rent was paid by a company controlled by Sarlie. Galliher was an American resident but spent the majority of his time in London where he had a house. In effect the plaintiff was seek-

---

27   See C. McLachlan, "Transnational Applications of *Mareva* Injunctions and *Anton Piller* Orders" (1987) 37 Int'l & Comp. L.Q. 669 at 679.

28   [1978] F.S.R. 442 (Ch.).

29   (1978) [1979] 1 Ch. 439.

ing an order to inspect the Paris premises to identify the value of assets held by Sarlie, and he was actively pursuing proceedings for a similar order in the United States. Templeman J. awarded the order to allow the plaintiff's agent to inspect the defendant's apartment in Paris. In doing so, Templeman J. stressed the need to establish a cause of action within the court's jurisdiction, and that the defendant must be personally amenable to the court's jurisdiction. In this case, Templeman J. was prepared to accept that the plaintiff may well establish a personal equity between himself and Galliher based on the apparent role that the defendant was playing in assisting Sarlie defeat his creditors. This equity related to the ownership of the flat and the chattels, the role of the first defendant, and whether there were sufficient assets to satisfy the judgment debts. The extent of this equity would justify an order supporting inspection. Presumably, taking custody of the chattels would not have been supported. The first defendant was clearly amenable to the court's jurisdiction by virtue of his residency in London, the fact that he was physically present in London at the time of the hearing, and because he had issued a notice of motion seeking a stay of proceedings.

The importance of having actual jurisdiction over the defendant before giving an order covering foreign property has been reiterated in the third case, *Altertext Inc.* v. *Advanced Data Communications Ltd.*[30] In that case the plaintiff had sought an *Anton Piller* order against six defendants, one of whom was a Belgian company, for alleged copyright infringement, passing off and breach of confidentiality. Scott J. was adamant that no such order should be granted against the Belgian company until such time as jurisdiction had been established.

There are as yet no reported decisions in Canada that have raised extra-territoriality and *Anton Piller* orders, nor has the issue been raised in the context of inter-provincial orders. In the context of a federal state there are good reasons to support the notion that an *Anton Piller* order granted by a court of one province will be enforceable over property in another province.[31] The utilisation by the plaintiff of an agent solicitor in another province to effect the order will ensure the same procedural safeguards which would have been applied had the order been sought before the court in the jurisdiction in which the property is located. Such an approach would be consistent with the Supreme Court of Canada's initiative in advancing greater cohesion; namely, provincial superior courts giving "full faith and credit" to each others'

---

30 [1985] 1 W.L.R. 457 (Ch. D.).

31 Mullan, above note 4 at 203 comes to the same conclusion.

superior courts' judgments.[32] There are precedents to this effect with respect to the granting of specific performance.[33] Finally, the plaintiff may have the choice of commencing its action in Federal Court, particularly for intellectual property matters, where jurisdiction is conceived as being the entire country. With respect to extra-territoriality concerning orders beyond Canada's borders, I believe Canadian courts will adopt the same cautious approach as the English courts. Only where the defendant is within the court's jurisdiction and the *in personam* approach can be enforced will the order be granted. Even then, the court should probably ask what impediments exist which prevent the plaintiff from simultaneously commencing proceedings for *Anton Piller*-type relief in the foreign jurisdiction, and whether these impediments render the *Anton Piller* order unlawful in the foreign jurisdiction, or merely admit to procedural inadequacies of that jurisdiction.

G. CONSEQUENCES OF NON-COMPLIANCE

A defendant who fails to comply with an *Anton Piller* injunction is liable to contempt of court. In addition, because the injunction is aimed at securing documents or property from destruction, the court is prepared to accept that where the defendant fails to allow the plaintiff access, an adverse inference can be drawn against the defendant regarding the existence and content of the documents or the existence of property. Another possible consequence is that the defendant could be barred from defending the proceedings. This possibility was alluded to in by Dillon L.J. in the *Mareva* case, *Derby & Co.* v. *Weldon (No. 6)*.[34]

H. CHARTER APPLICATION

There are potentially two areas where the *Anton Piller* injunction may impinge upon *Charter*[35] rights; the protection against unauthorized search and seizure, and the protection against incrimination.

---

32   See *Morguard Investments Ltd.* v. *De Savoye*, [1990] 3 S.C.R. 1077, and the discussion in chapter 6 on anti-suit injunctions.

33   See discussion in chapter 12, s. B., 4.

34   [1990] 1 W.L.R. 1139 at 1149 (C.A.).

35   *Canadian Charter of Rights and Freedoms*, Part I of the *Constitution Act, 1982*, being Schedule B to the *Canada Act 1982* (U.K.), 1982, c. 11.

Section 8 of the *Charter* confers a guarantee against "unreasonable search or seizure" by agents of the state. For this section to be applicable it is assumed that a solicitor as an officer of the court executing an *Anton Piller* injunction is an agent of the state. This assumption may be incorrect in that a solicitor acting for a private party in a common law action would be immune to *Charter* scrutiny under the principles enunciated in *Dolphin Delivery*.[36] Assuming that the action is subject to *Charter* scrutiny, the *Anton Piller* injunction requires the defendant to permit the plaintiff's solicitor entry and does not authorise the use of force. This was enough for Lord Denning M.R. to state that the order did not violate a common law right against search and seizure.[37] However in *Thomson Newspapers Ltd.* v. *Canada (Director of Investigation)*[38] a majority of the Supreme Court accepted that the demand for the production of documents under the threat of contempt proceedings could constitute a "seizure." The *Charter* prohibits unreasonable search and seizure. *Hunter* v. *Southam Inc.*[39] established that a search and seizure would be reasonable where it was the product of "prior judicial authorization from an impartial adjudicator acting judicially by reference to objective standards."[40] The criteria used by courts to determine whether an *Anton Piller* injunction should be granted would appear to meet this standard of *Charter* scrutiny, in that the order would constitute a reasonable search and seizure even without needing to resort to a section 1 analysis.[41]

Section 13 of the *Charter* provides protection against the use of incriminating evidence in any other proceeding. This section is similar to the *Evidence Act* provisions[42] and is subject to a similar analysis. The section speaks of a "witness" who is "testifying" in a "proceeding." An *Anton Piller* defendant satisfies none of these requirements. Nor does the section prevent compellability, but merely prevents subsequent use in a later proceeding.

---

36   *R.W.D.S.U., Local 580* v. *Dolphin Delivery Ltd.*, [1986] 2 S.C.R. 573.

37   See *Anton Piller*, above note 2, where Lord Denning M.R. disposed with the argument that the order violated the common law principle articulated in *Entick* v. *Carrington* (1765), 2 Wils. 275, 95 E.R. 807 (C.P.).

38   [1990] 1 S.C.R. 425.

39   [1984] 2 S.C.R. 145.

40   Mullan, above note 5 at 207.

41   In *Dominion Citrus & Drugs Ltd.* v. *Loconte Meat Market* (1983), 33 C.P.C. 105 (Ont. S.C. Masters), Master Donkin held, without discussion, that an *Anton Piller* order does not offend section 8 of the *Charter*.

42   See, for example, *Canada Evidence Act*, R.S.C. 1985, c. C-5, s. 5(2).

FURTHER READINGS

BERRYMAN, J., "*Anton Piller* Injunctions: An Update" (1985) 2 I.P.J. 49

BERRYMAN, J., "*Anton Piller* Orders: A Canadian Common Law Approach" (1984) 34 U.T.L.J. 1

DOCKRAY, M. & H. LADDIE "*Piller* Problems" (1990) 106 L.Q. Rev. 601

MULLAN, D.J., "*Anton Piller* Orders: Life at the Extremity of the Courts' Powers," in J. Berryman, ed., *Remedies: Issues and Perspectives* (Scarborough, Ont.: Carswell, 1991) 189

PACIOCCO, D.M., "*Anton Piller* Orders: Facing the Threat of the Privilege Against Self-Incrimination" (1984) 34 U.T.L.J. 26.

ROCK, A.M., "The '*Anton Piller*' Order: An Examination of its Nature, Development and Present Position in Canada" (1984) 5 Advocates' Q. 191

SHERIDAN, L.A., *Chancery Procedure & Anton Piller Orders* (Chichester, U.K.: B. Rose, 1994)

CHAPTER 6

INTERLOCUTORY INJUNCTIONS TO PREVENT COMMENCE-MENT OF LEGAL ACTION: ANTI-SUIT INJUNCTIONS

A. INTRODUCTION

At the outer extreme of judicial innovation in the field of interlocutory injunctions has been the anti-suit injunction. This injunction is designed to prevent a plaintiff from bringing a suit in another country. It is the product of globalized litigation and the fact that in many disputes there exists a potential for liability against numerous defendants in a number of jurisdictions. The usual legal mechanism for resolving these jurisdictional problems lies in the area of conflicts of laws and the doctrine of *forum non conveniens*. However, many jurisdictions, notably many European civil law countries and Texas, do not follow similar conflict rules. Plaintiffs have been drawn to these jurisdictions in the belief, often justified, that they will receive some procedural advantage (i.e., access to jury trial, different forms of proof such as strict liability rather than negligence, advantage of a contingent fee structure) — or that because of the greater availability of punitive damages the compensation granted will be significantly higher, than if they had continued to proceed in a more natural forum. In response, defendants have sought an anti-suit injunction, ordering the plaintiff to discontinue its suit in the foreign jurisdiction. For a court, adjudicating on such an issue is extremely problematic. At one level it appears as if the domestic court is being asked to pass judgment upon the capacity of a foreign court to administer justice. This issue transcends the litigants and raises questions concerning comity between national courts.

B. JURISDICTION AND CRITERIA FOR AWARD OF AN ANTI-SUIT INJUNCTION

Courts have always held jurisdiction to restrain a cause of action before the court by issuing a stay of proceedings. The obverse of this is an injunction restraining a party from proceeding in another jurisdiction. While there is evidence that such a power resided with courts from an early time, it was exercised sparingly and only with extreme caution, where the foreign proceedings were considered "vexatious or oppressive." With the emergence of much more multi-jurisdictional litigation and commensurate disputes about litigation forum, this position has changed; first in the United Kingdom,[1] and now in Canada.

In Canada the Supreme Court has provided a definitive test for the consideration of anti-suit injunctions in *Amchem Products Inc.* v. *British Columbia (Workers' Compensation Board).*[2] The appellants were persons who had suffered injury as a result of exposure to asbestos in the ship-building and construction industries. In 1988, nine individual appellants had commenced an action in a Texas court seeking damages from the respondent companies. After these actions were commenced the number of appellants swelled to 194. The British Columbian Workers' Compensation Board had a subrogated claim in most of these cases, although the individual appellants would receive any damages beyond the Board's interest. The appellants were residents of British Columbia, where their injuries were sustained. The respondents were all companies that held asbestos mining interests, but none had any particular connection with British Columbia other than as a supplier of asbestos. They were incorporated in the United States, although there was no concentration of respondents in any one state and no particular connection with Texas other than doing business within the state. The appellants' actions had been commenced in the Texas court, alleging various torts, including conspiracy in that the various respondents had failed to warn of the problems with asbestos exposure. The respondents had sought, unsuccessfully, a stay of proceedings before the Texas court, on the grounds of *forum non conveniens*. At the time Texas did not apply

---

1   See the development between *Castanho* v. *Brown & Root (U.K.) Ltd.* (1980), [1981] A.C. 557 (H.L.) and *Société Nationale Industrielle Aerospatiale* v. *Lee Kui Jak*, [1987] A.C. 871 (P.C.).

2   [1993] 1 S.C.R. 897 [*Amchem*].

the *forum non conveniens* doctrine.[3] The respondents then commenced the current proceedings before the British Columbia Supreme Court. The trial judge granted the injunction, which was upheld on appeal. Before the Supreme Court of Canada, the injunction was dismissed.

In prefatory remarks the Supreme Court recognized that a stay of proceedings and an anti-suit injunction are similar in nature but differ in one important respect: In the former, the domestic court is making a determination concerning whether it is the appropriate forum for the dispute. In the latter, the domestic court is making a determination on the appropriateness of a foreign court to hear an action, which raises an issue of comity between national courts.[4] Comity is the way it should be handled and therefore little resort should be necessary to an anti-suit injunction. A court will only be justified to interfere where a foreign court has departed from *forum non conveniens* to such an extent that the assumption of jurisdiction amounts to a serious injustice.

The test as formulated by the Supreme Court requires the following:

1) The domestic court should not entertain an application for an anti-suit injunction until such time as the foreign court has been given an opportunity to consider whether it is or is not an appropriate forum in which to bring the dispute. An applicant for an anti-suit injunction should thus commence proceedings for a stay of proceedings or similar order in the foreign court before resorting to an anti-suit injunction.

2) The domestic court can only consider an anti-suit injunction if it is alleged and shown by the applicant that it is the most appropriate forum in which to bring the dispute. This requires the domestic court to apply principles of *forum non conveniens*. The domestic court must ask itself whether there is another forum that is clearly

---

3   The *forum non conveniens* doctrine had been abrogated by the Texas Supreme Court in *Dow Chemical Co. v. Castro Alfaro*, 786 S.W.2d 674 (Tex. 1990). The doctrine has since been reintroduced in Texas by legislation enacted in 1993: see Tex. Civil Practice and Remedies Code Ann. §. 71.051 (West 1993).

4   In *Amchem*, above note 2 at 913-14, the Court adopted the definition of comity provided by the United States Supreme Court in *Hilton v. Guyot*, 159 U.S. 113 at 163-64 (1985), which was adopted by Estey J. in *R. v. Spencer*, [1985] 2 S.C.R. 278 at 283, and by La Forest J. in *Mortuard Investments Ltd. v. De Savoye*, [1990] 3 S.C.R. 1077 at 1096:"Comity" in the legal sense, is neither a matter of absolute obligation, on the one hand, nor of mere courtesy and good will, upon the other. But it is the recognition which one nation allows within its territory to the legislative, executive or judicial acts of another nation, having due regard both to international duty and convenience, and to the rights of its own citizens or of other persons who are under the protection of its laws.

more appropriate than the domestic court. When asking this question, the domestic court must be aware of the fact that the foreign court has already determined that it is an appropriate forum for the dispute, and that decision should be respected unless it is clear to the domestic court that the foreign court did not act on similar principles to *forum non conveniens*. If the foreign court, applying a doctrine of *forum non conveniens* or similar principles, "could reasonably have concluded that there was no alternative forum that was clearly more appropriate, the domestic court should respect that decision."[5]

3) Only where the domestic court has concluded that it is the appropriate forum, and that the decision of the foreign court should not be respected (either because the foreign jurisdiction does not recognize a *forum non conveniens* principle or similar rule, or because the foreign court did not apply the rules, such that its conclusion on jurisdiction could not reasonably be reached had it applied those principles) must the domestic court go onto the next phase of the inquiry and ask:

   a) Would it be wrong to deprive the plaintiff (party bringing the substantive litigation in the foreign court) of the advantage of the foreign jurisdiction?

   b) Would it be unjust to require the defendant (applicant for the anti-suit injunction) to submit to the foreign jurisdiction?

This third part of the test is peculiar to consideration of an anti-suit injunction rather than a stay of proceedings.

Applying this test to the facts in *Amchem* the Supreme Court differed with the decision of the lower courts in several respects. While the British Columbia Supreme Court, the domestic court, had concluded that it was a more natural forum for the dispute, it had concluded that it was not the *only* "appropriate forum" and that other states in the United States were equally "appropriate forums." Even though Texas did not follow a doctrine of *forum non conveniens*, nevertheless, it was fair to say that the selection of Texas could be justified on the basis that no other forum was clearly more appropriate. Even if the Texas court was not entitled to respect on the basis of *forum non conveniens*, the lower courts had misapplied the second aspect of the anti-suit injunction test in that the respondents had failed to prove that they would be deprived of a juridical advantage if forced to proceed in Texas.

The requirement that a domestic court should not entertain an application for an anti-suit injunction before the foreign court has been

---

5   *Amchem*, above note 2 at 932.

afforded an opportunity to determine whether it is an appropriate forum has been discussed by the Ontario Divisional Court in *Hudon* v. *Geos Language Corp.*[6] The plaintiff had entered into a contract with Geos to teach English in Japan. Geos Language was incorporated in British Columbia and was a subsidiary of Geos, a Japanese company. Under the plaintiff's contract of employment Geos was obliged to provide insurance coverage during the plaintiff's employment in Japan. The plaintiff was seriously injured in a car accident while she was taking a short break in China. As a result of her injuries she was left in a coma and was returned to Toronto, her place of residence. The plaintiff had received $110,000 insurance coverage pursuant to the policy Geos had arranged. However, compensation for her injuries would greatly exceed this amount. The plaintiff then commenced an action in Ontario against Geos, claiming that it had breached her contract of employment in failing to insure complete health and accident coverage, and that it had negligently misrepresented to the plaintiff the exact nature of the insurance coverage it had provided. Another clause in the contract stipulated that the contract was to be governed by the laws of Japan. Geos moved to stay the plaintiff's proceedings in Ontario. Before the Ontario court ruled on that motion, Geos also sought a declaration from the Japanese courts on the interpretation of the contract. They maintained that the Japanese suit would clearly demonstrate that under Japanese law Geos owed no duty to the plaintiff for what happened. The plaintiff sought from the Ontario court an anti-suit injunction to prevent Geos from proceeding with the Japanese court declaration. In support of her application the plaintiff provided an affidavit to the effect that she was in no condition, either physically or mentally, to travel to Japan to defend herself in the Japanese lawsuit.

In defence to the anti-suit injunction the defendant argued that under the test in *Amchem* the plaintiff must first seek a stay of proceedings before the Japanese court before commencing an action in Ontario. The Ontario court took the position that this requirement from *Amchem* was only the "preferable approach" and was not a condition precedent to any anti-suit injunction brought in Ontario. Moving to the next part of the test, the Ontario Divisional Court concluded that Ontario was the most appropriate forum, for five reasons:

1. evidence regarding the extent of the plaintiff's injuries would require Ontario witnesses to be called;

---

6   (1997), 34 O.R. (3d) 14 (Div. Ct.).

2. it was easier to bring witnesses from Japan to testify on the state of Japanese law if necessary than for all the parties to travel to Japan;
3. the allegations of negligence arose in Ontario where the contract was made;
4. the defendant had failed to show how it would be unjustly deprived of any legitimate juridical advantage; and
5. the plaintiff had shown a strong personal advantage to have the action tried in Ontario rather than being forced to travel to Japan.

The injunction was granted.

The Ontario Divisional Court's decision confronts the problem of how to reconcile the issue of justice for an individual litigant against the demands of comity, between nation states and courts. By placing the individual's claims ahead of the demands of comity a court awards justice to one individual at the possible expense of others who may have to litigate before foreign courts, for a lack of respect shown by Canadian courts will only engender disrespect by the foreign court. The court's decision in *Hudon* appears to be precipitous. The reason for not requiring the plaintiff to move for a stay of proceedings before the Japanese court is unconvincing: the plaintiff would hardly be required to make an appearance in person on such a motion, and could easily have briefed Japanese counsel. The Japanese courts would appear to have a similar doctrine to *forum non conveniens*.[7] The declaration on the position of Japanese law respecting the contract would be helpful to any action brought before the Ontario court. Finally, the Ontario court could still grant an anti-suit injunction after the Japanese court had ruled on the issue of appropriate forum, applying the full criteria of the *Amchem* test.

Although the anti-suit injunction appears to have been designed for transnational disputes it has also been applied in inter-provincial disputes.[8]

The anti-suit injunction is raised on an interlocutory motion, although the effect of the order is to act as a permanent injunction. The injunction can even be granted without a substantive cause of action or the commencement of proceedings by either of the parties in the domestic court. It is thus an exception to the rule that a permanent injunction can only be granted after a trial.

The second part of the *Amchem* test, that the domestic court can only consider an anti-suit injunction if it is the most appropriate forum

---

7   See E.L. Hayes, "*Forum Non Conveniens* in England, Australia and Japan: The Allocation of Jurisdiction in Transnational Litigation" (1992) 26 U.B.C. L. Rev. 41.
8   See *Gentra Canada Investments Inc. v. Lehndorff United Properties (Canada)* (1995), 174 A.R. 193 (C.A.).

in which to bring the dispute, has recently been discussed by the English courts. In *Airbus Industrie G.I.E. v. Patel*,[9] the appellant, Airbus Industrie, was the manufacturer of an aircraft in which the respondent, Patel, had been injured when it crashed during a domestic flight in India. Patel was an English national who had commenced suit in Texas against Airbus Industrie for negligence. There was no connection to Texas by any of the parties. Airbus had obtained an order from an Indian court preventing Patel from proceeding anywhere other than in India. As a matter of international law this order was not binding on Patel. Airbus had also successfully challenged the Texas court's actions, not on jurisdictional grounds, but on the grounds that as a company which was more than 50 percent owned by foreign governments it was entitled to claim sovereign immunity under U.S. legislation. The Texas trial court had upheld Airbus Industrie's immunity but this had been overturned on appeal. At the time of the present proceedings Airbus was appealing the Texas Court of Appeal's decision to the Texas Supreme Court. Although the first appeal had been heard in Texas, Airbus commenced proceedings in the United Kingdom for an anti-suit injunction against Patel. This had been refused by the trial judge, but was upheld in the English Court of Appeal.[10] In granting the injunction the Court of Appeal did not see its jurisdiction as being impeded by the fact that it was not an appropriate forum to hear the substantive litigation, nor did it see that it was acting to protect English jurisdiction. The court saw that it was the only jurisdiction which could control the actions of Patel as a national of the country and amenable to its *in personam* jurisdiction. The court acted under the impression that the Texas court would not make a ruling on jurisdiction because it did not acknowledge any rules of *forum non conveniens*. The Court of Appeal had concluded that it would be oppressive if Airbus was exposed to liability in Texas, a jurisdiction that was clearly not an appropriate one under any test.

In the House of Lords, the Court of Appeal's decision was overruled. Lord Goff, with whom the other Lords concurred, laid down the general rule:

> [B]efore an anti-suit injunction can properly be granted by an English court to restrain a person from pursuing proceedings in a foreign jurisdiction in cases of the kind under consideration in the present case, comity requires that the English forum should have a sufficient

---

9   (1998), [1999] 1 A.C. 119 (H.L. [*Airbus Industrie*].

10 [1997] 2 Lloyd's Rep. 8 (C.A.).

interest in, or connection with, the matter in question to justify the indirect interference with the foreign court which an anti-suit injunction entails.[11]

Much of Airbus Industrie's claim for relief had been built upon the inability of the Indian court to enforce it's order to prevent Patel from bringing suit in Texas. On this point Lord Goff stated:

> I am driven to say that such a course is not open to the English courts because, for the reasons I have given, it would be inconsistent with comity. In a world which consists of independent jurisdictions, interference, even indirect interference, by the courts of one jurisdiction with the exercise of the jurisdiction of a foreign court cannot in my opinion be justified by the fact that a third jurisdiction is affected but is powerless to intervene. The basic principle is that only the courts of an interested jurisdiction can act in the matter; and if they are powerless to do so, that will not of itself be enough to justify the courts of another jurisdiction to act in their place.[12]

The test formulated by Lord Goff is consistent with that articulated in *Amchem*, and was acknowledged as such by Lord Goff. In his analysis, he drew a distinction between "alternative forum" cases and "single forum" cases. The former raises a conflict when two jurisdictions, usually the domestic court and a foreign court, are relevant forums in which to bring the dispute. *Amchem* and *Airbus Industrie* are examples of this type, although in *Airbus Industrie* the alternative forums were two foreign courts, India and Texas.

Single forum cases arise when the domestic court is asked to grant an anti-suit injunction where the jurisdiction to bring the action only arises in the foreign court. An example of this type is the decision in *Midland Bank Plc. v. Laker Airways Ltd.*[13] The plaintiff, an English bank subject to English banking law, was requesting an anti-suit injunction to prevent the defendant, an English air carrier, from pursuing the plaintiff in an anti-trust proceeding commenced in the United States. The defendant had added the plaintiff to the United States action on the basis that the plaintiff had withdrawn its financial rescue operation of the defendant in circumstances that suggested the bank conspired with two other English transatlantic air carriers to put the defendant out of business. The court granted the anti-suit injunction. The dealings had

---

11 *Airbus Industrie*, above note 9 at 138.
12 *Ibid.* at 141.
13 [1986] Q.B. 689 (C.A.).

all taken place in England and at no stage had the plaintiff subjected itself or its dealings to scrutiny or control by United States authorities.

The principles articulated in *Amchem* cannot be applied in single forum cases because there is no issue of disputed appropriate alternative forums. Lord Goff, quoting Judge Wilkey of the United States,[14] states the justification for an anti-suit injunction in single forum cases as involving "consideration of the question whether an injunction is required to protect the polices of the English forum."[15] An appropriate test would "involve consideration of the extent to which the relevant transactions are connected with the English jurisdiction."[16] There appears as yet to be no reported case of a Canadian court considering the appropriate standard for granting an anti-suit injunction in a single forum case.

FURTHER READINGS

BLACK, V., "The Anti-Suit Injunction Comes to Canada" (1988) 13 Queens L.J. 103

GLENN, H.P., "The Supreme Court, Judicial Comity and Anti-Suit Injunctions" (1994) 28 U.B.C. L. Rev. 193

HARRIS, J., "Recognition of Foreign Judgment at Common Law — the Anti-Suit Injunction Link" (1997) 17 Oxford J. Legal Stud. 477

---

14   Judge Wilkey expressed the rationale for granting an anti-suit injunction as either to "to protect the jurisdiction of the enjoining court, or to prevent the litigant's evasion of the important public policies of the forum": *Laker Airways Ltd.* v. *Sabena, Belgian World Airlines*, 731 F.2d 909 at 927 (D.C. Cir. 1984).

15   *Airbus Industrie*, above note 9 at 139.

16   *Ibid.*

CHAPTER 7

PERPETUAL INJUNCTIONS: GENERAL PRINCIPLES

A. INTRODUCTION

An injunction can be sought and awarded as a final judgment of a court — either in equity's auxiliary jurisdiction, as a supplement to the common law, or in equity's exclusive jurisdiction, as the appropriate remedy for breach of an equitable right. The significant difference from interlocutory injunctions is that the court has now adjudicated on the plaintiff's substantive claim. Whereas the main objective for an interlocutory injunction is to ensure that effective relief can be rendered at trial, the objective of a perpetual injunction is to remedy an existing proven wrong, or to prevent the incursion of one in the future. The plaintiff must satisfy three criteria before a perpetual injunction will be granted:

- There is a cause of action.
- Damages are an inadequate remedy.
- There is no impediment to the court's discretion to grant an injunction.

B. A CAUSE OF ACTION

There are no limitations on what causes of action can support an injunction. However, a perpetual injunction will not be granted to protect a fanciful or unrecognized legal, equitable, or statutory right. Thus, a husband has been unable to get an injunction against his wife to prevent an abortion.[1] In some rare situations an applicant does not need a cause of action to gain a perpetual injunction; for example, where the plaintiff is simply seeking to restrain a wrongful arbitration[2] or to gain an anti-suit injunction which has permanent effect.

In the following chapters the typical causes of action which support the majority of perpetual injunctions are analyzed. The headings follow the approach adopted by Sharpe[3] and are also followed in the only Canadian published casebook on remedies.[4]

C. INADEQUACY OF DAMAGES

Historically, equity was subservient to the common law and only intervened where the latter was deficient in either substantive content or appropriate remedy. In the area of remedies the chief manifestation of subservience was the notion that an injunction was only available where damages were inadequate. Unfortunately, the concept of inadequacy has never been fully articulated in the law, and while there is still ritualistic reverence paid to the concept today, it is almost devoid of any prescriptive content.

Inadequacy of damages covers many forms. Cassels,[5] inspired by Rendleman,[6] suggests six possible meanings:

1) damage to person or property that is impossible to repair;
2) damage to an interest that is not easily susceptible to economic measurement;
3) a legal wrong that causes no financial or economic harm;
4) where damages are ascertainable but unlikely to be recovered;
5) a threat to an interest that is so important that a substitutionary remedy (damages) is inappropriate;
6) an injury that has not yet occurred or a wrong that is continuing.

---

1   See *Tremblay* v. *Daigle*, [1989] 2 S.C.R. 530. Nor does a foetus have rights to an injunction, it not being a "human being" within the law. See also *Paton* v. *British Pregnancy Advisory Service Trustees*, (1978) [1979] Q.B. 276.

2   See *Bremer Vulkan Schiffbau and Maschinenfabrik* v. *South India Shipping Corp.*, [1981] A.C. 909 & 962 (H.L.).

3   See R.J. Sharpe, *Injunctions and Specific Performance*, looseleaf (Aurora, Ont.: Canada Law Book, 1998).

4   See J. Berryman, et. al, *Remedies: Cases and Materials*, 3d ed. (Toronto: Emond Montgomery, 1997). c. 7.

5   *Ibid.*, 6.

6   See D. Rendleman, "The Inadequate Remedy at Law Prerequisite for an Injunction" (1981) 33 U. Fla. L. Rev 346.

We have already seen that the commensurate criterion of inadequacy in interlocutory injunctions, namely, the notion of irreparable harm, embodies many of these meanings depending on the particular objective pursued. Similarly, the particular type of inadequacy varies with perpetual injunctions — where this is still relevant, it will be discussed within the substantive causes of action in the following chapters.

Perhaps the strongest criticism of the irreparable injury rule has come from Laycock.[7] His thesis, based on an analysis of a vast number of American cases, is that the irreparable injury rule provides no guidance at all on how courts decide whether to grant or deny equitable relief. Laycock maintains that rather than one unifying concept there are a number of narrower rules serving their own particular policies. There is much in the Laycock thesis. But the criticism leveled at the irreparable injury rule seems to be a criticism that can be leveled at any large unifying concept. For instance, few would argue that the reasonable foresight test for damage assessment can accurately predict the damage quantification in any particular case, yet the test incorporates and communicates a powerful idea about the relationships of fault, risk and liability. I argue that the irreparable injury rule operates in a similar vein. Here (and in more detail in chapter 10 on the general principles of specific performance), it is suggested that the irreparable injury rule communicates ideas about efficiency and the appropriate utilization of coercive powers. While other particular rules may provide greater guidance in any particular instance, the irreparable injury rule is one that imbues most of equity practice in Anglo-Canadian law.

Academic criticism of the inadequacy criterion has also centred on the desirability of removing a presumption that favours common law damages and replacing it with a non-hierarchical plane which both maximizes and values the plaintiff's choice of preferred remedy. This choice is then subjected to judicial scrutiny and balanced against the countervailing arguments produced by the defendant against the plaintiff's choice. This does not necessarily mean that the frequency of injunctions will increase; rather, it focuses attention on more meaningful criteria that, it is suggested, lie at the heart of judicial discretion to award an injunction. What are those criteria?

---

7   See D. Laycock, "The Death of the Irreparable Injury Rule" (1989) 103 Harv. L. Rev. 687.

1) Inadequacy of Damages

Damages have at least two distinctive advantages over injunctions. Injunctions are either granted or denied — the plaintiff either gets complete relief or is denied relief altogether. Damages offer a much more flexible remedy, which can be adjusted to meet the demands of the particular case. The level of compensation can vary, punitive and aggravated damages can be added, and contributory causes by either the plaintiff or third parties can be accommodated.

The second advantage, although perhaps only in the eyes of the court and the defendant, is that damages are a passive response to right the plaintiff's wrong. Between judgment and final receipt of the assessed damages a great deal of time and energy can be engaged processing the judgment (on the appointment of receiver, judgment debtor examination, and bankruptcy). Compare this to the immediacy and intrusiveness of the contempt proceedings that follow violation of an injunction. The weakness of a damages remedy is the fact that it implies that any wrong can be equated to a monetary equivalent and thus suggests that all rights can be bargained as long as one party is prepared to pay compensation to the other.

The various meanings of inadequacy outlined above remain important. But whereas in the past, inadequacy of damages was considered a threshold which the plaintiff had to establish before moving onto other issues concerning the granting of an injunction, it is now merely one of a number of factors, albeit an important one, to be evaluated as part of a judicial discretion governing injunctions. Viewing it in this light also opens up possibilities of readily combining injunctive and damage remedies, such as damages in lieu of an injunction, suspensory injunctions (awarding an injunction but suspending its operation with compensation for the suspension), and compensatory injunctions (granting an injunction with compensation for the disruption it causes to the defendant).

2) Type of Right Infringed

The celebrated work of Calabresi and Melamed[8] has illustrated the inextricable link between choice of remedy and the protection accorded various rights. In their schema our most valued rights, our human rights and constitutional guarantees, are protected by criminal and constitutional law and cannot be bargained: they are regarded as

---

8   See G. Calabresi & A.D. Melamed, "Property Rules, Liability Rules, and Inalienability: One View of the Cathedral" (1972) 85 Harv. L. Rev. 1089.

being inalienable. Injunctions or "property rules" protect property rights; more particularly, real property. The only way these rights can be given up is through a consensual exchange with the owner. The injunction validates ownership by excluding all others. As we will shortly see, in the area of trespass to land an injunction is almost routinely awarded. Other rights, particularly contractual rights and rights to bodily integrity (avoidance of workplace, sporting, automotive accidents) the law protects through the awarding of damages as compensation. This is a "liability rule" and allows for the substitution of the right by a judicially determined damage remedy.

Calabresi and Melamed's approach is important because it sheds light on the malleability of the rights/remedy axis. The appropriate rule (inalienable, property or liability), will depend on more than the simple classification of the right infringed. Rather, it will be sensitive to the interests of the respective litigants. Thus, for example, the remedy for trespass to land may differ depending on the social utility of the trespasser's actions. Or, the remedy may differ if it is the attorney general seeking relief for a public nuisance as compared to an individual particularly affected by the same nuisance. In both examples, it is not simply the identification of wrong as trespass or public nuisance, or that they both affect realty, which predicates a single remedy. Rather, it is context and the balancing of the respective litigants' interests that determine what is an appropriate remedy.

3) Benefit and Burden

An important tool in risk assessment is cost-benefit analysis. This entails comparing the cost of compliance against the commensurate benefit to be obtained. To undertake such an analysis, benefit and burden need to be equated in monetary equivalents, and herein lies the difficulty. The plaintiff has chosen an injunction as a result of his own benefit-burden analysis, but that information is unlikely to be before the court. For example, the plaintiff may be pursuing an injunction because of concern about the defendant's solvency to pay damages. Alternatively, the plaintiff may be seeking to protect subjective aesthetic or public interest values that defy quantification, or he may be motivated out of sheer obstinacy to frustrate the defendant's activities. For the defendant, the cost of compliance is probably known — if the only litigious issue is appropriate remedy, the defendant's objection to the injunction is presumably based upon the burden of compliance. How is a court to undertake its own cost-benefit analysis in these circumstances? Yet, clearly this is an important tool that courts use in determining whether to order an injunction. In essence, a court substitutes its own evaluation for that of the plaintiff. Where the cost of compliance with an injunction would significantly exceed the damages a court would award in compensation, it is unlikely that an injunction will be granted. On the other hand, difficulty with quantifying the plaintiff's loss coupled with reasonableness in pursing an injunction will result in the injunction being granted, unless the burden on the defendant is overwhelming.

4) Supervision

Courts have been reluctant to make awards of both injunctions and specific performance where there is the possibility that the court will have to take an active part in the supervision of the order. Historically, this was seen as a major impediment to the granting of specific relief, although it has never operated as an absolute barrier. The court's perceived difficulties in supervising the enforcement of injunctions and specific performance can be grouped around four areas.

a) Problems Associated with the Possibility of Repeated Applications to Ensure Compliance

Courts are concerned that a few litigants do not monopolize scarce judicial resources. A court would sooner make a final determination of the issue and remedy between the parties than be engaged in a protracted process of ongoing applications for directions.

b) Problems Associated with the Engagement of Supervisors by Courts

Courts are concerned with how the supervision of specific relief is to be carried out. The courts do not have the available resources to recruit and administer people to supervise specific relief and must leave it up to the parties themselves, or to appoint a third party to undertake the supervision.

c) Problems associated with the Impact of the Court's Order beyond the Litigants

Courts are concerned with the escalation of their supervisory function into areas more properly the realm of government and administrative action.

d) Problems Associated with the Costs of Compliance Placed upon the Defendant

Courts are concerned that the more active their role on supervision of mandatory injunctions, the greater the cost imposed upon defendants. This is particularly so where the order lacks definition or where full impact of the order cannot be determined until other factual issues are made known during the course of the court's supervision.

One response to the above supervision problems was a clearer demarcation between prohibitive and mandatory injunctions. Historically, prohibitive injunctions were seen as being less intrusive than mandatory injunctions because they only gave the defendant the option of discontinuing his offending conduct. Mandatory injunctions required the defendant to undertake active steps as specified in the court's order. It soon became the practice of plaintiffs to frame affirmative relief in negative form. This position has since changed, such that courts now consider the effect of the order regardless of whether it is framed in negative or positive form.

Problems with supervision are still important today, but during the last few decades courts have grown accustomed to dealing with complex litigation requiring more active judicial intervention. For example, the appointment of receivers in corporate law can engage a court in years of ongoing involvement with litigants and receiver. In family law the supervision of custody and maintenance orders can span considerable periods of time and necessitate constant revisions. Canadian courts have also now experienced some of the complex issues involved in constitutional litigation requiring declaratory and mandatory orders.[9] The result of this new experience is that courts will no longer treat problems of supervision as an absolute barrier to injunctive relief but will identify ways in which the concerns can be minimized through careful drafting of the order.

5) Sundry Factors

Depending on the particular context and type of injunction sought, a number of other factors can have a varying influence on whether a court will grant a perpetual injunction. One such factor is the deliberateness of the defendant's conduct. If a defendant has flagrantly abused a plaintiff's rights, a court is more willing to intervene with an intrusive injunctive order.

Because an injunction will often have prospective effect, it is more willingly granted if it will avoid the danger of a multiplicity of future claims between litigants for a continuing wrong. Indeed, it is possible

---

9   See, for example, the Manitoba language case *Reference re Language Rights under s. 23 of Manitoba Act, 1870 and s. 133 of Constitution Act, 1867*, [1985] 1 S.C.R. 721.

in certain circumstances to get a *quia timet* injunction in advance of any injury having been caused to the plaintiff.

D. DISCRETIONARY FACTORS AFFECTING THE GRANT OF AN INJUNCTION

The above analysis of inadequacy of damages has suggested that courts are now willing to consider a variety of competing factors when determining whether to exercise their discretion to grant a perpetual injunction. Traditional formulations of inadequacy of damages that acted as a barrier have given way to a more discretionary balancing approach. To the discretionary factors already outlined, we can add the following; delay, unclean hands, and hardship. These latter factors are treated separately because they have been traditional concerns of equity that transcend the granting of injunctions and imbue many equitable remedies.

1) Delay[10]

Limitations statutes in all common law provinces create finite dates for particulars causes of action by which time litigation must be commenced. However, these statutes also provide a reservation preserving the rules of equity to the extent that they are not inconsistent with the Limitation Acts.[11] Thus, commencing an action seeking equitable relief for a cause of action covered in a limitation statue does not provide a way around statutory limitation periods. However, within a particular statutory period the special rules of equity pertaining to the limitations will still operate.

The imposition of limitation periods, although arbitrary, is done for sound policy reasons concerning the desirability to have closure of affairs between parties, and because of evidential problems after prolonged periods have taken their toll on witnesses' memories and availability.

---

10   The terms "delay," "acquiescence," and "laches" are used imprecisely and interchangeably. Laches normally connotes delay without prejudice to the plaintiff's position. Acquiescence usually implies a delay with prejudice to the defendant should he or she be required to return to the *status quo ante*. However, acquiescence has also been associated with the complete abandonment, estoppel, or waiver of equitable rights. Delay here simply means a passage of time that affects the granting of injunctive relief. See Sharpe, above note 3 at § 1.820 ff.

11   See J.S. Williams, *Limitation of Actions in Canada*, 2d ed. (Toronto: Butterworths, 1980) at 38; and G. Mew, *The Law of Limitations* (Toronto: Butterworths, 1991) at 23.

Delay plays an additional role concerning the availability of equitable relief. Plaintiffs must act promptly if they wish to seek an injunction once they are aware that a defendant is violating their rights. The reason for this is that a defendant may occasion further expenditure or change her position in some other way unnecessarily if it ultimately turns out that the plaintiff is proved correct in his claim. Unnecessary prejudice to the defendant is avoided by requiring the plaintiff to act promptly.

Two conditions must exist before delay will result in denial of equitable relief; one, an unreasonable period of time must have passed after the plaintiff becomes aware of the defendant's violation of the plaintiff's rights; and two, the defendant must suffer some prejudice if the relief is granted.

The plaintiff does not have to have actual knowledge that the defendant is committing a legal wrong. It is sufficient that the plaintiff has actual knowledge that would have made a reasonable person suspicious that the defendant is acting improperly. Even after the plaintiff has the requisite level of knowledge, the delay must still be unreasonable. There is no defined period when delay becomes unreasonable. A short delay may be unreasonable where the prejudice to the defendant is great and the violation obvious. Similarly, where the plaintiff is in doubt as to the nature of the violation and is proceeding cautiously, a longer period of time may pass before it is considered unreasonable.

The prejudice to the defendant must be such that the granting of the injunction will operate more harshly on the defendent than if it was granted without the delay. The prejudice to the defendant must be a real and substantial detriment and not merely trivial. The usual prejudice will be economic in that the defendant has incurred additional expenditure or liability during delay. However, loss of evidence or difficulties with mounting a defence to the plaintiff's action may also constitute prejudice. Even where delay is sufficient to decline an injunction remedy it may, nevertheless, still leave the plaintiff with an action for damages either in equity or at law.[12]

2)   Unclean Hands

The discretionary defence embodied in the maxim "who comes to equity must come with clean hands" has limited scope. The alleged act of impropriety being raised against the plaintiff must be linked to the very subject matter of the dispute.[13] Thus, an injunction will be refused if

---

12   See *Cadbury Schweppes Inc.* v. *FBI Foods Ltd.*, [1999] 1 S.C.R. 142.

13   See *Toronto (City of)* v. *Polai* (1969), [1970] 1 O.R. 483 (C.A.) aff'd (1972), [1973] S.C.R. 38.

- the right being asserted by the plaintiff has been obtained unlawfully,
- if the plaintiff has been guilty of equitable fraud in her dealings with either the defendant or a third party regarding the matter in dispute, or
- where the injunction would further a deception by the plaintiff on the defendant or a third party.[14]

3) Hardship

The factors discussed above, which a plaintiff must establish before being entitled to a perpetual injunction, already encompass some of the issues associated with hardship — it is rare that an injunction will be declined based solely on this ground. At the stage of considering a perpetual injunction the plaintiff has already shown that the defendant is a wrongdoer and that damages will not adequately meet the plaintiff's claim. Thus, before hardship can be raised as a discretionary reason for denial of relief, the defendant must prove that the hardship is of a serious nature and will be disproportionate to the injury experienced by the plaintiff if the injunction is denied. On rare occasions the court is prepared to consider hardship to a third party or the public as tipping the balance against an injunction or suspending its operation.[15]

4) Impossibility of Performance

Equity does not act in vain. Thus, it has been said that if an injunction would be impossible to perform; or would be futile, ineffective and pointless; or would be illegal, it will not be granted.[16]

Ultimately, the discretionary factors just discussed, together with the factors outlined under inadequacy of damages, must be placed in a balance of competing interests. This follows a similar pattern to that explicitly recognized in the granting of interlocutory injunctions. Indeed, many actions for a perpetual injunction originate in interlocutory proceedings, and merely order continuance of the interlocutory injunction as a final remedy.

---

14 See *Kettles and Gas Appliances Ltd.* v. *Anthony Hordern & Sons Ltd.* (1934), 35 S.R. (N.S.W.) 108 (S.C.).

15 See *Miller* v. *Jackson*, [1977] Q.B. 966 (C.A.).

16 See *Pride of Derby and Derbyshire Angling Ass.* v. *British Celanese Ltd.*, [1953] Ch. 149 at 181, Evershed M.R. See also *A.G.* v. *Guardian Newspapers Ltd.* (No. 2) (1988), [1990] 1 A.C. 109 (H.L.). ("Spycatcher" case) (Injunction refused because all possible damage had been done with initial publication and no useful purpose would be served by granting injunction.)

E. *QUIA TIMET* INJUNCTIONS

A *quia timet* injunction is a specialized perpetual injunction granted in advance of any injury having been caused to the plaintiff. It is because the plaintiff fears that an injury will happen that she seeks judicial intervention to prevent that occurrence. In essence, a *quia timet* injunction is the legal expression of the aphorism "an ounce of prevention can effect a pound of cure." Because it acts in advance of any injury, and keeping in mind that the plaintiff can always bring a common law action should loss come to pass, courts have been extremely circumspect in granting this form of injunction. It is not the injunction's prospective effect which justifies a cautious approach, as many injunctions are designed to prevent further future injury; it is that a court is being asked to extrapolate a factual scenario from conjecture rather than from some existing injury.

The test for a *quia timet* order involves two considerations: one, can the plaintiff show that the potential harm is imminent?; and two, can the plaintiff show that the harm, when it eventuates, will be substantial?[17] Unfortunately, the interaction of these two factors reveal many permutations, and thus it is not possible to define precisely in either a temporal or qualitative sense when a *quia timet* injunction will be granted.

1) Imminence

With respect to the issue of imminence the court looks the timeliness of the plaintiff's potential injury as well as its probability. If the injury is inevitable, although in the future, the injunction may be granted on the basis that the plaintiff has shown a high level of probability of loss. In *Hooper* v. *Rogers*[18] the defendant had bulldozed a track below the plaintiff's farmhouse. The impact of erosion on the track brought with it the real fear that the plaintiff's house would be undermined. At trial the plaintiff received damages in lieu of a *quia timet* injunction. The damages were assessed in equity pursuant to Lord Cairns' Act[19] (discussed in chapter 17), which allows equitable damages in lieu of an injunction. Without this provision damages could not have been awarded at common law, since no loss had actually been experienced

---

17   See *Fletcher* v. *Bealey* (1885), 28 Ch. D. 688.

18   (1974), [1975] Ch. 43 (C.A.).

19   *An Act to amend the Course of Procedure in the High Court of Chancery, the Court of Chancery in Ireland, and the Court of Chancery of the Country Palatine of Lancaster, 1858* (U.K.), 21 & 22 Vict., c. 27.

at the time the proceedings had been commenced. The defendant appealed on the grounds that the risk to the plaintiff was not imminent. In the Court of Appeal, Russell L.J. determined that imminence had to be measured in terms of whether the plaintiff's action was premature. The plaintiff was able to establish that the injury to the farmhouse was inevitable although the exact time of its occurrence could not be determined with certainty. However, more important was the fact that the plaintiff was able to prove that nothing less than the restoration of the natural slope of the track would arrest the erosion. The remedy sought would not differ if the plaintiff waited until further erosion occurred. In this sense the application was not premature, and the appeal was dismissed. All the factors necessary to the granting of the injunctive relief had been crystallized. Other cases have indicated that the plaintiff is entitled to an injunction if she has established a "strong case of probability."[20]

2) Seriousness of Harm

With respect to the issue of the seriousness of the harm, the plaintiff must show that the injury will constitute irreparable harm and be substantial.[21]

It is easier for a plaintiff to get a *quia timet* injunction where there is an existing infringement of the plaintiff's rights, (although because no injury has yet caused damage it is not actionable in common law), than where there is merely a threatened infringement and no injury. The lack of infringement increases the probability that no actionable injury will arise and thus relates back into the question of imminence.

The cautious approach to *quia timet* injunctions is justified on several policy grounds. Even where a *quia timet* injunction is not granted the plaintiff will still have his common law remedy available should the injury eventuate. Even if the initial application is premature, the plaintiff can bring a later application by which point the evidential proof may be overwhelming. Sharpe has also suggested that too readily accessible *quia timet* injunctions could stifle innovation. These injunctions frequently arise in the context of the law of nuisance where competing interests often pit the status quo against some new development or controversial use of land. In these cases it is preferable to adopt a wait-and-see attitude, whether the injury will eventuate and to the

---

20 See *A.G. v. Manchester (Corporation of)*, [1893] 2 Ch. 87.
21 See *Palmer v. Nova Scotia Forest Industries* (1984), 60 N.S.R. (2d) 271 (S.C.T.D.), where a serious risk to health would have constituted irreparable harm entitling a *quia timet* injunction.

extent that the plaintiff believes, rather than thwart what could otherwise be a development beneficial to society.[22]

F. MANDATORY INJUNCTIONS

A perpetual mandatory injunction obligates the defendant to undertake some affirmative work either to restore any damage caused by her wrong, or to continue to perform an obligation owed to the plaintiff. While the demarcation between prohibitive and mandatory injunctions has broken down, courts still pay particular attention to an injunctive order that requires additional expenditures by the defendant, rather than merely prohibits the defendant from pursuing a particular course of conduct or opportunity. Issues of benefit and burden are prominent when considering mandatory injunctions. In addition, the court will consider the conduct of the defendant. Where the defendant has acted wantonly and unreasonably in disregard to the plaintiff's rights then the court is more willing to order a mandatory injunction without regard to the cost involved or the value of the commensurate benefit to the plaintiff. Where the defendant has acted reasonably, then the cost of compliance is a relevant consideration to be weighed against the benefit of the injunction to the plaintiff. In *Jaggard* v. *Sawyer*,[23] Millett L.J. suggested that the key question to ask was — in all the circumstances, would it be oppressive to the defendant to grant the injunction? The defendant should not be "bound hand and foot to be subjected to any extortionate demands the plaintiff might make."[24] A mandatory order must also be expressed in language accurate enough that the defendant knows precisely what is expected of her to comply.

Coupling a mandatory order and a *quia timet* injunction heightens concerns over the cost of compliance. In *Redland Bricks Ltd.* v. *Morris*[25] the plaintiff sought an injunction requiring the defendant to restore support to the plaintiff's land that lay above the defendant's clay quarry and brick-making business. The defendant's activities threatened to undermine the plaintiff's market gardening business. The trial judge and Court of Appeal had both ordered a mandatory injunction. The defendant appealed on the basis that the cost of implementing the

---

22   See Sharpe, above note 3 at § 1.780.
23   [1995] 1 W.L.R. 269 (C.A.).
24   *Ibid.* at 288.
25   (1969), [1970] A.C. 652 (H.L.).

injunction (somewhere in the vicinity of £35,000) was completely disproportionate to the value of the plaintiff's threatened property (approximately £12,000). The House of Lords stated that the cost of compliance had to be considered where the defendant had acted reasonably although wrongfully, because at the time of the order the plaintiff had not yet suffered any loss which he had not already been compensated for, and, that the plaintiff always retained a right to sue in common law for any loss which subsequently eventuated. The trial judge had expressed the order in absolute terms, requiring the defendant to undertake restorative work so as to guarantee that the plaintiff's land would never erode in the future. The House of Lords said that while a reasonable expenditure could be justified to do some restorative work, the order being expressed in absolute terms meant that the defendant would incur too great an expenditure and was thus unreasonable.

FURTHER READINGS

SHARPE, R.J., *Injunctions and Specific Performance*, looseleaf (Aurora, Ont.: Canada Law Book, 1998)

SPRY, C.F., *The Principles of Equitable Remedies: Specific Performance, Injunctions, Rectification and Equitable Damages*, 5th ed. (Sydney: LBC Information Services, 1997)

CHAPTER 8

INJUNCTIONS TO PROTECT PROPERTY

A. INTRODUCTION

We saw in the previous chapter that the type of right infringed has a bearing on remedial choice. During much of the period spanning equity's formative development, equity traditionally accorded realty a reverence associated with the fact that it was the single most important asset held by an individual, defining both social status and wealth. Industrialization enhanced the value of land as a commodity upon which to build much needed housing, to carry utility services without impeding other uses of the land, to give support to adjoining structures, and for the minerals that could be mined. Faced with a violation of these property interests, the remedy in common law was deficient in one important respect. Common law damages could only be assessed for past wrongs, which left the property owner with the prospect of facing endless future actions for compensation. Equity's answer was to grant a perpetual injunction, prohibiting the trespass and restoring any damage that had been incurred. Only after *Lord Cairns' Act* was passed in 1858,[1] allowing damages in lieu of an injunction, could compensation be given for prospective damages not reflected in the diminution

---

1   *An Act to amend the Course of Procedure in the High Court of Chancery in Ireland, and the Court of Chancery of the Country Palatine of Lancaster, 1858* (U.K.) 21, & 22 Vict., c. 27.

of the property's market value. Against this state of affairs courts developed a distinct preference for injunctive relief. The injunction became synonymous with the protection of property and reified the notion that property could only be transferred through voluntary consensual exchange. However, equity did maintain the discretionary nature of the relief — there are examples where courts refused an injunction order can be found throughout the law reports of this era.[2]

Today we are more apt to conceptualize "property" as an abstract bundle of rights. The power of an owner to insist upon voluntary consensual exchange as the only means of appropriation by another has been truncated, particularly by legislation. For example, many crown agencies and municipalities have a statutory right of expropriation, with limited rights of objection by a property owner, that substitutes a fair market value for the lost property. Another important limitation on the rights of an owner is that of usage through zoning and other planning restrictions. Private restraints come through restrictive covenants and even mortgage documents. With this level of encumbrances on realty it is perhaps not surprising to find that courts are now re-appraising the use of injunctions in this area, particularly with respect to nuisance actions.

One of the main impediments to fashioning appropriate relief in this area is the binary nature of injunctive relief. If the injunction is denied then the court appears to be condoning a private right of expropriation on the tortfeasor. On the other hand, if the injunction is granted this may in fact inhibit an otherwise socially desirable activity. To overcome this impediment some courts have been willing to suspend the operation of an injunction, thus both validating the property holder's claim as well as the reasonableness of the defendant's activity. Another approach has been greater attention paid to the quantification of damages — either in lieu of an injunction, or as common law damages measured by a lost opportunity to bargain, or as restitutionary damages.

B. INJUNCTIONS AND TRESPASS

Trespass is an act of direct interference with the exclusive possession of another person's land, and an injunction has normally been granted in vindication of the property owner's exclusive rights. Thus, in *Lewvest Ltd.* v. *Scotia Towers Ltd.*,[3] a plaintiff successfully gained an injunction

---

2   See, for example, *Leader* v. *Moody* (1875), L.R. 20 Eq. 145 (C.A.).

3   (1981), 126 D.L.R. (3d) 239 (Nfld. S.C. (T.D.)) [*Lewvest*]. See also *Patel* v. *Smith* (W.H.) (Eziot), [1987] 1 W.L.R. 853 (C.A.).

preventing the defendant from swinging the boom of a crane over his property during the course of the construction of the defendant's building. Goodridge J. stated:

> Under our system of law, property rights are sacrosanct. For that reason, the rules that generally apply to injunctions do not always apply in cases such as this. The balance of convenience and other matters may have to take second place to the sacrosanctity of property rights in matters of trespass.
>
> What has happened here is that the third defendant, by trespassing on property of Lewvest Limited, can save itself, according to the evidence, close to half a million dollars. If it can save that money, so be it, but the Court is not going to give a right to use the plaintiff's property. That is a right that it must negotiate with the plaintiff.[4]

Where there is a temporary trespass, or one that does not occasion loss for the property owner, courts have stressed that the power of veto and exclusion is precisely the reason for favouring injunctive relief, even where the plaintiff is position has been described as "unneighbourly."[5]

Contrary to the above position are cases which have either granted but suspended an injunction, or have refused to enjoin the defendant and have confined the plaintiff to damages. This contrary line of cases tends to pick up on three factors:

- the social utility of the defendant's conduct;
- the deliberateness of the defendant's actions; and
- the permanence of the trespass.

Where the trespass is of a transitory and temporary nature, some courts are now more willing to confine the plaintiff to damages. In *Woollerton and Wilson Ltd.* v. *Richard Costain Ltd.*[6] the defendant was a contractor building a large post office building in a confined space in a congested downtown area. The jib of the defendant's crane swung over the plaintiff's land. The defendant had offered £250 compensation but the plaintiff had refused to accept this sum and had sought an injunction. The plaintiff had experienced no loss, a point raised by the defendant to suggest that the plaintiff should be confined to damages. The court did not accept the defendant's argument. In fact the absence of loss was a very good reason to favour injunctive relief on the grounds that clearly damages would be inadequate and that without the injunc-

---

4   *Lewvest*, above note 3 at 240.
5   See *Goodson v. Richardson* (1874), L.R. 9 Ch. App. 221.
6   [1970] 1 W.L.R. 411 (Ch.).

tion the court would, in effect, be licensing a trespass in return for a nominal payment. However, having granted the injunction the court then went on to suspend its operation until such time had passed that the defendant would have completed construction of the building. The justifications for suspension was that the defendant had inadvertently placed themselves in the position of being held up to ransom. The court accepted the evidence that in the past adjoining property owners had not objected to the crane's boom as long as the contractor had provided insurance coverage for any injury. The court remarked that in future, contractors should get the agreement of adjoining property owners before building. In addition, enjoining the defendant would necessitate a delay of over one year to redesign the plans so as not to commit the trespass. This delay would further exacerbate the congestion in the area as well as hold up the construction of an important development.

With respect to the deliberateness of the defendant's conduct, Stamp J. remarked on the fact that the defendant had acted inadvertently in *Woollerton* in justification of the suspension. In *Trenberth (John) Ltd. v. National Westminster Bank Ltd.,*[7] the defendant had to repair its building pursuant to an order issued by a local authority. The only way to effect repairs was to trespass on the plaintiff's premises. The plaintiff had steadfastly rejected any negotiations with the defendant to allow the trespass. Against this background the court held that the only possible remedy could be an injunction, particularly where the defendant had made a "flagrant invasion of another's rights of property."[8] It is not uncommon to find legislative intervention in this type of case that empowers a municipality to pass by-laws to allow temporary incursion on an adjoining property owner's land to effect repairs.[9]

With respect to the social utility of the defendant's conduct there is the suggestion, again in *Woollerton*, that the importance of the project, the building of a large general post office, had some bearing on whether the injunction should be suspended. Although Stamp J. did point out that, if the defendant had been deliberately trespassing on the assumption it was constructing an important building and therefore no court would enjoin the activity before completion, this would be a completely erroneous assumption to make and an injunction would have been granted.

---

7 (1979), 39 P. & C.R. 104 (Ch.) [*John Trenberth Ltd.*].
8 *Ibid.* at 106.
9 See, for example, Ontario *Municipal Act*, R.S.O. 1990, c. M.45, s. 210.64.

The correctness of *Woollerton* has been questioned in subsequent English cases[10] concerning whether suspension of the injunction was an appropriate exercise of the court's discretion. The decision has also been criticized by Sharpe[11] on the grounds that Stamp J. appeared to be of the opinion that the plaintiff had suffered no loss and therefore was not entitled to damages. Whether the defendant did in fact pay the £250 offered and described by Stamp J. as "substantial" is not known. However, it would seen only proper that the plaintiff receives some compensation for the trespass.

The difficulty in the area of trespass is the weakness of the common law remedies. In refusing an injunction a court appears to be granting a private power of expropriation to the defendant, often with little or no monetary compensation. Similarly, while the court is vindicating property rights in granting an injunction, it may also be exposing the defendant to exploitation at the plaintiff's hands, particularly where the trespass is the result of the defendant's inadvertence, and comes at a point in time where the defendant has few alternatives but to give in to the plaintiff's price.

An injunction protects the notion that property rights can only be exchanged through consensus. The law should protect and encourage bargaining of property rights. This can be achieved by disciplining deliberate trespassers who have adopted the approach that negotiation is futile and that any compensation will be less than the value of the advantage in trespassing. The court should grant an injunction in these cases. Any other remedy would, as Jessel M.R. pointed out, enable "the rich man to buy the poor man's property without his consent."[12] Even after the fact, the common law often grants punitive damages in these types of cases.[13]

Where the defendant has trespassed through inadvertence, different considerations come into play. The court could still routinely give an injunction on the basis that the plaintiff would then engage in post-judgment bargaining and negotiate the release of compliance for an appropriate payment. Unfortunately, the defendant will now be in a

---

10   See *Charrington v. Simons & Co.*, [1971] 1 W.L.R. 598 (C.A.); *John Trenberth Ltd.*, above note 7; and *Jaggard v. Sawyer*, [1995] 1 W.L.R. 269 (C.A.) [*Jaggard*].

11   *Injunctions and Specific Performance*, looseleaf (Aurora, Ont.: Canada Law Book, 1998) at § 4.610.

12   *Krehl v. Burrell* (1878), 7 Ch. D. 551 at 554.

13   See *Townsview Properties Ltd. v. Sun Construction and Equipment Co.* (1975), 7 O.R. (2d) 666 (C.A.); *Epstein v. Cressey Development Corp.* (1990), 48 B.C.L.R. (2d) 311 (S.C.); and *Austin v. Rescon Construction (1984) Ltd.* (1989), 57 D.L.R. (4th) 591 (B.C.C.A.).

position of greater vulnerability, and the sum negotiated is unlikely to mirror the amount which would have been negotiated had the defendant known he was trespassing when the infringement began. At that time the defendant could have taken other avoidance strategies, which may no longer be possible. The parties are in what economists call a bipolar monopoly because there are limited alternatives to dealing with each other if they are to avoid litigation. The price they settle for may be difficult to determine as each party attempts to extract the most they can from the other.[14]

Rather than allow the defendant to be held to ransom, a preferable approach would be for the court to create a reasonable exchange between the parties. One way to achieve this is to allow damages to be assessed on the basis of compensation for the plaintiff's lost opportunity to bargain the sale of the rights to trespass.[15] Another alternative is to allow restitutionary damages for waiver of tort.[16] These damages have the potential to equal the amount of the benefit obtained by the defendant, in actual profit made or expenditures saved, through the trespass. Even where the plaintiff does not seek this type of remedy it can be imposed on the plaintiff as damages in lieu of an injunction. The court can use these assessment approaches by analogy.

In some of the temporary trespass cases the court has actually recast the wrong as constituting a nuisance rather than as a trespass.[17] As we will shortly see, the courts have been more readily disposed to striking a compromise between the parties in nuisance cases and granting damages.[18]

Where the trespass is continuing and permanent, the plaintiff is more likely to seek a mandatory injunction requiring the defendant to demolish the infringing structure and remove it from the plaintiff's property. Where the defendant has acted deliberately, in accordance with the principles regarding mandatory injunctions from *Redland Bricks Ltd. v. Morris*,[19] the court is more inclined to grant the injunction, even if the defendant will be put to great expense in removing the

---

14 See the discussion in R.A. Posner, *Economic Analysis of Law*, 5th ed. (New York: Aspen Law & Business, 1998) at § 3.80.

15 See R.J. Sharpe & S.M. Waddams, "Damages for Lost Opportunity to Bargain" (1982) 2 Oxford. J. Legal Stud. 290.

16 See J. Berryman, "The Case for Restitutionary Damages Over Punitive Damages: Teaching the Wrongdoer that Tort Does Not Pay" (1994) 73 Can. Bar Rev. 320.

17 See *Hanson-Needler Corp. v. Kingsbridge Developments Inc.* (1990), 71 O.R. (2d) 636 (H.C.).

18 See *Bernstein of Leigh (Baron) v. Skyviews & General Ltd.* (1977), [1978] Q.B. 479.

19 (1969), [1970] A.C. 652 (H.L.).

trespass.[20] However, this is not a universal approach.[21] Where the defendant inadvertently trespasses, the court will put into balance the wasted expenditure the defendant will incur in complying with the injunction and may confine the plaintiff to damages. In *Jaggard* v. *Sawyer*,[22] Millett L.J. suggested that the question to be asked was whether, considering all the circumstances, it would be "oppressive" to the defendant to grant the plaintiff the injunction.

Where the defendant has made a *bona fide* mistake as to the ownership of land and has inadvertently built upon an adjoining property owner's land, legislation now provides for the court to order the defendant to pay compensation in return for a severance and transfer of the title to the infringed lands, or to a lien over the land for the value of the improvements.[23]

In some cases the court has commented upon the plaintiff's failure to seek an interlocutory injunction, and has used this as a supporting reason for declining a perpetual injunction and awarding damages in lieu.[24] As Sharpe has observed,[25] this approach places the plaintiff in a quandary. When seeking the interlocutory injunction the plaintiff will have to give an undertaking in damages. A defendant who is delayed in carrying out an activity can incur significant costs, that the plaintiff will be forced to pay on his undertaking where the court subsequently finds that there has been no trespass and the defendant was acting in accordance with her rights. On the other hand, a plaintiff who delays in bringing an interlocutory injunction, fearing the consequences of requiring an undertaking in damages, may well jeopardize his chance at getting an injunction and be required to settle for damages in lieu.

C. INJUNCTIONS AND NUISANCE

A nuisance is an indirect and continuing interference of the enjoyment of land by the actions of another. Nuisances differ from trespasses in that the actions of the defendant are not *per se* unlawful. The defendant is equally entitled to exploit his own land to the fullest extent permissible by law. Nuisance also differs in that the type of nuisance, com-

---

20 See *Gross* v. *Wright*, [1923] S.C.R. 214.
21 See *Dempsey* v. *J.E.S. Developments Ltd.* (1976), 15 N.S.R. (2d) 448 (S.C.T.D.).
22 Above note 10.
23 See Ontario *Conveyancing and Law of Property Act*, R.S.O. 1990, c. C.34, s. 37(1).
24 See *Jaggard*, above note 10.
25 Above note 11 at § 1.100 – 1.1010.

monly noise, air or water pollution, will often be widespread and the level of infringement of any one plaintiff may vary accordingly.

The traditional approach in the United Kingdom towards remedies for nuisance did not differ from that accorded the action of trespass. An injunction was routinely granted to protect quiet enjoyment as one of the incidence of property. However, where the nuisance was minor the English courts accepted that damages could be given in lieu of an injunction. In *Shelfer* v. *City of London Electric Lighting Co.*,[26] the plaintiff had sought an injunction restraining the defendant from causing vibrations and noise to his property. The defendant had built a power-generating facility next to the plaintiff's house, inconveniencing the plaintiff's sleep and causing some structural damage to his property. The trial judge declined to grant the injunction based upon the loss to the defendant, who would have been required to shut down his operations, when compared with the loss to the plaintiff. In the Court of Appeal, the trial judge was reversed. A. L. Smith L.J. gave what has become widely accepted as the appropriate criteria when considering an award of damages in lieu of an injunction enjoining a trespass or a nuisance. He said:

> [I]t may be stated as a good working rule that —
> 1) If the injury to the plaintiff's legal rights is small,
> 2) And is one which is capable of being estimated in money,
> 3) And is one which can be adequately compensated by a small money payment,
> 4) And the case is one in which it would be oppressive to the defendant to grant an injunction: —
> then damages in substitution for an injunction may be given.[27]

The court refused damages in lieu of an injunction because the injury to the plaintiff would have remained throughout the plaintiff's entire twenty-year lease, although the final injunction was suspended for a period of time.

Shelfer at least recognized the legitimacy of measuring benefit and burden to the protagonists as an approach to determining the appropriate remedy. However, it has not been until relatively recently that

---

26   (1894), [1895] 1 Ch. 287 (C.A.).

27   *Ibid.* at 322–23. The effect of granting damages in lieu of an injunction is to compensate for both past and future injuries such that it acts as a licensing of the impugned activity. The plaintiff is prevented from subsequently returning to court at a later time on the basis that a plaintiff cannot complain of that for which he has already been compensated. See *Jaggard*, above note 10 at 280, Bingham M.R..

English courts have been willing to adopt a more robust approach to measuring benefit and burden in determining the exercise of judicial discretion. *Miller v. Jackson*[28] is often seen as heralding a new approach. The plaintiff had purchased a house in a new housing estate adjoining a public park on which cricket had been regularly played for many years. Cricket balls frequently strayed onto the plaintiff's property and he sought an injunction restraining the playing of cricket. In the Court of Appeal Denning M.R. took the approach that there was no nuisance. The public interest in retaining the playing of village cricket outweighed the plaintiff's rights to quiet enjoyment. Geoffrey Lane L.J. found a nuisance and would have enjoined the playing of cricket. Cumming-Bruce L.J. also found a nuisance, but the public interest outweighed the plaintiff's interests such that he was confined to damages. The plaintiff, who had purchased his property adjoining the park for its obvious amenity value, had to expect a certain degree of burden flowing from the use of the park. In this case the court elevated the public interest as tipping the balance.

In *Kennaway v. Thompson*[29] the United Kingdom Court of Appeal took an even more robust approach in attempting to find a middle ground between the litigants. In that case the plaintiff had sought an injunction enjoining the defendant from conducting speedboat racing on a lake abutting the plaintiff's residence. The court granted the injunction to prevent the nuisance aspects of the plaintiff's complaint. However, it also partially accommodated the defendant's interest in speedboat racing by allowing a maximum of six boats per race on six days per year. At all other times the defendant was required to abide by a performance standard imposed as part of the court's order which restricted the noise level from boating activities to no more than 75 decibels.

Canadian courts have also vacillated on the appropriate balance between absolute protection of property rights and the relative benefit and burden to the litigants and other third parties. For Canadian courts these issues have been of particular concern touching environmental pollution of air and water in remote regions of the country where often the defendant industry is the single largest employer in the region. The traditional approach in these cases was to favour the individual property owner. In *Canada Paper Co. v. Brown*,[30] the plaintiff brought an action seeking to prohibit the production of sulphate fumes created by the defendant's paper mill operations. The injunction was granted and affirmed at all judicial levels. In the Supreme Court, Idington J. gave a

---

28   [1977] Q.B. 966 (C.A.).
29   (1980), [1981] Q.B. 88 (C.A.).
30   (1922), 63 S.C.R. 243.

strong defence of individual property rights, saying that it was inappropriate for the court to balance those rights against other public interest concerns which were more properly the function of the legislature. However, both Duff and Anglin JJ. were of the opinion that the impact of the order on the community at large could not be ignored when exercising a judicial discretion touching the grant or denial of an injunction. However, in this case both were of the opinion that the injunction would not lead to the closure of the defendant's paper mill and that other ways of manufacturing the sulphate of soda, which was not vital to the defendant's business, could be found.

Subsequently, in a series of cases involving water pollution, the courts adopted the usual course of granting an injunction and refusing to look at the impact of the award on the community.[31] These cases resulted in legislative intervention and the Ontario Water Resources Commission was created. However, there are also instances of later courts seizing upon Duff J.'s position and allowing the disproportionate harm to the defendant and third parties to tip the balance in favour of not granting an injunction and confining the plaintiff to damages.[32] Canadian courts have also approved of the criteria and approach in *Shelfer*.[33] In similar facts to *Miller v. Jackson* Canadian courts have not appeared to be so generously disposed towards communal benefits of sports over private property owners,[34] and there does not appear to be any equivalent judgment creating performance standards as in *Kennaway*.[35] One exception is the case of *Ward v. Magna International Inc.*[36] where the court granted extensive orders restricting the noise level to a certain decibel level, prohibited the playing of car radios, and restricted the expansion of sporting usage

31 See, for example, *K.V.P. Co. v. McKie*, [1949] S.C.R. 698; and *Stephens v. Richmond Hill (Village of)* [1955] O.R. 806 (H.C), aff'd [1956] O.R. 88 (C.A.).

32 See *Bottom v. Ontario Leaf Tobacco Co.*, [1935] O.R. 205 (C.A.); *Black v. Canadian Copper Co.* (1917), 12 O.W.N. 243 (H.C.), aff'd (1920), 17 O.W.N. 399 (Div. Ct.); and *Execotel Hotel Corp. v. E.B. Eddy Forest Products Ltd.*, [1988] O.J. No. 1905 (H.C.).

33 See *340909 Ontario Ltd. v. Huron Steel Products (Windsor) Ltd.* (1990), 73 O.R. (2d) 641 (H.C.), where the court gave slightly different criteria: i) severity of interference (nature, duration, effect), ii) character of locale, iii) utility of defendant's conduct, and iv) sensitivity of use interfered with.

34 See *Pardy v. Hiscock* (1977), 17 Nfld. & P.E.I.R. 71 (Nfld. S.C. (T.D.)); *Savoie v. Breau* (1973), 8 N.B.R. (2d) 512 (Q.B.); *Cook v. Lockeport (Town of)* (1971), 7 N.S.R. (2d) 191 (S.C.T.D.); and *Gauthier v. Naneff*, [1971] 1 O.R. 97 (H.C.).

35 But see *Walker v. Pioneer Construction Co. (1967) Ltd.* (1975), 8 O.R. (2d) 35 (H.C.), where an injunction was granted preventing the defendant from operating an asphalt plant between the hours of 9 p.m. and 7 a.m..

36 (1994), 28 C.P.C. (3d) 327 (Ont. Gen. Div.), supplementary orders reported at (1994), 28 C.P.C. (3d) 327 at 346 (Ont. Gen. Div.).

beyond the level of activity at the time of the order, in a park purchased by the defendant for the use of its employees.

The weakness in common law remedies again a difficulty in this area, as are problems with the process of private judicial adjudication. The weakness in common law remedies is similar to that experienced with trespass actions: awarding damages in lieu of the injunction appears to sanction the private expropriation of the plaintiff's property rights. While the approach in *Kennaway* is perhaps the most sensitive in striking a balance between competing uses of property, it will not work in all cases. We are only now coming to understand the cumulative effect of even small levels of pollutants and that the rights to discharge have to be worked out by looking at the ecosystem in its totality. Courts are not particularly well equipped to take cognizance of the interests of parties not represented before the court, or of the highly complicated scientific evidence upon which these decisions must be based. Creating performance standards for either water or atmospheric discharge cannot be worked out in isolation from others who are loading the environment with their own discharges.

Once interests of third parties are affected, and claims advanced in the public interest are made, we must ask ourselves who is best able to represent those parties or to make such claims? In the nuisance area, the more widespread the nuisance then the more likely it will be characterized as a public nuisance. As we will shortly see when looking at injunctions to protect public rights, in those cases different criteria apply to the granting of injunctions and in particular there is a significant role for the attorney general to play. Before granting an injunction enjoining a private nuisance that has widespread ramifications on parties beyond the litigants represented, it may be preferable for a court to seek input from the attorney general. On the other hand there is a bias and societal expectation that courts will protect individual property rights ahead of utilitarian arguments based on communal rights until the latter are articulated through legislation. The treatment of water rights illustrates that legislatures are willing to act where public opinion believes that the courts have miscalculated the benefit and burden of granting the injunctions. Yet another example is the right-to-farm legislation that inhibits a court's ability to grant an injunction for nuisances generated through normal farming practices.[37]

---

37   See Ontario *Farming and Food Production Protection Act*, S.O. 1998, c. 1, s. 2(2), which prevents a court from granting an injunction for any disturbance — defined as odour, dust, flies, light, smoke, noise and vibration — unless it is also subject to some other provincial provision controlling the generation of nuisances.

Another procedural problem with nuisance cases is the likelihood that not all aggrieved parties will be present before the court. Where the nuisance is widespread the intensity of the nuisance may fall indifferently on many parties. While some parties may be willing to incur the inconvenience and cost of commencing litigation, others will not. If damages are awarded then only those represented will receive compensation and thus the true cost of the nuisance will not be brought home to the defendant. Similarly, if the nuisance is small but nevertheless widespread, it is unlikely that any one individual will be willing to bring the matter on for trial if the result is likely to be a nominal amount of compensation. An injunction alleviates some of these problems concerning unrepresented parties.[38] Of course, the enactment of class action suits will also assist in overcoming procedural problems experienced in this type of litigation.

A pragmatic response by courts to the harshness of the binary nature of the injunction remedy is to grant the injunction but then suspend its operation for a period of time, during which the defendant is expected to take steps to abate the nuisance.[39]

At the outer extreme of remedial approach has been the suggestion adopted in one United States court of a compensatory injunction; an injunction granted to the plaintiff together with an order requiring the plaintiff to pay compensation to the defendant for the dislocation and inconvenience caused by the injunction. This type of order was imposed in *Spur Industries* v. *Del E. Webb Development Co.*[40] The plaintiff was a property development company that had purchased inexpensive land on the outskirts of Phoenix and had built a comprehensive residential housing complex. The defendant operated a feed lot on adjoining land that had been farmed since 1911 and had been a feed lot since 1959. The plaintiff complained about the nuisance created by the feed lot operation. The court granted an injunction but coupled it with an obligation to pay the defendant compensation for having to move the feed lot operation. On these facts such an order seems appropriate. The plaintiff has been advantaged by being able to purchase land for residen-

---

38 Admittedly, the injunction may create other representation issues where some putative plaintiffs freeload on the activities of the actual plaintiff, knowing that they will receive a benefit where the remedy is an injunction.

39 In *Corkum* v. *Nash* (1990), 98 N.S.R. (2d) 364 (S.C.T.D.), the court granted an injunction but suspended it for a period of six months to allow the parties to negotiate a settlement. The injunction was granted to protect the plaintiff's riparian rights that had been interfered with by the defendant.

40 494 P.2d 700 (Arizona S.C. 1972).

tial development at a far cheaper cost than was then currently available in Phoenix. The plaintiff is being required to share some of this fiscal advantage with the single party whose operation is being displaced.

But as a remedy for widespread application, the compensatory injunction has distinct limitations. Requiring the victim to pay the tort-feasor to remove the nuisance seems to fly in the face of our sense of justice and moral outrage. It would act as a powerful disincentive against bringing litigation. It would also be difficult to avoid significant problems with freeloaders if the nuisance was widespread and affected many individuals. If compensatory injunctions became routine it would undermine the prophylactic effect of tort law by diminishing the incentives for the tortfeasor to take steps to minimize the nuisance. Finally, if the solution was viable one would have expected to see more evidence of victims buying out tortfeasors so as to avoid the additional cost of litigation.

FURTHER READINGS

ROTHERHAM, C., "The Allocation of Remedies in Private Nuisance: An Evaluation of the Judicial Approach to Awarding Damages in Lieu of an Injunction" (1989), 4 Canterbury L. Rev. 185

TROMANS, S., "Nuisance — Prevention or Payment?" (1982) 41 Cambridge L.J. 87

CHAPTER 9

INJUNCTIONS TO ENFORCE PUBLIC RIGHTS

A. INTRODUCTION

In this chapter we examine the enforcement of public rights. These rights may derive from common law, statute or constitutional provisions. An important aspect of the enforcement of public rights is the role played by the attorney general, who, acting as *parens patriae,* has a broad jurisdiction to represent the public interest.[1] In some situations the attorney general may wish to invoke equity's jurisdiction to enjoin a public nuisance or in aid of the criminal law. In other situations a private citizen may wish to do the same. The law provides for an *ex relator* action in which the a private citizen is allowed to bring an action in the name of the attorney general. Often, legislation may specifically allow the individual to bring forward an injunction application to enforce public rights in his own capacity.

A different enforcement of public rights concerns the ability of an individual to seek an injunction against governmental and administrative action. Through prerogative writs and a general action for judicial review, administrative law has developed sophisticated and complex analytical policies with which to scrutinize governmental action. The adoption of injunctions and declarations, initially derived from private law adjudication, have become important remedies in the courts'

---

1   See *Ontario (A.G.) v. Dieleman* (1994), 20 O.R. (3d) 229 (Gen. Div.).

arsenal to ensure that administrative agencies stay within their statutory jurisdiction and carry out their mandates in accordance with the dictates of the rule of law. Of more recent origin is the use of injunctions to support rulings of administrative agencies. Lastly, we will review the important function played by injunctions as a remedy to protect constitutional and *Charter* rights.

B. INJUNCTIONS TO ENJOIN PUBLIC NUISANCES

An initial problem with public nuisance is defining its doctrinal parameters. A widely accepted definition is one given by Lord Denning:

> [A] public nuisance is a nuisance which is so widespread in its range or so indiscriminate in its effect that it would not be reasonable to expect one person to take proceedings on his own responsibility to put a stop to it, but that it should be taken on the responsibility of the community at large.[2]

This definition suggests that a public nuisance is merely a wider private nuisance. While there are many similarities between the two actions, a public nuisance encompasses more than a mere interference with private property. A public nuisance involves an unreasonable interference with public rights that may include health, safety, comfort and morality. Although rooted in the criminal law, there is now no longer a requirement that a public nuisance must also constitute a crime.[3] Traditional areas that have been held to constitute a public nuisance include the obstruction of highways,[4] the creation of excessive noise[5]

---

2   *A.G. ex. rel. Glamorgan County Council and Pontardawe R.D.C.* v. *P.Y.A. Quarries Ltd.* [1957] 2 Q.B. 169 at 191 (C.A.).

3   See the discussion by J. Cassels, "Prostitution and Public Nuisance: Desperate Measures and the Limits of Civil Adjudication" (1985) 63 Can. Bar Rev.764.

4   See *Tate & Lyle Industries Ltd.* v. *Greater London Council*, [1983] 2 A.C. 509 (H.L.); *British Columbia (A.G.)* v. *Mount Currie Indian Band* (1991), 54 B.C.L.R. (2d) 156 (C.A.); and *Ogden Entertainment Services* v. *U.S.W.A., Local 440* (1998), 159 D.L.R. (4th) 340 (Ont. Gen. Div.).

5   See *Manitoba (A.G.)* v. *Adventure Flight Centres Ltd.* (1983), 22 Man. R. (2d) 142 (Q.B.); and *Ontario (A.G.)* v. *Orange Production Ltd.*, [1971] 3 O.R. 585 (H.C.).

and large crowds,[6] the pollution of beaches,[7] and the control of soliciting for the purposes of prostitution.[8]

1) Actions Brought by the Attorney General to Restrain a Public Nuisance

As guardian of the public interest, the attorney general may bring an action to enjoin a public nuisance on his or her own initiative. More commonly, an action is brought by way of an *ex relator* action where the attorney general lends his or her name to a private individual who then brings the action. While the private individual bears the cost and carriage of the action, the attorney general may exercise a supervisory role, reviewing pleadings and discovery, and may also stay the proceedings or take control of them at any stage. The decision to bring a public nuisance action, or to allow an *ex relator* action, is the attorney general's alone and is not generally reviewable before the courts.[9]

The wrongs for which the attorney general normally brings an action for public nuisance usually involve either some interference with property or conduct already subject to some other criminal law process. The fact that injunctive relief is sought in the former mirrors similar actions brought by an individual for private nuisance, and the involvement of equity to protect property interests should come as no surprise. The involvement of equity as a supplement to the criminal law is more problematical and merits separate treatment (discussed below).

With respect to wrongs that infringe property, either public or private, courts have approached their discretion to grant an injunction in a similar fashion to that of private nuisance, save in the following respects. Whereas in private nuisance a court gives active consideration to confining the plaintiff to damages rather than grant an injunction, in a suit brought by the attorney general damages will rarely be awarded. A court is also less disposed towards considering arguments based on the defendant's hardship or claims of deleterious effect to the public interest flowing from granting the injunction — the public interest is

---

6   See *British Columbia (A.G.) ex. rel. Eaton v. Haney Speedways Ltd. and District of Maple Ridge* (1963), 39 D.L.R. (2d) 48 (B.C.S.C.); and *Dieleman*, above note 1.

7   See *R. v. The Sun Diamond* (1983), [1984] 1 F.C. 3 (T.D.); and *Hickey v. Electric Reduction Co. of Canada* (1970), 2 Nfld. & P.E.I.R. 246 (Nfld. S.C.).

8   See *British Columbia (A.G.) v. Couillard* (1984), 11 D.L.R. (4th) 567. See also *Nova Scotia (A.G.) v. Beaver* (1985), 67 N.S.R. (2d) 281 (S.C.A.D.).

9   See *Gouriet v. Union of Post Office Workers* (1977), [1978] A.C. 435 (H.L.), but see discussion on standing below.

now represented, and therefore conjecture on this issue is avoided. Nor does the attorney general have to show that common law remedies are inadequate: once the attorney general demonstrates that there has been an infringement of the law, deleterious effect on the community at large is assumed.

Where the alleged public nuisance is so widespread that a private nuisance action would not exist for any individual property owner, a suit by the attorney general for an injunction can take on the appearance of a form of judicial land-use zoning. For example, in *British Columbia (A.G.) v. Couillard*[10] McEachern C.J. ordered an injunction against known prostitutes, and others who were made aware of the order, from plying their trade in a broad geographical area defined as the West End of Vancouver. While the injunction was aimed at restraining the particular nuisance aspects of prostitution, namely, the soliciting and importuning of pedestrians, the net effect of the order was to drive the prostitution trade to adjoining suburbs and thereby create a prostitution-free zone in the area covered by the injunction. In a subsequent action brought by two individual property owners whose hotel businesses adjoined the area covered by the injunction, and who now suffered the nuisance of the displaced prostitution trade, the injunction was denied on the basis of lack of the individual litigants' standing.[11]

2) Actions Brought by an Individual to Restrain a Public Nuisance

Individuals may pursue an action for a public nuisance in their own capacity if they can satisfy the appropriate standing requirement. To establish standing an applicant must show either that the public nuisance also constitutes a private nuisance on the applicant's property, or that the applicant has suffered some special or particular injury over and above that suffered by the community at large. In Canada the special damage requirement has been interpreted as requiring the applicant to establish an injury which is direct and substantial, and of a type that is a difference in kind and not merely degree from the injury suffered by the public at large.[12] For example, in *Hickey v. Electric Reduc-*

---

10   Above note 8.

11   See *Stein v. Gonzales* (1984), 14 D.L.R. (4th) 263 (B.C.S.C.).

12   See L.N. Klar, *Tort Law*, 2d. ed. (Toronto: Carswell, 1996) at 531.

tion Co. of Canada Ltd.[13] the plaintiff claimed that the defendant had polluted the waters of Palacentia Bay by discharging various toxic by-products into the water, which had rendered fish in the bay inedible. The plaintiff was a commercial inshore fisherman. Although the obvious impact of the defendant's action was much more severe on the plaintiff the court did not give the plaintiff standing to bring a private nuisance. Because the damage was common to all those who fished the waters of Palacentia Bay, and the right to fish was one given to all citizens, the plaintiff could not establish any peculiar damage distinct from the community at large. Simply because the injury was more severe for the plaintiff, affecting the plaintiff's business interest, this alone did not give standing.

Once this threshold is met there is no additional barrier to the granting of an injunction to restrain a public nuisance than those applied to the normal case of an injunction to restrain a private nuisance.[14]

C. INJUNCTIONS IN AID OF THE CRIMINAL LAW

1) Actions Brought by the Attorney General in Aid of the Criminal Law

Historically, equity exercised no criminal jurisdiction, and injunctions were not available to provide additional enforcement to deter and prevent criminal conduct. However, as the number of regulatory offenses and other quasi-criminal statutory provisions increases, courts have shown a willingness to grant injunctive relief in aid of penal provisions so as to prevent continual flouting of the law

- where the statutory penalty is inadequate to deter,[15]
- where the statute provides no penalty for violation,[16] or

---

13 Above note 7. See also W. Estey, "Public Nuisance and Standing to Sue" (1972) 10 Osgoode Hall L.J. 563; and J.P.S. McLaren, "The Common Law Nuisance Actions and the Environmental Battle — Well-Tempered Swords or Broken Reeds?" (1972) 10 Osgoode Hall L.J. 505.

14 See *MacMillan Bloedel Ltd.* v. *Simpson*, [1996] 2 S.C.R. 1048.

15 See *Ontario (A.G.)* v. *Grabarchuk* (1976), 11 O.R. (2d) 607 (Div. Ct.); and *Alberta (A.G.)* v. *Plantation Indoor Plants Ltd.* (1982), 34 A.R. (C.A.), rev'd on other grounds [1985] 1 S.C.R. 366.

16 See *Ontario (A.G.)* v. *Harry* (1979), 22 O.R. (2d) 321 (H.C.); and *Ontario (A.G.)* v. *Yeotes* (1980), 28 O.R. (2d) 577 (H.C.), rev'd (1981), 31 O.R. (2d) 589 (C.A.), leave to appeal refused to S.C.C. (1981), 37 N.R. 356n. Both cases involved violation of the Ontario *Planning Act* (R.S.O. 1990, c. P. 13) provisions relating to subdivision approval.

- where there is a serious threat to public safety.[17]

Such intervention is not based on the protection of any proprietary right or irreparable harm suffered by the attorney general, but is based on the public interest of all citizens to see that the law is obeyed. The attorney general does not have to prove that all other remedies have been exhausted[18] before being granted an injunction.

However, the courts are concerned that the attorney general does not make precipitous resort to an injunction to enjoin criminal behaviour. In *Nova Scotia (A.G.)* v. *Beaver*,[19] the attorney general had commenced proceedings for an injunction to enjoin prostitutes from operating in downtown Halifax. The injunction was brought to prevent a public nuisance. The Court noted that much of the activity described by the attorney general as a public nuisance was also covered by the Criminal Code and that the effect of the injunction would be in support of the criminal law. The trial judge had declined to grant the injunction. The Court of Appeal affirmed that decision. Hart J.A., commenting upon the approach to be adopted when granting an injunction to uphold the criminal law, said:

> In my opinion, a judge when being asked by an attorney general to grant such an injunction must consider whether it is really necessary in the light of other procedures available to accomplish the same end. He should consider, as well, the damages of eliminating criminal conduct without the usual safeguards of criminal procedure available to an accused. He should also consider whether the evil complained of should more properly be eliminated by a change in legislation. Only in very exceptional cases where by reason of lack of time or otherwise no other suitable remedy is available should such an injunction be granted to prevent the commission of a crime.[20]

Where the attorney general is seeking an injunction to prevent the violation of a statute but there is no evidence of continual flouting by the defendant, the courts have required the attorney general to establish all three aspects of the *American Cyanamid* test. In *Ontario (A.G.)* v. *Ontario Teachers' Federation*,[21] the court did not grant an injunction

---

17   See *A.G.* v. *Chaudry* [1971] 1 W.L.R. 1614 (C.A.); *Metropolitan Corporation of Greater Winnipeg* v. *Radio Oil Ltd.* (1964), 48 D.L.R. (2d) 596 (Man. Q.B.).

18   See *Saskatchewan (Minister of the Environment)* v. *Redberry Development Corp.*, [1987] 4 W.W.R. 654, aff'd [1992] 2 W.W.R. 544 (Sask. C.A.).

19   Above note 8.

20   *Ibid.* at 293.

21   (1997), 36 O.R. (3d) 367 (Gen. Div.).

preventing the violation of the *School Boards and Teachers' Collective Negotiations Act.*[22] Although the attorney general could show a serious question to be tried — the lawfulness of the teachers' withdrawal of labour to protest the Provincial Government's enactment of Bill 160,[23] which amended Ontario's Education Act — he could not prove any irreparable harm at the time the matter came before the court. The proof of irreparable harm was seen as a necessary requirement because without evidence of flouting there was no basis to argue that the defendant was demonstrating an extreme contempt for the law. In holding that there was no evidence of irreparable harm, MacPherson J. noted that under the Ontario *School Boards and Teachers' Collective Negotiations Act* there was provision for the Education Relations Commission to determine when the closure of schools would jeopardize the successful completion of the students' school year. Thus, the Act itself had an enforcement mechanism which the attorney general had not restored to. MacPherson J. also noted that in the past the Commission had only given such advice after a strike of at least twenty-seven days.

While not having to go on to the balance of convenience test, MacPherson J. also indicated that the balance lay against the attorney general. The court considered the negative consequences which flowed from not awarding the injunction — namely, public perception of apparently sanctioning law-breaking, the perception that individuals who have lawful means of expressing their views can resort to more problematic avenues, and the perception that the attorney general alone does not represent the public interest in law enforcement. These concerns had to be weighed against the fact that the attorney general had ignored the enforcement mechanism contained within the statute and the severe penalties provided therein. In the past courts had only granted an injunction in exceptional cases where the defendant had flouted the law, or where the breach of law was clear, or where the enforcement provisions had proved ineffective. None of these had been demonstrated in this case and the application was premature.

Where the attorney general is seeking an injunction in aid of a *Criminal Code*[24] violation, Canadian cases exhibit a tendency towards greater scrutiny of the claim and only in exceptional circumstances will an injunction be granted.[25] In the "flouting" cases, the paradigm model

---

22 R.S.O. 1990, c. S.2 (rep. by S.O. 1997, c. 31, s. 178).
23 *Education Quality Improvement Act*, 1997, S.O. 1997, c. 31.
24 R.S.C. 1985, c, C-46.
25 See *Robinson v. Adams* (1924), 56 O.L.R. 217 (C.A.); and *Canadian H.W. Gossard Co. v. Tripp* (1967), [1968] 1 O.R. 230 (H.C.).

involves an inadequate fixed penalty and the use of an injunction can be justified as a way of avoiding a multiplicity of prosecutions. But the *Criminal Code* typically offers a range of indictable offences, often dependent upon the magnitude of the crime and the deliberate nature of the accused's conduct. Against this backdrop the need for additional civil remedies is far less pressing. There is also a real concern that the accused will be subject to

- double jeopardy (prosecuted criminally and civilly for the same event),
- punishment in excess of the statutory prescription (violation of the injunction can be met with civil or criminal contempt of court — discussed below), and
- be tried without any of the accepted procedural safeguards normally associated with a criminal trial (where the crown is the required to meet higher burden of proof, the accused has a right to a jury trial, and a right to remain silent; all three are lost in civil proceedings).

Before granting an injunction a court has to be satisfied that the defendant is indeed guilty of an offence or some other illegal conduct.[26]

2) Actions Brought by an Individual to Enforce the Criminal Law

A private individual has a right to bring a private prosecution; however, the attorney general may stay the proceedings or take control of them at any stage.[27] Even if an individual is allowed to continue with a private prosecution, this gives no additional right to seek an injunction in aid of the criminal law. A second way for a private individual to pursue a private prosecution is through an *ex relator* action, in the attorney general's name. Again, this is subject to the overall scrutiny of the attorney general and does not confer any greater right to injunctive relief in aid of the criminal law. However, it does raise the issue as to what is the position where the attorney general, in exercise of his or her discretion, refuses to allow a private individual an *ex relator* action. Can individuals pursue their own actions for an injunction to enforce a public right arising from a penal statute, and can an individual challenge the attorney general's exercise of discretion?

---

26   *League for Life in Manitoba Inc.* v. *Morgentaler* (1985), 19 D.L.R. (4th) 703 (Man. Q.B.).

27   *Dowson* v. *R.* (1981), 62 C.C.C. (2d) 286 (Ont. C.A.), rev'd [1983] 2 S.C.R. 144.

The English House of Lords gave definitive answers to these questions in *Gouriet* v. *Union of Post Office Workers*.[28] The plaintiff, a private citizen, sought an injunction against the defendant trade union that had ordered its members not to handle mail destined for South Africa. The actions of the defendant, if carried out by its members, would have constituted a violation of the *Post Office Act,* 1953[29] although when the plaintiff commenced his suit no crime had been committed. The plaintiff had initially sought approval from the attorney general to bring an *ex relator* action but the attorney general declined to give his approval. The plaintiff then commenced the action in his own name. At first instance, the injunction application was denied. The plaintiff immediately appealed the decision, seeking to add the attorney general as a joint defendant and to challenge the attorney general's exercise of discretion to deny an *ex relator* action. In the Court of Appeal both actions were denied, although the court allowed the plaintiff to amend his pleadings and seek a declaration. An appeal was then taken to the House of Lords.

The plaintiff was unsuccessful on his appeal. In the opinion of all the Lords, the issue before the court concerned who was the appropriate person to guard the public interest arising in a dispute that raised very controversial political and social issues. To this question their Lords replied that it lay with the attorney general alone to enforce public rights by way of request for a civil preventative remedy.

Lord Wilberforce justified his approach on two grounds. One; an assessment of the wider public interest and the desirability of seeking civil remedies was best left to a public official who could take into account conflicting considerations, (such as what was the best way to handle the dispute, of particular concern in the industrial context; would the injunction merely exacerbate matters; and would preventative action assist or hinder negotiations?)

Two; if, in making decisions identifying public interest the courts were to step into a highly-charged political arena and assess matters beyond their traditional determination of legal rights and fact, this would undercut the court's standing in the eyes of the public.

On the issue of whether the attorney general's discretion to allow an *ex relator* action was reviewable before the courts, both Lords Dilhorne and Edmund-Davies expressly reaffirmed the position expressed in *London County Council* v. *A.G.*[30] that it was not.

---

28 Above note 9.
29 U.K., c. 36.
30 [1902] A.C. 165 (H.L.).

The dominant position in Canada with respect to standing to challenge the attorney general's discretion appears to mirror that applied in *Gouriet*: an individual citizen has no right to pursue a civil remedy to uphold the law unless falling within the established exceptions to *Gouriet* (see discussion below).[31] However, it is possible that Canadian courts may be more willing to extend standing to an individual citizen beyond the stringent standard adopted in *Gouriet*. In a number of cases the Supreme Court has been willing to extend standing to individuals and groups who are claiming to advance public rather than private interests, and who are challenging the constitutionality of some legislative provision or action.[32] This more generous notion of standing has also been extended to those who seek to challenge the statutory authority for some administrative action.[33] It can be argued, extrapolating from the direction the Supreme Court has taken on standing, that an applicant should be accorded the ability to enforce public rights, or to challenge the attorney general's decision either not to enforce the law or to decline an *ex relator* action, without having to bring herself within the recognized exceptions to *Gouriet*. In *League for Life in Manitoba* v. *Morgentaler*[34] Kroft J. rejected the argument that the plaintiff should be given standing to seek a preventative injunction against Dr. Morgentaler from performing abortions in a clinic opened specifically to provide women with access to this medical procedure. The plaintiff was a pro-life group who had first sought from the attorney general the right to bring an *ex relator* action. The attorney general had declined to allow the action based on the fact that criminal charges had already been laid against the defendant. The plaintiff then commenced these

---

31   See *Carruthers v. Langley* (1984), 13 D.L.R. (4th) 528 (B.C.S.C.), aff'd with additional reasons at (1985), 23 D.L.R. (4th) 528 (B.C.C.A.), leave to appeal to S.C.C. refused (1986), 70 B.C.L.R. xl.; and *Delher v. Ottawa Civic Hospital* (1979), 25 O.R. (2d) 748 (H.C.), aff'd (1980), 29 O.R. (2d) 677 (C.A.), leave to appeal to S.C.C. refused [1981] 1 S.C.R. viii. See D.J. Mullan, *Administrative Law*, 3d ed. (Toronto: Carswell, 1996) § 490.

32   See *Thorson v. Canada (A.G.)* (1974), [1975] 1 S.C.R. 138; *Nova Scotia (Board of Censors) v. McNeil*, [1976] 2 S.C.R. 265; and *Canada (Minister of Canada) v. Borowski*, [1981] 2 S.C.R. 575, where it was held that an applicant has standing where three elements are satisfied: (a) there is a justiciable issue appropriate for judicial determination; (b) a serious issue is raised and the applicant has a genuine interest in the issue; (c) there is no other reasonable and effective manner in which the issue may be brought before the court.

33   See *Finlay v. Canada (Minister of Finance)*, [1986] 2 S.C.R. 607; and *Canadian Council of Churches v. Canada (Minister of Employment and Immigration)*, [1992] 1 S.C.R. 236.

34   Above note 26.

proceedings for its own injunction in its own name. Although noting the liberalization of standing in Canada, Kroft J. saw "no binding or compelling reason why one citizen should be granted the standing to sue another and to invoke civil remedies simply on his assertion that the enforcement of the criminal law is inherently good and therefore sustainable in the civil courts".[35] Kroft J. also alluded to a distinction that should be drawn between a request for a declaration and an injunction when considering the liberalization of standing requirements. The former, being less obtrusive, may warrant a more generous standing threshold.[36]

The dominant position represented by *Gouriet*, that courts jealously guard the attorney general's discretion to determine where the public interest lies, either to lay criminal charges[37] or to seek civil preventative injunctive orders to enforce the law, is subject to a number of specific exceptions.

The first exception arises where the interference to the public right also constitutes an interference with the plaintiff's own private property rights. In *MacMillan Bloedel Ltd.* v. *Simpson*,[38] the actions of protesters in preventing the plaintiff access to its lands from the public highway constituted sufficient interference such that the plaintiff had standing to seek an injunction to prevent the protesters' obstruction. The injunction was granted in spite of the fact that the attorney general had taken the decision not to lay charges against environmental groups engaged in civil disobedience.

---

35   *Ibid.* at 713.

36   A similar approach to declaratory relief and standing was applied in *Mathias Colomb Band of Indians* v. *Saskatchewan Power Corp.* (1994), 111 D.L.R. (Man. C.A.), leave to appeal to S.C.C. refused (1994), 111 D.L.R. (4th) vii, where it was suggested that standing to gain a declaratory order to enforce a statutory prohibition would be more broadly drawn than if the relief sought were damages. See also S. MacIntyre, "Above and Beyond Equality Rights: *Canadian Council of Churches v. The Queen*" (1992) 12 Windsor Y.B. Access Just. 293 at 303 ff.

37   It is possible that an individual may seek mandamus to compel enforcement of the law although even in these cases the court is reluctant to interfere with the exercise of discretion to lay charges. See *R.* v. *Metropolitan Police Commissioner, ex parte Blackburn* (No. 3), [1973] Q.B. 241 (C.A.); *R.* v. *Power*, [1994] 1 S.C.R. 601 where the court held that it would only interfere with an attorney general's discretion to prosecute where there was conspicuous evidence of improper motives or bad faith, or where the an act violates the conscience of the community. See also *Kostuch* v. *Alberta (A.G.)* (1995), 174 A.R. 109 (C.A.).

38   Above note 14. See also *Boyce* v. *Paddington Borough Council,* [1903] 1 Ch. 109 at 114, Buckley J., rev'd [1903] 2 Ch. 556 (C.A.), restored (*sub nom. Paddington Corp.* v. *A.G.*) (1905), [1906] A.C. 1 (H.L.).

A second exception is where the plaintiff does not suffer an interference to any private right, but that in respect of a public right, the plaintiff suffers special damage over and above that experienced by the public at large.[39] Two difficulties arise with respect to this exception. One, the difficulty of defining "special damage," has already been commented upon in the context of a suit for public nuisance. The other difficulty is how to identify a justiciable public right.

With respect to public rights it is possible for legislation to specifically confer upon an individual or body a civil right of enforcement, in addition to creating a penalty offense.[40] A particularly useful example of this is contained in section 328 of the Ontario *Municipal Act*,[41] which grants to every ratepayer within a municipality the right to seek injunctive relief to prevent contravention of municipal bylaws.[42] The right can also be inferred[43] although it is difficult to do so if the statute provides a complete code of remedies for its enforcement.[44] The plaintiff must also be able to show that the statute was enacted to provide a benefit or confer a protection on a particular class of individuals and not merely to prevent the accused from committing the wrong.[45]

This last requirement has been construed strictly in the United Kingdom, where it has been said that on the true construction of the legislation there is an intention by the legislature to confer upon mem-

---

39   It is not sufficient to have a "special interest" in the outcome of the alleged unlawful act. The plaintiff must demonstrate how she will suffer some special damage or injury: see *Manitoba Naturalists Society Inc.* v. *Ducks Unlimited Canada* (1991), 86 D.L.R. (4th) 709 (Man. Q.B.).

40   See, for example, section 50.2 of the Ontario *Law Society Act*, R.S.O. 1990, c. L.8 (enacted by the Law Society Amendment Act, 1998, S.O. 1998, c. 21, s. 24), which confers a statutory right on the Law Society to seek an injunction to bar a person from practicing law without a licence. See also *Law Society of Upper Canada* v. *Junger* (1991), 85 D.L.R. (4th) 12 (Ont. Gen. Div.), aff'd (1996), 133 D.L.R. (4th) 287 (Ont. C.A.); and Ontario *Environmental Bill of Rights, 1993*, S.O. 1993 c. 28, s. 84.

41   R.S.O. 1990, c. M.45.

42   See *Zanzibar Tavern Inc.* v. *Las Vegas Restaurant & Tavern Ltd.* (1994), 22 M.P.L.R. (2d) 225 (Ont. Gen. Div.).

43   See *Argyll (Duchess of)* v. *Argyll (Duke of)* (1964), [1967] Ch. 302.

44   See *Seneca College of Applied Arts and Technology* v. *Bhadauria*, [1981] 2 S.C.R. 181 and *Frame* v. *Smith*, [1987] 2 S.C.R. 99.

45   See *Lonrho Ltd.* v. *Shell Petroleum Co. (No. 2)* (1981), [1982] A.C. 173 (H.L.); and *Roth* v. *Roth* (1991), 4 O.R. (3d) 740 (Gen. Div.).

bers of the protected class a civil cause of action.[46] This would appear to be the position in Canada as well. In *Whistler Cable Television Ltd.* v. *IPEC Canada Inc.*,[47] Braidwood J. had to consider whether a plaintiff, who held an exclusive license to operate a cable television distribution system in a defined geographical area, could seek injunctive relief against another operator based on an alleged infringement of the *Broadcasting Act*.[48] The other operator did not hold a license but furnished similar services to a number of hotels, apartments and hospitals in the plaintiff's exclusive area. Braidwood J. suggested that the following questions should be asked to determine whether the legislation conferred a right to a civil remedy.

> I am of the opinion that the Broadcasting Act should be examined to determine:
>
> (1) for whose benefit was the Act passed;
> (2) whether it was passed in the interest of the public at large or for a particular class of persons or both;
> (3) whether the plaintiff is within a class of persons the Act was designed to benefit;
> (4) whether the damages suffered by the plaintiff were the kind of damage the statute was intended to prevent;
> (5) whether the penalties prescribed in the Act are adequate; and
> (6) does the Act set up a scheme designed to exclusively carry out the objects of the Act.[49]

Applying these criteria, Braidwood J. held that the plaintiff had a legitimate cause of action to support an injunction and thus declined to strike the injunction action out.

The dilemma for a court is to find a legitimate justification for acting when the legislature has criminalized a particular type of infringing conduct but has declined to provide for civil liability at the same time. In addition, an aggrieved plaintiff always retains the option of pursuing a private prosecution, although only after the fact.

---

46 See *Pickering* v. *Liverpool Daily Post and Echo Newspapers Plc.*, [1991] 2 A.C. 370 at 420, Lord Bridge (H.L.). See also *C.B.S. Songs Ltd.* v. *Amstrad Consumer Electronics Plc.* (1987), [1988] Ch 61 (C.A.), aff'd on other grounds [1988] A.C. 1013 (H.L.). This approach is in contrast to the now-repudiated position of Lord Denning who took a much more liberal construction in *Ex Parte Island Records Ltd.*, [1978] Ch. 122 (C.A.).

47 [1993] 3 W.W.R. 247 (B.C.S.C.) [*Whistler Cable*].

48 S.C. 1991, c. 11.

49 *Whistler Cable*, above note 47 at 261.

A third exception, or variation on the second exception, concerns suits brought by a competitor who is complying with some legislative licensing regime and who seeks to enjoin another competitor who is not in legislative compliance. For a legitimate business operator, licensing can amount to a considerable business overhead cost: if a competitor is not similarly meeting the licensing requirements, he may gain a significant competitive advantage. Courts have divided on whether this constitutes sufficient special interest on the legitimate business operator's behalf to support an injunction. Key to the courts' determination is whether the legislative regime grants an applicant an individual right of enforcement, or whether this is held only by the public body empowered to regulate businesses. This issue is resolved by looking at the underlying purpose of the licensing requirement, and whether the creation of restrictions on licencees is an integral part of the legislative objective. Thus, in cases where the intent of the legislation is to create monopolies or restrictions on competition so as to advance its particular legislative goals, an injunction will be granted at the suit of a legitimate competitor. Instances of this approach are restrictions on broadcasting which are seen as being important to carry out the legislative goals of Canada's telecommunication sector.[50] However, if the legislation does not aim to create restrictions on competition, but intends rather to advance some other goal, such as public safety or the abeyance of a nuisance not directly affecting the applicant's property, an injunction will be refused on the grounds of the applicant's lack of standing.[51]

D. THE USE OF INJUNCTIONS IN ADMINISTRATIVE LAW

In this part we consider the use of injunctions in administrative law. The intent is not to extensively review administrative law principles

---

50 See, for example, *Terra Communications Ltd.* v. *Communicomp Data Ltd.* (1973), 1 O.R. (2d) 682 (H.C.); and *Whistler Cable*, above note 47. See also *Swan River-The Pas Transfer Ltd.* v. *Manitoba (Highway Traffic and Motor Transport Board)* (1974), 51 D.L.R. (3d) 292 (Man. C.A.), where the court considered whether an injunction should be granted to protect a carrier's right to haul goods. The legislation provided for restrictions on carriers to ensure the profitability and continuity of service to remote parts of northern Manitoba.

51 See, for example, *Shore Disposal Ltd.* v. *Ed DeWolfe Trucking Ltd.* (1976), 16 N.S.R. (2d) 538 S.C.A.D.

but simply to bring attention to the role that both interlocutory and permanent injunctions can play as a remedy in judicial review of administrative action. However, it should also be recalled that the Supreme Court of Canada has done much to liberalize the laws of standing to allow an individual to commence proceedings for unlawful administrative action in her own right, and, presumably, seek interlocutory relief.[52] Throughout this section it is important to keep in mind certain principles relating to the role of courts in administrative law and the nature of administrative law itself.

The development of administrative law governs the relationship between citizen and state. Special rules have been created, out of recognition of the pervasive role played by government in all aspects of our modern society and from societal expectations that government should be beyond reproach in its dealings with the citizenry. Unfortunately, it is no longer possible to draw clear lines between governmental action and public law, and the traditional sphere of private activity governed by private law. Much of government is carried out by private actors, under the authority of some legislative overlay. Should judicial review be available in these situations? Much government action simply mirrors private commercial activity. Should this activity be subject to judicial review? Similarly, some private parties, trade unions or professional associations for example, act as if they are a public institution in their dealings with members. Should their activity also be subject to judicial review?

An initial inquiry requires one to ask whether the issue raised is in fact a public law issue amenable to judicial review. Generally, if the source of the power is either statute, subordinate legislation, or prerogative, or the nature of the power engages functions which have public law overtones, then it will be amenable to judicial review.[53] Assuming that the issue raised is one of public law an applicant may be required to exhaust any statutory avenues of appeal before being permitted to proceed with an application for judicial review.[54] It is also important to understand the limited role that courts should play in administrative law. It is not the role of courts to second-guess or substitute their

---

52   On standing, see Mullan, above note 31 at § 627–31; and W.A. Bogart, "Understanding Standing, Chapter IV: *Canada (Minister of Finance) v. Finlay*" (1988) 10 Supreme Court. L.R. 377.

53   See *R. v. Panel on Take-overs and Mergers, ex parte Datafin Plc.*, [1987] Q.B. 815 (C.A.); and *Volker Stevin N.W.T. ('92) Ltd. v. Northwest Territories (Commissioner)*, [1994], N.W.T.R. 97 (C.A.).

54   See *Canadian Pacific Ltd. v. Matsqui Indian Band*, [1995] 1 S.C.R. 3.

decision for that of the administrative actor; rather, it is to ensure adherence to procedural safeguards and standards when administrative decisions affecting an individual's rights and entitlements are made.

There are four main areas where injunctions may play a role in administrative law: one, the availability of injunctive relief as a permanent remedy on a judicial review application; two, the use of interlocutory or interim injunctions pending an application for judicial review; three, the possibility of granting an injunction to further the aim of an administrative tribunal; and four, the use of injunctions to enjoin the Crown.

1) Injunctive Relief as a Remedy for Judicial Review

Historically, judicial review was carried out by commencement of a prerogative writ for

- *certiorari* (requiring the statutory authority to submit the record of the impugned proceedings before a superior court to be assessed for jurisdictional error),
- prohibition (preventing proceedings or making a decision by an administrative actor),
- *mandamus* (compelling an administrative actor to perform its legal duties),
- *habeas corpus* (bringing before a superior court a person who is held in custody) and
- *quo warranto* (questioning a person's entitlement to exercise public office).

The private civil law remedies of injunction and declarations supplemented these writs if the applicant could establish an infringement of some private right or the occasion of some special damage. The prerogative writ of *mandamus* and action for a mandatory injunction are similar — the former is the more usual remedy although examples of the latter can be cited.[55] A similar conclusion can be made with respect to the writ of prohibition and a prohibitive injunction.[56]

---

55   See *Smoling v. Canada (Ministry of Health and Welfare)* (1992), 95 D.L.R. (4th) 739 (F.C.T.D.) [*Smoling*].
56   See *David Hunt Farms Ltd. v. Canada (Minister of Agriculture)*, [1994]. 2 F.C. 625 (C.A.).

In those jurisdictions that have created a standardized application for judicial review by statute[57] the prerogative, injunction, and declaration remedies have been rolled into one streamlined process that is launched by commencement of an application for judicial review rather than by way of either writ or action. This would appear to have subsumed the availability of injunctions and declarations within the grounds for judicial review provided in the applicable legislation — in Ontario, for example, the availability of injunctions and declarations will be contingent upon the impugned act flowing from an exercise of a statutory power.[58]

2) Interlocutory Injunctions Pending an Application for Judicial Review

Historically, prerogative writs did not provide for any interlocutory process that would stay proceedings before a decision maker pending the outcome of an application for judicial review. The filing of a writ neither prevented the implementation of decisions already taken nor stopped a tribunal from continuing with its proceedings. The statutory reforms introducing a general application for judicial review now typically authorize the granting of interlocutory relief pending the determination of an application for judicial review. Even in the absence of a specific authorization, courts have begun to grant a stay of proceedings pending the determination of a judicial review application, as part of the court's inherent jurisdiction.[59] The criteria used to determine interlocutory relief here is the same as applied in other interlocutory injunction applications, save in one respect. There is a public interest element in the efficient and timely exercise of administrative action, and this must be given appropriate weight when weighing up the balance of convenience. However, if a respondent administrative actor provides no evidence of irreparable harm, and does not challenge the assertion of the applicant on where the balance of convenience lies, then a court will grant an interlocutory injunction[60] staying enforcement of the administrative ruling, pending the outcome of an application for judicial review.

---

57   See Ontario *Judicial Review Procedure Act*, R.S.O. 1990, c. J.1; British Columbia *Judicial Review Procedure Act*, R.S.B.C. 1996, c. 241; Prince Edward Island *Judicial Review Act*, R.S.P.E.I. 1988, c. J-3; Alberta *Rules of Court*, parts 56 and 56.1; and Canada *Federal Court Act*, R.S.C. 1985, c. F-7, s. 18(1).

58   See *Masters v. Ontario* (1994), 18 O.R. (3d) 551 (Div. Ct.).

59   See *Manitoba (A.G.) v. Metropolitan Stores (MTS) Ltd.*, [1987] 1 S.C.R. 110.

60   See *Smoling*, above note 55.

The courts have also been concerned that the applicant does have a justiciable issue, one that is amenable to judicial resolution. The courts are naturally reluctant to allow their forum to become a vehicle to simply second-guess the original decision maker. Courts are not particularly well equipped to hear arguments relating to science, politics or social policy, matters more properly dealt with in the administrative realm of government where due consideration and expertise can take account of the multi-dimensional facets of policy making.[61]

Some legislation establishing administrative tribunals contains privative clauses protecting the tribunals' decision-making ability. For these tribunals, the grounds for judicial review are higher, requiring proof that the tribunal's decision is patently unreasonable. Before being granted an interlocutory injunction staying the tribunal's order pending an application for judicial review, courts have required an applicant to prove a strong *prima facie* case threshold exists.[62]

3) Injunctions in Support of an Administrative Agency

It is possible for empowering legislation to confer injunction-granting powers on an administrative agency, although there are constitutional limits on the extent to which this can clothe an administrative tribunal with the full panoply of judicial remedies.[63] More often, legislation makes provision for an administrative agency to determine orders regarding specific actions rather than conferring broad injunctive power; cease and desist orders as part of a labour relations board, for example, or reinstatement as part of an order granted by a human rights commission.[64] Where the empowering legislation does not provide an exhaustive schedule of remedial powers, or where the legislation is simply silent on some aspect of remedies, such as the ability to grant interim relief, an emerging trend has been to seek judicial intervention to support the working of an administrative agency.

In *Canada (Human Rights Commission)* v. *Canadian Liberty Net*,[65] the Supreme Court ruled on whether the Federal Court had jurisdiction to grant an interlocutory injunction pending a determination by a human rights tribunal. The Human Rights Commission had sought an injunction to prevent the defendant from using a voice mail system

---

61   See *Cummins* v. *Canada (Minister of Fisheries and Oceans)*, [1996] 3 F.C. 871 (T.D.).
62   See *Sobeys Inc.* v. *U.F.C.W., Local 1000A* (1993), 12 O.R. (3d) 157 (Div. Ct.).
63   *Re Residential Tenancies Act of Ontario*, [1981] 1 S.C.R 714.
64   See, for example, *Canadian Human Rights Act*, R.S.C. 1985, c. H-6, s. 53(2); and Ontario *Labour Relations Act*, 1995, S.O. 1995, c. 1, Schedule A, s. 99(6).
65   [1998] 1 S.C.R. 626.

alleging that such activity constituted a discriminatory practice under the *Canadian Human Rights Act*.[66] The defendant had created a number of voice mail options that broadcast racist and anti-Semitic messages. The Canadian Human Rights Commission, believing such activities constituted a discriminatory practice, had empanelled a tribunal to rule on the matter. At the same time the Commission sought interlocutory relief from the Federal Court. In the trial court, Muldoon J. granted the injunction. This decision was subsequently overturned on appeal. Before the Supreme Court the specific issue was moot and the court declined to rule on whether the injunction should or should not have been granted. However, it did clarify the principles on which such a determination should be made. Both the majority and dissenting minority were agreed that it lay within the authority of a provincial Superior Court to grant such an injunction. This ruling reaffirmed the position taken in *Brotherhood of Maintenance of Way Employees Canadian Pacific System Federation* v. *Canadian Pacific Ltd.*,[67] where it was held that the court had within its inherent jurisdiction the power to grant a "free-standing" injunction, that is, one that was not dependent upon the substantive cause of action being within the court's jurisdiction as long as the substantive issue would come before some competent tribunal for determination, where it was "just and convenient" to do so. The key issue was whether the Federal Court, as a statutory court, held a similar jurisdiction. That matter turned on the interpretation of the *Federal Court Act*[68] and whether the power to grant an injunction "in addition to any other relief" was expansive or contained a limitation.[69] The minority interpreted the term narrowly, requiring

---

66   R.S.C. 1985, c. H-6.
67   [1996] 2 S.C.R. 495.
68   R.S.C. 1985, c. F-7.
69   The argument here concerning the Federal Court's juinsdiction to grant an interlocutory injunction is part of the application of the wider test adopted in *ITO-International Terminal Operators Ltd.* v. *Miida Electronics Inc.*, [1986] 1 S.C.R. 752 requiring the applicant to demonstrate that the Federal Court had jurisdiction by satisfying the following three grounds: [i] there must be a statutory grant of jurisdiction by the federal parliament, [ii] there must be an existing board of federal law which is essential to the disposition of the case and which nourishes the statutory grant of the jurisdiction, and [iii] the law on which the case is based must be a law of Canada as the phrase is used in section 101 of the *Constitution Act, 1867* (U.K., 30 & 31 Vict., c. 3, reprinted in R.S.C. 1985, App. II, No. 5. In addition to the argument based upon jurisdiction deriving from the *Federal Court Act*, the applicant had also argued that the *Human Rights Act* itself granted jurisdiction to the Federal Court by implication. The Supreme Court declined to accept this argument on the basis that the implication of jurisdiction was not "necessary" for the administration of the terms of the legislation.

the court to be able to hear the matter itself such that the award of some "other relief" was purely ancillary. Because the legislation gave the Human Rights Tribunal exclusive jurisdiction to hear the substantive claim, the Federal Court had no jurisdiction to grant an injunction. The majority took the position that because the Federal Court held a jurisdiction to supervise, control, and enforce federal administrative tribunals, and because orders of the Human Rights Tribunal could in fact be transformed into Federal Court orders, these powers amounted to "other relief" such that the court had jurisdiction to grant interlocutory injunctions in aid of the Commission's mandate.

On the basis that the Federal Court had jurisdiction, the majority went on to express their opinion on which test was applicable in the exercise of discretion to grant an interlocutory injunction, in a case involving limitations upon speech. Because the issue was now moot the majority merely indicated the inappropriateness of the *American Cyanamid* standard and the need for constitutional compliance when considering relief which impugned a constitutional protection of freedom of expression.[70]

Canadian Liberty Net is a logical extension to the position taken by the Supreme Court in *Brotherhood of Maintenance of Way Employees Canadian Pacific System Federation* in widening the jurisdiction of all superior courts to grant ancillary and supportive interlocutory relief. The Supreme Court is eschewing jurisdictional debates in favour of framing the arguments as going to a court's discretion whether to grant interlocutory relief. However, it is important to remember that the relief sought here is in aid of an administrative tribunal's jurisdiction and is not intended to supplant it.

4) Injunctions Against the Crown

At common law there was a general immunity preventing the granting of an injunction against the Crown itself. The apparent rationale for this approach was in the difficulty of enforcement by one emanation of the Crown (the courts), against another, and in the general notion that the Crown "could do no wrong." The impact of modern legislation has greatly altered the Crown's immunity from suits brought by the citizenry. Legislation in both the federal[71] and provincial arenas provides

---

70   See above, chapter 3 S.E. "Interlocutory Injunctions to Restrain Defamation and Injunious Falsehood."

71   See *Crown Liability and Proceedings Act*, R.S.C. 1985, c. C-50, s. 22.

for Crown liability save in one important respect concerning the availability of injunctive relief. Section 14(1) & (2) of the Ontario *Proceedings Against the Crown Act*,[72] provides that in any proceedings against the Crown, or servant of the Crown where the effect would be tantamount to ordering an injunction against the Crown itself, the court will not grant an injunction or specific performance, but may order a declaration in lieu. Similar legislation is found in the other provinces.[73] Practically speaking, a declaration will be just as effective as an injunction, few governments or Crown actors will wish to risk public opprobrium for disobeying a court decree.

However, the absence of a jurisdiction to give interlocutory declaratory relief means that there is an apparent lacuna in the law.[74] Courts have begun meeting the apparent gap in remedies in this area by resorting to a number of interpretative strategies.

The first strategy concerns the interpretation of the term "Crown" and distinguishes between the exercise of a power held by the Crown itself and the grant of a power specifically allocated to be exercised by a minister, agent, or servant in their own name. In the former case, the legislation will confer immunity from being subject to an injunction. In the latter case, although the minister, agent, or servant may well be classified as servants of the Crown, they are not exercising a power or function as if they were acting for the Crown itself. Rather, they are exercising a power specifically allocated to the office they hold in their own capacity as minister, agent, or servant. To hold otherwise would be to extend Crown immunity preventing the granting of compulsory remedies into many areas where it has traditionally not been held to

---

72 R.S.O. 1990, c. P.27.

73 See British Columbia *Crown Proceedings Act*, R.S.B.C. 1996, c. 89, s. 11(2) & (4); Prince Edward Island *Crown Proceedings Act*, R.S.P.E.I. 1988, c. C-32, s. 13(2) & (4); Alberta *Proceedings Against the Crown Act*, R.S.A. 1980, c. P-18, s. 17(1) & (2); Manitoba *The Proceedings Against the Crown Act*, R.S.M. 1987, c. P140, s. 14(2) & (4); New Brunswick *Proceedings Against the Crown Act*, R.S.N.B. 1973, c. P-18, s. 14(2) & (4); Newfoundland *Proceedings Against the Crown Act*, R.S.N. 1990, c. P-26, s. 15; Nova Scotia *Proceedings Against the Crown Act*, R.S.N.S. 1989, c. 360, s. 16(2) & (4); and Saskatchewan *Proceedings Against the Crown Act*, R.S.S. 1978, c. P-27, s. 17(2) & (4).

74 See *Francis v. Mohawk of Akwesasne Band of Indians* (1993), 62 F.T.R. 314 (T.D.).

apply. It would, in effect, prevent the issuing of *mandamus* or injunctions against any governmental actor.[75]

A second strategy deals with the jurisdiction of the court to enjoin Crown conduct where the constitutionality of the Crown's actions is being questioned (see discussion below).[76]

A third strategy deals with the courts' jurisdiction to enjoin Crown conduct that is either illegal or *ultra vires* the empowering statutory authority. Under the principle that the Crown "can do no wrong," it has been accepted that a government officer, agent, or servant undertaking an act that is *ultra vires* (that is, outside the statutory duties assigned by the legislature) cannot claim Crown immunity. This is on the basis that the empowering statute could not have authorized an improper act.[77] Once the person is outside the jurisdiction of the empowering Act, they have forfeited Crown immunity and the court has power to grant both an interlocutory or permanent injunction against them.

Courts are resistant to extending. Crown immunity beyond that which is reasonably justifiable to govern the country.[78] There is a natural allure to the notion of equality and that the Crown should be treated as any other defendant is before the law. This view is particularly strong in actions brought against Crown agents whose activities mirror that of many private businesses.[79] Nevertheless, there is still power in the Crown's immunity that can have a particular impact when considering an application for interlocutory relief.

---

75   See *Canada (A.-G.)* v. *Saskatchewan Water Corp.* (1993), 106 D.L.R. (4th) 250, Bayda C.J. (Sask. C.A.); Canada (*Conseil des Ports Ntionaux*) v. *Langelier* (1968), [1969] S.C.R. 60; M. v. *Home Office* (1993), [1994] 1 A.C. 377 (H.L.) [*Home Office*]; H.W.R. Wade, "Injunctive Relief Against the Crown and Ministers" (1991) 107 L.Q. Rev. 4; and P.W. Hogg, *Liability of the Crown*, 2d. ed. (Toronto: Carswell,1989) at 26. But note that in *Mundle* v. *Canada* (1994), 85 F.T.R. 258 (T.D.), it was held that a judicial review application before the Federal Court was not a "proceeding against the Crown," such that any protection against the granting of injunctions against the Crown contained within section 22 of the *Crown Liability and Proceedings Act*, above note 71, was not applicable.

76   See *RJR-MacDonald Inc.* v. *Canada (A.G.)* [1994] 1 S.C.R. 311.

77   See *Rattenbury* v. *British Columbia (Land Settlement Board)*, [1929] S.C.R. 52; *Lodge* v. *Canada (Minister of Employment and Immigration)*, [1979], 1 F.C. 775 (C.A.); *Saugeen Band of Indians* v. *Canada (Minister of Fisheries and Oceans)*, [1992] 3 F.C. 576 (T.D.); and *Hughes* v. *Canada* (1994), 80 F.T.R. 300 (T.D.).

78   See the comments by Dickson J. in *R.* v. *Eldorado Nuclear Ltd.*, [1983] 2 S.C.R. 551 at 558.

79   See *Baton Broadcasting Ltd.* v. *Canadian Broadcasting Corp.* [1966] 2 O.R. 169 at 174, Grant J. (H.C.).

E. INJUNCTIONS AND CONSTITUTIONAL LITIGATION

In this part, we focus upon permanent injunctions to enforce constitutional rights, and in particular rights derived from the *Charter*.[80] The enforcement of these rights creates novel yet difficult problems for courts. One immediate difference from established private law models on equitable remedies is the almost total irrelevance of the inadequacy of damages criteria as part of the test to determine what constitutes an appropriate remedy. The test is meaningless for the practical reason that there is little established jurisprudence on damages as an appropriate remedy for constitutional violation.[81] On a philosophical level, constitutional rights are usually regarded as being inalienable, and therefore the law has eschewed attempts to suggest that they can be quantified in a monetary and substitutionary fashion. Constitutional litigation tends to be more forward-looking and concerned with future constitutional compliance rather than with compensation for past transgressions. Constitutional litigation is more often concerned with group rights, or where the decision made between the actual litigants may impact on many other similarly situated individuals.[82]

Where the applicant is merely seeking to prevent the enforcement of unconstitutional laws and actions, the issuing of a prohibitive injunction will mirror the concerns present in private adjudication when granting a similar order, save in one important respect. Finding unconstitutional a law that has been acted upon for some time may carry with it profound repercussions beyond the litigants, and warrants the court in restraining any finding of invalidity until such time as reparative steps have taken place. Where the court takes a role in defining those reparative steps, it crosses into making a mandatory injunction (also referred to as a "reparative injunction"). Where the court is unable to define the reparative steps without further investigation, or where the court is engaged in ongoing supervision of the decree, then we cross into what has been

---

80 *Canadian Charter of Rights and Freedoms*, Part I of the *Constitution Act, 1982*, being Schedule B to the *Canada Act 1982* (U.K.), 1982, c. 11.

81 In spite of the able efforts of K. Cooper-Stephenson, *Charter Damages Claims* (Toronto: Carswell, 1990); and K. Roach, *Constitutional Remedies in Canada* (Aurora, Ont.: Canada Law Book, 1994), there are few cases where damages have been awarded for constitutional violation.

82 See A. Chayes, "The Role of the Judge in Public Law Litigation" (1976) 89 Harv. L. Rev. 1281.

termed a "structural injunction."[83] A final variant, where the court specifically addresses the reparative steps to the legislature and requires legislative action, has been termed a "legislative injunction."[84]

Prohibitive injunctions in constitutional settings are uncontroversial and in fact extremely rare. The more likely remedy is a declaration under section 24 (or as a pre-*Charter* remedy preserved under section 26) of the *Charter,* or a declaration of invalidity under section 52 of the *Constitution Act,*[85] which itself may be delayed.[86] The difficulty with a declaration under section 24 is that it is not enforceable on the parties, although there is a legitimate perception that a government agency will comply. Nor does a court remain seized of the issue, preventing the applicant from returning for further mandatory orders or use of the contempt-of-court power. Any order that engages the court in supervision becomes more problematical, for the following reasons:

1) For mandatory injunctions in private law, the courts have mandated a form of cost-benefit analysis with which to evaluate the benefit to be gained by the plaintiff when weighed against the cost of compliance to the defendant. A similar approach cannot be undertaken in a constitutional setting if the notion of entrenched and inalienable rights is to have any meaning.

2) The description and content of many of the constitutional rights being protected is of a more fluid nature in Canada because they are subject to a section 1 analysis as well as the notwithstanding override contained in section 33 of the *Charter.* This can be contrasted with the American constitutional provisions that tend to be cast in more absolute terms. As a result, a reparative or structural injunction ordered by a Canadian court to bring governmental practice into constitutional compliance can take numerous directions. It thus violates the notion that the defendant is entitled to have clear instructions of what he must do to comply with the court's order. On the other hand, these distinctive aspects of the Canadian *Charter* can act as an argument to embolden courts into remedial creativity.

---

83   This terminology is taken from O.M. Fiss, *The Civil Rights Injunction* (Bloomington, Ind.: Indiana University Press, 1978).

84   See R.A. Schapiro, "The Legislative Injunction: A Remedy for Unconstitutional Legislative Inaction" (1989) 99 Yale L.J. 231.

85   *Constitution Act, 1982,* being Schedule B to the *Canada Act 1982* (U.K.), 1982, c. 11.

86   See H.S. Fairley, "Private Law Remedial Principles and the *Charter*: Can the Old Dog Wag this New Tail?" in J. Berryman, ed., *Remedies: Issues and Perspectives* (Scarborough, Ont.: Carswell, 1991) 313.

3) One problem more likely to arise as the intrusiveness of the courts' orders intensify, is where courts are perceived as impinging on traditionally governmental functions. A court ordering an injunction requiring public expenditure is not in a position to evaluate the priority that order has as against other governmental claims for funds, nor is the court in a position to evaluate or audit the effectiveness of the expenditure.

The emergence of more intrusive injunctions in Canada has mirrored similar developments in the United States. From a fairly early stage there has been recognition of a need to develop reparative injunctions to correct harms caused by past constitutional violations. The decision of the Supreme Court in *Reference re Language Rights under s. 23 of Manitoba Act, 1870 and s. 133 of Constitution Act, 1867*[87] is widely cited as the first significant remedial development of intrusive constitutional injunctions.[88] Following the finding that all unilingual enactments of the Manitoba Legislature were invalid, the Court had a choice of remedies. The simplest approach would have been a declaration of invalidity, that the laws were of no force or effect.[89] For the Court, the prospect of the ensuing "legal vacuum [and] consequent legal chaos"[90] necessitated a different response. The Court then declared a state of emergency, and that all unilingual acts of Manitoba would be deemed valid until the "expiry of the minimum period necessary for translation, re-enactment, printing and publishing."[91] Subsequently, the court held a hearing to determine what would be an appropriate time span in which to translate the unilingual legislation. Even after this period had been determined the court retained jurisdiction and was subsequently asked on two occasions to extend the translation period for various orders in council and instruments incorporated by reference in laws.[92]

---

87   [1985] 1 S.C.R. 721 [*Language Rights Reference*].

88   See Roach, above note 81 at § 13.420: R.W. Kerr, "The Remedial Power of the Courts After the Manitoba Language Rights Case" (1986) 6 Windsor Y.B.Access Just. 252; and W.A. Bogart, "'Appropriate and Just': Section 24 of the *Canadian Charter of Rights and Freedoms* and the Question of Judicial Legitimacy" (1986) 10 Dal. L.J. 81.

89   This approach had been suggested by some of the litigants, who hoped to put leverage on the Manitoba Legislature to pass a constitutional amendment that had earlier failed to pass.

90   *Languages Rights Reference*, above note 87 at 747.

91   *Ibid.* at 767.

92   See *Re Manitoba Language Rights Order*, [1990] 3 S.C.R. 1417.

Throughout this translation period the litigants worked harmoniously in coming to agreements to put the Supreme Court's order into effect.

The injunction in the *Language Rights Reference* was reparative of the minority francophone language rights. After determination of the substantive issue, the government willingly complied with the court's decree and the issue of what the court would have done had the government been delinquent did not have to be broached. Where governments have acted in a recalcitrant manner the American experience has been to resort to further intrusive injunctive orders, namely structural injunctions. In these orders the court, faced with a recalcitrant governmental agency, seeks to transform the institution so that it will act in constitutional compliance in the future. The order seeks to eradicate the systemic barriers that have caused the constitutional rights of a group or class of individuals to be infringed.

Often, a court is called upon to make a conscious policy preference to attain constitutional compliance. A cursory inspection of the way American courts have had to supervise desegregation of schools,[93] or reform mental hospitals and prisons[94] will give an idea of the magnitude of these types of orders. However, such orders have only come as a last resort for courts, and only in the face of continual belligerency and delay on behalf of the impugned agency in remeding the problem. Even after assuming control, courts have looked to the institutions themselves to come forward with plans of how to go about the reforming process and only reluctantly has the court itself appointed someone to undertake the supervision and implementation of the order.

Fortunately in Canada, the incidence of recalcitrant government agencies has been infrequent. By and large, the impugned agencies have complied with the courts' orders even where they have been issued as mere declarations. However, there are a number of cases involving minority language education, where the activities of particular education boards, who have failed to provide French language education, has tried the patience of several courts in a number of provinces. In *Marchand v. Simcoe County Board of Education*,[95] the court ordered the defendant to provide to the plaintiff, representing francophone parents, equivalent instruction and facilities as enjoyed by English language students. In granting this mandatory order the judge noted that the Board

---

93   See *Green v. County School B. of New Kent Country, Va.*, 391 U.S. 430 (1968); *Morgan v. Kerrigan*, 401 F. Supp. 216 (D. Mass. 1975); and *Swann v. Charlotte-Mecklenburg Board of Education*, 402 U.S. 1 (1971).

94   *James v. Wallace*, 406 F. Supp. 318 (M.D. Ala. 1976).

95   (1986), 55 O.R. (2d) 638 (H.C.) [*Marchand*].

of Education had maintained a negative attitude towards minority language education and that the government had delayed in proceeding with implementing rights first declared by the Court of Appeal in 1984.[96] A year later the Board of Education returned to get clarification of the court's order. In the intervening period the Ontario Legislature had enacted changes creating French Language Education Councils (FLECS). In the county of Simcoe, the FLEC board had proposed a way to provide for French language education but the capital funding for the plan was disputed by the Government, the Simcoe Board of Education and FLEC. This issue was put to the trial judge who simply endorsed the FLEC proposal as meeting the objectives set out in the court's original judgment. In other examples on the provision of minority language education the respective boards of education have similarly complied with court orders after expressions of initial frustration at having been called to account for their actions.[97]

At the outer extreme of intrusive orders to ensure constitutional rights is the legislative injunction. American courts

- have used this form of injunction to force a legislature to enact some form of enabling legislation,[98] or to increase appropriations to fund reform.[99]

This order brings courts into conflict with the role traditionally occupied by legislatures, where courts have usually refused relief based upon crown immunity or infringement of parliamentary privilege. Many of these have usually concerned whether an injunction can be ordered to prevent the legislature from passing legislation where it is alleged that the proposed legislation will be *ultra vires* when enacted.[100]

---

96 See *Reference re Education Act of Ontario and Minority Language Education Rights* (1984), 47 O.R. (2d) 1 (C.A.).

97 See *Marchand v. Simcoe Board of Education (No.2)* (1987), 61 O.R. (2d) 651 (H.C.). See also *Lavoie v. Nova Scotia (A.G.)* (1988), 84 N.S.R. (2d) 387 at 388 (S.C.T.D.) rev'd. (1988), 91 N.S.R. (2d) 184 (S.C.A.D.); and *Société des Acadiens du Nouveau-Brunswick Inc. v. New Brunswick Language School Board No. 50* (1983), 48 N.B.R. (2d) 361 (Q.B.T.D.), additional reasons at (1983), 50 N.B.R. (2d) 41 (Q.B.), aff'd (*sub nom. Assn. of Parents for Fairness in Education, Grand Falls District 50 Branch v. Minority Language School Bd. No. 50*)(1987), 82 N.B.R (2d) 360 (C.A.), aff'd [1968] 1 S.C.R. 549.

98 See *Spallone v. United States*, 493 U.S. 265 (1990).

99 See *Missouri v. Jenkins*, 495 U.S. 33 (1990).

100 See *Merricks v. Heathcoat-Amory and Minister of Agriculture, Fisheries and Food*, [1955] Ch. 567; and *Home Office*, above note 75.

The closest examples of legislative injunctions in Canada occur around the cases disputing electoral boundaries. In *Dixon* v. *British Columbia (A.G.)*,[101] McLachlin C.J.S.C. held that the British Columbia electoral boundaries were unconstitutional on the grounds that the inequality of voter parity within the current system did not accord with the section 3 *Charter* "right to vote" provision. With respect to remedy, McLachlin C.J.S.C. gave a declaration of invalidity but suspended its operation for a temporary period with the hope that the British Columbia legislature would enact legislation that would survive *Charter* scrutiny. In *ex curia* comments McLachlin C.J.S.C. admitted that she had deferred the really difficult question. What would happen if the legislature did not act? However, she also indicated that there existed a closer relationship of deference and cooperation between judicial and legislative arms of government in Canada, as against the confrontational route prevalent in the United States.[102]

Consistent with McLachlin J.'s description of the underlying basis of the relationship between judicial and legislative arms of government, as yet no court in Canada has been required to answer her difficult question. In other examples where the potential for confrontation has arisen, courts have acted cautiously. In *Perry* v. *Ontario*[103] the Court of Appeal did not allow a mandatory injunction to stand requiring the province to negotiate with Indian groups to structure an enforcement policy on hunting and fishing which complied with section 35 of the *Constitution Act* 1982 (Recognition of existing aboriginal and treaty). Unlike the protection of minority language rights, which had been explicitly delineated, court-ordered negotiation was inappropriate where the definition of the constitutional rights was still in an embryonic form. In *Mahé* v. *Alberta*,[104] the Supreme Court preferred to issue a declaration outlining what was required to meet the provisions of section 23 of the *Charter*. The declaration outlined rights of management and control over minority language education, rather than mandating by injunction the enactment of legislation to achieve that result. The chosen approach preserved the right of the legislature to explore how the policy guidelines provided by the court could be implemented.

---

101   (1989), 59 D.L.R. (4th) 247 (B.C.S.C.).

102   See B.M. McLachlin, "The *Charter*: A New Role for the Judiciary" (1991) 29 Alta. L. Rev. 540.

103   (1997), 33 O.R. (3d) 705 (C.A.), leave to appeal to S.C.C. refused (1997), 110 O.A.C. 400. See also *Delgamuukw* v. *British Columbia* (1993), 104 D.L.R. (4th) 470 (B.C.C.A.), new trial ordered [1997] 3 S.C.R. 1010.

104   [1990] 1 S.C.R. 342.

At present there are no reported cases where a Canadian court has been required to go to the same lengths as American courts to enforce either a structural or legislative injunction. Hopefully, Canadian governmental agencies will continue to voluntarily implement court orders respecting constitutional compliance. However, if a point is ever reached where government intransigence threatens the maintenance of constitutional rights, Canadian courts should meet the challenge through the cautious application of structural injunctions.

FURTHER READINGS

COOPER-STEPHENSON, K.D., *Charter Damages Claims* (Calgary: Carswell, 1990)

ESTEY, W., "Public Nuisance and Standing to Sue" (1972) 10 Osgoode Hall L.J. 563

FRIEDLANDER, L., "Must the Law Be Obeyed? The Attorney-General's Response to Flouting" (1995) 17 Advocates' Q. 80

GILLESPIE, N., "Charter Remedies: The Structural Injunction" (1990) 11 Advocates' Q. 190

MULLAN, D.J. *Administrative Law*, 3d ed. (Toronto: Carswell, 1996)

ROACH, K., *Constitutional Remedies In Canada* (Aurora, Ont.: Canada Law Book, 1994)

SPECIFIC PERFORMANCE: GENERAL PRINCIPLES

A. INTRODUCTION

Specific performance is an equitable remedy that orders a defaulting promisor to keep her contractual bargain under pain of contempt of court. The popular notion is that it is a presumptive remedy in the enforcement of realty contracts and of a secondary nature in any other contract setting. As we will see, neither of these premises accurately records the full scope of the remedy.

Specific performance is a remedy that has been shaped by historical practice and many of the rules pertaining to its availability seem strange today without some appreciation of the past development of the remedy. In the first part of this chapter we will briefly explore these historical antecedents. In recent times there has been renewed interest in specific performance as a remedy which most closely approximates to "complete" compensation for breach of contract and much ink has been expended reconciling equity's chosen contractual remedy with the compensatory goal of damages. These arguments will also be explored in this chapter. As will emerge, the dominant arguments inhibiting specific performance are concerns over its relationship with the common law remedy, of changes and perceptions about the inability of courts to undertake supervision of what is perceived as being an intrusive and coercive order. As with other equitable remedies, there are also a number of discretionary barriers to the granting of specific performance — these will be discussed in chapter 11. In subsequent chapters, specific performance will be looked at in a number of discrete areas of contracting.

B. A BRIEF HISTORY OF THE DEVELOPMENT OF SPECIFIC PERFORMANCE

Where a promisor's obligations remain unfulfilled it appears natural for the promisee to seek specific performance. In that way the promisor will get complete relief for that which was promised. Why then has the common law favoured substitutionary relief over specific performance?

To answer this question, one has to appreciate the nature of contracting through history.[1] If one were to take a look at the manner of contracting in the sixteenth century one would make several observations.

- The first would be the variety of courts in which litigants could bring an action, which lead to much forum shopping: Chancery, the Law Merchant, Admiralty Courts and Courts of Request all provided some form of relief for parol (oral) contracts. Indeed, most of these courts had superior process for handling parol contracts than did the common law courts, and as a result proved very attractive to litigants. Many of these courts were influenced by European approaches, practiced by merchants and traders throughout Europe as part of the Law Merchant, and by the workings of the earlier Ecclesiastical Courts, from where the chancellors were often drawn. An important tenet of the Ecclesiastical Courts was the notion that a person who had failed to honour his promise imperiled his soul before God. The only way to remedy this spiritual imbalance was to make the promisor observe his promise. This tenet was carried over to Chancery Courts by ecclesiastically-trained chancellors. In common law, however, the main form of contracting was through either the action of covenant, which required specialty (a deed under seal), or the action of debt, by way of penal or conditional bond. A promisor would create an obligation by entering a penal bond that was discharged by actually performing the promise on the stipulated date, or by forfeiting the penal bond. It is in these early roots than one sees emerging the idea of a monetary payment as being a substitution for actual performance.

---

1   See H. Hazeltine, "Early History of Specific Performance of Contract Law in English Law" reproduced in *Rechswissenschaftliche beitrage Juristische festgabe des auslandes zu Josef Kohlers* (1909); A.W.B. Simpson, A *History of the Common Law of Contract: The Rise of the Action of Assumpsit* (Oxford: Clarendon Press, 1975); and P.S. Atiyah, *The Rise and Fall of Freedom of Contract* (Oxford: Clarendon Press, 1979).

- Next, one would observe the total absence of suits based on executory parol contracts in common law courts. It would be another 200 years before the common law finally developed the writ of *assumpsit* (because he promised) which would elevate the promise as being a central tenet of contract law.
- Third, one would note the importance accorded realty, and the fact that only in chancery (through the notion of the passing of a "use," or benefit, thus creating a proprietary interest held by the promisee), would a purchaser be protected specifically against a vendor's breach. In common law, title to land would only pass on conveyance, which required the strict observance of particular formalities.

If one were to advance forward and view a snapshot of contracting in the seventeeth century, the picture would appear quite similar. For contracts concerning realty, chancery courts played a decisive role in enforcement. There were two reasons for explain this phenomenon.

- First, realty carried with it not only its economic worth but also political power and authority, as well as social status.[2] Thus, a conpensatory remedy, which merely substituted damages for actual performance, would not result in the transfer of these ephemeral qualities.
- The second reason was the subordination of contract by property concepts. Chancery, which had created the passing of a use to denote when property had exchanged, was inextricably tied to what Horowitz has called a "title theory of exchange."[3] Entrapped in this conceptual framework, chancery courts were slow to react to the nascent ideas of the bilateral executory contract[4] that were about to emerge, and which became so important in the creation of new forms of property. Realty still formed the single most important form of property that could be bargained, and this ensured the continued impor-

---

2   See D. Cohen, "The Relationship of Contractual Remedies to Political and Social Status: A Preliminary Inquiry" (1982) 32 U.T.L.J. 31, who points out the inextricable link between land ownership and political enfranchisement at the time.

3   See M.J. Horwitz, *The Transformation of American Law, 1780–1860* (Cambridge: Harvard University Press, 1977). Central to a title theory of exchange is the notion that the contract is being enforced because it alone effects an exchange of ownership in the property, which is the subject of the contract. The simple presence of a promise within the contract is not the reason justifying specific enforcement. In this sense, equity mirrored the old common law by creating a proprietary interest, the equitable interest, and ordered its conveyance.

4   A bilateral executory contract is a contract in which the reciprocal exchange of promises between two parties is the immediate consideration for enforcement without the need for any steps of actual performance having taken place.

tance of chancery's remedies. In common law, the enactment of the *Statute of Frauds* in 1677,[5] while freeding the enforcement of land and other important contracts from the need to prove specialty, still required the formalities of a signature, and thus again inhibited the creation of enforceable parol contracts at common law.

Advancing a further 100 years, both the manner of contracting and remedies for breach are dramatically different. By the eighteenth and nineteenth centuries the common law had developed the bilateral executory contract, and contracting not only functioned to effect a transfer in title to property, but also became an important instrument to protect against changes in supply and price in a market economy. The emergence of the bilateral executory contract also created a new form of property — namely the expectation interests of a promisee. Specific performance would seem to be a perfect remedy to vindicate the expectation interest, and one would expect it to have become the remedy of choice for disappointed promisees, but this did not happen.

Two reasons account for this curtailment of specific performance. A latent aspect of equity jurisprudence at the time were the notions of "fairness" and "good conscience." In contract law this translated into a doctrine of "just price," and accounted for much of chancery's development of the doctrine of relief against penalties imposed under conditioral or penal bonds. Where the particular commodity subject to a contract does not fluctuate wildly in price, it is unlikely that enforcing the contract specifically will reveal any conflict between doctrines of just price and title theory of exchange. However, where the contracted commodity is dependent upon the market price on the day, a contract analysis built around a title theory of exchange, which treats the property as having passed to the promisee on the day the promise was made, is likely to violate notions of "just price" if the market is riding high on the day appointed for judicial enforcement. The emerging notions of contracting, built around protection of expectations and the new type of property such doctrines created, made the established contract doctrines of chancery appear anachronistic. The second reason for chancery's waning importance over newer forms of contractual undertakings was the general decline in the expeditious processing of claims before chancery courts. This was the period on which Charles Dickens wrote his condemnatory assessment of chancery practice in *Bleak House*.[6]

---

5   *An act for prevention of frauds and perjuries, 1677* (U.K.), 29 Car. II, c. 3.
6   I have pursued these argument much more fully in J. Berryman, "The Specific Performance Damages Continuum: An Historical Perspective" (1985) 17 Ottawa L. Rev. 295.

During the nineteenth century, the paradigmatic bilateral executory contract dominated discourse on the law of contract. This model appealed to advocates of legal formalism, the conceptualization of law as a science governed by immutable doctrinal principles. Legal formalism included finding an appropriate role for damages as a primary remedy for breach of contract. Prior to the 1800s the assessment of damages for breach of contract lay exclusively within a jury's domain and few rules existed to proscribe a jury's damage assessment. This all changed with the decision in *Hadley v. Baxendale*,[7] which imposed limits on the recoverability of consequential losses, particularly speculative profits. Another article of faith concerning damage assessment was the innocent party's obligation to mitigate his loss: a plaintiff was not to be allowed to "saddle on the defendant the consequences of his own stupidity, laxity, or inertia."[8] Nor did these doctrines distinguish between executed and executory contracts. Of course, these rules can now be justified on economic grounds concerning the apportionment of risk and how to identify the best loss-avoider, and who can most expeditiously prevent the further incursion of losses between the contracting parties. But, at least for executory contracts, it is not obvious why specific relief should not be favoured to protect a promisee's expectations unless the law manifested some antipathy towards the complete protection of the promisor's interest. We will return to these arguments in the next section.

In terms of our historical analysis, the adherents to legal formalism held a deep suspicion of specific performance. Holmes took it as a self-evident principle that the "only universal consequence of a legally binding promise is, that the law makes the promisor pay damages if the promised event does not come to pass."[9] As Gilmore has pointed out, for Holmes specific performance was to be avoided and damages for breach were to be purely compensatory and never punitive.[10]

Once the Holmesian view of contract had taken hold, the availability of specific performance became an anachronism. For the legal formalists, the free-wheeling discretionary nature of equity was also anathema. Legal theorists and judges of the time who conceived law as a science erected doctrinal limitations on equity's intervention. Chief

---

7   (1854), 9 Ex. 341, 156 E.R. 145. See also R. Danzig, "*Hadley v. Baxendale*: A Study in the Industrialization of the Law" (1975) 4 J. Legal Stud. 249.

8   G.T. Washington, "Damages in Contract at Common Law" (1932) 48 L.Q. Rev. 90 at 106.

9   O.W. Holmes, *The Common Law* (London: Macmillan, 1909) 301.

10   See G. Gilmore, *The Death of Contract* (Columbus, Oh.: Ohio State University Press, 1974) at 14.

amongst these developments was the re-emergence of the notion that equity only stepped in to supplement the common law. This principle, enshrined in the adequacy of damages test, had always been latently present, but for most of the earlier period only lip-service had been paid to it. Now it became a dominant assessment of the relationship between common law and equity.

Equity did retain pre-eminence over land contracts, however, this was partly due to the historical antecedents that had placed many land contracts within chancery's purview.[11] It is also important to note that even as late as 1874 over 80 percent of the land in Great Britain was owned by fewer than 7000 people.[12] As a form of property for investment its potential would only be realized much later, after the repeal of the Corn Laws had taken hold. The notion of uniqueness of land *per se* explained why specific performance remained the presumptive remedy for contracts involving realty. And if specific performance was made available to a purchaser the doctrine of affirmative mutuality assured that it should be made available to a vendor.

Specific performance was also restrained by concerns about the difficulties of supervision. This restraint arose in the context of personal service contracts as well as building and repair contracts. Throughout the 1800s, contradictory judgments surround this restraint.[13] As Pound suggested, the conservatism in making decrees for the affirmative performance of anything beyond a single act was an attempt by the chancellors to maintain credibility in the jealous eyes of the common law courts, by ensuring that what was decreed could in fact be performed.[14]

There are three lessons to be learnt from this brief history of specific performance. First, the modern restraints on the availability of

---

11   The doctrine of uniqueness probably links back to the passing of a use doctrine in chancery. As Jekyll M.R. stated in *Lechmere* v. *Earl of Carlisle* (1733), 3 P. Wms. 211, 24 E.R. 1033 (Ch.), of the passing of the use doctrine: "[a] rule so powerful it is, as to alter the very nature of things; to make money land, and on the contrary, to turn land into money."

12   See E. Spring, "Landowners, Lawyers, and Land Law Reform in Nineteenth-Century England" (1977) 21 Am. J. Legal Hist. 40 at 50.

13   See for example, the judgment of Wood V.C. in *Kay* v. *Johnson* (1864), 2 H. & M. 118, 71 E.R. 406 (V.C.) who thought that the authorities were all opposed to granting specific performance to enforce a building contract; and contrast with the judgment of James V.C. in *Wilson* v. *Furness Railway Co.* (1869), L.R. 9 Eq. 28, who stated that a court would struggle with any amount of difficulty to uphold performance of a building contract.

14   See R. Pound, "The Progress of the Law — Equity" (1920) 33 Harv. L. Rev. 420 at 434.

this equitable remedy are rather recent in origin. Second, current restraints may simply be the outcome of some earlier conflict between chancery and common law courts and have little bearing today. Third, the availability of specific relief is inextricably linked to the dominant contractual paradigm of the day and the particular weight it accords to protecting the varying interests of promisees.

C. THE SUPREMACY OF DAMAGES

It is generally accepted that contractual remedies exist to protect the promisee's expectations. The law's aim is to place the plaintiff in the position she would have been in had the contract been performed according to its terms. To accomplish this task requires a process to determine and assess a promisee's expectation, and then to choose an appropriate remedy to effect the protection accorded by the law.

Whether the expectation interest should be protected is beyond the scope of this book, although some cursory observations need to be recorded. The protection of expectations is a necessary part of modern capitalist society in that it supports individual autonomy concerning the creation and accretion of capital, and the ability to undertake long-range forward planning. Given the importance of protecting expectations, one would assume that the law would strive for completeness in remedial choice wherever possible. Of course, in many cases of breach of contract the particular losses are unavoidable and it only remains for the court to provide a substitutionary remedy in damages. Seeking either a pre-emptive specific performance remedy to avoid breach, or specific performance relief after breach, is simply not an option. However, even in these cases it is important to note that the law has for various policy reasons imposed restraints on the quantification of damages. Thus, the doctrine of remoteness, which largely aims to curb liability for consequential losses by limiting recoverable damages to those that the defendant either knew of, or could have reasonably been expected to know of, is a fundamental limitation on completeness of remedy. On other occasions, and with varying intensity, courts have imposed limits on the recovery of non-pecuniary damages arising from breach; the ostensible justification being the difficulty in quantifying what are regarded as idiosyncratic losses, or, because they are too remote. However, even after removing these contractual actions there remains a plethora of situations where specific performance could operate as a remedy and would come closer to ensuring completeness. Why is this not acknowledged in our remedial taxonomy?

1) Economic Efficiency

Much modern debate about the relationship of specific performance to damages for breach has centered on identifying the most economically efficient result. Protagonists argue both for and against specific relief as being economically efficient. Underlying most economic arguments is the principle that after identifying a set of distributive entitlements,[15] economic optimality is attained "if no change in that distribution can be made that leaves no one worse off and at least one person better off."[16] An alternative way of expressing the same sentiment is that "efficiency means exploiting economic resources in such a way that 'value' — human satisfaction as measured by aggregate consumer willingness to pay for goods and services — is maximized."[17] The law's role is to assist in achieving this result by overcoming barriers, particularly transactional costs (such as the cost incurred in negotiating voluntary exchanges, identifying parties to transactions, and collecting information to exercise choice), that inhibit economic efficiency. Law also affects initial distributive entitlements. Wealth maximization means that the person who puts the greatest value on a commodity is probably the most economically efficient user of that commodity.

Those who suggest[18] that the current law's approach to remedies helps attain economic efficiency, argue that damages as a paramount remedy for breach of contract ensures that a breaching promisor can resell a commodity to a person who clearly places a greater value on that commodity than the present promisee. As long as the promisee's expectations are satisfied by a substitutionary damages remedy (which clearly the promisee will take because at the point of receiving damage compensation the promisee would prefer to have the damages to the specific commodity. Otherwise the promisee would have been willing to pay more for the commodity to insist upon specific performance in the first place), all parties walk away happy from the transaction and an economically efficient result has been attained. Cases where specific performance is available, for example, because the commodity is unique, are justified on the basis that substitutionary damages would

---

15   Distributive entitlements describe the distribution of wealth in any society and are governed by political, religious, philosophical, and moral imperatives. Differing sets of entitlements will have their own economically efficient distribution.

16   R.M. Dworkin, "Is Wealth a Value" (1980) 9 J. Legal Stud. 191 at 193.

17   R.A. Posner, *Economic Analysis of Law*, 5th ed. (New York: Aspen Law & Business, 1988) at 13-17.

18   See, for example, A.T. Kronman, "Specific Performance" (1977) 45 U. Chi. L.Rev. 351.

be problematic because court cannot find any similar market in which to calculate an award of damages. The risk of under- or over-compensation can be avoided by awarding specific performance.

Those who argue that specific performance should be more freely available also defend their position on efficiency grounds.[19] Assuming that the law generally seeks to provide complete recovery, they argue that a damages remedy systematically under-compensates a promisee for loss, and that the routine availability of specific performance would avoid the incursion of litigation costs associated with quantifying damages. Of course, the routine availability of specific performance violates the notion that a promisor is free to breach his contract provided he pays damages in substitution — it would require the promisor to negotiate the release of the specific performance obligation so that the promisor could sell his commodity to another party, who places a higher value on it. The promisee would be placed in an exploitative position, able to seek some of the profits that will inure to the promisor through breaching and entering into a contract with the third party. This argument assumes that the ability to provide cover (satisfy the promisee's expectations from a different source) is less costly for the promisee to undertake than the promisor. In a competitive market there is no reason to support this assumption. Where cover is difficult to provide then this would suggest that the costs of calculating damages as a substitute remedy would be just as high, if not higher than if specific performance had been made available. Where cover is impossible, obviously specific performance will be favoured, even if damages are the dominant remedy.

It would seem that the economic efficiency arguments concerning the relationship of specific performance to damages are inconclusive. Much turns on the underlying assumptions made in the respective analyses and in particular the actual costs associated with "transaction costs." The supremacy of one remedy over the other is justified if it minimizes the costs incurred in negotiating around an inefficient remedy. Unfortunately, empirical quantification of these costs and incorporation into a workable legal principle has not been achieved. Nevertheless, important contributions from the economic efficiency arguments can inform our understanding of the relationship between damages and specific performance. Two of these aspects are explored next.

---

19   See, for example, A. Schwartz, "The Case for Specific Performance" (1979) 89 Yale L.J. 271.

2) Efficient Breach

The strict notion of efficient breach is built around the Holmesian view of contract, that the "only universal consequence of a legally binding promise is, that the law makes the promisor pay damages if the promised event does not come to pass." Implicit in this approach is the notion that the damages paid to the promisee to compensate for breach will be less than the profit obtained by the promisor as a result of the breach. This uncoupling of a promisee's losses from a promisor's gains is the demarcation line between using restitutionary remedies to protect contracts as against particular contractual remedies which substitute damages for breach. Restitutionary remedies are not generally supported in contract because they result in the promisor being forced to share the benefits of breaching her contract with the promisee, often in circumstances where the measure of monetary compensation has no bearing on the promisee's actual losses.

Decreeing specific performance, which in effect gives the promisee exactly what was contracted, is seen as over-compensating the promisee if he does not actually value the performance. In this sense the notion of efficient breach favours the promisor, where the cost of protecting the promisee is less than the gain to be made through breach. Obviously, where the promisee is seeking specific performance, this act alone may be taken as evidence that the promisee does in fact value performance at the actual cost of performance to the promisor. In those circumstances, it is arguable that the decree should always be granted (see discussion below on consumer surplus).

However, the promisee's actions in seeking specific performance may simply mask another objective, and that is to extract from the promisor some of her expected benefits of breach — the promisee is willing to bargain compliance with the decree for some of the promisor's expected profits.[20] The law has been reluctant to allow restitutionary principles that measure the promisor's gain and award that to the promisee, although there is a growing recognition that in the case of opportunistic breach, a restitutionary remedy may be appropriate. Similarly,

---

20   From an economic efficiency point of view, such bargaining activity is neutral. The issue as to who benefits from breach — either the promisor exclusively, or whether the promisor must also share that benefit with the promisee as part of the price of breach — is simply a distributive question and will not alter the actual economically efficient outcome of who gets the commodity. See I.R. Macneil, "Efficient Breach of Contract: Circles in the Sky" (1982) 68 Va. L. Rev. 947.

there is reluctance to arm the promisee with a remedy that may lead to a monetary payment in excess of the promisee's actual losses.

Courts have often indicated that the aim of contract damages is to compensate the plaintiff for his actual losses, and not to remove the benefits of breach from the defendant.[21] If specific performance was routinely available it would result in the promisor being forced into either pre- or post-judgment negotiations to arrange a release of the specific performance decree. These negotiations are likely to be more problematic than negotiating the damages that the promisor must pay for breach. In the latter negotiations, objective external reference points in the marketplace help identify the value of the promisee's expectations. In the former, there are no external reference points on which to determine how much of the profit the promisee will be willing to settle for, and, indeed, the promisee may have no knowledge of what the actual profit amounts to. Where damage negotiations are problematic, because there is no marketplace, specific performance is per se justified.

There is an additional problem with either pre- or post-judgment negotiations; such negotiations must happen prior to the passing of the commodity to a third party. For a third party the outcome of negotiations between promisor and initial promisee is a matter of indifference. The outcome has obvious distributive concerns between promisor and promisee, but will not alter the price paid by a third party. However, what is of concern to a third party is the timeliness of performance. The convenience of a substitutionary remedy is that the commodity moves quickly into the hands of the party who places the greatest value on it, and thus collectively maximizes wealth. Prolonged negotiations around specific performance can only delay that outcome. Finally, it would seem somewhat unjust if the ability to extract profit from the promisor for breach was conferred on those who through happenstance were still able to pursue specific performance, whereas other promisees, for whom specific relief was not an option, were confined to compensatory damages.

3) Consumer Surplus

A central tenet of the efficient breach argument is that a promisee's expectation can always be substituted by payment of a monetary equivalent. By and large this is an accurate reflection of commercial contracts, where there is an available market on which in secure substitute

---

21   See *Tito v. Waddell (No. 2)*, [1977] Ch. 106 at 332.

performance, or where the commodity, even if unique, is being acquired for its economic or investment value rather than for any intrinsic value it may possess. In these circumstances the promisee is probably the best person to arrange cover, that is, the substitute performance, rather than placing the burden on the promisor, because she will do so at a lower cost. The promisee would have already acquired market information in determining to accept the promisor's contract and is thus in the best position to identify an alternative supplier. The promisee also knows what she will accept as a substitute performance. If the costs were lower for the promisor, we would expect that party to freely negotiate a release from the contract by arranging a substitute performance, and thus avoid the cost of litigating this type of dispute. However, where a market does not exist, or where the promisee's expectations include the acquisition of the intrinsic value of a commodity, confining the promisee to damage compensation may systematically under-compensate.

Where a promisee's expectations are derived from the intrinsic value of a commodity, such as a family heirloom or unique good, a failure to award specific performance will deprive the promisee of this value. The idiosyncratic value attached to a particular commodity is often termed "consumer surplus."[22] It represents the subjective value one individual places upon the performance of the contract because the performance has unique meaning to that individual. It will often exceed any objective market value, presuming one can be found. It is a real loss to the particular individual and, arguably, merits compensation if only to approach completeness in remedial selection. Of course, difficulties in damage quantification are avoided if specific performance is granted.

Part of the problem concerning consumer surplus is that our traditional paradigm of contract, the Holmesian view, tends towards a myopic view of contracting dominated by commercial interests. Consumers, because they more readily place value on acquisitiveness rather than investment potential, are apt to have their interests ignored in this paradigm. The law has always been suspicious of idiosyncratic values, perceiving them as bogus claims designed to inflate compensatory damage awards resulting in a windfall to the plaintiff. Nevertheless, there has been an emerging trend toward recognizing consumer surplus. It also arises in determining whether to give a plaintiff damages assessed on the basis of cost of restoration, or merely on diminution in value, where a plaintiff's

---

22   See D. Harris, A. Ogus, & J. Phillips, "Contract Remedies and the Consumer Surplus" (1979) 95 L.Q.Rev. 581.

property has been damaged. Specific performance is one way in which consumer surplus can be protected without unduly burdening the defendant. In fact, it may be the preferable approach in a contract setting because it avoids having to quantify damages for an highly subjective interest.

It would appear that the relationship struck between specific performance and damages has much to commend itself as being economically efficient. The supremacy of damages is defensible in commercial transactions where an operating market allows for quick substitution of the promisor's breached performance. Where the lack of a marketplace makes damage quantification problematic, or where the promisee accords particular value on the actual performance, the awarding of specific performance is appropriate. The economic efficiency arguments are realized in legal doctrine by requiring the plaintiff to prove that damages are an inadequate remedy. This is a threshold test that the plaintiff must surmount before gaining access to specific performance.

4) Uniqueness

We have seen in the previous section that the concept of uniqueness has traditionally been linked to the notion that for a contract concerning unique goods, damages are seen to be inadequate. The mark of "uniqueness" in this sense is that the contracted good cannot readily be replaced by a substitute. However, this conception of uniqueness is rather narrow. It applies to objects of art where there is only a single article in existence. Another conception of uniqueness, referred to above as "consumer surplus," is the individual intrinsic value placed by a plaintiff on a particular article because it carries with it certain associative memories, although the article itself may not be rare at all. Family heirlooms are an example of this category. This form of uniqueness has also been termed *pretium affectionis*. Yet another notion of uniqueness is built around difficulties in securing a substitute because of transient problems in a marketplace. For example, securing oil during the Arab oil embargo of the 1970s, or securing a long-term supply of low-sulphur-producing coal to satisfy environmental emissions standards. In these examples the actual commodity is not rare, rather, the transactional context renders the commodity unique. This has been termed "commercial uniqueness" in the United States. These notions of uniqueness will be explored in later chapters.

The uniqueness concept has been particularly persuasive with respect to realty contracts, where there is a commonly-held belief that specific performance is the presumptive remedy. Historically, the uniqueness argument concerning realty stems from the passing of the "use" in land between vendor and purchaser, which in chancery courts happened at the time a contract for valuable consideration was entered. The more popular notion of uniqueness as referring to particular geographical or physical attributes of the property only came later and probably as an attempt to differentiate between contracts of realty and personalty.[23] The continued veracity of the uniqueness argument with respect to realty contracts has been questioned in Canada, in light of the contemporary role placed on realty that readily sees land as a exchangeable commodity. These issues are explored more fully in chapter 12.

5) Mitigation

Whether damages are an adequate remedy depends in part on the availability of a market in which to assess the damages. In effect we are concluding that the plaintiff must accept a market-price rule (i.e. the difference bewteen contract price and market price at the date of breach) for damage assessment. The market-price rule incorporates the mitigation concept, assuming that the plaintiff would have sought an alternative performance in the marketplace at the date of breach, or as soon as is reasonably practicable. Where a plaintiff seeks specific performance, there is no obligation to mitigate. One requirement for the decree is that the plaintiff must always be ready and willing to perform her side of the contract — it would thus be inconsistent to also impose on the plaintiff an obligation to mitigate. Specific performance may seem more attractive in that it avoids this limiting factor on an award of damages. This may suggest that a plaintiff can speculate at the defendant's risk rather than be required to crystallize her loss. The temptation to speculate is controlled by the inadequacy of damages threshold test, which places an evidentiary burden on the plaintiff to establish that damages really are truly inadequate. As we will see in later chapters, the courts have developed guidelines on how a plaintiff can satisfy this test.[24]

---

23 See above note 6.
24 See D. Clark, "Rethinking the Role of Specific Relief in Contractual Settings" in J. Berryman, ed., *Remedies: Issues and Perspectives* (Scarborough, Ont.: Carswell, 1991) 139, who argued that a plaintiff should be at liberty to determine herself whether to seek specific performance without having to satisfy the inadequacy of damages test, and that this would better ensure "completeness" of relief. To reconcile with the obligation to mitigate, Clark suggests that the duty to mitigate should only be conditionally suspended, such that if the plaintiff is merely seeking the remedy to speculate at the defendant's risk, and voluntarily abandons seeking the relief, then the obligation to mitigate would be retroactively resurrected.

6) Sundry Areas Where Damages Are an Inadequate Remedy

There are a number of other areas where specific relief will be favoured over damages, but which do not follow any precise doctrinal boundaries.

a) Avoidance of a Multiplicity of Suits

In a breach of contract action where the contract performance amounts to the payment of an annuity, or contemplates similar ongoing acts of performance, the court faces the prospect that the plaintiff will have to return to court, bringing multiple actions to recover damages for acts of continuing breach. In these circumstances, and to minimize the possibility of multiple legal action a court will favour specific performance. Thus in *Beswick* v. *Beswick*[25] the House of Lords held that where a widow, administratrix of her husband's estate, was entitled to receive payments of an annuity, the court would award specific performance to force the annuity scheme rather than confine the plaintiff to bringing a series of actions to enforce each payment as it fell due. Such a result may differ today, where a monetary damages remedy could be used to purchase an equivalent annuity scheme in substitution for the breached scheme.

b) Enforcement of Obligations Owed to a Third Party

Where a contract obligation is owed to a third party, the law of contract is deficient in appropriate remedies. For the contracting party to whom the promise to benefit a third party was made, damages are often unsatisfactory because the promisee may have experienced no actual loss as a result of the breach: The third party beneficiary, who does not enjoy any privity of contract, will be denied any remedy based on the contract's breach. Equity has allowed the promisee to seek specific performance in these cases even though the actual loss to the third party could have readily been compensated in damages.[26]

c) Insolvency

The prospect of the promisor becoming insolvent raises the issue whether that fact alone can justify the conclusion that damages would be inadequate and therefore specific performance must be granted the promisee. With respect to injunctions, courts have been prepared to consider the financial responsiveness of the defendant as a reason to

---

25   (1967), [1968] A.C. 58 (H.L.) [*Beswick*].

26   See *Beswick*, above note 25; *Woodar Investment Development Ltd.* v. *Wimpey Construction U.K. Ltd.*, [1980] 1 W.L.R. 277 (H.L.); and *Rattrays Wholesale Ltd.* v. *Meredyth-Young & A'Court Ltd.*, [1997] 2 N.Z.L.R. 363 (H.C.).

conclude that damages are an inadequate remedy and that the injunction should be granted. However, these situations do not advance the plaintiff's position over other third party creditors. It is this prospect, that if a successful plaintiff gains specific performance, and thus gains title to the good or property, he will have gained an advantage over other creditors, that has lead courts to exercise caution in this area. Where the plaintiff has a justification to support a claim for specific performance other than the defendant's insolvency (either actual or impending), or where the plaintiff is the sole creditor of the defendant, the court may grant specific performance. This claim will be strengthened if the plaintiff has a proprietary interest in the subject matter of the contract.[27] However, if the sole reason for requesting specific performance is the insolvency or likely insolvency of the defendant, and if the granting of the remedy would prejudice other creditors of the defendant, specific performance will be denied.[28]

D. PROBLEMS WITH SUPERVISION[29]

At the turn of the century, it was almost an article of faith that a court would decline to award specific performance where the order may result in the court being asked to provide ongoing supervision of the decree. The apparent rationale for this view was concern over the use of judicial resources to determine what was actually required to be done under the order, how to determine if the defendant had complied,

---

27 See I.C.F. Spry, *The Principles of Equitable Remedies: Specific Performances, Injunctions, Rectification and Equitable Damages,* 5th ed. (Sydney: LBC Information Services, 1997) at 68; R.J. Sharpe, *Injunctions and Specific Performance,* looseleaf (Aurora, Ont.: Canada Law Book, 1998) § 7.290; and G.H. Jones & W. Goodhart, *Specific Performance,* 2d ed. (London: Butterworths, 1996) at 34.

28 See *Anders Utkilens Rederi A/S* v. *O/Y Lovisa Stevedoring Co. A/B, The Golfstraum,* [1985] 2 All E.R. 669 (Ch.).

29 The discussion in this section is built around a contract paradigm which focuses upon discrete transactions — contracts between atomistic individuals who contract with regard to their own self-interest. This paradigm ignores the important contribution of Ian Macneil, who has described much of modern contracting as taking place inside a relational contract paradigm: see *The New Social Contract: An Inquiry into Modern Contractual Relations* (New Haven, Conn: Yale University Press, 1980). Relational contracts see any particular discrete transaction as part of a complex matrix of relationships between the contracting parties and others. Parties seek ways to harmonize and preserve the relationship for mutual benefit.

and concern over repeat applications by a plaintiff where the contract performance envisaged performance over a long period. However, as a rule of universal application it was indifferently applied. In *Ryan* v. *Mutual Tontine Westminster Chambers Ass.*, a case dealing with the specific performance of a landlord's obligation to appoint a porter for the benefit of his tenants,

- the English Court of Appeal asserted that,

> Ordinarily the Court will not enforce specific performance of works, such as building works, the prosecution of which the Court cannot superintend; not only on the ground that damages are generally in such cases an adequate remedy, but also on the ground of the inability of the Court to see that the work is carried out.[30]

But seven years later, in the same count, in *Wolverhampton Corp.* v. *Emmons*,[31] Smith M.R. commented that he had never seen the force of Kay L.J.'s objection to specific performance of building contracts. Collins L.J. confessed that he could not understand "the principle upon which the Courts of Equity have acted in sometimes granting orders for specific performance in these cases, and sometimes not."[32] In this case the court gave specific performance to enforce a contract in which the defendant had agreed to build eight houses within a certain period of time on land sold to him by the plaintiff.

Underlying supervision problems are several strands of thought that must be unwoven. Some of these concerns mirror the same issues confronted when considering mandatory injunctions.

1)   Problems Associated with the Possibility of Repeated Applications to Ensure Compliance

This will be a particular problem where the court is unable to describe precisely what the defendant must do to carry out the decree, leaving the plaintiff embroiled in repeated attempts to clarify both what is required and whether the defendant has actually completed the task described. However, unlike the injunction setting where the court is required to identify both the nature and extent of the order, with specific performance the contract itself should provide some structure in which to fashion a decree.

---

30   [1893] 1 Ch. 116 at 128, Kay L.J [*Ryan*].
31   [1901] 1 K.B. 515 (C.A.).
32   *Ibid.* at 523–24.

A second aspect concerns contracts that span a long period of time. With respect to building contracts the courts have from an early date distinguished between building contracts which contemplated a single act of performance, where specific relief was generally available, and those which included obligations of continuing maintenance, where specific relief was declined. This also has repercussions for other long-term contracts such as long-term supply agreements. These are discussed in chapter 13.

2) Problems Associated with Court Supervision

A damages remedy is self-administered. A plaintiff, as judgment creditor, must take active steps to move enforcement of the court order along and will incur the incidental costs of doing so. Breach of a specific performance decree amounts to a contempt of court, and engages the court's attention to enforcement, although a large part is still played by the plaintiff, who has to initiate contempt proceedings. The prospect of the court being required to actively supervise, possibly with its own personnel, is viewed as a significant burden to the granting of specific performance. However, this fear is perhaps overstated. As Sharpe has pointed out,[33] the plaintiff will still have a significant self-interest in monitoring the defendant to ensure that the contemplated contractual performance is pursued with due diligence and in a proper manner, and it will be the plaintiff who alerts the court to any failure to comply. The key issue is whether there is sufficient definition of what is required of the defendant, so that compliance, or the lack of it, can be readily determined.

Another concern with court supervision is the feeling that the public cost of judicial administration will be higher for specific relief than that for damages. There is no empirical study to support this feeling. We simply do not know the likelihood of ongoing judicial involvement in administering specific relief, nor the comparative costs of that involvement compared to the cost of administering a damage assessment and collection process. However, it should be remembered that the denial of specific relief based on a visceral opinion on the cost of administration comes at a stage when there has already been a determination that damages are an inadequate remedy. The denial of specific relief at this stage must be balanced against the prospect of imperfect justice being administered concerning the quantification of damages.

---

33   Above note 27 at § 7.460.

Given the apparent willingness of the public to bear the burden of judicial administration costs in the areas where injunctive relief has been granted to accord justice, I would suggest the additional cost/burden of granting and administering specific performance would be marginal, if at all, and one the public is willing to bear to attain a more just result.

3) Problems with Enforcement of Specific Performance through Contempt of Court Power

The prospect of enforcing non-compliance of a specific performance decree with contempt of court is viewed as being heavy-handed. Contempt of court, leading to possible imprisonment, is the most coercive power in the courts' arsenal. To use such power for what amounts to a breach of contract appears unwarranted. However, while the prospect of imprisonment remains an option there are other possible coercive steps that a court may take to ensure compliance. For example, the court can impose a fine, or order sequestration of the defendant's property. Again, in this area, there is no empirical data that suggests the freer availability of specific relief would ultimately result in the resurrection of a latter-day debtors' prison.

4) Problems Associated with Placing the Cost of Compliance on the Defendant

Here the concern is that the cost of compliance placed on the defendant may be out of all proportion to the benefit obtained by the plaintiff. This is a real consideration when considering the awarding of mandatory injunctions, where the courts have insisted that the injunction be framed with sufficient precision that the defendant knows what is required and the cost of compliance can be determined. In some respect, the same result should prevail when considering specific performance. Indeed, the task of evaluating cost and providing specificity in the order should be made easier because resort can always be made to the contract's terms.

5) Problems Associated with Forcing the Recalcitrant Defendant Back Into the Contract

Where relationships have soured over contractual performance there is a natural reluctance to force the parties back into a situation that may only lead to further acrimony. In some way, by pursuing specific performance the plaintiff has expressed her own assessment of the risks inherent in forcing a recalcitrant defendant back to perform, and has been prepared to accept the risk. However, if the plaintiff is only pursuing specific performance to maximize her own post-judgment bargaining powers and extract some of the defendant's gains through breach, the court will deny specific relief.

Where the contract entails personal services the courts have been reluctant to grant specific relief for fear that the order takes on the appearance of involuntary servitude. In addition, it may be more difficult to ensure the defendant's compliance because the nature of the contract may involve subjective assessments, for example a contract to play football or to sing in an opera. Similarly, a contract built upon trust and confidence requires reciprocity. If that has been lost, it is hardly likely to be recreated by court order and coercion. However, reinstatement has become a common labour remedy and it would seem that human rights and labour tribunals have been able to overcome the problems associated with difficulties of supervision. Personal service contracts are dealt with in chapter 14.

The movement away from the strict line taken in *Ryan*[34] has been pursued with vigor by Megarry V.C. in a number of cases. In *Giles (C.H.) & Co.* v. *Morris*,[35] the plaintiff sought specific performance of a contractual obligation to appoint him as a director of a certain company, and to enter into service contracts with the plaintiff in the case of another company. The plaintiff had been involved in the workings of both companies and it had been the wish of the owner before his death, as evidenced by a contract between the owner and the plaintiff, that the plaintiff succeed him as manager. Certain directors of both companies, who also administered the deceased's estate, were objecting to the plaintiff's appointment. Megarry J. ordered specific performance of the agreement. In doing so, he distinguished between a decree that simply obliged the defendants to execute a complex contract of sale and management of the companies — the appointment of the plaintiff being simply one part of the agreement — and one that required the court to actually supervise the personal services provided by the plaintiff. As this case dealt with the former, Megarry J. was prepared to order specific performance. However, even if it was of the latter type, Megarry J. opined:

> One day, perhaps, the courts will look again at the so-called rule that contracts for personal services or involving the continuous performance of services will not be specifically enforced. Such a rule is

---

34 Above note 30.
35 [1972] 1 W.L.R. 307 (C.A.).

plainly not absolute and without exception, nor do I think that it can be based on any narrow consideration such as difficulties of constant superintendence by the court. Mandatory injunctions are by no means unknown, and there is normally no question of the court having to send its officers to supervise the performance of the order of the court. Prohibitory injunctions are common, and again there is no direct supervision by the court. Performance of each type of injunction is normally secured by the realisation of the person enjoined that he is liable to be punished for contempt if evidence of his disobedience to the order is put before the court; and if the injunction is prohibitory, actual committal will usually, so long as it continues, make disobedience impossible. If instead the order is for specific performance of a contract for personal services, a similar machinery of enforcement could be employed, again without there being any question of supervision by any officer of the court.[36]

In *Shiloh Spinners* v. *Harding*,[37] Lord Wilberforce also suggested in *obiter dicta* the need to rethink the issue of impossibility of court supervision as a reason for denial of specific relief. Megarry V.C. returned to the same theme in *Tito* v. *Waddell (No. 2)*.[38] In *Posner* v. *Scott-Lewis*,[39] the facts of which are almost identical to *Ryan*, Mervyn Davies J. granted specific performance in light of the direction taken in the aforementioned cases. In 1964, the plaintiffs had entered into 99-year leases, part of which included the requirement that the lessor furnish the services of a resident porter to undertake specific tasks outlined in the leases. Mervyn Davies J. provided the following criteria upon which a decision to grant specific relief should be made:

(a) Is there a sufficient definition of what has to be done in order to comply with the order of the court?
(b) Will enforcing compliance involve superintendence by the court to an unacceptable degree?

---

36 *Ibid.* at 318.
37 [1973] A.C. 691 at 724 (H.L.). In *Co-operative Insurance Society Ltd.* v. *Argyll Stores (Holdings) Ltd.* (1997), [1998] 1 A.C. 1, Lord Hoffmann, the other lords concurring, intimated that Lord Wilberforce's remarks in this case had been misunderstood. In Lord Hoffmann's opinion Lord Wilberforce was only addressing the issue of compliance with repair covenants in the situation where a tenant is seeking relief against forfeiture of a lease. It is no barrier to granting relief against forfeiture if compliance with a covenant to repair, requiring supervision by the court, is made part of the court's order.
38 Above note 21 at 321.
39 (1986), [1987] 1 Ch. 25.

(c) What are the respective prejudices or hardships that will be suffered by the parties if the order is made or not made?[40]

Applying that criteria Mervyn Davies J. saw considerable inconvenience if a resident porter wasn't appointed, in that the plaintiffs would be deprived of a service they had been given and had come to expect for the last twenty years, and which rendered the apartments a 'luxury' apartment building.

The apparent liberalization evident in the case just discussed has come under fire from a recent decision of the House of Lords. In *Co-operative Insurance Society Ltd.* v. *Argyll Stores (Holdings) Ltd.*[41] two experienced commercial entities had entered into a long term commercial lease in which the tenant, Argyll, was obliged to "keep open" their supermarket during usual hours of business for the locality. Argyll, who ran a major chain of supermarkets throughout the U.K., was in fact the anchor tenant in the plaintiff's (Co-operative Insurance Society Ltd.), shopping complex. After undertaking a review of its business operations Argyll decided to close down its store in the plaintiff's mall. This decision was made as part of a restructuring in which twenty-seven loss-making or marginally profitable stores were closed. The defendant's store in the plaintiff's mall had been running an annual loss of £70,000. In the trial court, the plaintiff had sought specific performance requiring the defendant to continue to keep its store open for the remainder of the lease — approximately nineteen years. The trial judge had rejected the plaintiff's request, confining it to damages, and citing a long-established rule against granting specific relief requiring a person to continue running a business. In the Court of Appeal, the majority granted the specific performance decree, paying particular attention to the "gross commercial cynicism" and "wanton" and "unreasonable conduct" of the defendant.[42]

The House of Lords reversed the Court of Appeal and restored the trial judge's original order. In doing so, Lord Hoffmann, with the other lords concurring, sought to clarify the law regarding specific performance and difficulties with supervision. On one level Lord Hoffmann confirms Megarry V.C.'s position that the prospect of constant court supervision is not the reason for restraint in granting the decree. However, what does justify restraint is the interplay of coercive powers — committal for contempt, and the prospect of repeated breaches of the

---

40 *Ibid.* at 36.
41 Above note 37.
42 *Ibid.* at 18.

order requiring a multiplicity of suits. In Lord Hoffmann's opinion, the threat of committal for contempt adversely impacts on the defendant's commercial reputation, creating an inimical climate in which to operate a business. Further, the seriousness of the finding will result in a heightened sense being accorded the litigation, leading to expensive and possible repeated actions before the court over a prolonged period of time. Lord Hoffmann used the latter reason as a justification for distinguishing between orders that required a defendant to carry on an activity, as in running a business, and orders that required the defendant to achieve a result, as in completing a building. The prospect of repeated applications is viewed as being more real in the former than in the latter. In addition, it is probably harder to frame an order to ensure compliance in regard to an activity as against a result. It is not enough that the contractual obligation is described in sufficiently precise terms so as to escape scrutiny under the doctrines of contractual uncertainty — a higher level of exactitude is required. Lord Hoffmann was also concerned that granting specific performance would arm the plaintiff with a means to extract a higher price in return for releasing the defendant from the "keep open" obligation. The lease did allow for an assignment, an act that had in fact taken place before the appeal to the House of Lords. On this point, Lord Hoffmann reiterated that damage compensation was a measure of the plaintiff's actual losses rather than a mechanism to extract profits made by the defendant through breach, and should not be undermined by an order for specific performance.

The *Argyll* decision has been criticized by Professor Tettenborn.[43] He argues that, with respect to Lord Hoffmann's first argument, the need for precision of language in the order, the requirement would appear to be satisfied in the facts of this case, as much as it has been satisfied in cases on the enforcement of building contracts where specific relief has often been made available. With respect to Lord Hoffmann's second argument, the prospect of repeated breaches, Tettenborn argues that in the facts of *Argyll* there was no evidence to support the view that the defendant would do other than comply with the order, if only out of a regard for economic self-interest and commercial reputation. These findings had underpinned the majority in the Court of Appeal and had not been refuted by Lord Hoffmann. Rather, Lord Hoffmann had resorted to a principled objection based on hypothetical difficulties should a defendant fail to observe a court's

---

43   See A. Tettenborn, "Absolving the Undeserving: Shopping Centres, Specific Performance and the Law of Contract" [1998] Conv. & Prop. Law 23. See also the criticism of *Argyll* by Spry, above note 27 at 668.

decree, or, if required to run a business face insolvency at some later stage. Tettenborn also points out that courts have other means at their disposal, such as costs, to deter repeated unmeritorious applications by the plaintiff for committal.

The net effect of the *Argyll* decision is to dismiss judicial concerns over the deployment of actual resources to supervise a specific performance decree, but to elevate concerns over the prospect of repeated applications by the plaintiff to ensure compliance. Based on these concerns, the House of Lords has made a demarcation between specific performance of an "activity" as against a "result" that makes it very problematic to ever get specific performance requiring a defendant to continue operating a business. One immediate rejoiner is the obvious point that some activities, while spanning a long time, can be quite simple in nature and clearly susceptible to an order. It also begs the question, when does a "result" become an "activity"?

The few Canadian cases so far that have discussed *Argyll* have simply endorsed its principles. In *Centre City Capital Ltd.* v. *Bank of East Asia (Canada)*,[44] the plaintiff requested specific performance of an obligation to occupy leased premises and operate a bank in the plaintiff's building. At the time of the suit, the plaintiff had commenced an action for an interlocutory mandatory injunction, the defendant was making lease payments but had deferred taking actual occupancy. The court denied relief on the basis that the order envisaged "would require supervision, numerous rulings by the court as to whether the Order is being followed, motions for contempt and various other scenarios."[45]

Even before *Argyll*, there had been a number of Canadian decisions concerning the enforcement of shopping-centre leases brought against tenants, seeking specific performance of obligations to remain in business.[46] These decisions have usually resulted in a denial of specific relief, although not uniformly.[47] In *566719 Ontario Ltd.* v. *New Miracle Food Mart Inc.*[48] the plaintiff sought specific performance of a lease obliging the defendant to operate a "first-rate supermarket." The defendant was

---

44   [1997] O.J. No. 5218 (Gen. Div.).

45   *Ibid.* at para. 13.

46   See *Weyburn Square Developments Ltd.* v. *Liggett Drug Ltd.*, [1988] 6 W.W.R. 401, (Sask. Q.B.); *Islington Village Inc.* v. *Citibank Canada* (1992), 27 R.P.R. (2d) 100 (Ont. Gen. Div.), aff'd [1992] O.J. No. 2953 (C.A.); and *566719 Ontario Ltd.* v. *New Miracle Food Mart Inc.* (1994), 41 R.P.R. (2d) 22 (Ont. Gen. Div.).

47   See *Centre City Capital Ltd.* v. *Great Atlantic & Pacific Co. of Canada* (2 August 1988), Toronto RE 1247/88 (Ont. H.C.); *Propriétés Cité Concordia Ltée* v. *Banque Royale*, [1981] C.S. 812 (C.S. Qué), rev'd [1983] R.D.J. 524 (C.A. Qué).

48   Above note 46.

the anchor tenant in a mall and had attempted to assign the remaining term of the lease, pursuant to a term of the agreement permitting assignment, to tenants whom the landlord believed did not have sufficient business acumen nor financial resources. The court upheld the landlord's right to refuse the assignment but did not award specific performance. Farley J. drew a distinction between the "conveyancing" and "business operation" aspects of a lease. The conveyancing aspect, which included the rental payment obligation, would lend itself to specific relief in a similar fashion to a sale of a land contract. The business operation aspect of the lease, which Farley J. likened to a "franchise" agreement, would lead to a denial of specific performance because the agreement contemplated a continuing relationship, and because there was no "natural, automatic, or causal" relationship which would dictate specific performance in these circumstances. Interestingly, at an earlier point in his judgment, Farley J. expresses support for the idea that a business defendant's commercial reputation, its "pride and integrity not to let its standards slip," may be enough to take care of any supervision questions.[49] This is an argument accepted by a majority in the Court of Appeal, but rejected by the House of Lords, in *Argyll*.

It would appear that problems with supervision are still potent arguments against the awarding of specific relief, particularly if *Argyll* is closely followed in Canada. What is lost sight of in many of the judgments is that arguments about supervision only surface after a finding that damages are considered an inadequate remedy.[50] It is against this background, of an imperfect remedy at law being granted, that problems with supervision should be considered. It seems to further an injustice if the plaintiff is now denied a more perfect remedy than damages simply because of some perceived problems about future supervision. It is even more intolerable that the problems are speculative and hypothetical and based on the perceptions of judges about litigants generally rather than being particularized to the problems confronted by the individual adversaries before the court.

---

49   *Ibid.* at 34.

50   Assessing damages in keep open lease clauses can be very problematical. There are a variety of clauses. Often, the rental payment, or part thereof, is determined as a percentage of the store's revenues. Thus the impact of the loss of one store, particularly an anchor store, on the revenue of other stores in a shopping complex can be difficult to gauge. In addition, the keep-open clause can also reflect the shopping mall owner's desire to keep a certain store mix so as to make the total venture desirable to consumers. These less tangible attributes are difficult to quantify. See A.M. Kaufman, "Operating Clauses in Shopping Centre Leases: Lights Out for the Vacating Tenant" (1991) 18 C.B.L.J. 245.

Part of the difficulty in *Argyll*[51] concerning problems with supervision may have been the opinion of the House of Lords that once a specific performance decree has been awarded it is considered final. This opinion results in the inability of the litigants ever returning to court to seek a change in the court's order based on changed circumstances and where the continued enforcement of the order would constitute oppression. Of concern in *Argyll* was the issue that if a defendant was required to continue operating its store at a loss it may at some subsequent time face insolvency. In the actual case there was no suggestion that the defendant, a national food chain, would face insolvency if forced to keep open the store in question. This aspect of the judgment has been criticized by Tettenborn.[52] It also appears to be inconsistent with the House of Lords' own judgment in *Johnson* v. *Agnew*.[53] There, the non-performance of a specific performance decree remained a continuing breach of the contract, conferring upon the plaintiff the right to bring an action in common law for breach and to seek damages. In Ontario, the *Court of Appeal*[54] has recently affirmed the notion that once specific performance has been decreed the contract comes under the management and control of the court, and presumably can be changed at any time on the suit of either party. Thus, it seems quite appropriate for a court to grant specific relief, where the problems with supervision remain hypothetical and constitute speculation, until such time as any difficulty is incurred by the parties. At that stage the court could reassess its decision to persevere with the contract and bring the relationship to an end by requiring the plaintiff to crystallize its loss in damages. Where problems with supervision arise immediately (the inability to describe what has to be done would be one instance), the court should refuse the specific performance decree forthwith.

E. MUTUALITY

The concept of mutuality of remedies is easily stated although its continued vitality is much debated. Negative mutuality states that a plaintiff will be denied specific relief if the defendant would be ineligible to

---

51   Above note 37 at 18.
52   See Tettenborn, above note 43 at 36; and Spry, above note 27 at 671.
53   (1979), [1980] A.C. 367 (H.L.).
54   See *Lubben* v. *Veltri & Sons Corp.* (1997), 32 O.R. (3d) 65 (C.A.).

get specific relief of the plaintiff's obligations.[55] In this formulation, mutuality serves as a way to protect the defendant from being straddled with a court order requiring her compliance, yet having no assurance that the plaintiff will perform his or her reciprocal obligations, other than her remedy at common law. It is under this guise that a plaintiff has been denied specific performance of a contract to purchase land in return for acts of personal services: the ostensible reason being that the court could not grant specific performance of the plaintiff's obligations, based on the fact that the court will not grant specific relief where it would entail problems of court supervision.[56] Similarly, in a suit by an infant of a contract for the purchase of land, specific performance has been denied based upon lack of mutuality since the defendant could not equally enforce the contract against the infant.[57]

Affirmative mutuality states that a plaintiff will be granted specific relief if the defendant would be granted specific relief of the plaintiff's obligations. In this guise, it has commonly been argued that mutuality of remedies requires that a vendor be granted specific performance in spite of the fact that damages would appear to be an adequate remedy.[58]

Obviously, these formulations of the doctrine of mutuality contradict each other, as Corbin pointed out,[59] this may explain why the doctrine has never had the cogency in the United States as it has assumed in other common law countries.[60] In other countries, mutuality has at

---

55   The rule has been expressed by J.B. Ames, "Mutuality in Specific Performance" in J.B. Ames, *Lectures on Legal History and Miscellaneous Legal Essays* (Cambridge: Harvard University Press, 1913) 370 at 371, as "Equity will not compel specific performance by a defendant if, after performance, the common-law remedy of damages would be his sole security for the performance of the plaintiff's side of the contract."

56   See *Cooke* v. *Gay* (1956), 4 D.L.R. (2d) 146 (N.S.S.C.).

57   See *Flight* v. *Bolland* (1828), 4 Russ. 298, 38 E.R. 817 (Ch.).

58   See *Landmark of Thornhill Ltd.* v. *Jacobson* (1995), 25 O.R. (3d) 628, at 636, McKinlay J. (C.A.). The likely historical reason for reciprocity of remedies in these circumstances is linked to the bifurcated jurisdiction of chancery and common law courts. In the common law courts, where damages were assessed by a jury, a vendor would have no certainty of gaining a just result after a chancery court had decreed specific performance. This would take on an added significance in the case of a sale of land contract if the plaintiff's obligations failed to adhere to the minimum requirements of the *Statute of Frauds* and there were no acts of part performance upon which the defendant could gain enforcement of the plaintiff's obligations to pay the contract price.

59   See A.L. Corbin,*Corbin on Contracts*, vol. 5A (St. Paul, Minn.: West, 1964) § 1178.

60   See, for example, for instance the perfunctory treatment accorded in the *Restatement on the Law Second, Contracts* 2d (St. Paul, Minn: American Law Institute, 1981) § 363; [*Restatement*] and by Cardozo J. in *Epstein* v. *Gluckin*, 233 N.Y. 490 (1922).

times taken on the appearance of an independent doctrine going to a court's jurisdiction whether to grant specific performance and constitutes an absolute defence;[61] although, it is now accepted that it is a question which goes to a court's discretion whether to grant specific performance.[62] Both Spry[63] and Sharpe[64] have argued that mutuality is an adjunct of the discretionary defence to specific relief based on hardship to the defendant. (Hardship is discussed in the next chapter.) They argue that the hardship concern, which the doctrine of mutuality addresses, is to avoid the defendant from being left to an unsatisfactory remedy, or no remedy, if ordered to give specific performance to the plaintiff. However, denial of specific performance on this ground can also constitute a hardship to the plaintiff, where the specific relief is denied based upon perceived problems about his own performance to the defendant wrongdoer. If the legitimate concerns of the defendant can be met in some other way so that she can be protected, then specific relief should not be denied the plaintiff. The question is, how can the defendant be legitimately protected?

A conservative response to the question just asked is to determine the issue of mutuality at a time when there is still a risk to the defendant of the plaintiff's default. If that risk has passed, as in when the plaintiff's obligations have been executed, then there is no reason to deny the plaintiff specific performance based on any lack of mutuality which may have been present at the time of contracting. This issue has been addressed in the important case of *Price* v. *Strange*.[65] The plaintiff, Price, was a builder who occupied a maisonette leased from the defendant, Strange. Price was holding over as his tenancy had expired. Price was in breach in a number of respects of his tenancy, in that he was sharing the accommodation with others and was keeping two cats. However, Strange, who held a 99-year lease of the tenanted premises, was also in breach of a number of covenants to kept the leased premises in good repair and had been given notice by her landlord that the premises had to be repaired. Strange then entered into an agreement with Price. In return for Price effecting several major repairs on the premises, Strange would grant Price a further tenancy for the remainder of

---

61 This is the way that E. Fry, in *A Treatise on the Specific Performance of Contracts, Including Those of Public Companies* (Philadelphia: T. & J.W. Johnson & Co., 1858) at 108, expressed the position.

62 See *Price* v. *Strange* (1977), [1978] Ch. 337 (C.A.) [*Price*].

63 Above note 27 at 91 ff.

64 Above note 27 at § 10.480.

65 Above note 62.

Strange's term of the lease at the annual rent of £600, and would vary the terms of the tenancy to reflect Price's changed domestic circumstances. Pursuant to this new agreement, Price undertook repair work to the interior part of the premises but was stopped by Strange from completing the exterior work. Strange, purporting to terminate the new agreement, had made her own arrangements to finish the exterior work. Thus, at the time of trial the plaintiff was seeking specific performance of the obligation to execute a renewal of the tenancy at a time when all the outstanding work had in fact been completed.

If the proposition proffered by Fry,[66] that mutuality of remedy had to be determined at the time of contracting, prevailed, the plaintiff would not be entitled to specific performance. The plaintiff faced two impediments. One was the fact that his agreement with the defendant was oral and therefore did not comply with the *Law of Property Act, 1925*[67] which requires the agreement to be evidenced in writing. The second impediment was because the contract entailed repair work, the defendant would have been refused specific performance on the grounds that the agreement would require the constant superintendence of the court. The Court of Appeal ruled that Fry's understanding of the law was incorrect and that mutuality had to be determined at the time of making the proposed order. Therefore, because nothing remained to be performed by the plaintiff, specific performance requiring the defendant to execute the tenancy was ordered, subject only to a monetary adjustment to reflect the fact that the defendant had incurred the cost of the external repairs rather than the plaintiff.

A second component of the issue of how to protect the defendant's legitimate expectations of performance is to appreciate the role that waiver can play. It is possible for the defendant to waive the defence of mutuality. In *Price* the fact that the defendant had not stopped the plaintiff from commencing the interior repairs, and had demanded and accepted payment of the increased rent even after purportedly repudiating the oral contract, constituted sufficient acts to amount to a waiver of any defence of want of mutuality.[68]

The result in *Price* is obviously to be commended because there is nothing for which the defendant needs protection; however, this need

---

66   Above note 61.

67   (U.K.), 15 & 16 Geo. V, c. 20.

68   The same actions were also said to create an "equity" against the defendant. Spry argues that rather than amounting to a waiver these actions go to determine the issue of hardship, and that mutuality always remains relevant to the exercise of a court's discretion whether to grant specific performance: above note 27 at 96.

not be true in all cases. It is possible to devise other ways to protect the defendant from the risk of non-performance of executory obligations owed to him by the plaintiff. For example, the order itself can be made conditional upon the plaintiff first rendering the performance owed to the defendant.[69] Alternatively, a form of monetary security could be furnished by the plaintiff, or a simple undertaking may suffice. It may be that the court will be happy to confine the defendant to a potential suit for damages should the plaintiff not perform, where the likelihood of the plaintiff's default is remote. Finally, it may be possible for the court to use the services of a third party to protect the defendant. In *Jones* v. *Tucker*[70] the plaintiff, a resident of the United States, sought specific performance of a contract for the sale of land located in Saskatchewan in return for the conveyance of land he owned in Iowa. Anglin J. suggested that any concerns about ensuring that the defendant received title to the land in Iowa could be met by placing the defendant's own land in the control of a court officer and releasing it to the plaintiff only when the officer had been satisfied that the defendant had received a good and clear title to the Iowa land.

F. PARTIAL PERFORMANCE

In a number of cases there are statements to the effect that unless specific performance can be ordered of the entire contract, it will not be awarded of part of it. One of the strongest statements of this kind is the judgment in *Ryan* v. *Mutual Tontine Westminster Chambers Assn.*[71] The court refused specific performance of a lease obligation to hire and supervise a porter primarily on the grounds of difficulty with supervision. In addition, it also refused to enforce a lesser obligation requiring the landlord merely to appoint a porter on the grounds that "when the

---

69   See *Jones* v. *Tucker* (1916), 53 S.C.R. 431. This approach is also adopted in the *Restatement*, above note 60 at § 372, although it was rejected by Goff L.J. in *Price*, above note 62 at 350. However, Goff L.J.'s rejection was probably based on the fact that the plaintiff's performance also constituted part performance and the court would not grant an injunction or make a conditional order to allow the plaintiff to establish part performance so that he was then entitled to equitable relief to surmount the lack of a written contract. Goff L.J. suggested the situation would be different if there had already been some acts of part performance before the plaintiff's action had commenced.

70   Above note 69.

71   Above note 30.

Court cannot compel specific performance of the contract as a whole, it will not interfere to compel specific performance of part of a contract."[72] However, even at the time *Ryan* was decided other decisions evidenced an ambivalence to this restriction. Thus in *Lytton v. Great Northern Railway Co.*[73] the court specifically enforced an obligation to build a railway siding in return for the conveyance of land but would not specifically enforce the covenant to maintain the siding. Elsewhere, courts have interpreted the contractual obligations as being independent and severable, specifically enforcing part even when the remedy was not available for the other obligations.[74]

The issue confronted here is similar to the underlying basis of the mutuality doctrine. How can the parties be protected from suffering a loss from unfulfilled contractual obligations? If the defendant is in default there seems to be no reason to deny the plaintiff specific relief if the plaintiff is prepared to accept a lesser performance. In addition, the plaintiff should be entitled to compensation to cover any deficiency in performance. The defendant is not prejudiced by such action where he has received that which was contractually promised by the plaintiff. Indeed, as we shall see in chapter 12, equity has readily moved towards granting specific performance of land contracts with an abatement of the purchase price to reflect that the actual conveyance is of a lesser interest than that promised by the vendor. There are even instances where a vendor will be granted specific performance, imposing a property onto a purchaser and requiring the purchaser to accept compensation for the deficiency where the deficiency is not essential (see chapter 12, section C, "Vendor's Application"). However, it is another matter to force the defendant to accept a lesser performance by the plaintiff in return for the court granting specific performance on the plaintiff's action. Unless the defendant can be protected against the prospect of the plaintiff's partial non-performance, specific relief should be refused. However, if the defendant can be protected, perhaps by similar solutions as those given for the problem of mutuality, specific performance should be granted. Indeed, there are instances where the defendant is required to accept damages for deficiencies by the plaintiff of inessential terms. (This is discussed below).

It may be that on closer inspection all that is required for the court to order is the execution of a document rather than be concerned with the particular enforcement of some of the obligations contained within

---

72   *Ibid.* at 123, Lord Esher M.R.
73   (1856) 2 K. & J. 394, 69 E.R. 836 (V.C.).
74   See *Holliday v. Lockwood*, [1917] 2 Ch. 47.

the ensuing contract. Thus, in *Giles (C.H.) & Co.* v. *Morris*[75] the court was prepared to grant specific performance of a contract for the sale of a controlling interest in a business. Part of the contract required the defendant to appoint the plaintiff to its board of directors. Because the obligation itself only required the execution of a document, and did not entail the supervision of a contract of personal services, specific performance could be ordered. It did not matter that the defendants could immediately dismiss the plaintiff after execution of the appointment. Perhaps the most glaring example of courts abrogating the notion of not ordering performance of part of a contract is in the use of injunctions to enforce negative covenants, thereby effecting specific performance in a roundabout way. This type of order is discussed in chapter 15.

G. REMEDY STIPULATION

At common law contracting parties will sometimes use a liquidated damages clause to express what they believe is the most appropriate remedy for breach of contractual obligations. The courts have generally enforced such clauses where the clause

- represents a genuine pre-estimate of loss,
- is not disproportionate to the actual losses, and
- does not amount to a penalty.[76]

Do similar considerations prevail where the parties stipulate for specific relief, and what consequences flow with respect to the granting of equitable relief when the parties have included a liquidated damages clause in their contract?

There are few cases where parties have expressly stipulated for specific relief[77]—such a clause would be superfluous if the *raison d'être* of contract was to ensure actual performance. Of course we know that a significant part of our contractual paradigm is built on the ability to breach and substitute with compensation in damages. And herein lies the answer to the courts' reluctance to enforce express party stipulations requiring specific performance: such an action would circumvent the notion of efficient breach and make redundant the issue of damage

---

75   Above note 35.

76   See *Dunlop Pneumatic Tyre Co.* v. *New Garage & Motor Co.*, [1915] A.C. 79 (H.L.); and *H.F. Clarke Ltd.* v. *Thermidaire Corp.* (1975), [1976] 1 S.C.R. 319.

77   I have only found one, *Tritav Holdings Ltd.* v. *National Bank of Canada* (1996), 47 C.P.C. (3d) 91 (Ont. Gen. Div.).

inadequacy as a threshold requirement for the availability of equitable relief.[78] A second reason is that equitable remedies are always seen as being discretionary — the strict compliance with a party stipulation of specific performance would abrogate a court's discretion.

A party stipulation for specific performance may still have relevance in an evidentiary capacity. The clause can be seen to alert a court to possible difficulties in quantifying damages as a suitable remedy. An admission by the party against whom the order is sought that specific relief is necessary to ensure a plaintiff receives the benefits of the contract should not be set aside lightly. In light of the Supreme Court's requirement that a plaintiff must prove that damages are inadequate even in real estate transactions (see discussion below), a remedies stipulation may assist the plaintiff in doing so.

The evidentiary impact of a remedy stipulation appears to be the approach taken where a court has been asked to enforce a negative stipulation by injunction. In the leading case in this area, *Warner Brothers Pictures Inc.* v. *Nelson*,[79] the plaintiff had claimed an injunction to prevent the actress Bette Davis from breaching her agreement by working for another film studio. The agreement contained a clause in which the defendant acknowledged that her services were "of a special, unique, extraordinary and intellectual character" that gave them a particular value, "the loss of which cannot be reasonably or adequately compensated in damages" so that a breach may "cost the producer great and irreparable injury and damage," and would entitle the employer to bring an action for an injunction.[80] On the effects of this acknowledgment and remedy stipulation Branson J, said:

> Of course, parties cannot contract themselves out of the law; but it assists, at all events, on the question of evidence as to the applicability of an injunction in the present case, to find the parties formally recognizing that in cases of this kind injunction is a more appropriate remedy than damages.[81]

---

78   Sharpe, above note 27 at § 7.780, also suggests that other external factors may motivate concern by the court to resist routine enforcement of party-stipulated remedies. Such would be the case if a personal service contract contained such a clause. There, the court would be reluctant to allow its processes to enforce the party stipulation merely because the employee agreed to it. This would invoke the spectre of involuntary servitude and may be difficult to supervise without the expenditure of an unwarranted amount of judicial resources.

79   (1936), [1937] 1 K.B. 209.

80   *Ibid.* at 220.

81   *Ibid.* at 221.

This principle is echoed in the recent judgment of Gotlib J. in *Tritav Holdings Ltd.* v. *National Bank of Canada*.[82] This case would appear to be the only one where the parties have expressly provided for the granting of specific performance in their remedy stipulation clause. The plaintiff, a landlord of a commercial shopping plaza, was seeking an interim injunction requiring the defendant to reopen its bank in the plaza. The lease contained a clause titled "Failure of the Tenants to Carry on Business" that included a "keep open" provision, a liquidated damages provision, and the tenants's recognition and consent to the landlord seeking injunction and specific performance to restrain and compel the tenant to reopen the premises. Commenting upon the remedy stipulation clause Gotlib J. remarked that the "parties cannot contract out of the law as it exists."[83] The injunction was denied because the plaintiff was unable to show that it would suffer irreparable loss. The tenant had vacated the premises for over three months without protest from the plaintiff, who only commenced legal action for an interlocutory motion some six months after the defendant had moved out.

When the parties have specifically included a liquidated damage clause in their contract, the presence of the clause does not prevent the plaintiff from bringing an equitable action for injunction or specific performance. The argument that the clause should be interpreted as the parties agreeing that damages are an adequate remedy[84] has not been successful. The courts have accepted that a liquidated damage clause is an accurate way to assess damages for past losses. However, the plaintiff should still be at liberty to argue that for prospective losses damages may still be an inadequate remedy, thus warranting the grant of either an injunction or specific performance.[85] Where the liquidated damages clause is also designed to compensate for future losses, the granting of specific performance would appear to amount to over-compensation. In these circumstances the plaintiff must elect between specific relief and liquidated damages. However, even after this election, a plaintiff can still maintain an action for equitable damages in lieu of an injunction or specific performance up to the time of judgment and may still be granted *in specie* relief for the future. Dickson J. summarized the

---

82   Above note 77.

83   *Ibid.* at 95.

84   The contrary result would prevail if it is clear from the interpretation of the liquidated damages clause that the parties intended the defaulting party to have an election, either to perform the contract or to be released from performance on payment of the liquidated damages.

85   See *Elsley Estate* v. *J.G. Collins Insurance Agencies Ltd.*, [1978] 2 S.C.R. 916.

position in *Elsley Estate* v. *J.G. Collins Insurance Agencies Ltd.*, a case dealing with the enforcement of a restraint of trade clause in a contract of employment, as follows:

1) Where a fixed sum is stipulated as and for liquidated damages upon a breach, the covenantee must elect with respect to that breach between liquidated damages and an injunction.

2) If he elects to take the liquidated damages stipulated he may recover that sum irrespective of his actual loss.

3) Where the stipulated sum is a penalty he may only recover such damages as he can prove, but the amount recoverable may not exceed the sum stipulated.

4) If he elects to take an injunction and not the liquidated sum stipulated, he may recover damages in equity for the actual loss sustained up to the date of the injunction or, if tardy, up to the date upon which he should have sought the injunction, but in either case, not exceeding the amount stipulated as payable upon a breach.

5) Where a liquidated damages sum is stipulated as payable for each and every breach, the covenantee may recover this sum in respect of distinct breaches which have occurred and he may also be granted an injunction to restrain future breaches.[86]

FURTHER READINGS

BURROWS, A.S., *Remedies for Torts and Breach of Contract*, 2d ed. (London: Butterworths, 1994)

COVELL W. & K. LUPTON, *Principles of Remedies* (Sydney: Butterworths, 1995)

JONES, G.H. & W. GOODHART, *Specific Performance*, 2d ed. (London: Butterworths, 1996)

---

86   *Ibid.* at 938.

CHAPTER 11

SPECIFIC PERFORMANCE: DISCRETIONARY DEFENCES

A. INTRODUCTION

In this chapter we will explore a number of discretionary defences to the granting of specific performance. Some of these defences are intimately connected to issues of contract formation and enforceability. Others are related to equity's method and approach — in particular, they build upon notions of fairness and avoidance of unconscionable behavior. Finally, some are simply historical anachronisms that may have outlived their usage. Although these matters have traditionally been dealt with under a heading of "defences" they do not necessarily all operate as would a defence in say, criminal law. They do not invariably lead to denial of all equitable relief, although that can happen; rather, they operate as signposts alerting a court to matters that may affect the justice of awarding equitable relief. In many of these areas we are dealing with gradations of a person's conduct that must be analyzed in the particular context of the litigants' dispute. Often, a number of these "defences" will arise, and it is the totality or cumulative effect which is ultimately determinative of the court's discretion.

Historically, the denial of specific relief could have a serious impact on the eventual remedy granted a plaintiff. It would be of little consequence if the denial of equitable relief, based on some discretionary ground due to the plaintiff's improprieties, simply meant that the plaintiff would receive equivalent justice in common law damages. But this was not the case while determination of damages was left to juries who ameliorated their awards to reflect the plaintiff's conduct. Thus, the denial of specific relief carried with it significant risk of the plaintiff being under-compensated as well as having the expense and inconvenience of starting a new action at common law. Now, since control is has been placed on jury damage assessments and chancery and common law procedures have been fused, some of the discretionary defences appear anachronistic. It is probably fair to say that the factors that motivate a court in denying specific relief are also considered in the assessment of damages.[1] However, where specific performance would amount to a more complete justice, because damages are inadequate, denying the plaintiff her remedy of choice will have a significant impact.

B. ISSUES RELATING TO CONTRACT FORMATION AND ENFORCEMENT

Before specific performance can be decreed there must be a contract in existence. (For an explanation, see the discussion below on estoppel.) Thus, any intervention that makes the contract void or voidable will also deny specific performance as a remedy. Equity plays a significant role in contract law through a number of doctrines in addition to the granting of specific performance — in particular, rescission for fraud, undue influence, unconscionability, misrepresentation or mistake which operates to bring the contract to an end. There is some controversy as to the extent of these interventions, but the net effect is to bring the contractual obligations to an end and to restore the parties to their original positions. Historically, a common feature to equity's intervention in these areas was that it would arise even though at com-

---

1   In one study undertaken in the United States the authors concluded that where specific relief has been denied based on some equitable defence it is in fact a final denial of the case. It is very rare for a plaintiff to be able to resort to a common law remedy after denial of specific performance. See J. P. Frank & J. Endicott, "Defenses in Equity and 'Legal Rights'" (1954) 14 La. L. Rev. 380. E. L. Sherwin, "Law and Equity in Contract Enforcement" (1991), 50 Md. L. Rev. 253, suggests, that where an equitable defence has resulted in the denial of specific performance, then, based on the same grounds, a court will often resort to compensating the promisee for his lost reliance interest rather than his expectation interest. The former damages will be lower. The decision in *Jacobs* v. *Bills*, [1967] N.Z.L.R. 249 (S.C.) would appear to exemplify this suggestion: the plaintiff was denied specific performance but then allowed to recover damages based upon the old rule of *Bain* v. *Fothergill* (1874), L.R. 7 H.L. 158 (limiting damages to the cost of exploring the title) rather than for his loss of the property value under the contract.

mon law the contract could be treated as valid. This was based on the fact that chancery's notion of what conduct constituted impropriety, often referred to as "equitable or constructive fraud,"[2] was wider in ambit than equivalent common law doctrines. Whether it is still relevant to maintain a distinction between treatment of contracts at common law and in equity with respect to substantive doctrines on formation and enforcement is beyond the scope of this book. If a contract is rescinded *ab initio* it appears futile to suggest that it could have remained enforceable at common law, and in any case, this has nothing to do with the availability of specific performance. The dominant issue in most of these cases is whether either party has a right to rescission. This section looks at the question, under what circumstances will specific performance be denied and the plaintiff left to damages at common law? which was recognized as a possible scenario before the enactment of the Judicature Acts.[3]

1) Mistake

Where the parties have entered into a contract under a common mistake the contract will not be specifically enforced if the mistake is so fundamental that it prevents the formation of an agreement. Where the parties have entered into a contract in which the defendant has made a unilateral mistake, which was known by the plaintiff or induced by the plaintiff's conduct, then the contract will be rescinded. Where the defendant has made a unilateral mistake that is neither known nor contributed to by the plaintiff, the contract will be enforced unless there are some other circumstances present that make enforcement an hardship amounting to injustice.[4] Apart from cases where rescission is granted, where the denial of specific performance logically follows,

---

2   In the case of misrepresentation, equity's intervention is justified even for an innocent misrepresentation before the contract has been executed. See generally G. H. L. Fridman, *The Law of Contract in Canada*, 3d ed. (Scarborough, Ont.: Carswell, 1994) at 808 *ff*.

3   See R. J. Sharpe, *Injunctions and Specific Performance*, looseleaf (Aurora, Ont.: Canada Law Book, 1998) § 10.100; and I.C.F. Spry, *The Principles of Equitable Remedies: Specific Performance, Injunctions, Rectification and Equitable Damages*, 5th ed.(Sydney: LBC Information Services, 1997) at 156 – 7.

4   See *Tamplin v. James* (1880), 15 Ch. D. 215 (C.A.); and *Foderaro v. Future Homes Construction Ltd.* (1991), 17 R.P.R. (2d) 258 (Ont. Gen. Div.); [*Foderaro*] Sharpe, above note 3 at § 10.110; G. H. Jones & W. Goodhart, *Specific Performance*, 2d ed. (London: Butterworths, 1996) at 105; and Spry, above note 3 at 157.

there are few cases of mistake (either common mistake, or unilateral mistake by the defendant), where specific performance has been denied and the plaintiff left to his remedies at common law.

Hope v. *Walter*[5] would appear to be one such case. The plaintiffs were trustees for sale of a property where, unbeknown to them, their tenant had been convicted of running a brothel. On learning this, the purchaser did not want to complete the sale. The court denied the vendor specific performance, on the grounds that it would not require the purchaser to complete in circumstances where the purchaser could be exposed to a criminal conviction for knowingly renting property in which a brothel was operating. The court confirmed that the vendor could still proceed at common law for damages.

More often, the enforcement of a contract in which the defendant has made a mistake can constitute hardship, and thus the court will refuse specific performance on this ground (see discussion below). In other situations, the plaintiff has been required to treat the contract as rescinded; or else to agree to rectification of the agreement in accordance with the defendant's understanding of the terms, after which specific performance will follow. It is also possible for the court to grant the plaintiff specific performance but to give some abatement of the purchase price to reflect the fact that the purchaser is not getting exactly what she thought she was purchasing (see discussion in chapter 12, section D.1 "Purchaser's Action").

2) Misrepresentation

Where the plaintiff has induced the defendant into entering a contract by making a misrepresentation of fact, either innocently or fraudulently, the defendant may have a successful defence to a suit for specific performance and may be able to have the contract rescinded. It does not matter whether the plaintiff believed in the truth of the statement, although the court will be more disposed to effecting rescission in the case of fraud than for innocent misrepresentation. Thus, as with mistake, so with misrepresentation; specific performance is intertwined with the availability of rescission.[6] However, from an early date it was said that even it a misrepresentation was not serious enough to support rescission of the contract, it could, nevertheless, justify a denial of specific performance.[7]

---

5   [1900] 1 Ch. 257 (C.A.).
6   See Fridman, above note 2 at 293 – 311.
7   See *Cadman* v. *Horner* (1810), 18 Ves. Jun. 10, 34 E.R. 221 [Ch.]; *Re Terry and White's Contract* (1886), 32 Ch. D. 14 (C.A.); and *Holliday* v. *Lockwood*, [1917] 2 Ch. 47.

It is possible that the defendant may lose the right to rescind a contract through delay, lack of ability to restore the parties, or because the contract has been executed, yet still have a valid argument to justify the court refusing specific performance and confining the plaintiff to damages.[8] Thus, in *Panzer* v. *Zeifman*[9] the vendor had, through his agent, represented that his property had a private driveway and parking location, although in fact the driveway was shared in common with the adjoining owner. The purchaser was unaware of this at the time of signing the agreement. The purchaser did not immediately go to his solicitor but sought to secure mortgage financing. Being unable to secure financing, he requested permission from the vendor to offer his equity for sale. After the time had elapsed for making requisitions on the property, the purchaser hired a solicitor. The problems over the driveway were then revealed and the purchaser sought to rescind the agreement. The vendor brought an action for specific performance. The trial judge found that the representation had induced the purchaser to buy the property, but that the right to rescind was gone based on the purchaser's affirmation of the contract. The vendor was awarded specific performance. In the Court of Appeal, the trial judge's decision on rescission was upheld, but the decision to award specific performance was reversed on the grounds that the vendor had misrepresented the property and had not come to the court with clean hands (see discussion below). The court, however, did confirm the right of the vendor to seek damages at common law for the purchaser's failure to close.

A similar argument has been accepted in a case of non-disclosure where the vendor failed to reveal to the purchaser that the liquor licenses of the hotel he was selling was about to be revoked.[10] Spry also argues that in exercising their discretion to grant specific performance, a court may well deny *in specie* relief when the misrepresentation relates to matters of opinion or of law, or of future conduct, which would not give rise to grounds for rescission. This is on the basis that all these issues go to the question of hardship that may be imposed if the defendant is required to specifically perform the contract.[11]

In realty contracts, an additional factor is brought to bear on the exercise of a court's discretion. Where the misrepresentation amounts to a mis-description of the property (such as a minor defect in title or the physical characteristics of the land) contained in the contract, in

---

8   See Spry, above note 3 at 164.
9   (1978), 20 O.R. [2d] 502 (C.A.).
10   See *Summers* v. *Cocks* (1927), 40 C.L.R. 321 (Austl. H. C.).
11   See Spry, above note 3 at 162.

addition to rescission or specific performance the court may order specific performance with compensation for the error. This additional option makes it less likely that the court will deny specific performance and leave the plaintiff to an action for common law damages.

3) Problems Associated with Consideration — "Equity Will Not Assist a Volunteer"

The equitable maxim that "equity will not assist a volunteer" is meant to indicate that equity will not perfect an imperfect gift or trust, nor create a contract in which no consideration has been provided. The extent to which this notion is adhered to in contract law appears to be changing. Historically, it meant that a contract made under seal, and therefore enforceable at common law, was, nevertheless, unenforceable by specific performance in equity if there was no consideration. This position has been upheld in Canada.[12] However, a nominal consideration can constitute good consideration and will be sufficient in equity, so that in *Mountford* v. *Scott*[13] the United Kingdom Court of Appeal was prepared to hold that the payment of a nominal consideration of £1 was sufficient consideration to support specific performance of an option agreement. In fact, the judgment of Russell L.J. suggests that a contract made under seal alone would now be enforceable in equity.

However, inadequacy of consideration may be evidence of an improvident bargain leading to a finding of some unconscionable dealings and thus the contract may be set aside and specific performance denied.[14]

---

12   See *Savereux* v. *Tourangeau* (1908), 16 O.L.R. 600 (C. A.); and *Riches* v. *Burns* (1924), 27 O.W.N. 203 (H.C.). In the latter case the agreement acknowledged that the option was given in consideration of the sum of $1, although the evidence revealed that it had never been paid. On this basis the court said that consideration had not been provided in fact and thus specific performance could not be decreed. The judgment appears at odds with the decision of the Supreme Court of Canada in *Davidson* v. *Norstrant* (1921), 61 S.C.R. 493, in which the option agreement acknowledged that it had been granted in return for consideration of $100 "now paid." Again the evidence revealed that in fact the $100 had not been paid. Nevertheless, the court held that the promise to pay was the consideration because it stood as a debt due. *Riches* v. *Burns* has recently been followed without question in *Rapattoni* v. *McDonald*, [1988] O.J. No. 1461 (Dist. Ct.).

13   [1975] Ch. 258 (C.A.).

14   See *Black* v. *Wilcox* (1976), 12 O.R. (2d) 759 (C.A.); *Baxter* v. *Rollo* (1912), 18 B.C.R. 369 (S.C.) aff'd (1913), 18 B. C. R. 369 at 372 (C. A.); and *Turner Estate* v. *Bonli Estate*, [1990] 5 W.W.R. 685 (Sask. C.A.).

4) Equitable Estoppel

The basis of any estoppel is the notion that a representor is not allowed to deny the truth of a representation already made to and acted upon by a representee. In equity this can create either promissory estoppel or proprietary estoppel. In either case, it can arise when one party seeks to enforce his strict legal rights after having previously indicated in word or actions that he would not do so, but would put them into abeyance. Estoppel prevents the representor from enforcing his strict legal rights if it would be inequitable to do so. Promissory estoppel, it is usually argued, can only be used as a "shield and not as a sword" and therefore cannot be used to found an action to enforce a promise in the absence of consideration. However, other decisions have suggested that the distinction between shield and sword cannot be maintained, and convey the impression that promissory estoppel can found an action.[15] If this is so then it must be arguable that specific performance should be available to ensure enforcement. Indeed, in the absence of consideration and an enforceable contract, there is no common law remedy, and specific performance or equitable damages may be the only remedy.

Proprietary estoppel (sometimes known as estoppel by acquiescence) applies where one party encourages another to believe that the latter will receive an interest in land in return for laying out resources to the former's benefit, or the latter's detriment. It often arises where one party makes improvements to the other's land, with the encouragement or acquiescence of the other person, and where it would be unconscionable for the other person to rely on her existing legal rights and to deny the former person relief. This form of estoppel does create a cause of action[16] and would therefore appear to support a decree of specific performance.

In *Hong Kong (A.G.)* v. *Humphreys Estate (Queen's Gardens) Ltd.*[17] the Government of Hong Kong entered into an agreement to exchange

---

15   The issue has recently been discussed in *Reclamation Systems Inc.* v. *Rae* (1996), 27 O.R. (3d) 419 (Gen. Div.), wherein all the relevant cases are cited. Cummings J. concluded that the shield/sword distinction was still a part of Canadian law despite suggestions to the contrary. This approach would also be consistent with the judgment of the Supreme Court in Canada in *Saskatchewan River Bungalows Ltd.* v. *Maritime Life Assurance Co.,* [1994] 2 S.C.R. 490; which reaffirmed the role of consideration as a prerequisite for creating enforceable promises in a discussion on the application of waiver.

16   The relevant cases are discussed in *Zelmer* v. *Victor Projects Ltd.* (1997), 147 D.L.R. (4th) 216 (B.C.C.A.).

17   [1987] 1 A.C. 114 (P.C.).

lease and development rights over a piece of crown land in return for the conveyance of an apartment building and cash. The agreement was "subject to contract." The arrangement was complex and both parties undertook certain actions and made considerable expenditures, prior to a concluded contract but on the basis that an agreement would eventually be worked out. As it turned out, the respondents withdrew from the agreement and never signed a formal contract. The respondents then commenced an action to recover possession of their property and repayment of the moneys advanced to the Government as part of the planned exchange. The Government defended the action arguing that the respondents were estopped from denying the contract and seeking its enforcement. The Privy Council held that the Government's action failed because it could not prove that the respondents had created or encouraged an expectation in the Government that there would be no withdrawal from the arrangement. In light of the express reservations about "subject to contract" it was not unfair, unjust, or unconscionable for the respondents to refuse to proceed. However, in the course of the judgment Lord Templeman, speaking for the Privy Council, intimated that it would be quite conceivable for a court to award specific performance where an agreement had become binding by estoppel, and further, that even in the face of a "subject to contract" provision it would be possible that the parties could be bound to the agreement.[18]

In an important decision, *Waltons Stores (Interstate) Ltd.* v. *Maher,*[19] the High Court of Australia has suggested that both promissory estoppel and propriety estoppel are cut from the same cloth and the law is capable of being formulated into principles of general application. In that case the respondents, Maher, had entered into discussions with Waltons concerning a lease of a commercial store to be built to Waltons' specifications. Discussions had advanced to the stage of a formal agreement being drafted by Waltons' solicitor, who had sent it to Maher. In conversations with Waltons' solicitor, Maher had been led to believe that the final agreement was a formality. Anxious to commence construction, and having been given certain assurances by Waltons' solicitor that the deal was to go ahead, Maher demolished an existing building and commenced construction on the building to be leased to Waltons. Waltons then decided not to proceed with the lease but did not inform Maher for over seven weeks. Upon learning that Waltons did not wish to proceed, Maher commenced proceedings for a declara-

---

18   *Ibid.* at 120, 127 – 8.
19   (1988), 164 C.L.R. 387 (Austl. H.C.) [*Waltons Stores*].

tion that a binding lease existed, and requested specific performance. In both the trial court and the lower Court of Appeal, Maher won, although damages were granted in lieu of specific performance.

The High Court of Australia affirmed the lower courts, but on different grounds. The basis of the estoppel was the fact that it would be unconscionable for Waltons' to withdraw from the assumption which their actions had created in Maher; namely, that a contract would be completed, and upon which Maher had acted to its detriment.[20] At first blush this decision can be seen as significantly undermining the need for consideration, leading to enforcement of gratuitous promises in the name of preventing unconscionable conduct. However, to meet this concern, the High Court sought to limit the area in which an estoppel could be raised. Such limitation came from the fact that purely gratuitous promises do not create reasonable expectations of enforcement in promisees.[21] That expectation can only come about where the defendant has acted in some unconscionable way so as to create an impression in the other party that the defendant's promise can be relied upon. And then, the remedy provided should be in proportion to the detriment occasioned by the plaintiff as a direct result of the unconscionable conduct.

---

20   The grounds upon which the estoppel is raised are described by Brennan J., *ibid.* at 428–29, as follows:

[T]o establish an equitable estoppel, it is necessary for a plaintiff to prove that (1) the plaintiff assumed that a particular legal relationship then existed between the plaintiff and the defendant or expected that a particular legal relationship would exist between them and, in the latter case, that the defendant would not be free to withdraw from the expected legal relationship; (2) the defendant has induced the plaintiff to adopt that assumption or expectation; (3) the plaintiff acts or abstains from acting in reliance on the assumption or expectation; (4) the defendant knew or intended him to do so; (5) the plaintiff's action or inaction will occasion detriment if the assumption or expectation is not fulfilled; and (6) the defendant has failed to act to avoid that detriment whether by fulfilling the assumption or expectation or otherwise. For the purposes of the second element, a defendant who has not actively induced the plaintiff to adopt an assumption or expectation will nevertheless be held to have done so if the assumption or expectation can be fulfilled only by a transfer of the defendant's property, a diminution of his rights or an increase in his obligations and he, knowing that the plaintiff's reliance on the assumption or expectation may cause detriment to the plaintiff if it is not fulfilled, fails to deny to the plaintiff the correctness of the assumption or expectation on which the plaintiff is conducting his affairs.

21   Accepting the position adopted by Goff J. in *Amalgamated Investment and Property Co. (in liquidation)* v. *Texas Commerce International Bank Ltd.* (1981), [1982] Q.B. 84; at 403 and *Waltons Stores*, above note 19, 427.

In some situations, this may justify the enforcement of the promise; in others a compensatory payment of expenditures will be enough.[22] The area of equitable estoppel highlights the fact that specific performance is granted of "promises" rather than "contracts." In an interesting aside in the *Waltons Stores* case, Brennan J. remarked that equitable estoppel "complements the tortious remedies of damages for negligent misstatement or fraud and enhances the remedies available to a party who acts or abstains from acting in reliance on what another induces him to believe."[23] The link between equity and tort has been noted in other areas.[24] It alludes to the notion that in the area of promises, equity acts to establish a normative standard of behavior no longer dependent upon the voluntary assumptions of consensual obligations.

5)   The *Statute of Frauds* and the Doctrine of Part Performance

Excluding Manitoba, all the common law provinces have some form of Statute of Frauds.[25] The statute requires a disposition of realty to be manifest by a note or memorandum in writing and signed by the party to be charged to be enforceable. There are numerous cases on the statute's interpretation and not all can be reconciled. In essence, the statute requires the memorandum to come into existence prior to any litigation in which lack of compliance with the statute may be raised — it does not have to be contemporaneous with the alleged contract itself. The memorandum should include a record of the property that is being transacted, the price paid, and the parties involved, although it does not have to be a formal document created for this exact purpose. There is considerable divergence in the cases as to what degree of certainty is required over these matters, which are considered essential, and any

---

22   The High Court of Australia returned to this point in *Commonwealth of Australia* v. *Verwayen* (1990), 170 C.L.R. 394 (Austl. H.C.). See particularly Mason C.J. at 415 — 6, and Brennan J. at 429.

23   *Waltons Stores*, above note 23 at 427.

24   See, for example, the arguments raised by J. D. McCamus, "Prometheus Unbound: Fiduciary Obligation in the Supreme Court of Canada" (1997) 28 C. B. L. J. 107, who argues that the developments in the area of equiable compensation are creating a type of equitable tort.

25   See, for example, Ontario *Statute of Frauds*, R. S. O. 1990, c. S. 19. In British Columbia, the *Law and Equity Act*, R. S. B. C. 1996, c. 253 provides greater flexibility on what constitutes sufficient memorandum in writing and widens the application of the doctrine of part performance. In Manitoba, the *Statute of Frauds* has been repealed: *An Act to Repeal the Statute of Frauds*, S. M. 1982-83-84, c. 34.

other necessary conditions of the agreement.[26] The memorandum does not have to be signed by both parties, only the one against whom the action is brought. Where the Statute of Frauds is not satisfied the contract is unenforceable rather than void: the contract can remain valid for some purposes but it cannot support an action for specific performance[27] — except through the doctrine of part performance.

The doctrine of part performance is based upon the wider notion of fraud, applied in equity to prevent a person from using a statutory provision to perpetrate a fraud. This notion of equitable or constructive fraud is linked to the concept that it would be unconscionable conduct for a defendant to take advantage of the lack of a written memorandum to avoid her obligations.

The following criteria, formulated by Guest[28] and accepted in Canadian courts,[29] need to be satisfied in order to successfully raise part performance:

1) the acts of part performance relied upon must be referable to some contract; they prove the existence of some contract, and are consistent with the contract alleged;
2) the acts of part performance relied upon have been performed by the plaintiff;
3) the contract must be one that, if it had been evidenced in writing, would have been specifically enforceable; and,
4) there must be clear and proper evidence of the existence of a contract.

With respect to point 1) there has been much discussion on what evidence constitutes sufficient acts of part performance and whether that evidence must unequivocally relate to the specific contract alleged, or whether it is sufficient that the evidence is referable to some contract.[30] Thus, for example, mere payment of money (as in a deposit) has not constituted a sufficient act of part performance under the former narrower view, because such an act is equally consistent with a loan or a gift. Under the latter wider view, the payment of money can amount to part performance. This debate has largely been fuelled by the House of

---

26   See the discussion in P. M. Perell & B. H. Engell, *Remedies and the Sale of Land*, 2d ed. (Toronto: Butterworths, 1998) at 12.

27   See *Maddison* v. *Alderson* (1883), 8 App. Cas. 467 (H.L.).

28   See A. G. Guest *Anson's Law of Contract*, 24th ed. (Oxford: Clarendon Press, 1975) at 84–88

29   *Deglman* v. *Guaranty Trust Co. of Canada*, [1954] S. C. R. 725; and *Taylor* v. *Rawana* (1990), 74 O. R. (2d) 357 (H. C.), aff'd (1992), 10 O. R. (3d) 736 (C. A.).

30   See the discussion on this issue in *Alvi* v. *Lal* (1990), 13 R. P. R. (2d) 302 (Ont. H. C.).

Lords' decision in *Steadman* v. *Steadman*.[31] That decision gave voice to the wider view and appears to be the position adopted by some courts in Canada,[32] whereas in decisions made before *Steadman* the narrower view had consistently been relied upon by the Canadian Supreme Court.[33] In a recent case before the Supreme Court, the court extensively cited *Steadman* in support, although it made no comment on this particular issue.[34]

With respect to point 3), that the contract must be one that, if it had been evidenced in writing, would be capable of specific performance — it has been accepted that if specific performance is unavailable no resort can be made to common law damages.[35] The doctrine of part performance only makes the contract susceptible to equitable remedies — it does not allow the application of common law damages. However, resort can be made to equitable damages, in lieu of specific performance and injunctions, under the *Lord Cairns'* Act provisions.[36] This is perhaps an unfortunate result because it means that if specific performance was available but denied on discretionary grounds, equitable damages could nevertheless be substituted. However, if specific performance was unavailable from the outset, perhaps because the defendant no longer owned the property, then no damages could be

---

31   (1974), [1976] A.C. 536 (H.L.).

32   See, in British Columbia, *Currie* v. *Thomas* (1985), 19 D.L.R. (4th) 594 (B.C.C.A.); and in Newfoundland, see *Hollett* v. *Hollett* (1993), 106 Nfld. & P.E.I.R. 271 (Nfld. S. C. (T. D.)).

33   See *Brownscombe* v. *Vercamert Estate*, [1969] S.C.R. 658; and *Thompson* v. *Guaranty Trust Co. of Canada* (1973)[1974] S.C.R. 1023.

34   See *Hill* v. *Nova Scotia* (*A. G.*), [1997] 1 S.C.R. 69. The case dealt with whether the province of Nova Scotia could rely upon a statutory provision requiring any interest over a highway to be expressed in writing, to defeat a claim brought by a farmer whose land had beeen expropriated some twenty-seven years ago. The farmer claimed that as part of the expropriation he had been promised the right to allow his cattle to cross between the two parts of his farm that had been divided by the creation of the highway. The province had installed gates and had maintained the farmer's access way for most of the period leading up to the dispute. By analogy to the *Statute of Frauds*, the court indicated that the province could not set up the writing requirement so as to defeat the landowner's equitable right. The writing requirement in this case served the same purposes as that in the *Statute of Frauds*, and was thus subject to the doctrine of part performance so as to avoid the inequitable operation of the statute.

35   See *Lavery* v. *Pursell* (1888), 39 Ch. D. 508, followed in Canada in *Carter* v. *Irving Oil Co. Ltd.*, [1952] 4 D.L.R. 128 (N.S.S.C.); *Pearson* v. *Skinner School Bus Lines (St. Thomas) Ltd.*, [1968] 2 O.R. 329 (H.C.); and discussed in *James* v. *Alcock* (1996), 143 Nfld. & P.E.I.R. 106 (Nfld. S.C.(T.D.)).

36   See Spry above note 3 at 256.

awarded in either common law or equity. This tends to keep the debate alive as to which issues go to jurisdiction and which to discretion in equity. It would be better to accept the anachronistic nature of the doctrine of part performance, and view it as meeting evidential concerns about the existence of a contract.

Canadian courts may have further ameliorated the consequences of this limitation by making a generous construction on the availability of specific performance: as long as the contract was at some time capable of being specifically performed, or was a type of contract that routinely supported a specific performance decree, then damages in lieu of specific performance can be granted. This position applies even if at the time of commencing the litigation, or at trial, specific performance was an impossibility.[37]

6) Certainty

There are two aspects to certainty. One is the law of contract's requirement that a contract must be certain enough that it can be interpreted and performed. Lack of certainty here renders the contract void. A second aspect of certainty is that already discussed in chapter 10 with respect to difficulties with court supervision: the contract must be certain enough for the court to instruct the defendant in what exactly she is required to comply. It is possible for the contract to be certain in the first sense, yet, nevertheless, be deemed too uncertain because of problems with supervision. This argument has commonly been used against the enforcement of building contracts and long term supply contracts (see discussion below). However, this uncertainty with supervision should not be confused with uncertainty in the result, which may flow from properly enforcing a contractual term. Thus, in *Dynamic Transport Ltd.* v. *O.K. Detailing Ltd.*[38] the Supreme Court of Canada was prepared to grant specific performance of an obligation imposed upon the vendor to act in "good faith and to take all reasonable efforts" to secure planning approval from a local municipality so that the conveyance of a piece of land could be effected. The outcome of the approval process was uncertain, yet the order could be enforced. The court went on to identify how damages would be assessed if the vendor failed to carry out his obligations.

---

37   See *Starlite Variety Stores Ltd.* v. *Cloverlawn Investments Ltd.* (1978), 22 O.R. (2d) 104, aff'd (1979), 27 O.R. (2d) 256 (C.A.); and *Christy v. Mohl*, [1985] B.C.J. No. 1623 (S.C.).

38   [1978] 2 S.C.R. 1072.

C. ISSUES RELATING TO THE PLAINTIFF'S CONDUCT

In this section we are looking at issues relating to the plaintiff's conduct that affect the granting of the remedy directly as distinguished from the formation of the contract itself.

1) Plaintiff Must Be "Ready, Willing, and Able" to Perform

By making a request for specific performance, the plaintiff affirms that he wants to proceed with the contract — therefore, it is a requirement that the plaintiff must be "ready, willing and able" to perform his own contractual obligations. Where the plaintiff is invoking equity's jurisdiction he "must not blow hot and cold, or be dilatory in the performance of his obligations; he must show that at all times he was desirous, prompt and eager to complete the contract."[39] In the normal course of a real estate transaction, the plaintiff would tender documents (although tendering is not a prerequisite to bringing a specific performance application[40]) on the day set for completion, being the day that she must be ready, willing and able to perform. If tendering is refused, then the plaintiff can elect either to: accept the repudiation of the contract; terminate the contract and sue for damages; or, affirm the contract and seek specific performance. The date for completion is further complicated by the approach adopted in respect to stipulations of time.

A time stipulation must be construed as any other term of a contract would be. If time is of the essence, and is an essential term of the contract, then non-satisfaction will constitute a breach and thus entitle the innocent party to treat the contract as discharged. If time is of the essence, but it is not an essential term, then the innocent party will have an action for damages but will not be able to repudiate the contract for breach. As with any other term, an innocent party may waive a breach of a time stipulation if it is expressed as being for the innocent party's sole benefit. The innocent party may waive compliance with a time stipulation clause altogether; alternatively, she may waive only the initial breach, and, upon giving reasonable notice, she may return to treating time as being of the essence. It is possible for the parties to explicitly express in their contract that time is of the essence — in

---

39   *Wandoan Holdings Ltd.* v. *Pieter Vos Ltd.* (1974), 4 O.R. (2d) 102 at 108, Weatherston J. (H. C.).

40   See *Kloepfer Wholesale Hardware & Automotive Co.* v. *Roy*, [1952] 2 S.C.R. 465.

some situations the law will normally presume (in mercantile agreements, for example); and in others, it must be made so by the parties giving notice to that effect.[41]

Time stipulations used to be treated differently in common law and equity. In the former, they were strictly construed and usually always treated as being of the essence; whereas in the latter, they were only treated as of the essence once a party had given notice to that effect. In *United Scientific Holdings Ltd.* v. *Burnley Borough Council*[42] one hundred years after the passing on the *Judicative Acts*, the House of Lords finally reconciled the disparate positions of common law and equity. This decision has been followed in Canada.[43]

The interplay of "time of the essence" and "ready, willing and able" leads to the following permutations:

a) Where Time is of the Essence at Date of Completion

If time is of the essence at the date of completion, then the plaintiff must be ready, willing and able to complete at that time to be able to maintain an action for specific performance. The alternative is to accept the breach, and, if it is of an essential term, to bring the contract to an end and treat it as discharged for breach. If it is not of an essential term, then the plaintiff must continue with performance of the contract and be ready, willing and able to complete to maintain an action for damages.

b) Where Time is of the Essence at Date of Completion but Plaintiff Has Waived the Term

If the plaintiff has waived the time stipulation, then he is estopped from later arguing that the other party was in breach of contract for failure to observe that stipulation — however, performance must take place in a reasonable time period. Alternatively, the plaintiff can restore the importance of timely performance by giving reasonable notice that time is, once again, of the essence.[44] If at the new time set for completion the plaintiff is now not ready, willing and able to perform, then he will be in breach himself. It is no defence to a suit by one party to say that the other had not been ready, willing, and able to complete at the original time set for completion. This is so because it

---

41   See Fridman, above note 2 at 524; and Perell & Engell, above note 26 at 43.

42   (1977), [1978] A. C. 904 (H.L.).

43   See *Sail Labrador Ltd.* v. *The Challenge One* (1998), [1999] 1 S. C. R. 265.

44   See *King* v. *Urban & Country Transport Ltd.* (1973), 1 O.R. (2d) 449 (C.A.)[*King*]. It is possible that commencement of a suit for specific performance can constitute reasonable notice, in which case the date for compliance will be set by court order.

does not lie in the mouth of one party, now in default, to complain about the prior deficiencies of another. In addition, if the contract remains on foot, the plaintiff not having elected to rescind for the earlier breach but rather having waived the breach of the other party, then it remains on foot for the benefit of both parties.[45]

c) Where Time is of the Essence at Date of Completion but Neither Party Is Able to Complete

What is the situation where neither party was ready, willing and able to perform at the time originally stipulated for performance? It was commonly said that for a plaintiff to maintain an action, she must plead both that she was ready, willing, and able to complete at the time originally set for completion, and that she continued to remain ready, willing, and able to complete at the time of the court order. However, the cases have now established that it is the latter which is important. Thus, in *Basra* v. *Carhoun*[46] the British Columbia Court of Appeal held that readiness, willingness, and ability to perform only had to be pleaded and proved at the date set for completion by the court order. It was not essential for the plaintiffs to be able to prove that they were ready, willing, and able to perform at the original date set in the contract and continued to remain so throughout the time period until the date of the court order. In that particular case, the plaintiffs had sought to purchase all the shares in a motel business. At the time set for completion the purchasers were unable to show that they were ready, willing, and able to complete because they had yet to get the approval of the debenture holder of the motel business for their assumption of the liabilities. Nor were the vendors ready, willing, and able to complete, because they had failed to furnish the appropriate documentation as required under the contract. The purchasers successfully sought specific performance, and the court viewed that as constituting reasonable notice that time was again of the essence. Although the plaintiffs were still not in a position to complete the deal, they had made all the appropriate overtures to the debenture holder and were awaiting its approval.

---

45   See *Mehmet* v. *Benson* (1965), 113 C.L.R. 295 (Austl. H. C.) [*Mehmet*] cited with approval in *Basra* v. *Carhoun* (1993), 82 B.C.L.R. (2d) 71 (C.A.).

46   Above note 45.

In granting specific performance, the court basically granted an extension of time upon which to satisfy the contract.[47]

Where both parties are unable to complete at the time set for completion, and "time is of the essence," the contract remains in agreement. If neither party is able to put themselves in a position of being ready, willing, and able in the future to complete, the contract will be treated as being abandoned and unenforceable by either side.[48] However, one party can resurrect the "time of the essence" clause by proving that they are now ready, willing, and able to perform.[49] If a party who was not ready, willing, and able to complete on the date of completion purports to terminate the contract before a new date for completion is set, without resurrecting the "time of the essence" clause (namely, being ready, willing, and able to complete), he will be treated as having breached the contract.[50]

2) Plaintiff in Breach of Other Contractual Obligations

As a general rule, before a plaintiff can seek specific performance they must be in compliance with their own contractual obligations. This has been said to be part of the equitable maxim of "he who seeks equity must do equity."[51] Obviously, a party who has breached their own obligations, to the extent that the other party can treat the contract as discharged for breach, is not allowed to recover specific performance. This is based on the principle that a party cannot take advantage of their own wrong.[52] However, it is possible for the plaintiff to be in

---

47   The order is somewhat strange. In effect, the plaintiffs are not ready, willing, and able to perform at the time of the court order, nor may they be when the new time set for completion in the court's order comes about. In this sense the plaintiffs are being given an extension to work out the details of the contract and, presumably, may still bring it to an end if they are unsuccessful in getting the approval of the debenture holder. The court suggests that orders for specific performance may be elaborate. In addition, the court appears to have wanted to save the parties in this case from the folly of their respective counsel who were described as being incompetent.

48   See *Zender v. Ball* (1974), 5 O.R. (2d) 747 (H.C.). Under these circumstances the defendant, if purchaser, will still be entitled to recover his deposit on the basis that because the vendor cannot complete he has no right to keep the deposit. The right to forfeiture under the agreement is dependent upon the vendor not being in breach. See also *Taylor v. Aramenko* (1994), 100 B.C.L.R. (2d) 245 (C.A.).

49   See *King* above note 44; and *Meadowland Development Co. v. Haverstock Estate* (1990), 96 N. S. R. (2d) 214 (S. C. T. D.)

50   See *Domicile Developments Inc. v. MacTavish* (1999), 45 O.R. (3d) 302 (C.A.).

51   See *Oxford v. Provand* (1868), L.R. 2 P.C. 135.

52   See *Australian Hardwoods Pty. Ltd. v. Railways Commissioner*, [1961] 1 W. L. R. 425 (P.C.); and *Konjevic v. Horvat Properties Ltd.* (1998), 40 O.R. (3d) 633 (C.A.).

breach of contract of inessential terms or of a trivial nature and still recover specific performance.[53] It is also possible for a vendor in a contract for the sale of land to force an imperfect performance upon the purchaser with an abatement of the purchase price (see below), provided that the discrepancy is small or trifling.[54]

3) Delay[55]

Prior to the passing of statutory Limitation Acts the common law had no developed doctrine on limitation periods. This can be contrasted with the position in equity, where the doctrines of laches and acquiescence had developed to restrict the time frame in which a plaintiff could prosecute her action. Every province now has a Limitation Act, which controls the period in which an action must be commenced.[56] However, most provincial legislation also provides a reservation preserving the rules of equity to the extent that they are not barred by virtue of the Act. In the context of specific performance, which is part of equity's ancillary jurisdiction, the Limitation Acts provide an outer limit in which the claim must be made. However, the equitable doctrine of delay will control the availability of specific performance within that statutory limitation period.[57]

The doctrine of delay as a defence to an action for specific performance is built on the notion that it would be inequitable to allow a plaintiff to recover equitable relief where his delay has occasioned prejudice to the defendant. It is the fact of prejudice to the defendant, and not merely the dilatory prosecution of the action by the plaintiff, that

---

53   See *Mehmet*, above note 45 at 307, Barwick C.J.:

> The question as to whether or not the plaintiff has been and is ready and willing to perform the contract is one of substance not to be resolved in any technical or narrow sense. It is important to bear in mind what is the substantial thing for which the parties contract and what on the part of the plaintiff in a suit for specific performance are his essential obligations.

54   See *LeMesurier v. Andrus* (1986), 54 O.R. (2d) 1 (C.A.).

55   The terms "delay" "acquiescence," and "laches" are not used consistently. Laches often refers to the situation where the plaintiff has simply delayed in bringing his action, where as acquiescence can refer to delay accompanied by actual prejudice to the defendant. Acquiescence is also used to refer to estoppel and waiver. In this section the simple term "delay" will be used.

56   See, for example, Alberta *Limitations Act*, S. A. 1996, c. L – 15.1; British Columbia *Limitation Act*, R. S. B. C. 1996, c. 266; and Ontario *Limitations Act*, R. S. O. 1990, c. L.15.

57   See J. S. Williams, *Limitation of Actions in Canada*, 2d ed. (Toronto: Butterworths, 1980) at 38; and G. Mew, *The Law of Limitations* (Toronto: Butterworths, 1991) at 23.

gives rise to the defence. Thus, it has been said that "specific performance [is not] to be regarded as a prize, to be awarded by equity to the
zealous and denied to the indolent."[58]

Two conditions must be fulfilled to invoke the defence of delay:

1) there must be unreasonable delay in the commencement or prosecution of proceedings, and
2) in all the circumstances the consequences of delay must render the
grant of relief unreasonable or unjust.[59]

The latter condition has also been expressed as that there "must be
such a change of position as would make it inequitable to require the
defendant to carry out the contract."[60] The delay will usually arise
between the date set for performance of the contract and the time at
which the plaintiff decides to commence proceedings. If the plaintiff
fails to commence proceedings in a timely fashion, the court may consider the plaintiff to have acquiesced to the breach.[61] There is no defi-
nite time period over which it can be said that the defence of delay is
met: the issue will turn on the context of the dispute and the prejudice
caused the defendant. A period of a few weeks may constitute delay
where it involves the sale of a speculative property whose price fluctu-
ates,[62] whereas in one case a delay of over twenty years was not considered fatal to bringing an action for specific performance.[63]

Prejudice to the defendant may arise from him having made
expenditures on the property after believing that the deal had fallen
through, or from a belief that the plaintiff was not going to seek specific performance but only resort to damages.[64] Other prejudice that
has favoured the defendant is where the property has escalated in
value over the period of the delay such that it would be unfair to grant

---

58 *Lazard Brothers & Co.* v. *Fairfield Properties Co. (Mayfair)* (1977), 121 Sol. J. 793 at
     793, Megarry V.C. (Ch.)
59 *Ahone* v. *Holloway* (1988), 30 B.C.L.R. (2d) 368 (C.A.) at 378 per McLachlin J. (C.A.)
60 *Bark-Fong* v. *Cooper* (1913), 49 S.C.R. 14 at 23, Duff J.
61 Before acquiescence can arise the plaintiff must know that her rights are being
     violated. This is a general requirement for delay to operate as a defence, and it may
     be decisive in other contexts of equitable rights and remedies. For specific
     performance it is difficult to conceive where the plaintiff would not be aware of a
     violation of her contractual rights of performance. But see *Crampsey* v. *Deveney*
     (1968),[1969] S.C.R. 267.
62 See *Edgar* v. *Caskey (No. 2)* (1912), 7 D.L.R. 45 (Alta S.C. (T. D.)).
63 See *Fitzgerald* v. *Masters* (1956), 95 C.L.R. 420 (Austl. H. C.).
64 See *370866 Ontario Ltd.* v. *Chizy* (1987), 57 O.R. (2d) 587 (H.C.).

specific performance,[65] or where the defendant would be unable to mount a suitable defence through loss of evidence to meet the claim.[66]

It is also possible that the plaintiff will be excused any delay if the defendant's own conduct has contributed to that delay, or if the parties have been engaged in attempting to negotiate a resolution to their dispute.[67]

4) Clean Hands

The colourful equitable maxim, "he who comes to equity must come with clean hands," is often referred to in the cases although it is seldom determinative of whether or not to grant equitable relief. It is often seen as convenient shorthand to encompass a number of other applicable defences touching the exercise of the court's discretion. While historically it may have referred to the general moral turpitude of the plaintiff, it now clearly requires that "the depravity, the dirt in question on the hand, has an immediate and necessary relation to the equity sued for"[68] In most cases where unclean hands is raised, the defendant will be able to resist the plaintiff's request for specific performance based on a defence of the plaintiff being guilty of breach of contract, or the author of a contract formation fault. However, there are situations where the conduct of the plaintiff will not constitute a breach or amount to a contractual formation fault, where specific performance is nevertheless denied because of unclean hands. Typically, these cases arise where the plaintiff is trying to take advantage of her own wrong or is guilty of wishing to pursue some illegal purpose.[69] The conduct of the plaintiff is not looked at in isolation from the conduct of the defendant. Thus in *Brett* v. *Brett*[70] the plaintiff vendor was granted specific performance despite the fact that he had tried to deceive his estranged spouse about the full price of the sale. The defendant purchaser had

---

65   See *Verheyen* v. *Harrison*, [1989] O.J. No. 1217 (Dist. Ct.) [*Verheyan*].

66   See *Grauer Estate* v. *Canada* (1986), 1 F.T.R. 51 (T. D.) citing *Halsbury's Laws of England*, vol. 16, 4th ed. (London: Butterworths, 1980) at 832, para. 929.

67   See *Newfoundland Farm Products Corp.* v. *Newfoundland Ass. of Public Employees* (1995), 132 Nfld. & P.E.I.R. 38 (Nfld. S.C.(T.D.)).

68   *Hongkong Bank of Canada* v. *Wheeler Holdings Ltd.*, [1993] 1 S.C.R. 167 at 188, Sopinka J. giving the decision of the court and citing with approval the quote from *Moody* v. *Cox and Hatt,* [1917] 2 Ch. 71 at 87 – 88 (C.A.). See also *Toronto (city of)* v. *Polai* (1969) [1970] 1 O.R. 483 (C.A.), aff'd (1992) [1993] S.C.R. 38.

69   See *Cerilli* v. *Klodt* (1984), 48 O.R. (2d) 260 (C. A.), (1986), 55 O.R. (2d) 399n; and *Zimmermann* v. *Letkeman* (1977)[1978] 1 S.C.R. 1097. (H. C.)

70   (1996), 7 R.P.R. (3d) 90 (Ont. Gen. Div.).

actively participated in the scheme of deception, and Kiteley J. found it inappropriate to punish the plaintiff for his moral turpitude where that would have the effect of rewarding the defendant for the same conduct.

D. UNFAIRNESS AND HARDSHIP

The notion of unfairness focuses upon the plaintiff's conduct, but with specific reference to the particular circumstances of the defendant. A plaintiff cannot take advantage of a defendant if, through age, poverty, sickness, infirmity of body or mind, lack of capacity or education it would be unconscionable and unfair to do so. In Canada, where the substantive jurisprudence on unconscionability and contract is well developed, it is difficult to conceive of a situation where an equitable remedy would be denied based on hardship but the contract would still be left open to enforcement in common law.[71] The simple reality is that if hardship operates to deny *in specie* relief it will probably either lead to the rescission of the agreement in equity, or make it void or will be unenforceable at common law.

The notion of hardship differs from unfairness in that it focuses upon the actual impact the order would have on the defendant if it were made. Where the specific performance decree would have the effect of amounting to severe hardship, it will be denied, and the plaintiff left to his remedy in damages. The defence of hardship is not dependent upon any wrongdoing on the plaintiff's behalf, although it can accompany other defensive claims where the plaintiff's conduct may be in question. Rather, it is the consequences of the remedy on the defendant, where the hardship imposes an unjust and unreasonable burden. Although potentially wide-reaching in effect courts have exercised caution in this area, so that they do not award relief merely because the defendant has made an improvident bargain or because performance has become more onerous than originally contemplated.[72]

---

71 *McCorkell* v. *McFarlane*, [1952] O.W.N. 653 (H.C.) would appear to be one case, although the plaintiff was only awarded the return of his deposit and out of pocket expenses and not any damages for loss of the bargain. In *Victoria Wood Development Corp.* v. *Ondrey* (1978), 22 O.R. (2d) 1 at 12 (C.A.), Arnup J. A. , for the court indicated that he could find no case in Canada or England where without mistake, misrepresentation, intoxication, "trickiness", or feeble-mindedness specific performance had been refused yet the contract still remained in force and was capable of being sued upon in common law.

72 See *O'Neil* v. *Arnew* (1976), 16 O.R. (2d) 549 (H.C.).

The type of hardship that triggers the defence must be severe and extreme. In *Patel* v. *Ali*[73] at the time of contracting the defendant vendor was in good health, married, and had one child, although she spoke little English. By the date of judgment, some four years after the original completion, the vendor had been diagnosed with bone cancer leading to the amputation of her leg and the fitting of a prosthesis, her husband had been adjudged a bankrupt and had spent time in prison, and she was pregnant with a third child. The defendant was also very reliant upon the support of local friends and relatives who lived within the immediate vicinity of her current house. Under these changed circumstances the court denied specific performance because the hardship amounted to "extraordinary and persuasive circumstances" amounting to injustice. However, in denying the order, the court required the defendant to lodge £10,000 into court to secure the payment of damages after an inquiry. Failure to observe this part of the order would result in the instigation of the original specific performance order.

In *Stewart* v. *Ambrosina*,[74] the hardship experienced by the vendor was also a change in circumstances subsequent to signing the agreement. By the time for completion the vendor had been made a widow, her husband having committed suicide after an extended period of marital difficulties, in care of six children, and solely dependent upon government assistance for support. In this case Cory J. held that hardship subsequent to the contract coming into existence could not be used to determine whether equitable relief should be denied. His reasoning in this regard appears to be out of a concern that such a defence could erode certainty of contract, particularly in an environment of price inflation. In addition, the hardship to one party had to be weighed against the hardship to the other if specific performance were denied[75]. In this case the purchaser would equally have experienced difficulty securing an alternative house given the inflationary pressures on the housing market at the time.

In a recent decision of the Ontario Court of Appeal, *Re 1110049 Ontario Ltd.* v. *Exclusive Diamonds Inc.*,[76] specific performance of the sale of a jewelry store was denied, partially on the grounds that at the time of the sale the defendant vendor had recently suffered the loss of

---

73   [1984] Ch. 283 [*Patel*].

74   (1975), 10 O.R. (2d) 483 (H. C.), aff'd (1977), 16 O.R. (2d) 221 (C.A.).

75   See also *Da Costa* v. *Barbieri*, [1990] O.J. No. 376 (Dist.Ct.), where the hardship to the defendant was said to be out of proportion to the hardship to the plaintiff, and thus specific performance should be denied.

76   (1995), 25 O.R. (3d) 417 (C.A.).

his wife, who had been brutally murdered and who had been an equal partner in running the business. There was no evidence of an inadequate price having been paid for the store or improper pressure, only that because of the loss of his wife, the vendor would have been more susceptible to selling his business than at other times. Although the conditions for hardship existed at the time of the contract, namely the distraught state of the vendor, it was the prospect of subsequent "substantial hardship" if the vendor was forced to sell his business, that he now wanted to continue operating, that determined the court's decision. This decision is troubling in that the level of hardship does not seem to be "extraordinary" when compared to other decisions in the area. It is also difficult to reconcile with the position taken in *Stewart* with respect to the relevance of subsequent hardship, although in this respect, it is a desirable outcome. There seems no reason to deny the relevance of subsequent hardship. An equitable decree takes effect from the time the court grants it — it seems strange not to "balance the equities" at that time. The denial of specific relief in these circumstances does not lead to the denial of damages. The damages will be awarded as a measure of protecting the plaintiff's bargain, and it is only the additional interest in having specific performance that is being denied. The denial of specific performance under these circumstances cannot be viewed as undermining the sanctity of contracts, in as much as the routine awarding of damages for breach is not equally viewed as impinging upon the sanctity of contracts.

Where hardship, and delay attributable to the plaintiff's dilatoriness, come together, the courts appear to be more willing to give credence to the hardship experienced by the defendant.[77] Courts are also prepared to look at a party's subsequent expenditure on the property as amounting to hardship if the party is now required to convey the property,[78] although this could also be accommodated by requiring the plaintiff to pay additional compensation in return for specific performance.[79] A court will not take account of hardship to third parties unconnected with the property unless the defendant is in some legal or moral relationship with the third parties and the court's order would impede its execution.[80]

---

77   See *Verheyen*, above note 65.

78   See *Babcock v. Carr* (1981), 34 O.R. (2d) 65 (H. C.).

79   See *Foderaro*, above note 4.

80   See *Patel*, above note 73, citing Isaacs J. in *Gall v. Mitchell* (1924), 35 C.L.R. 222 at 230 (Austl. H. C.).

E. IMPOSSIBILITY AND FUTILITY

Specific performance is not available if it is impossible for the defendant to perform. This will commonly arise where the defendant has sold, or has created third party rights in the property, and where those parties were unaware of the plaintiff's prior claim.[81] This is part of the traditional support that equity has accorded *bona fide* purchasers for value without notice.[82] There are some rare situations where equity has bound a third party to acknowledge the prior contractual claim of a purchaser even though the third party had no notice of the purchaser's claim. In *Canadian Medical Laboratories Ltd.* v. *Windsor Drug Store Mc.*,[83] the plaintiff had entered into a lease agreement that contained an exclusivity clause. The plaintiff operated a medical laboratory in the defendant's medical centre. The defendant purported to terminate the lease, and the plaintiff did vacate, after they had a dispute over the degree of contribution each should pay to attract a doctor to the medical centre. By the time of the litigation the defendant had entered into another agreement to lease space to a competitor of the plaintiff. The court granted an injunction requiring the lessor to honour the plaintiff's exclusivity clause and to reinstate the plaintiff's business: further, the competitor was ordered to vacate the premises. The latter order was made even though the court held that the competitor was not aware of the plaintiff's lease with the building's owner.

---

81   See *Eastwalsh Homes Ltd.* v. *Anatal Developments Ltd.* (1990), 72 O.R. (2d) 661 (H. C.), rev'd (1993), 12 O.R. (3d) 675 (C. A.), leave to appeal to S. C. C. refused (1993), 15 O.R. (3d) xvi (note). However, where the subsequent purchaser is aware of the prior claim, and even where they have taken possession and have made expenditures on the property, specific performance will still be granted the first purchaser. See *MacIntyre* v. *Commerce Capital Mortgage Corp.* (1981), 34 O.R. (2d) 104 (H.C.), but contrast with the result in *Warmington* v. *Miller*, [1973] Q.B. 877 (C.A.), where the prospect of the defendant breaking a term in the head lease was used as a reason to deny the plaintiff specific performance of a subletting.

82   Martland J, quoting with approval from E. Fry, A Treatise on the Specific Performance of Contracts, 6th ed. by G. R. Northcote (London, Stevens and Sons, 1921) § 205 – 06, said in *Canadian Long Island Petroleums Ltd.* v. *Irving Industries (Irving Wire Products Division) Ltd.* (1974) [1975] 2 S.C.R. 715 at 737: "Generally a stranger to the contract is not a proper defendant to an action for enforcing it. But this general rule is subject to exceptions. If a stranger to the contract gets possession of the subject-matter of the contract with notice of it, he is or may be liable to be made a party to an action for specific performance of the contract upon the equitable ground of his conscience being affected by the notice."

83   (1992), 99 D.L.R. (4th) 559 (Ont. Gen. Div.).

Impossibility may also arise where government action has inter-vened, as in an expropriation[84] or non-compliance with legislation.[85] Perhaps a more liberal approach to impossibility is that afforded in *Wroth* v. *Tyler*.[86] There, the court would not order specific performance requiring the husband to bring uncertain litigation demanding his wife to relinquish her interest in the matrimonial home so that it could be conveyed to the purchaser, despite the opinion of Megarry J. that such litigation would probably be successful.

A plaintiff can protect herself against the possibility of third party rights adversely impacting on the availability of specific performance for realty contracts by registering a certificate of pending litigation (for-merly known as a *lis pendens*) on the title. Under the various provincial codes of civil procedure there is provision for a party to register a cer-tificate of pending litigation, which, once registered, is treated as notice to all subsequent parties who deal with the land that a prior claim has been made.[87] Such an order can be made *ex parte*. The significance of a certificate can be quite profound because without it there is little to prevent the vendor selling, or otherwise disposing of the property. For this reason there is a great deal of litigation on the granting and dis-charging of these certificates.[88] Because the proceedings are essentially an interlocutory action, with the defendant usually seeking the dis-charge of the certificate, the criteria applied by courts mirror that for interlocutory injunctions; namely, a measure of the plaintiff's claim together with the balance of convenience test. (In Ontario, a master has jurisdiction to order a certificate of pending litigation.)

Under the first part of the test, a plaintiff must show that he has "a reasonable claim to an interest in the land." (In Ontario, see *Courts of*

---

84   See *E. Johnson & Co. (Barbados) Ltd.* v. *N.S.R. Ltd.,* [1997] A.C. 400 (P.C.).

85   See *St. Thomas Subdividers Ltd.* v. *639373 Ontario Ltd.* (1996), 91 O. A. C. 193 (C.A.).

86   (1973) [1974] Ch. 30.

87   In Ontario, see *Courts of Justice Act*, R.S.O. 1990, c. C.43, s. 103 Manitoba *The Court of Queen's Bench Act*, S.M. 1988-89, c. 4, s. 58; and *The Queen's Bench Act, 1998*, S.S. 1998, c. Q-1.01, ss. 46-47.

88   An interesting issue has been raised with respect to "rights of first refusal". Unlike options which create an immediate equitable interest in the holder, a right of first refusal is a mere contractual right until such time as the grantor has received an offer which it intends to accept. At that time it has been held that an equitable interest crystallizes, and takes precedence over any equitable right created in the purchaser under the contract which triggered the first right of refusal. See *McFarland* v. *Hauser* [1979] 1 S.C.R. 337, and *McLeod* v. *Castlepoint Development Corp.* (1997), 31 O.R. (3d) 737 (C.A.), leave to appeal to S. C. C. refused [1997] S.C.C.A. No. 191.

Justice Act[89] section 103(6)(a)(ii).) The plaintiff does not reach this standard by simply showing that his claim is neither frivolous nor vexatious, but nor does it appear to require *prima facie* proof.[90] The plaintiff's claim must also show that specific performance is necessary to protect an interest that would not be protected solely with damages.

Under the second part of the test, the following factors have been itemized to aid in the determination of the court's discretion:

1) whether the land is unique
2) the intent of the parties in acquiring the land, i.e., for purposes of investment or occupation
3) whether there is an alternative claim for damages
4) the ease or difficulty to quantify damages
5) the presence or absence of another purchaser
6) whether damages would be a satisfactory remedy
7) whether the plaintiff is a shell company
8) the harm to each party if the certificate is maintained or removed.[91]

In addition, the plaintiff must make full and frank disclosure on an *ex parte* motion,[92] and where the contract specifically restricts the plaintiff from bringing motion for a certificate of pending litigation, that will be honoured.[93]

Specific performance will also be refused where the order would be futile. This concept is embodied in the equitable maxim that "equity does not act in vain"[94] Thus, enforcement will not be ordered of a lease for a term that has already expired.[95] Futility is not an absolute and admits to questions of degree. In *Tito v. Waddell (No. 2)*,[96] Megarry V. C. refused enforcement of a contract that would have required the defendant to restore plots of land and to plant various island fruits on a Pacific island that had been extensively mined for phosphate. This was

---

89   Above note 87.
90   See *Chippewas of Kettle & Stony Point v. Canada* (1994), 17 O.R. (3d) 831 (Gen. Div.); and *Allan Candy Ltd. v. Canadian Imperial Bank of Commerce Mortgage Co.*, [1994] O.J. No. 1300 (Gen. Div.).
91   See *572383 Ontario Inc. v. Dhunna* (1987), 24 C.P.C. (2d) 287 (Ont. S. C. Masters), and cited with approval in *931473 Ontario Ltd. v. Coldwell Banker Canada Inc.* (1991), 5 C.P.C. (3d) 238, add'l reasons (1991), 5 C. P. C. (3d) 271 (Ont. Gen. Div.).
92   See *Cimaroli v. Pugliese* (1988), 25 C.P.C. (2d) 10 (Ont. S.C. Masters).
93   See *Chiu v. Pacific Mall Develolments Inc.* (1998), 73 O. T. C. 161 (Ont. Gen. Div.).
94   See *New Brunswick & Canada Rly & Land Co. v. Muggeridge* (1859), 4 Drew. 689, 62 E.R. 263 at 268, Kindersley V. C.
95   See *McMahon v. Ambrose*, [1987] V.R. 817 (S.C.).
96   [1977] Ch. 106 at 326.

partially because doing so would amount to a waste of time and money, as the plots could never be restored or bear fruit as envisaged by the plaintiffs.

In some rare situations, equity will grant an injunction to enforce a negative stipulation that adversely affects third party rights.

F. ELECTION

The notion of election arises when a promisee is required to determine in which direction she wishes to proceed following actual breach or anticipatory breach by the promisor. Following actual breach the promisee is essentially given two choices: one is to accept the breach and repudiate the contract, the other is to affirm the contract and seek its specific enforcement.[97] Obviously, these are diametrically opposite outcomes. In the case of an anticipatory breach the promisee will have the same two options; however, it may also be possible for the promisee to unilaterally continue with performance of her own promises and thus effectively force a performance onto the defaulting promisor.[98] Purchasers have a third option — the restoration of benefits, and in particular a demand for the return of a deposit. The request for return of a deposit will be treated as bringing the contract to an end and the promisee will not be entitled to specific performance.[99] Similarly, a claim for damages alone will be seen as accepting the promisor's breach, repudiating the contract and thus bringing it to an end so that specific performance is rendered legally impossible. The law cannot enforce what is dead.[100]

An election by a promisee requires no formal documentation, thus caution must be exercised if the promisee wishes to preserve her options for as long as possible. It is possible for the promisee to plead in the alternative, requesting both specific performance and

---

97   See *Semelhago* v. *Paramadevan*, [1996] 2 S.C.R. 415 at 425, Sopinka J.

98   The difficulty in this area is to justify why a plaintiff should be able to impose an unwanted performance on to the defendant rather than be required to accept the anticipatory breach and crystallize his loss in damages. See *White & Carter (Councils) Ltd.* v. *McGregor* (1961), [1962] A.C. 413 (H.L.).

99   See *MacNaughton* v. *Stone* [1949] O. R. 853 (H.C.); and *Arbutus Garden Homes Ltd.* v. *Arbutus Gardens Apartments Corp.*, [1996] 7 W.W.R. 338 (B.C.SC.). Even if the request for return of the deposit is not satisfied, the promisor cannot later opt for specific performance.

100   See *Johnson* v. *Agnew* (1979), [1980] A.C. 367 at 392, Lord Wilberforce (H.L.).

damages,[101] although at some stage an election will have to be exercised. The problem is that the promisee's actions can also be construed as a waiver of the promisor's breach, giving rise to an estoppel and thus impacting upon the promisee's cause of action and remedial choices. Sharpe[102] has argued that the doctrine of election probably derived from estoppel, and that greater flexibility would be attained if the link was restored. One essential feature of estoppel is that it requires acts of detrimental reliance or change of position by the defendant to be operative. In the context of election, Sharpe argues that the plaintiff should be given flexibility to change initial election of remedies until such time as the defendant has detrimentally relied upon a particular election. The net effect of such a proposal would be to allow a plaintiff who has precipitously sought return of a deposit, or elected to take damages, to be able to renounce that election in favour of specific performance as long as the defendant had not detrimentally relied upon the plaintiff's initial choice. The plaintiff would still have to meet the threshold justifications for specific performance; a task probably made more difficult by the initial election.

Where the promisee pleads in the alternative, or simply maintains an action for specific performance, he must continue to be ready, willing, and able to perform (see discussion above). The contract remains alive for both parties, and the defendant is allowed to take advantage of any subsequent actions of the plaintiff to discharge or alter her obligations in ways that may impact upon the plaintiff's remedial choices. However, the defendant cannot abrogate or pre-empt the plaintiff's right to elect by agreeing to submit to specific performance after initially breaching the contract. In *Beauchamp v. Coastal Corp.*[103] the plaintiff had entered into a contract for the purchase of the defendant's ship. The defendant had initially defaulted and the plaintiff commenced proceedings, pleading in the alternative for specific performance. The plaintiff later informed the defendant that it would elect to take damages and had only pleaded the specific performance claim because the defendant was contesting the court's jurisdiction *in rem* over the ship. The defendant then brought a motion, confessing to judgment and seeking the court to impose specific performance on the plaintiff. In both trial court and Court of Appeal the defendant lost. It is difficult to reconcile this case with the dicta of Sopinka J. in *Semelhago v. Paramadevan*, where he wrote that

---

101   See *Dobson v. Winton & Robins Ltd.*, [1959] S.C.R. 775.
102   Above note 3 at § 10.840–10.880.
103   [1986] 2 F.C. 298 (C.A.).

the claim for specific performance can be seen as reviving the contract to the extent that the defendant who has failed to perform can avoid a breach if, at any time up to the date of judgment, performance is tendered.[104]

I would suggest that a distinction must be maintained between pleadings, proof, and election of remedy. Pleadings can be worded in the alternative even if both ultimately cannot prevail. In this sense, pleadings alone cannot constitute an election. Proof narrows choice in that the claim to a remedy will be dependent upon establishing breach of contract, or that the contract is still capable of specific performance, or that the plaintiff has established his entitlement to the remedy. Elements of proof arise throughout the relationship of the contracting parties. Election of remedy may exist up until judgment, subject to what has been found during the proof stage. Indeed, it is possible that circumstances can contrive to render the voluntary election moot. This would occur, for example, where third party rights have been created over the property prior to judgment, as in *Johnson* v. *Agnew*.[105] Thus, it is possible for the plaintiff to have made an election, or rather have the factual circumstances determine an election for him, prior to judgment. In this sense, Sopinka J. is correct in asserting that the defendant can cure his breach by tendering performance at any time subject to damages for delay, inconvenience, or abatement, which renders the notion of an election redundant. In *Beauchamp* it would be better to conclude that the actual election was made when the plaintiff advised the defendant that it was intending to seek damages and had only pleaded specific performance to maintain the jurisdiction in the Federal Court. After that point in time the defendant could not impose a contract on the plaintiff by confession to judgment.

Although an election to seek damages is irrevocable, the same cannot be said of an election for specific performance. Even after judgment for specific performance has been granted, it is possible for the plaintiff to discontinue seeking the defendant's compliance with the order, and elect to take damages for breach. In *Johnson* the plaintiff vendor, after initially being successful in gaining a decree of specific performance, was later unable to effect its own performance, largely because the failure to complete had exacerbated the plaintiff's financial condition such that the mortgagee had exercised its power of sale. The plaintiff then elected to take damages. Lord Wilberforce confirmed this right: "if the

---

104 Above note 97 at 426.
105 Above note 100, and discussion below.

order for specific performance is not complied with by the purchaser, the vendor may *either* apply to the court for enforcement of the order, *or* may apply to the court to dissolve the order and ask the court to put an end to the contract."[106]

In this case it is something of a misnomer to speak of an election, because the intervention of the mortgagee effectively exercised the election for the plaintiff.

Hetherington[107] has questioned whether the plaintiff must return to seek the court's permission to dissolve the contract. The defendant's action in not complying with the decree for specific performance is not only a contempt of court, but continues to be in breach, or else constitutes a new breach of contract. This act alone establishes the right of the plaintiff to seek compensation at common law without the need for judicial sanction. However, the Ontario Court of Appeal has recently endorsed the notion that the court maintains a supervisory role once judgment has been rendered. In *Lubben* v. *Veltri & Sons Corp.*[108] the plaintiff vendor had successfully claimed specific performance against the purchaser. The contract contained a clause giving the purchaser a unilateral right to assign the contract anytime prior to closing, and after the specific performance decree was granted the purchaser purported to assign the deal to an impecunious numbered company. Both the trial court and the Court of Appeal indicated that once the decree had been granted the contract came under the "court's management and control." The decree compelled the purchaser to personally carry through their contractual obligations under the court's guidance. It would be contrary to common sense and public policy to allow the purchaser to avoid its obligations by now allowing the assignment.

FURTHER READINGS

ZARNETT, B., "Specific Performance" [1995] Spec. Lect. L.S.U.C. 193

---

106   *Ibid.* at 394 [emphasis in original].
107   See M. Hetherington, "Keeping the Plaintiff Out of His Contractual Remedies: The Heresies that Survive *Johnson* v. *Agnew*" (1980) 96 L.Q. Rev. 403 at 408.
108   (1997), 32 O.R. (3d) 65 (C.A.). See also *Gaspari* v. *Creighton Holdings Ltd.* (1984), 52 B.C.L.R. 30 (S.C.).

CHAPTER 12

SPECIFIC PERFORMANCE: SALE OF LAND

A. INTRODUCTION

It has been repeatedly said that land is considered unique and therefore there is a presumption that specific performance will be granted of any contract involving realty. The justification for this position is that no two pieces of land are identical and that each has a special and peculiar value to a purchaser.[1] With respect to the vendor's position, the doctrine of affirmative mutuality has created an equivalent presumption that specific performance will be granted to a vendor despite the ease in assessing damages. This may still accurately reflect the position in other common law countries; however, since the Supreme Court of Canada's judgment in *Semelhago* v. *Paramadevan*,[2] it cannot be assumed to accurately reflect the position in Canada.

---

1   See *Adderley* v. *Dixon* (1824), 1 Sim & St. 607, 57 E.R. 239 at 240–41, Leach V.C (Ch.).
2   [1996] 2 S.C.R. 415 [*Semelhago*].

B. PURCHASER'S APPLICATION

1) Adequacy of Damages

Recall from chapter 10 that the main argument supporting the paramount position of damages in our remedial taxonomy is the relative efficiency of resolving disputes. However, this efficiency can create an injustice where the quantification of particularly subjective interests forms an important part of the plaintiff's motivation for entering the contract. With respect to the sale of land, there has been a presumption that a purchaser's motivation towards a particular piece of property always carries with it a desire to satisfy a number of subjective goals. We can all readily identify with wishing to acquire our "dream home;" once we had found it, we would not readily part with it even for a king's ransom. Unfortunately, when we put this argument to scrutiny we quickly realize that it does not accord with the contemporary marketplace or our participation in that market. The market is far more dynamic than the law presumes.

The choice to purchase is not made because one particular property, romanticially viewed, meets our dream home ideal. Rather, the cold reality of what a person can afford, location, and number of bedrooms gives us a number of options unrelated to the unique characteristics of any individual home. We rarely reside in one house during our entire life. The advertisers' siren call to purchase a "starter home" or "handyman's special," or, at the other end of the life cycle, to realize savings from a now-too-large family home, all belie the uniqueness of those properties. The boring similarity of our suburban housing developments, made famous by Pete Seeger's rendition of Malvina Reynolds' song "Little Boxes" also undercuts any notion of uniqueness. The fact that people in urban centres are more likely to rent than own has created vast scope for property investors guided by principles of market return and the commodification of property as simply another investment vehicle.

Despite prior authority that confirmed the presumptive nature of specific performance,[3] the Supreme Court of Canada has revised this position in *Semelhago*.[4] The appellant vendor had refused to close a real-estate transaction for the sale of his residential home. The respondent had agreed to buy the appellant's home for $205,000. The deal

---

3   See *Kloepfer Wholesale Hardware & Automotive Co.* v. *Roy*, [1952] 2 S.C.R. 465; and *Bashir* v. *Koper* (1983), 40 O.R. (2d) 758 (C.A.).

4   Above note 2.

was to be financed by a cash payment of $75,000 and $130,000 raised on a mortgage of the purchaser's existing home. The purchaser intended to sell his existing home within a six-month period of completion on his new home, and had taken an open mortgage over his existing home for this period. At the time of completion, in October 1986, the purchaser's existing home was worth $190,000. At the time of trial, November 1990, it was worth $300,000. The vendor's home was worth $325,000 at the date of trial. At the trial the purchaser elected to take damages rather than specific performance. The trial judge awarded the purchaser $120,000, being the difference in contract price and market value of the vendor's home at the date of trial. Such an assessment was in keeping with the Ontario Court of Appeal's decision in *306793 Ontario Ltd.* v. *Rimes*.[5]

The vendor appealed. He argued that such an award amounted to a windfall. The purchaser not only received the increase in value of the property he was going to buy, but also kept the increase in value of the house that he already owned, but which was to be sold to finance the purchase of the new home. An alternative assessment proposed by the vendor, but rejected by the trial judge, would simply have computed the difference between the increase experienced by the vendor on his house and the increase experienced by the purchaser retaining his existing house. Another alternative, suggested by the purchaser, would have computed the increase in value on the vendor's house and subtracted the costs incurred by the purchaser to achieve that increase. Thus, the carrying costs of the $130,000 mortgage between closing and trial dates, and the notional interest the purchaser would have made on investing the cash payment of $75,000 for the same period would have to be factored in. This would give damages as $80,810. The Court of Appeal had accepted this last alternative.

The vendor appealed to the Supreme Court of Canada. The issue before the Supreme Court was simply the appropriate damage assessment principle. The Supreme Court reluctantly affirmed the approach taken by the Court of Appeal. However, Sopinka J., speaking for the majority, also took the opportunity to comment on the appropriateness of seeking specific performance. LaForest J. declined to address this issue without the advantage of argument. Sopinka J. first suggested that any generosity in damage assessment in these types of cases be only justified if the property is unique:

---

5   (1979), 25 O.R. (2d) 79 (C.A.).

While at one time the common law regarded every piece of real estate to be unique, with the progress of modern real estate development this is no longer the case. Residential, business and industrial properties are all mass produced much in the same way as other consumer products. If a deal falls through for one property, another is frequently, though not always, readily available.

It is no longer appropriate, therefore, to maintain a distinction in the approach to specific performance as between realty and personalty. It cannot be assumed that damages for breach of contract for the purchase and sale of real estate will be an inadequate remedy in all cases.

Courts have tended, however, to simply treat all real estate as being unique and to decree specific performance unless there was some other reason for refusing equitable relief ...

Specific performance should, therefore, not be granted as a matter of course absent evidence that the property is unique to the extent that its substitute would not be readily available.[6]

Sopinka J. went on to endorse the approach taken by Estey J. in *Asamera Oil Corp.* v. *Sea Oil & General Corp.*[7] to the that there must be "some fair, real and substantial justification" for the claim to specific performance. Had Sopinka J. been trying this case *de novo*, the purchaser would not have met this standard. The parties had both been content to present the case on the basis that the purchaser had been entitled to specific performance.

The Supreme Court's position is not entirely new. Prior to the decision in *Semelhago* a number of lower court decisions had distinguished the availability of specific performance for contracts where the property was being purchased for investment purposes.[8] In the cases subsequent to *Semelhago* courts have readily conceded that there has been a sea change in approach to the discretion to grant specific performance. Generally, courts now require the plaintiff to adduce some evidence of uniqueness of the property before being entitled to specific perfor-

---

6   *Semelhago*, above note 2 at 428–29.

7   (1978), [1979] 1 S.C.R. 633.

8   See *Heron Bay Investments Ltd.* v. *Peel-Elder Developments Ltd.* (1976), 2 C.P.C. 338 (Ont. H.C.); and *Chaulk* v. *Fairview Construction Ltd.* (1977), 14 Nfld. & P.E.I.R. 13 (Nfld. C.A.). See also J. Berryman, "Specific Performance, Uniqueness and Investment Contracts: A Canadian Perspective" [1984] Conv. & Prop. Law. 130; and P.J. Brenner, "Specific Performance of Contracts for the Sale of Land Purchased for Resale or Investment" (1978) 24 McGill L.J. 513.

mance.[9] However, few courts have systematically explored varying concepts of uniqueness.

For the plaintiff to prove that she has some fair, real and substantial justification for specific performance, she must now demonstrate that damages are an inadequate remedy. This approach will presumably reconcile the availability of specific performance with the position taken when seeking other equitable remedies. It also requires courts to articulate inadequacy criteria in a much more systematic way than in the past.

2) Uniqueness

Perhaps the best articulation of the varying concepts of uniqueness is a lower court decision by Adams J. in *Domowicz* v. *Orsa Investments Ltd.*[10] Together with other family members, the plaintiff, a lawyer, had started investing in apartment buildings. They entered into the purchase of an apartment complex from the defendants, to close in 1986. The sale did not in fact close and the plaintiffs were successful in gaining summary judgment for specific performance in 1987. The Court of Appeal set that judgment aside. The matter then came back on trial in 1993. The parties were unable to resolve their dispute and brought the action forward to determine whether specific performance was available, and what damages would follow if it were not. On the availability of specific relief, Adams J. cited extensively from academic commentaries about the nature of contracting and the supremacy of damages as a remedy. The common law has always sought to limit a promisee's damages by requiring certainty and foreseeability, and by denying recovery for avoidable losses. Specific performance frustrates all three limitations, but particularly that relating to avoidable losses, or the obligation to mitigate. After reviewing the case law which supported a presumption of specific relief, Adams J. saw reconciliation with contract doctrine on the basis that the specific relief presumption should be rebuttable and dependent upon a real exploration of the inadequacy of monetary relief.

What types of inadequacy of monetary relief will count? In reviewing the facts of this case, Adams J. pointed to at least three attributes

---

9   See, for example, *Triopiano* v. *Stonevalley Estates Inc.* (1997), 36 O.R. (3d) (Gen. Div.) (giving specific performance of a ravine lot); and *Fossum* v. *Visual Developments Ltd.*, [1997] A.J. No. 1255 (Q.B.) (specific performance of highly valued historic property in the heart of the city).

10   (1993), 15 O.R. (3d) 661 (Gen. Div.), add'l reasons (1994), 20 O.R. (3d) 722 (Gen. Div.), aff'd (1998), 40 O.R. (3d) 256 (C.A.) [*Domowicz*].

that may have supported the plaintiffs' right to specific performance. First were the particular physical characteristics of the property. In their evidence the plaintiffs had tried to suggest that this property had unique features that made it particularly desirable as an apartment block. Some of these characteristics were its street level parking, its red brick rather than white glazed brick exterior, its state of good repair, its lack of close proximity to other similar high-rise buildings, its east/west location, and its suite mix. Adams J. singularly dealt with each of these matters and concluded that other properties on the market in the vicinity had comparable characteristics. Some of these characteristics Adams J. dismissed as *post facto* reasons raised to justify pursuit of specific performance. Second, were the particular transactional characteristics of this property. Much turned on the ability of new owners to seek rent review as a way to increase the return on the property; although subsequent legislative changes dramatically altered this potential. This argument proved to be something of a two-edged sword for the plaintiffs. Adams J. saw in the financing and rent review increases an incentive to quickly turn the building over, which went to undermine the plaintiffs' assertions that they intended to hold onto the property for a long period. Third, were the personal or subjective attributes of the plaintiffs in wishing to purchase this particular building. The plaintiffs asserted that the building was being acquired for one of the plaintiffs' retirement. Again, this proved unconvincing in light of that plaintiff's age (late thirties), and the fact that another property had been purchased the same day by the plaintiffs and sold a year later. As Adams J. pondered, why wasn't that kept for the plaintiff's retirement? Adams J. summed up the plaintiffs' attempt: "While an admirable attempt was made to characterise this apartment building as physically and commercially unique, the evidence in this respect is insufficient."[11]

Adams J. alluded to at least three types of inadequacy of monetary relief, or characteristics of uniqueness:

- the physical attributes of the property,
- the commercial or transactional attributes, and
- personal factors of the purchaser.

---

11   *Ibid.* at 688. In the subsequent action on the damages assessment, Adams J. confined the plaintiffs to damages measured as the difference in contract and market price assessed at a reasonable period after the breach, being three months. At this point the plaintiffs could have reasonably been expected to find a similar investment property in mitigation of their losses. Damage assessment reported at 20 O.R. (3d) 722 (Gen. Div.).

Traditionally, our civil law has confined itself to the first, and these are likely to remain important; however, other types of inadequacy should be recognized. The recognition of commercial uniqueness, should be welcome, although this will probably carry significant evidential burdens. Certainly the evidence adduced in *Domowicz* appears to have been quite extensive on this point. In addition to the plaintiff's evidence on the uniqueness of the property the defendant vendor also introduced numerous comparison sales to show that other buildings provided a similar return and were available in the market.

We should be careful not to immediately conclude that a plaintiff should be confined to damages when purchasing realty for investment purposes. That is an easy temptation to follow, but can only be justified if other properties existing at the time of contract completion presented comparable investment opportunities. In particular, it may be the surrounding contextual features (for example, the ability to get rent increases or a particular planning consent), which take an otherwise mundane building and colour it as being commercially unique. The plaintiff should be given an opportunity to prove this if specific performance is desired.

With respect to personal factors, it is impossible to predetermine what might influence a court. Perhaps one example is in *Fossum v. Visual Developments Ltd.*[12] The plaintiff was successful in getting an order for specific performance of an agreement to purchase a property in downtown Edmonton. The property was described as being part of the most "valuable retail space in Edmonton." It had on-site parking, also rare in Edmonton, as well as usable retail space in the basement. These particular physical attributes make the property unique; however, the most significant factor was that the plaintiff's existing property adjoined the purchased property, separated only by a laneway that the plaintiff desired to have closed. This latter feature is an example of one that is peculiar and personal to the plaintiff.

Inadequacy of monetary relief may take other forms — difficulties in damage quantification may be one such feature. The financial incapacity of the defendant to pay may be another. These characteristics have not normally carried a great deal of weight when considering specific performance, although they have been considered when determining the availability of injunctions. These issues may become more important as aspects of the plaintiff's "personal circumstances."

---

12   Above note 9.

Although the Supreme Court of Canada and lower courts may still speak of a presumption favouring specific relief in real estate contracts, it would appear that the plaintiff carries much of the burden to prove a fair, real, and substantial justification in seeking the remedy. The burden of proving this threshold requirement in other equitable remedies, notably injunctions, clearly lies on the plaintiff. In *Domowicz* itself, much of the evidence appeared to have originated with the plaintiffs with respect to uniqueness, although there was also considerable evidence from the defendant, which was ultimately preferred.

The approach now favoured in Canada had earlier been summarily dismissed in Australia.[13] It has also been criticised in the United Kingdom,[14] on the basis that it does not protect subsequent sub-purchasers of the property should the purchaser now be confined to damages rather than being granted specific performance. Other criticisms are that without specific performance purchasers are discouraged from making sub-sales before completion, and that the purchaser may not have their resale profits protected if they are not reasonably foreseeable. Some of these criticisms can be met by encompassing the expanded notion of uniqueness criteria suggested above: subsequent resale should be viewed as either a "transactional attribute" or a "personal circumstance" of the plaintiff.

In this sense, the decision in *Chaulk v. Fairview Construction Ltd.*[15] is open to criticism. In that case the purchaser's actual resale of properties bought from the vendor was used as a reason to deny specific performance. The purchaser had proved by his own actions that the property was being acquired solely for investment and speculative purposes. The decision is wrong. Even in an assessment of damages a plaintiff is not expected to sacrifice accrued property rights nor violate the interests of third parties as acts of mitigation. Rather, the very existence of those factors make specific performance appropriate because of the unique situation confronting the plaintiff. Where the resale is a mere possibility rather than a reality, the question becomes why a speculator in property should be favoured over traders in shares or other commodities?[16]

---

13   See *Pianta v. National Finance & Trustees Ltd.* (1964), 180 C.L.R. 146 Austl. H.C.

14   See G.H. Jones & W. Goodhart, *Specific Performance*, 2d ed. (London: Butterworths, 1996) at 130.

15   Above note 8.

16   See R.J. Sharpe, *Injunctions and Specific Performance*, looseleaf (Aurora, Ont.: Canada Law Book, 1998) at § 8.70.

3) The "Interest" in Land

Although the most common action for specific performance concerning land is the enforcement of an agreement of sale and purchase, the remedy is, available for other more transient interests in land. For example, in *Verrall v. Great Yarmouth Borough Council*[17] the National Front, a political party known for its xenophobic views, had applied to a local Conservative-controlled municipal council to be permitted to hold their annual conference utilizing a municipal hall. The council had been aware that the National Front conference would bring with it protests, nevertheless, it went ahead and rented the hall. Local elections changed the composition of the municipal council and a new Labour-led majority purported to rescind the previous council's decision to rent the hall. The National Front sought to rent alternative halls but could not find any community prepared to rent to them. It therefore brought an action for specific performance against the council. The trial judge had awarded specific performance, and the Court of Appeal affirmed the trial court's decision. Although earlier authority had suggested that you could not get specific performance of short-term leases,[18] this was no longer good law. In this case, factors such as the importance of allowing political parties a right to organize and operate, freedom of expression, and the fact that organizing a conference of this nature entailed a long lead-up time to make arrangements for delegates, justified the awarding of specific performance.

No doubt the more transient the interest in the property, the more difficult it becomes to satisfy the threshold test and prove that damages would be an inadequate remedy. It is the surrounding factors in *Verrall*, factors which are either transactional or personal characteristics, which lift this case from the routine. There is no reason to have arbitrary restrictions on lesser interests in land if all other criteria can be satisfied.

4) Specific Performance of Foreign Land

The general approach to conflict of laws questions concerning foreign land are that the law of the place where the land is situated governs the rights over the property (*lex situs*). However, from an early English case,[19] courts recognized that equity's *in personam* jurisdiction could apply to a defendant amenable to court service, even if her property lay

---

17   (1980), [1981] Q.B. 202 (C.A.).
18   See *Glasse v. Woolgar & Roberts (No.2)* (1897), 41 Sol. J. 573.
19   See *Penn v. Lord Baltimore* (1750), 1 Ves. Sen. 444, 27 E.R. 1132 (Ch.).

abroad. Thus, it is now accepted in Canada that where a plaintiff has a dispute justiciable within the court's jurisdiction, the defendant can be held liable to specific performance concerning land held in another jurisdiction. This is the position providing that service can be effected because the defendant is present within the court's jurisdiction, or can be served under the appropriate provincial rules relating to service outside the court's jurisdiction. This approach is said to be based on the fact that equity acts *in personam*: thus, it is the defendant *in person* who is being directed to transfer the land to the plaintiff, rather than the court directly on the property itself. Four criteria must be met before a local court will exercise this jurisdiction:

1) The court must have *in personam* jurisdiction over the defendant. The plaintiff must be able to effect service or the defendant must agree to submit to the court's jurisdiction.
2) There must be a personal obligation running between the parties. The defendant's conscience must be affected if he were to insist upon his strict legal rights. This will be found where there is a contract, trust or other equitable obligation in existence.
3) The domestic court must be able to supervise the execution of the judgment.
4) The court will not exercise jurisdiction if the order would be of no effect in the foreign country, although it will act if the only impediment is that the foreign jurisdiction would not recognize the personal obligation upon which jurisdiction is based.[20]

The last criterion will only have effect where what is being proposed in the domestic court's order would be illegal in the foreign jurisdiction. The fact that the order of the domestic court acts *in personam* will usually take the plaintiff outside this criterion.

The distinction between acting *in personam* and directly adjudicating on the rights concerning real property can be illustrated in the enforcement of the court's order. If the land was situated within the court's jurisdiction, the court could ultimately order a transfer of the property to the plaintiff by judicial sale. However, if the land is situated in a foreign country there is no way to ensure compliance without the agreement of the court in the country where the land is situated. In a similar situation, Canadian courts would not reciprocate by recognizing a foreign equitable *in personam* decree.[21] The distinction between

---

20 Accepted in *Catania* v. *Giannattasio* (1999), 174 D.L.R. (4th) 170 (Ont. C.A.), paraphrasing J. G. McLeod, *The Conflict of Laws* (Calgary: Carswell, 1983) at 323–24.
21 See *Duke* v. *Andler*, [1932] S.C.R. 734.

acting *in personam* rather than adjudicating on the rights over the property directly may be difficult to maintain, and justifies a circumspect approach in this area.

Where the action arises in one province, but the land is situated in a different province the courts have subjected the dispute to the test articulated in *Amchem Products Inc.* v. *British Columbia (Workers' Compensation Board)*[22] and *Tolofson* v. *Jensen; Lucas (Litigation Guardian of)* v. *Gagnon*[23] to establish the appropriate forum to hear the dispute. On resolution of this issue specific performance can be granted, relying upon the *in personam* nature of the relief, requiring the defendant to convey the property situated in the other province.[24] Alternatively, a stay of proceedings may be issued, requiring the plaintiff to commence his action in the more appropriate forum where there is a real and substantial connection.[25]

C. VENDOR'S APPLICATION

A vendor's action for specific performance appears to contradict the notion that a plaintiff should be left her damages remedy if that is adequate. The vendor's claim is only for the loss of the expectancy on the sale. If the purchaser has breached, the vendor should be expected to mitigate her loss, similar to any other sale agreement that is breached.[26] However, in spite of the obvious logic of this argument, there are numerous instances where a vendor has been granted specific performance.[27] The rationale for this has been based on affirmative mutuality,[28] a now discredited doctrine. It is possible that much of our understanding in this area will have to be revised in light of the Supreme Court of Canada's ruling in *Semelhago*.[29] The cases subsequent to that decision do appear to have a slightly different nuance, in

---

22 [1993] 1 S.C.R. 897.

23 [1994] 3 S.C.R. 1022.

24 See *War Eagle Mining Co.* v. *Robo Management Co.* (1995), [1996] 2 W.W.R. 504 (B.C.S.C.), admitting of the possibility of an order but declining jurisdiction in favour of Saskatchewan, where the property was located.

25 See *Avenue Properties Ltd.* v. *First City Development Corp.* (1986), 32 D.L.R. (4th) 40 (B.C.C.A.), stay refused.

26 See *LeMesurier* v. *Andrus* (1986), 54 O.R. (2d) 1 (C.A.), leave to appeal to S.C.C. refused [1986] 2 S.C.R. v. [*LeMesurier*].

27 See *Landmark of Thornhill Ltd.* v *Jacobson* (1995), 25 O.R. (3d) 628 (C.A.).

28 Discussed in chapter 10.

29 Above note 2.

which the vendor is expected to provide evidence of why damages would be an inadequate remedy rather than rely upon any presumption to that effect.

In *Westwood Plateau Partnership* v. *WSP Construction Ltd.*[30] the vendor had entered into a complex agreement to sell land in two stages. Stage one was completed. It was the intention of the purchaser to develop the lands. Before granting subdivision approval, the local municipality required the construction of a drainage channel. The vendor constructed the channel, but the purchaser refused to complete the deal on the basis that the vendor had materially altered the lands when building the drainage ditch. In addition, the purchaser claimed the vendor could not convey adequate title to certain creek beds that had run across the land. The court awarded the vendor specific performance. In doing so Sigurdson J. noted that this agreement was not executory but rather partly executed. The purchaser had been in possession for a considerable period of time and had in fact made significant improvements to the property in expectation that the deal would close.[31]

In *Hoover* v. *Mark Minor Homes Inc.*[32] the vendor had agreed to sell a two-acre block of land to the purchaser. Prior to completion the purchaser became aware that part of the property had been used as an abattoir and contained a blood pit on it. Changes were made to the agreement obliging the vendors to fill the blood pit with sand. While doing that work, the vendor had trucked clay fill onto the property and had demolished the blood pit rather than filling it. The purchaser refused to close claiming that the agreement had been breached, and sought recovery of a mortgage she had advanced to the vendor. The vendor then counter-claimed for specific performance. After the vendor had received notice that the purchaser intended to repudiate the contract, he had sought unsuccessfully to sell the property. Evidence from two local real-estate brokers indicated that it was a unique property with a limited market, and that the price the vendor had attempted to sell it for had been reasonable. Under these circumstances, Leitch J. granted the vendor a decree of specific performance, stating that the unique circumstances surrounding this property made

---

30   (1997), 37 B.C.L.R. (3d) 82 (S.C.).

31   See also *Scully* v. *Cerney* (1996), [1997] 2 W.W.R. 222 (B.C.C.A.).

32   (1998), 75 O.T.C. 165 (Ont. Gen. Div.). See also *Comet Investments Ltd.* v. *Northwood Logging Ltd.* (1998), 22 R.P.R. (3d) 294 (B.C.S.C.), awarding specific performance to a vendor who had assembled a four-acre block especially for the purchaser.

damages inadequate and that the risks of resale should transferred to the purchaser.[33]

In both of these cases it would appear that the courts are developing criteria with which to scrutinize the vendor's claim that damages would be inadequate. A similar analysis to that in *Domowicz*[34] can be applied. In *Westwood Plateau Partnership* the personal circumstances of the vendor, the fact that it is a partially completed deal, and that the vendor has let the purchaser into early possession, justify the awarding of specific performance. In *Hoover* both the unique characteristics of the property and the transactional aspect, the fact that there is a limited market for this type of property in its location, justify specific performance.

Hoover also suggests that difficulty in selling the property alone may justify shifting the risk of resale onto the purchaser. This harkens back to an earlier justification for granting a vendor specific performance, namely, that the award gives the vendor the complete contract price immediately rather than requiring her to reassume the risk of the marketplace before bringing suit against the purchaser. However, while the lack of a market in which the land is readily saleable may make damage quantification more difficult, there is no reason why a vendor of land should be treated differently than other sellers of goods. Rarely would there be absolutely no market available, and the damages remedy will always protect the vendor's expectation, that is, the difference between the contracted price and what the vendor has realised in the marketplace.

Regrettably, the decision of the Ontario Court of Appeal in *Landmark of Thornhill Ltd.* v. *Jacobson*[35] would seem at odds with recent developments, although it was decided before *Semelhago* was rendered. In this case the appellant, a developer of condominiums, had sold the respondents a condominium to be financed by a vendor take-back mortgage, which the purchaser would assume on closing. The purchasers had refused to close, raising uncertainty about the mortgage in light of a court ruling which had questioned this type of financing as being in breach of the *Condominium Act*[36] — an appeal of that ruling was before the Court of Appeal at the time. The parties attempted to resolve their dispute touching the validity of the financing scheme. The vendor wanted to protect its right to recover the mortgage interest payments if

---

33 Compare with *Taylor* v. *Sturgeon* (1996), 156 N.S.R. (2d) 147 (S.C.), where the vendor failed in an action for specific performance because it could not establish that the land was unique and thus did not have a readily available market.

34 Above note 10.

35 Above note 27.

36 R.S.O. 1990, c. C.26.

an appeal upheld the validity of the scheme, while the purchasers wished to be free to arrange their own financing without incurring any liability for interest owed on the vendor take-back mortgage. The purchasers moved into the condominium on an interim basis pending the eventual closing, and tendered performance on their terms, which was refused. They then treated the contract as having been repudiated. The purchasers did not want to submit to the vendor's mortgage, despite having initially agreed to it, and they were attempting to use the validity ruling to avoid the arrangement. The vendor, reluctant to forego the advantage of the mortgage, sued for specific performance of the original contract. The purchasers requested the return of their deposit. The trial judge had held for the purchasers on the basis that the original agreement had been amended to exclude the vendor take-back mortgage.

The Court of Appeal disputed the trial judge's finding, indicating that there was nothing in the evidence to suggest that the vendor had given up this right. On the right to specific performance the court said:

> In spite of the fact that a vendor of real property is getting nothing unique from his side of the bargain, specific performance has traditionally been awarded to vendors of real property as well as purchasers, on the basis of mutuality of remedies.
>
> It was argued by counsel for the purchasers that condominium apartments in modern multi-unit buildings are in no way unique, and should not, therefore, be subject to specific performance decrees at the plea of either vendor or purchaser. However, while many condominium units are of the mass-produced carbon copy variety, there are many which are truly unique. It is clear that uniqueness is an important factor for the court to consider in the exercise of its discretion to grant specific performance. However, the non-defaulting party should not be put in the position of having to prove the uniqueness of realty in order to succeed. On the other hand, a defaulting party should be required to prove any lack of uniqueness on which it wishes to rely.
>
> In determining whether or not to exercise discretion in favour of specific performance, the court should look not only at the nature of the property involved, but also the related question of the inadequacy of damages as a remedy. In addition, because of the equitable nature of the remedy, the court should take into account the behaviour of the parties.[37]

---

37   *Ibid.* at 636.

It is unfortunate that the type of uniqueness on which the Court of Appeal focuses is only the particular characteristics of the property. It seems strange that in order to resist specific performance the burden is cast on to the purchaser to prove that the property is not unique. There is no reason why the vendor should be advantaged in this way by being the recipient of a presumption in his favour.[38] It would have been better for the Court of Appeal to have relied upon the difficulty the vendor was facing in reselling the property in light of the collapse of the condominium market at the time.

D. SPECIFIC PERFORMANCE WITH ABATEMENT

1) Purchaser's Action for Specific Performance with Abatement or Compensation

It is possible for the purchaser to accept less than what was promised by the vendor and to seek an abatement of the purchase price or compensation for the deficiency. The purchaser commonly has to elect to either rescind the contract for breach or accept the performance tendered by the vendor and seek abatement — the corollary of this is for the purchaser to seek specific performance and abatement simultaneously. Obviously, there is room for abuse in allowing such a claim. A purchaser may wish to recover for what has turned out to be an improvident bargain by claiming that the vendor promised more in the contract than has been tendered. For this reason the courts have closely scrutinized abatement claims. The purchaser must show that the abatement arises from either a deficiency in respect to title or for some other contractual term of the agreement that has not been fulfilled[39] — the vendor is unable to convey all the property described in the contract, for example, or that some encumbrance affects the property, which the vendor has not disclosed or cannot remove. The plaintiff has not been allowed to base the abatement on an innocent misrepresentation because this would be tantamount to giving damages for an innocent misrepresentation, an action still prohibited at

---

38 And see the comments of Lax J. in *11 Suntract Holdings Ltd.* v. *Chassis Service & Hydraulics Ltd.* (1997), 36 O.R. (3d) 328 at 349 (Gen. Div.) [*11 Suntract Holdings*].

39 See *Sokoloff* v. *5 Rosehill Avenue Developments Inc.* (1998), 21 R.P.R. (3d) 176 (Ont. Gen. Div.) (failure of condominium developer to build according to agreed specifications)

common law.[40] The purchaser's only choice in this situation is rescission. Similarly, where the plaintiff was aware of the defects at the time of contracting it has been assumed that the purchaser entered the agreement knowing of, and accepting, those deficiencies.[41] A final restraint on the purchaser's action is that it appears that a request for abatement is lost after the contract has been fully executed.[42]

The quantification of the abatement can be difficult. The courts speak of compensation rather than damages, which may suggest that some measure other than the purchaser's expectancy should be used.[43] Since the fusion of law and equity this debate appears to have become somewhat sterile. In *Sokoloff* v. *5 Rosehill Avenue Developments Inc.*[44] a condominium developer, anxious to secure sales, had agreed to provide the services of an architect and to incorporate certain internal structural features. The developer failed to incorporate these features to the purchaser's satisfaction, but had forced the purchaser to take possession on a without-prejudice basis. At the time for tendering performance, the purchaser sought an abatement of the purchase price. Gans J. allowed the abatement. Compensation was to be quantified on the following principles:

a) Assessing compensation is, for all intents and purposes, the same task as assessing damages for breach of contract.

b) In instances involving specific performance, a purchaser, in so far as such is possible, is to be placed in the same position as if the contract had been performed — in this respect, the purchaser can recover damages for loss of bargain.

c) Damages for loss of bargain can be established by:
   i)   providing the purchaser with a rateable reduction from the purchase price without regard to the actual value of the land,
   ii) reimbursing the purchaser for the cost of remediation,
   iii) providing the purchaser with the difference between the value of the land without the defect and with the defect,
   iv) providing the purchaser with the difference between the purchase price and the value of the land without the defect.

---

40   See *Rutherford* v. *Acton-Adams*, [1915] A.C. 866 (P.C.) [*Rutherford*].
41   See *Bullen* v. *Wilkinson* (1912), 3 O.W.N. (C.A.).
42   See *Di Cenzo Construction Co.* v. *Glassco* (1978), 21 O.R. (2d) 186 (C.A.).
43   For example, it has been suggested in *Grant* v. *Dawkins*, [1973] 1 W.L.R. 1406 (Ch.), that abatement compensation cannot exceed the amount of the purchase price. See also the criticism by Jones & Goodhart, above note 14 at 286.
44   Above note 9.

d) In cases of this nature, the court is not wedded to any particular methodology so long as it has regard to the material circumstances, including the intention of the parties, in determining the purchase price at first instance.[45]

Gans J. accepted the evidence of a real estate agent as to the diminished value of the condominium with the defects, and assessed the abatement as $55,215 representing 13.5 percent of the original purchase price.

It is common to find that the right of the purchaser to seek abatement is qualified or restricted by an express term in the agreement of sale and purchase. The term, or annulment clause, entitles the vendor to terminate a contract and return the purchaser's deposit, if the vendor is unable or unwilling to meet an objection or requisition on title made by the purchaser. Indeed, the clause has been included to preclude the purchaser's action for specific performance and abatement, and has the effect of preventing the plaintiff imposing a judicially-determined abatement of purchase price on the vendor.[46] The Supreme Court of Canada has held that such a clause does not excuse a vendor from making "genuine efforts," or from acting "capriciously or arbitrary," to obtain what is necessary to carry out the contract, nor from "repudiating a contract; for a cause which he himself has brought about."[47]

This has been interpreted as creating two distinct duties on the vendor. The first, applicable at the time the agreement is entered into, requires the vendor to not act recklessly or with "unacceptable indifference" toward the purchaser. (Reckless behaviour would be, for example, knowing of an irremovable defect at the time of contracting but, nevertheless, entering into an agreement with the hope of being able to deliver a clear title.) The second duty, applicable at the time of conveyance, requires the defendant to use reasonable efforts to carry the contract to fruition.[48]

2) Vendor's Action for Specific Performance with Abatement or Compensation

It may appear strange, but it is possible for the vendor to impose a less than complete performance upon a purchaser subject to abatement in

---

45 *Ibid.* at 183–84.
46 See *Louch v. Pape Avenue Land Co.*, [1928] S.C.R. 518; and *Selkirk v. Romar Investments Ltd.*, [1963] 1 W.L.R. 1415 (P.C.).
47 *Mason v. Freedman*, [1958] S.C.R. 483 at 486, Judson J.
48 See 11 Suntract Holdings, above note 38.

the contract price. This action stems from the fact that equity looks at the "substance and not merely at the letter of the contract."[49] If the vendor can convey "substantially" what the purchaser contracted for, then the vendor will be entitled to specific performance with abatement.[50] Substantial compliance is a matter of objective assessment, although it cannot be divorced from the legitimate subjective requirements of the purchaser.[51] In *LeMesurier v. Andrus*[52] the vendor was unable to convey a narrow strip abutting a private driveway amounting to 0.16 percent of the total property area. Such a discrepancy was regarded as being minor, and would have supported the vendor's claim for specific performance with abatement. In *Stefanovska v. Kok*,[53] the vendor could not remove a storm-water easement in favour of the municipality that ran along the boundary of the property. The easement affected 3.5 percent of the property but did not restrict use and enjoyment. Moldaver J. held such a defect was not substantial. In *Green v. Kaufman*[54] the Ontario Court of Appeal held that a purchaser could not repudiate the contract when the only impediment on title was a construction lien equivalent to 0.002 percent of the purchase price, which could be solved by a simple adjustment in the purchase price.

E. SPECIFIC PERFORMANCE OF BUILDING CONTRACTS

The specific performance of building contracts has often given rise to anomalous results. Because these types of contracts threaten to raise complex issues of court supervision, specific performance has often been denied. However, at the turn of the last century a number of railway cases arose in which a plaintiff vendor had sold land to a railway company in return for the erection of a station or siding on the land. Having acquired the land, the railway company would default on the remainder of the promise, and the vendor would sue. In a surprising

---

49   *Rutherford*, above note 40 at 869, Viscount Haldane.
50   See *LeMesurier*, above note 26.
51   See *Stefanovska v. Kok* (1990), 73 O.R. (2d) 368 (H.C.).
52   Above note 26.
53   Above note 51.
54   (1996), 95 O.A.C. 183 (C.A.).

number of these cases the vendors were successful.[55] Even prior to this period the courts had been quite imaginative in overcoming supervision problems. In *Allen v. Harding*, Lord Cowper decreed specific performance of a building contract with the following arrangement for supervision: "each Side to choose two Commissioners, neighbouring Gentlemen; and if they cannot agree, then resort to the Ordinary of the Diocese to settle the Matter between them."[56] And in *Mosely v. Virgin*[57] the court instructed the Master in Chancery to supervise. The anomaly of this position became more apparent after the decision of *Ryan v. Mutual Tontine Westminster Chambers Assn.*[58] purported to clarify the issue of problems of supervision as grounds for refusing specific performance. Some seven years later, in a judgment devoid of all but one authority, Romer L.J. laid down what has become the classic test for specific performance of building contracts:

> There is no doubt that as a general rule the Court will not enforce specific performance of a building contract, but an exception from the rule has been recognised. It has, I think, for some time been held that, in order to bring himself within that exception, a plaintiff must establish three things. The first is that the building work, of which he seeks to enforce the performance, is defined in the contract; that is to say, that the particulars of the work are so far definitely ascertained that the Court can sufficiently see what is the exact nature of the work of which it is asked to order the performance. The second is that the plaintiff has a substantial interest in having the contract performed, which is of such a nature that he cannot adequately be compensated for breach of the contract by damages. The third is that the defendant has by the contract obtained possession of land on which the work is contracted to be done.[59]

With respect to the third criteria it is no longer a requirement that the work has to be performed on the land acquired by the defendant pur-

---

55 The impatience of the courts is perhaps best noted in the comments of James V.C. in *Wilson v. Furness Railway Co.* (1869), L.R. 9 Eq. 28 at 33: "It would be monstrous if the company, having got the whole benefit of the agreement, could turn round and say, 'This is the sort of thing which the Court finds a difficulty in doing, and will not do.' Rather than allow such a gross piece of dishonesty to go unredressed the Court would struggle with any amount of difficulties in order to perform the agreement.'

56 (1708), 2 Eq. Cas. Abr. 17, 22 E.R. 14 at 14 (L.C.).

57 (1796), 3 Ves. Jr. 184, 30 E.R. 959 (Ch.).

58 [1893] 1 Ch. 116 (C.A.).

59 *Wolverhampton Corp. v. Emmons*, [1901] 1 K.B. 515 at 524–25 (C.A.).

suant to the disputed contract. It is sufficient that the defendant is in possession of land upon which the work has to be done.[60]

A slightly wider proposition has been accepted in Canada. In *Tanenbaum* v. *W.J. Bell Paper Co.*[61] the plaintiff had sold a part of his land to the defendant. The contract required the defendant to build a road over the land he acquired to provide access to the remaining part of the plaintiff's land. The road was to be of a certain quality. In addition, the defendant was to provide a six-inch water main to the plaintiff's land. The plaintiff desired these conditions so that it could develop its remaining land as a commercial or industrial site. After acquiring the land the defendant built an inferior quality road and installed an undersized two-inch water main. The plaintiff sought specific performance. Gale J. accepted the proposition taken from *Williston on Contracts*:

> The basis of equity's disinclination to enforce building contracts specifically is the difficulty of enforcing a decree without an expenditure of effort disproportionate to the value of the result. But where the inadequacy of damages is great, and the difficulties not extreme, specific performance will be granted and the tendency in modern times has been increasingly towards granting relief, where under the particular circumstances of the case damages are not an adequate remedy.[62]

The focus of Williston's approach is on the inadequacy of damages rather than difficulties with supervision. In *Tanenbaum*, the defendant had alleged that the plaintiff would be adequately compensated in damages. The plaintiff refuted this argument by pointing out the difficulty in being able to quantify the effect inadequate servicing would have on the marketability of his remaining land. In addition, the contract had no covenant binding the defendant to keep the road in repair. It was impossible to quantify the repair costs, even presuming that the plaintiff would be able to effect repairs to the road still under the defendant's control. The court accepted the plaintiff's position and awarded specific performance. The defendant was required to remove the existing substandard road and install one according to the contract's description, and to lay an appropriately-sized water main.

The damage proportionality argument is particularly apposite where the defendant is being required to bring a defective performance

---

60   See *Carpenters Estates Ltd.* v. *Davies*, [1940] Ch. 160 at 164, Farwell J.

61   [1956] O.R. 278 (H.C.).

62   *Ibid.* at 307, quoting from *Williston on Contracts* vol. 5, rev. ed. by S. Willistion & G.J. Thompson (New York: Baker, Voorhis & Co., 1937) § 1423.

up the contract specifications.[63] Another way of effecting a similar result is to adjust the contract specifications with an abatement of the purchase price. In *Greenbaum* v. *619908 Ontario Ltd.*,[64] the plaintiff had entered into a contract with the defendant builder for construction of a home in an high-class subdivision. The house was to be 3700 square feet in size and to have a number of options specifically requested by the buyer. One of the contract's terms allowed the builder to make minor variations, and to terminate the contract if the house could not be built according to the applicable municipal bylaws. Another term restricted the purchaser's right to register notice of the agreement or a caution on the title of the land. A dispute arose between the parties and the buyer lodged a certificate of pending litigation on the title. The buyer sought specific performance of the original agreement, while the builder sought the lifting of the certificate of pending litigation, and summary judgment dismissing the buyer's claim. While the matter was being litigated the builder continued to build the home although the square footage of the design was reduced to 3536 square feet. Sutherland J. ordered the removal of the certificate of pending litigation. However, he also went on to consider the plaintiff's claim for specific performance. On this point Sutherland J. indicated that the plaintiff should not be entitled to insist upon a house of 3700 square feet. The foundations of the house and parameter walls had been built. Nor could it be determined in these proceedings whether the smaller home still complied with the contract specifications. However, the plaintiff could still indicate whether she wanted to proceed with the home being built, or to proceed with her action for damages alone. If she elected to pursue the house as being constructed she still had the right to go to trial and prove breach and thus request an abatement of the purchase price.

Sutherland J.'s decision on the availability of specific performance was based on the inadequacy of damages, the ability to determine what was specified under the contract, and the presence or absence of enmity between the parties. There was obvious cost involved if the foundations had to be pulled out and new ones installed for a larger home. The contract specifications still had to be determined, as was whether the builder had a right to vary the square footage of the home. The other details of the home could be supervised in that the home was still a builder's model and other homes provided comparisons in workmanship and amenities. As most of the remaining work was to be

---

63 Similar arguments are used to determine whether to award damages on a cost of reinstatement basis or to confine the plaintiff to diminution in value.

64 (1986), 11 C.P.C. (2d) 26 (Ont. H.C.).

performed by subcontractors, the enmity that existed between the parties would not be insurmountable.

Sutherland J. described his approach as being consistent with the "demonstrated trend toward a more flexible approach on the part of the Courts to the granting of specific performance of contracts, such as construction contracts involving detailed questions of compliance and supervision."[65] The facts in *Greenbaum* are somewhat unique in that Sutherland J. is really trying to provide a framework in which the parties can negotiate a settlement of their dispute before coming on for a full trial of the merits. However, his remarks on the availability of specific performance continue the liberalization commenced in *Tanenbaum*.

Another novel approach to building contracts was attempted in *Webster v. Garnet Lane Developments Ltd.*[66] The plaintiff successfully sought specific performance of a building contract for a new home. The court was concerned about the problems that may have arisen if the defendant, a building developer, was required to build the home. The court ordered that the defendant entrust sufficient funds to build the plaintiff's homes with a trustee, who would employ a third party to build the home according to the original specifications. In the Court of Appeal the plaintiff asked to substitute damages for the trial court's order. The Court of Appeal agreed, noting that damages would be a preferable remedy in the circumstances.

FURTHER READINGS

CHAPMAN, J.J., "A Stacked Deck: Specific Performance and the Real Estate Transaction" (1994) 16 Advocates' Q. 240 & 273

DA SILVA, O.V., "The Supreme Court of Canada's Lost Opportunity: *Semelhago v. Paramadevan*" (1998) 23 Queen's L.J. 475

DI CASTRI, J.V., *The Law of Vendor and Purchaser: The Law Practice Relating to Contracts for Sale of Land in the Common Law Provinces of Canada*, 3d ed. (Toronto: Carswell, 1989)

---

65   *Ibid.* at 54.
66   (1989), 70 O.R. (2d) 65 (H.C.), rev'd (1992), 10 O.R. (3d) 576 (C.A.), leave to appeal to S.C.C. refused [1992] S.C.C.A. No. 501.

HARPUM, C., "Specific Performance with Compensation as a Purchaser's Remedy — A Study in Contract and Equity" (1981) 40 Cambridge L.J. 47

HERSCHORN, A., "Specific Performance of Agreements for the Purchase and Sale of Land" (1991) 12 Advocates' Q. 171

PERELL P.M. & B.H. ENGELL, *Remedies and the Sale of Land*, 2d ed. (Toronto: Butterworths, 1998)

CHAPTER 13

SPECIFIC PERFORMANCE: SALE OF CHATTELS AND SHARES, AND AGREEMENTS FOR THE PAYMENT OF MONEY

A. INTRODUCTION

In this chapter we look at a number of discrete contracts concerning the sale of chattels, shares, and agreements for the payment of money. The area is complicated by certain statutory provisions which purport to impact upon the availability of *in specie* relief. In addition, apart from the situation of sale of goods of rare beauty and distinction, there has never been a strong argument for specific performance based on uniqueness or inadequacy of damages.

B. SALE OF GOODS

1) Background To the *Sale of Goods Act* Provisions

Prior to the enactment of the *Sale of Goods Act*, 1893[1] there were numerous examples of specific performance being granted for goods of rare beauty and distinction,[2] or those that had some other high subjective value to the buyer, such as a family heirloom.[3] These contracts

---

1   (U.K.), 56 & 57 Vict., c. 71.
2   See, for example, *Fells v. Read* (1796), 3 Ves. Jr. 70, 30 E.R. 899 (Ch.) [*Fells*] (silver altarpiece); and *Falcke v. Gray* (1859), 4 Dr. 651, 62 E.R. 250 (V.C.) [*Falcke*] (old jars).
3   See *Pusey v. Pusey* (1684), 1 Vern. 273, 23 E.R. 465 (Ch.) [*Pusey*].

supported specific performance because the goods were seen to be unique, and therefore damages were an inadequate remedy. In 1856 the United Kingdom enacted *The Mercantile Law Amendment Act, 1856*,[4] an Act requested by mercantile groups and designed, among other things, to make specific performance more readily available. The Act adopted practices from Scottish law, itself inspired by Roman law.[5] However, the legislation was never resorted to prior to its repeal in 1893, when it was replaced by section 52 of the *Sale of Goods Act, 1893*.[6]

Section 50 of the Ontario *Sale of Goods Act* states:

> In an action for breach of contract to deliver specific or ascertained goods, the court may, if it thinks fit, direct that the contract be performed specifically, without giving the defendant the option of retaining the goods on payment of damages, and may impose such terms and conditions as to damages, payment of the price, and otherwise, as to the court seems just.[7]

This section has been controversial. Despite the fact that its legislative purpose was supposedly to make *in specie* relief more readily available,[8] this has not happened. Spry points out that the section was meant to be *in addition* to any other rights the buyer may have had to specific performance in equity.[9] This construction of the legislation is favoured because the legislative goal was to expand availability[10] and, contrary to popular misconception, the Act cannot be viewed as a complete code of

---

4   (U.K.), 19 & 20 Vict., c. 97.

5   See W.E. Masterson, "Specific Performance of Contracts to Deliver Specific or Ascertained Goods Under the English Sale of Goods Act and the American Sales Act", in M. Radin & A.M. Kidd, eds., *Legal Essays in Tribute to Orrin Kip McMurray* (Berkeley: University of California Press, 1935) 439.

6   Above note 1.

7   R.S.O. 1990, c. S.1 Equivalent provisions can be found in other provincial statues: see Alberta *Sale of Goods Act*, R.S.A. 1980, c. S-2, s. 52; British Columbia *Sale of Goods Act*, R.S.B.C. 1996, c. 410, s. 55; Manitoba *The Sale of Goods Act*, R.S.M. 1987, c. S10, s. 53; Newfoundland *Sale of Goods Act*, R.S.N. 1990, c. S-6, s. 53; New Brunswick *Sale of Goods Act*, R.S.N.B. 1973, c. S-1, s. 49; Nova Scotia *Sale of Goods Act*, R.S.N.S. 1989, c. 408, s. 53; Prince Edward Island *Sale of Goods Act*, R.S.P.E.I. 1988, c. S-1, s. 52; and Saskatchewan *Sale of Goods Act*, R.S.S. 1978, c. S-1, s. 51.

8   See G.H. Treitel, "Specific Performance in the Sale of Goods" [1966] J. Bus. Law 211.

9   See I.C.F. Spry, *The Principles of Equitable Remedies Specific Performance, Injunction, Rectification and Equitable Damages*, 5th ed. (Sydney: LBC Information Services, 1997) at 55.

10 See the comments of Michaud C.J.K.B. in *George Eddy Co. v. Corey*, [1951] 4 D.L.R. 90 at 108 S.C.(A.D.) (N.B.) for an expansionist interpretation of the *Sale of Goods Act* provision.

equitable remedies touching sale of goods. The section is silent as to both a purchaser's right to interlocutory injunctive relief, and a vendor's right to specific performance.[11] Nevertheless, some courts have given a restricted interpretation to the provision particularly concerning what is understood to be "specific or ascertained" goods.

2) Non-ascertained Goods

Most academic commentaries suggest the leading case on the interpretation of the section is *Re Wait*.[12] The plaintiff sub-purchased 500 tons of wheat from the defendant. The shipment was part of a larger load, approximately 1000 tons, purchased by the defendant and shipped from North America. Prior to its arrival, the defendant went into bankruptcy. The receiver claimed the full shipment of wheat for all the creditors while the plaintiff brought an action for specific performance claiming entitlement to 500 tons of the load. The plaintiff had given its cheque for the wheat prior to its arrival. The problem is common enough — a clash between creditors and who in particular can claim priority over the bankrupt's assets. The plaintiff's main argument was brought on the grounds that the goods were "specific and ascertained," within the *Sale of Goods Act* and therefore it was entitled to specific performance. By a majority, the Court of Appeal rejected this submission. The legislative intent behind "specific and ascertained" was that the goods had been appropriated to the purchaser, in that they had been identified as the purchaser's goods at the time of sale ("specific" is defined this way in the *Act*), or in accordance with the agreement after the contract had been made.

The position on the *Act* in *Re: Wait* has been recently reaffirmed in *Re Goldcorp Exchange Ltd.*,[13] a decision of the Privy Council on appeal from New Zealand. In that case a group of purchasers had taken part in a scheme promoted by Goldcorp Exchange to allow smaller investors to purchase bullion and other precious metals. Under the scheme, Goldcorp Exchange would purchase bullion in bulk but would hold it for individual investors who were then issued a certificate indicating how much gold was held in their name. At no stage was the gold actually broken up into allotments. The inevitable happened — Goldcorp Exchange went bankrupt and there was insufficient gold to meet the demands of

---

11   See R.J. Sharpe, *Injunctions and Specific Performance*, looseleaf (Aurora, Ont.: Canada Law Book, 1998) § 8.300.

12   (1926), [1927] 1 Ch. 606 (C.A.).

13   (1994), [1995] 1 A.C. 74 (P.C.).

the investors or of other secured creditors. One of the investor's arguments was that a proprietary title had vested in them at the time of entering into the purchase agreements; or at the latest, when Goldcorp Exchange had acquired some bullion, by virtue of the agreement.

The Privy Council, Lord Mustill delivering the judgment, said they found the decision of the majority in *Re Wait* irresistible. Non-ascertained goods could be broken into two subgroups. One, "generic goods," are sold on terms that allow the seller to determine both how and from what source he will obtain the goods answering the contractual description. Two, goods sold "ex-bulk" that allow the seller to determine from a larger known source how much will be appropriated to meet the buyer's contract. In both categories, unless the parties create a different intention in their contract, no equitable title passes until the goods are ascertained. The creation of an equitable interest in the property in favour of the buyer, as when title has passed, is not a requirement for the granting of specific performance, but it does appear to be a significant factor in determining whether *in specie* relief will be granted.[14]

Undoubtedly, in the context of a bankruptcy these decisions are correct.[15] It would be wrong for the parties to use specific performance as a way to advance a proprietary interest over other creditors — although it is interesting to note that other equitable progeny (i.e., remedial constructive trust and declaration of trust by vendor) have been used in these same circumstances to do just that. However, this is not a reason to apply the same principles universally to all sale of goods settings. A number of earlier Canadian cases appear to contradict the direction of *Re Wait*. In *Fraser* v. *Kee*[16] the court awarded the purchaser specific performance of a contract to deliver five railway cars of potatoes. After the first four carloads were delivered the seller defaulted on delivering the fifth, claiming a dispute over where the potatoes were to be inspected. The contract provided for inspection on delivery; the defendant now wanted inspection to be at his cellars for fear that the buyer would reject an unusually large number of the potatoes. The

---

14   See *Redler Grain Silos Ltd.* v. *BICC Ltd.*, [1982] 1 Lloyd's Rep. 435 (C.A.) (injunction given preventing seller from selling goods after title had passed to the buyer).

15   The rationale offered by Atkin L.J. in *Re Wait*, above note 12 at 640 concerned the effect such an order would have on financing sales transactions. If an equitable interest was created merely because the interest of a sub-purchaser had been notified to a bank, banks would be extremely reluctant to loan finance on the security of holding the legal title by way of the bill of lading if that interest could be defeated through an action for specific performance.

16   (1916), 9 W.W.R. 1281 (B.C. Co. Ct.).

court awarded the purchaser specific performance pursuant to the *Sale of Goods Act*. From the judgment, it would appear that the defendant had more than five carloads of potatoes available for delivery, and that the goods only became ascertained in the *Re Wait* sense when they were loaded onto the cars. Nevertheless, the court accepted that the contract was specifically enforceable from its outset, following the law as articulated in *Holroyd* v. *Marshall*.[17] In that case Lord Westbury was prepared to give specific enforcement of contracts that fell into Lord Mustill's second category of "ex-bulk" agreements.[18]

A greater challenge to *Re Wait* has emerged in *Sky Petroleum Ltd.* v. *V.I.P. Petroleum Ltd.*,[19] a case dealing with the request for an interlocutory injunction of a long-term supply agreement. In that case the plaintiff, a retailer of petrol, had entered into a ten-year supply agreement with the defendant. The defendant was the sole supplier of the plaintiff's needs. During the Arab oil embargo, the defendant stopped supplying the plaintiff. The plaintiff had little chance of securing another supplier and would likely have had to declare bankruptcy. He brought an action for an interlocutory injunction. Goulding J. granted the injunction. In doing so, Goulding J. admitted that he was going against the "well-established and salutary rule" that specific performance would not be granted for a contract to sell and purchase chattels not specific or ascertained. However, he felt that this doctrine was based on the fact that in the case of an ordinary contract for non-specific or ascertained goods, damages were usually a sufficient remedy. In this case, faced with the prospect that an alternative supply could not be secured, and that the action was for interlocutory relief, such an order was justified.

Specific performance of long-term supply agreements and injunctions to enforce negative stipulations are both discussed later; however, these cases suggest that courts will go against the "well-established rule" that specific performance is not available for non-specific or

17   (1862), 10 H.L. Cas. 191, 11 E.R. 999 (H.L.).
18   Atkin L.J. criticized this aspect of Lord Westbury's judgment: see *Re Wait*, above note 12 at 634. Other Canadian cases that support an expansive interpretation of the *Sale of Goods Act* provision are *Re Western Canada Pulpwood & Lumber Co.* (1929), 38 Man. R. 378 (C.A.) (contract for lumber which was treated as ascertained after it was marked by the purchaser); and *George Eddy Co.* v. *Corey*, [1951] 4 D.L.R. 90 (N.B.) S.C. (A.D.) (sale of "all the mill cut" for a certain period). Both cases deal with the issue whether the goods were "ascertained." At the time of contract the goods were not "specific" but under the contract the goods became ascertained when the timber was assembled. In both cases, the purchaser is taking the entire output of the seller and thus there is no act of "selecting."
19   [1974] 1 W.L.R. 576 (Ch.) [*Sky Petroleum*].

ascertained goods.[20] It is also interesting to note that these cases originate as injunction applications, where the operation of the inadequacy of damages threshold is more apparent. What is needed in this area, as in the context of sale of land, is a more developed and systematic approach to the inadequacy of damages/uniqueness threshold. This area is being explored in the United States under the Uniform Commercial Code (U.C.C.) with the development of commercial uniqueness.

3) Commercial Uniqueness

The concept of "commercial uniqueness" is used to describe the circumstances that take an otherwise prosaic good, which under normal circumstances would never give rise to a decree of specific performance, and lift it into a unique good, based on the surrounding commercial context of the sale. It has been defined in a decision in New Zealand by Hammond J. (who is, incidentally, a former legal academic) as follows:

> By that [commercial uniqueness] is meant goods which are, in some sense, essential to the plaintiff's business and for which the procurement of substitutes would cause disruption to that business for some reason or other. Severe delay would be one such reason; lack of expertise would be another; or high transaction costs (to a successful plaintiff) still another. This at least may be a concept that is capable of carrying the law forward, and it has some affinities with the developed North American concept of an "inability to cover." The traditional law has an aesthetic quality (which is appropriate in very particular, but quite rare, cases); commercial uniqueness is a broader concept, and capable of reaching a much wider range of cases.[21]

Commercial uniqueness is a concept that has found favour in the United States under the U.C.C. § 2-716. The provision reads:

---

20   For other Canadian injunction cases that have discussed the possibility of granting an injunction which amounts to specific enforcement of the contract, see *Baxter Motors Ltd. v. American Motors (Canada) Ltd.* (1973), 40 D.L.R. (3d) 450 (B.C.S.C.) (enforcing a franchise agreement to continue to deliver cars for the plaintiff to sell); and *Burnside Industrial Packaging Ltd. v. Canada Post Corp.* (1994), 131 N.S.R. (2d) 181 (S.C. T.D.) (injunction denied seeking to enforce Canada Post to continue servicing retail outlets operated by the plaintiff).

21   *Butler v. Countrywide Finance Ltd.*, [1993] 3 N.Z.L.R. 623 at 636 (H.C.) (considering specific performance of light fixtures sold as security in a scheme to finance a motel business). Ultimately, the remedy was declined because of vagueness in describing the fixtures covered by the agreement.

1) Specific performance may be decreed where the goods are unique or in other proper circumstances.

2) The decree for specific performance may include such terms and conditions as to payment of the price, damages, or other relief as the court may deem just.

3) The buyer has a right of replevin for goods identified to the contract if after reasonable effort he is unable to effect cover for such goods or the circumstances reasonably indicate that such effort will be unavailing ....

The official commentary states that "this Article seeks to further a more liberal attitude than some courts have shown in connection with the specific performance of contracts of sale," and that:

[i]n view of this Article's emphasis on the commercial feasibility of replacement, a new concept of what are "unique" goods is introduced under this section. Specific performance is no longer limited to goods which are already specific or ascertained at the time of contracting. The test of uniqueness under this section must be made in terms of the total situation which characterizes the contract.

Under U.C.C. § 2-716 one of the key determinants to specific performance is the assessment of ability to replace. The provision is not restricted to impossibility of replacement but allows a buyer to bring an action for specific relief where she would experience considerable difficulty, expense, or delay to replace, or where there is market scarcity of the contracted goods. Courts in the United States have enforced long-term supply contracts for the provision of propane gas to a subdivision,[22] the supply of carrots[23] and cotton,[24] agreements for the supply of aviation fuel in short provision during the Arab oil embargo,[25] the supply of cryolite needed for aluminum production which was in short supply,[26] and to enforce a contract for the supply of low-sulphur coal

---

22 See *Laclede Gas Co. v. Amoco Oil Co.*, 522 F.2d 33 (8th Cir. 1975), rev'd on other grounds 531 F.2d 942 (8th Cir. 1976).

23 See *Campbell Soup Co. v. Wentz*, 172 F.2d 80 (3rd Cir. 1948), but declining specific performance because it would be harsh to impose it on the buyer under the circumstances.

24 See *R.N. Kelly Cotton Merchant Inc. v. York*, 494 F.2d 41 (5th Cir. 1974).

25 See *Eastern Air Lines. Inc., v. Gulf Oil Corp.*, 415 F. Supp. 429 (S.D. Fla. 1975).

26 See *Kaiser Trading Co. v. Associated Metals & Minerals Corp.*, 321 F. Supp. 923 (N.D. Cal. 1970).

so that a public utility could meet its environmental emission targets.[27] In all these cases it is the surrounding circumstances, creating shortages in supply, that justify the awarding of specific performance.

The approach adopted in the U.C.C., coupled with an expanded notion of commercial uniqueness as described by Hammond J. would do much to liberalize the remedy of specific performance in sale of goods. Together with the new direction being followed in the sale of land, adopting this approach would bring these areas together to provide some uniformity. The analysis of uniqueness which I suggest flows from *Domowicz* v. *Orsa Investments Ltd.*[28] would be equally applicable in the context of sale of goods. In many of these cases, the initial action is an interlocutory injunction to restrain breach of contract or to seek a mandatory injunction of some aspect of the contract. The action at the interlocutory stage begins in a setting where inadequacy of damages is a significant threshold requirement and where courts have generally been willing to entertain varying conceptions of that criterion. While the remedial purposes of interlocutory and final judgment (although many of these cases stop at the interlocutory proceedings) the evidential record and legal arguments are likely to be duplicated. Harmonizing, the applicable test with respect to adequacy of damages for these equitable remedies will simplify litigation, improving both litigation costs and timeliness of relief.

4) Specific and Ascertained Goods

Where the goods are specific or ascertained, specific performance has been more readily granted where the buyer can prove that they are unique. This has certainly been the approach in the case of family heirlooms and other items of rare beauty and distinction,[29] although the issue is still one for the court's discretion.[30] Where the goods are specific or ascertained the courts are far more willing to consider other factors (besides the particular characteristics of the goods themselves), when considering whether damages would be an adequate

---

27   See *Orange and Rockland Utilities Inc.* v. *Amerada Hess Corp.*, 324 N.Y.S.2d. 494 (S.C. 1971).

28   (1993), 15 O.R. (3d) 661 (Gen. Div.).

29   See *Fells*, above note 2; *Falcke*, above note 2; *Pusex*, above note 3.

30   See *Cohen* v. *Roche* (1926), [1927] 1 K.B. 169 (specific performance refused of a contract to sell an antique chair of no special value or interest); and *Taylor* v. *Eisner*, [1993] 4 W.W.R. 98 (Sask. C.A.) (specific performance of a herd of elk refused because they were not unique).

remedy and whether the goods are unique. In particular, courts have looked at transactional characteristics surrounding the goods. Thus, in an Australian case, *Dougan* v. *Ley*,[31] the court awarded specific performance in the sale of a car, not because the vehicle was unique, but because it carried with a taxi licence which, owing to regulation, was severely restricted in supply. In *Behnke* v. *Bede Shipping Co.*[32] the court awarded specific performance of the sale of a ship because, although old, the ship had new boilers and motors installed which allowed the buyer, a German company, to immediately register it on the German registry. In this sense the ship had particular value to the buyer.[33] In *Simmons & McBride Ltd.* v. *Kirkpatrick*[34] the court awarded specific performance in the sale of a car because, despite the buyer's best efforts, another one could not be found at the time. In *Kristian Equipment Ltd.* v. *Urano Rentals Ltd.*[35] the court granted specific performance of a contract for the sale of generating equipment, subject to a determination of a third party's security interest. The plaintiff was able to give three justifications favouring specific relief. One, the generator's particular characteristic being able to generate large amounts of power in isolated mining communities, meant that there was a "very limited potential market" for the equipment. Two, the buyer had made substantial payments on the equipment and there were doubts as to the seller's solvency. Three, the buyer wished to proceed with the transaction.

While the two latter cases suggest that scarcity of market and inability to find a replacement favour a buyer, the courts have downplayed these issues in other cases. Thus in *Société des Industries Métallurgiques S.A.* v. *Bronx Engineering Co.*[36] specific performance was refused of a contract for the sale of a slitting machine, despite the fact that a replacement machine would take nine to twelve months to build,

---

31   (1946), 71 C.L.R. 142 (Austl. H.C.)

32   [1927] 1 K.B. 649 [*Behnke*].

33   It has been said that a plaintiff is *prima facie* entitled to specific performance of a contract to buy a ship, see *Behnke*, *ibid.* This is no longer a universal rule and the plaintiff will now have to show that damages are inadequate and that the ship has particularly unique characteristics: see *Gleason* v. *Ship Dawn Light* (1997), 130 F.T.R. 284 (T.D.), overruled on another point (1998), 223 N.R. 155 (F.C.A.); and *C.N. Marine Inc.* v. *Stena Line A/B and Regie Voor Maritiern Transport, The Stena Nautica (No. 2)* [1982] 2 Lloyd's Rep. 336 (C.A.).

34   (1945), 61 B.C.R. 467 (S.C.).

35   (1988), 68 Sask. R. 134 (Q.B.).

36   [1975] 1 Lloyd's Rep. 465 (C.A.).

and where the court admitted that the plaintiff would experience difficulties in quantifying damages.[37]

With some exceptions, the cases on specific performance of specific and ascertained goods appear to be cognizant of the wider commercial setting in which the dispute arises, and to formulate an appropriate remedial response including *in specie* relief. Although not explicitly articulating the argument, courts are considering aspects of commercial uniqueness and adequacy of damages criteria, beyond the traditional focus on particular physical attributes of the goods. Physical attributes, transactional and personal characteristics, together with assessments on ability to replace because of market shortage, all inform the exercise of the court's discretion.

5) Sellers Action for Specific Performance

The interest a seller has in performance is to secure the price of the goods sold. Section 47 of the Ontario *Sale of Goods Act*[38] makes express provision for the seller to maintain an action for the price, where property in the goods has passed (section 47(1)), or where the contract expressly specifies when the price is to be paid regardless of when property is to pass (section 47(2)).[39] Under this provision, the seller could also maintain an action for the cost of storage when the buyer refuses to take delivery under section 36 — this will be tantamount to specific performance. Where property has not passed, the seller is left to her action for non-acceptance of the goods. Under section 48, she may maintain an action for damages which will be measured as the difference in price between the contract and market price at the date of breach. The *Act* is silent on whether the seller can maintain an action for specific performance where property has not passed to the buyer and where section 42(2) does not apply: in this situation the Act would appear to confine the seller to damages. However, as pointed out by Spry[40] and Sharpe,[41] the *Sale of Goods Act* is not a comprehensive code

---

37 This case has been criticized for its unfairness: see G.R. Stewart, "Enforced Performance of Contracts of Sale of Goods — Trends Toward Greater Flexibility and Usefulness" (1981–82) 3 Advocates' Q. 18; and G.H. Jones & W. Goodhart, *Specific Performance*, 2d ed. (London: Butterworths, 1996) at 145.

38 Above note 7.

39 See G.H.L. Fridman, *Sale of Goods in Canada*, 4th ed. (Toronto: Carswell, 1995) at 349.

40 Above note 9.

41 Above note 11.

of remedies and there seems no reason why a seller should be refused specific performance if she can mount the traditional threshold of "inadequacy of damages." Such a case may be where the seller is building a certain item to specifications, and there is little chance of resale to another buyer. Presumably, the seller could recover damages, which at the outside would be the contract price plus any other consequential losses incurred. However, this would still be subject to an obligation to mitigate. Where the seller wishes to shift the entire risk of mitigation and resale onto the buyer, specific performance may be the most effective form of relief.[42]

6)   Specific Performance under the United Nations Convention on Contracts for the International Sale of Goods

Canada and the respective provinces have enacted the United Nations Convention on the International Sale of Goods (CISG).[43] The CISG covers the formation and performance of all international sale of goods transactions, and was designed to provide its member states with a harmonized body of trade law respecting sales. In the area of specific performance, the CISG has attempted a compromise between the positions adopted in civil law countries, where specific relief is preferred over damage substitution, and common law countries, where damages are favoured over *in specie* relief.

Article 46 of the CISG outlines a buyer's remedies and includes the following:

1) The buyer may require performance by the seller of his obligations unless the buyer has resorted to a remedy which is inconsistent with this requirement.

---

42   This would appear to have been the case in an unreported New Zealand judgment, *Bates v. Western* (1 November 1993), Auckland CP 305/93 (H.C.), and discussed in R. Ahdar, "Specific Performance in the Sale of Goods Revisited" (1994) 22 Austl. Bus. L. Rev. 305.

43   See Ontario *International Sale of Goods Act,* R.S.O. 1990 c.I.10; Manitoba *The International Sale of Goods Act,* S.M. 1989-90, c. 18; Alberta *International Conventions Implementation Act,* S.A. 1990, c. I-6.8; New Brunswick *International Sale of Goods Act,* S.N.B, 1989, c.I-12.21; Nova Scotia, *International Sale of Goods Act,* S.N.S. 1988, c. I3; British Columbia *International Sale of Goods Act,* R.S.B.C. 1996, c.236; Saskatchewan *International Sale of Goods Act,* S.S. 1990-91, c.I-10.3; and Canada *International Sale of Goods Contracts Convention Act,* S.C. 1991, c. 13.

2)   .... [the buyer may require substitute goods where the goods do
not conform with the contract.]

3)   .... [the buyer may require the seller to repair and remedy any
non-conformity with the contract.]

Article 62 outlines the seller's remedies, and states:

> The seller may require the buyer to pay the price, take delivery or
> perform his other obligations, unless the seller has resorted to a rem-
> edy which is inconsistent with this requirement.

These provisions differ appreciably from equivalent *Sale of Goods Act*
provisions, in that they are not restricted to specific or ascertained
goods. The convention is also worded to give the buyer the right to
require the seller to perform, which does not appear to be conditional
on finding damages to be inadequate or proving that the buyer cannot
secure a replacement in the marketplace. This would tend more to the
civil law position. However, article 28 of the CISG qualifies the granting of specific performance. It states:

> If, in accordance with the provisions of this Convention, one party is
> entitled to require performance of any obligation by the other party, a
> court is not bound to enter a judgment for specific performance
> unless the court would do so under its own law in respect of similar
> contracts of sale not governed by this Convention.

This qualification, added in recognition of the different approach to specific performance practiced in common law countries, modifies the
rigid "require performance" standard of article 46. Article 28 limits specific performance "in respect of similar contracts of sale not governed
by this Convention." The interpretation of this provision is made difficult by the application of article 2 of the Convention. Article 2 excludes
from the Convention contracts dealing with the sale of stocks and
investments, ships or aircraft, and any consumer transactions. Thus,
these forms of contract can not be treated as "similar." To apply article
28 a domestic court must consider whether specific performance would
be made available in the case of a particular contract that could have
been made under the Convention if that contract had come within article 1. Article 1 states, "This Convention applies to contracts of sale of
goods between parties whose places or business are in different states."

Another interesting argument concerns the interplay between article 46(2) & (3) and article 28. In the case of a fundamental breach,
where the seller has delivered goods that fail to meet the contract
description, article 46 (2) provides the buyer with a right to require the
seller to substitute goods that filfull the contract. Article 46(3) pro-

vides the buyer with a right to require the seller to repair goods that fail to meet the contract description where it is reasonable to do so. Because these provisions deal with specific instances of defective performance, Honnold[44] has argued that they are *lex specialis* and therefore may qualify the general provisions contained in article 28. This would be a fairly astounding result, in that it would give buyers the right to correct defective performance without the need to prove either that damages are inadequate or that there was no possibility of securing an alternative supply in the marketplace. Apart from situations where the seller has failed to tender performance, which would therefore fall under article 46(1), this interpretation would tend to eviscerate much of article 28.

However, if article 28 is interpreted to import the restrictive interpretation given to the *Sale of Goods Act* by *Re Wait*,[45] then little reconciliation has been achieved. Certainly Canada would be more restrictive than the United States in this regard, which could only increase the prospect of forum shopping. It is hoped that the adoption of CISG can add to the impetus to relax the availability of specific performance, and that the approach taken in *Sky Petroleum* will be favoured.[46] Neither the rigidity of the "require performance" standard of article 46 nor the inflexible interpretation of the *Sales of Goods Act* should dominate this area. Rather, the inherent flexibility of the discretionary nature of equitable relief should be allowed to flourish.

7) Replevin and Interim Orders for Recovery of Personal Property

The common law action of replevin allows a person who is the owner of goods, or who had an immediate right to possession, to expeditiously recover the property. In Ontario the action is now caught under section 104 of the *Courts of Justice Act*[47] and rule 44 of the *Rules of Civil*

---

44   See J.O. Honnold, *Uniform Law for International Sales Under the 1980 United Nations Convention,* 2d ed. (Deventer, Neth. Kluwer Law and Taxation, 1991) generally at §§ 191 & 279, and specifically at § 285.

45   Above note 12.

46   Above note 19. See P. Schlechtriem, *Commentary on the UN Convention on the International Sale of Goods (CISG),* 2d ed., trans. G. Thomas (Oxford: Clarendon Press, 1998) at 190, 375; S. Walt, "For Specific Performance Under the United Nations Sales Convention" (1991) 26 Tex. Int'l L.J. 211; and J.M. Catalano, "More Fiction than Fact: The Perceived Differences in the Application of Specific Performance under the United Nations Convention on Contracts for the International Sale of Goods" (1997) 71 Tul. L. Rev. 1807.

47   R.S.O. 1990, c. C. 43.

Procedure.[48] The order allows a plaintiff to recover possession of the property and then prove lawful entitlement to ownership. Because the proceedings are commenced at an interlocutory stage, courts have insisted that the plaintiff provide "substantial grounds" of proof of ownership, together with evidence that the property was unlawfully taken, or is being unlawfully detained, by the defendant. "Substantial grounds" has been interpreted as being more than "reasonable or probable grounds" but less than "*prima facie*" grounds.[49] Traditionally, a plaintiff must have had possession of the goods at some time prior to claiming replevin.[50] However, other cases have indicated that it is sufficient for the plaintiff to prove an equitable title[51] or even a contractual right to possession[52] without ever having actually taken possession of the property. In *Canada (A.G.)* v. *Hoverlift Systems Ltd.*[53] the plaintiff sought replevin of an ice-breaking machine that was being manufactured by the defendant. The contract contained a clause that upon breach by the defendant the plaintiff could require delivery of the work, any work in progress, and other parts and material. The defendant breached the contract while constructing the equipment. The court ordered replevin of the partially-completed machine without determining whether title in the goods had passed to the plaintiff. Without the replevin action, the plaintiff would presumably have resorted to an interlocutory mandatory injunction and specific performance. But the plaintiff could not be assured of these remedies based on earlier case law (see discussion above, at section 4, "Specific and Ascertained Goods.") and certainly would have faced a higher threshold test of proof that damages were an inadequate remedy.[54]

The action for replevin is not without its own difficulties in execution. Ontario Rule 44 is quite detailed as to how the applicant is to go

---

48   R.R.O. 1990, Reg. 194. See British Columbia *Law and Equity Act*, R.S.B.C. 1996, c. 253, s. 57; Manitoba *The Court of Queen's Bench Act*, S.M. 1988–89, c. 4, s. 59(1); Manitoba *Court of Queen's Bench Rules*, r. 317; Alberta *Rules of Court*, r. 427; and Saskatchewan *Queen's Bench Regulations*, O.C. 433/1999, 23 June 1999, c. C-1.01 Reg 1, r. 4.6.

49   See *Clark Door of Canada Ltd.* v. *Inline Fiberglass Ltd.* (1996), 45 C.P.C. (3d) 244 (Ont. Gen. Div.).

50   See *Susin* v. *297509 Ontario Ltd.* (1978), 6 C.P.C. 206 (Ont. S.C. Masters); and *Manitoba Agricultural Credit Corp.* v. *Heaman* (1990), 70 D.L.R. (4th) 518 (Man. C.A.).

51   See *Carter* v. *Long & Bisby* (1896), 26 S.C.R. 430.

52   See *Canada (A.G.)* v. *Hoverlift Systems Ltd.* (1981), 36 A.R. 331 (Q.B.).

53   *Ibid.*

54   See G.R. Stewart, "Remedies — Replevin — Recovery in Specie" (1984) 62 Can. Bar Rev. 418.

about executing the order. In particular, the plaintiff must provide security in an amount equal to at least twice the value of the property subject to the order, or such other amount that the court may direct. The sheriff undertakes the actual replevin.

C. LONG-TERM SUPPLY AGREEMENTS — REQUIREMENT CONTRACTS

It is common for commercial entities to enter into long-term supply agreements. "Requirement contract" is the term used to describe contracts in which one supplier agrees to furnish all a buyer's needs for a particular commodity. An "output contract" is an agreement where the buyer contracts to take all the output from a supplier; for example, all the crop yield from the supplier's farm. These contracts have obvious advantages for both parties. Perhaps the most significant is that these agreements tend to iron out price fluctuations, which could work to either the advantage or disadvantage of both parties. Another advantage is the ability to maximize forward planning — in manufacturing, for example, ensuring the price and availability of a necessary commodity may be crucial to justify a large capital expenditure. In other situations, the agreement may be the product of buyers or sellers acting in consort to shore up bargaining power against a powerful single entity on the other side, as in franchise agreements. Common to most of these types of agreements is that they are relational contracts. Typically, the parties have had prior dealings, there may be a high amount of integration between the parties' operations, and the parties will be aware of the high costs involved should they breach the contract, necessitating a search for an alternative market or supplier. These agreements also tend to be for rather common goods, where it is the integration of the transactional features of the agreement that make it of particular value to the parties.

Upon breach of a long-term supply agreement the plaintiff will be entitled to her normal contract damage remedy. Where an alternative supplier or buyer can be found who will deal on similar if not identical terms, then the plaintiff should be willing to enter into a new agreement and allow the difference in contract price to be a measure of the damages. However, in many cases the market is either non-existent or inactive, such that reliable comparisons cannot be made or reasonable alternatives secured. This will be particularly problematical where the anticipated contract life is long, possibly including a price escalation clause, and where there is a high level of co-operation and integration between the parties. In these cases specific performance becomes more desirable, and, if available, even a court-ordered readjustment of the agreement's terms. Unfortunately, Anglo-Canadian law seems to lag behind the United States in providing *in specie* relief in these situations.

We saw in the previous section that Anglo-Canadian law generally resisted awarding specific performance of non-specific or non-ascertained sale of goods contracts. This result was generally based on the perception that similar goods could be readily acquired on the market, and that mere difficulty in being able to quantify damages would not in itself justify specific performance. A similar picture holds for the specific enforcement of long-term agreements.

In *Dominion Iron & Steel Co.* v. *Dominion Coal Co.*[55] the plaintiff had contracted to purchase all its coal supplies from the defendant. A dispute arose concerning the quality of the coal delivered, its suitability for steel making, and some periods of short delivery by the defendants. At the time of breach the contract price was below the market price of the coal and the defendant had started selling its coal to other buyers. The plaintiffs had been forced to purchase from alternative suppliers at a higher price. The Nova Scotia trial court and appellate courts both ordered specific performance of the supply agreement. In their minds this was a situation where damages were clearly an inadequate remedy. based upon the difficulty in quantification. The agreement had some 90 years to run and thus it was impossible to predict future market prices over so long a period. Even if that was done, the setting of appropriate discount (a measure of the effect of inflation and interest rates over a prolonged period) would be complex and difficult, and the eventual damages assessed so huge that it could cause the defendant's financial ruin (and thus in the plaintiff going uncompensated). The contract did provide for arbitration after each five-year period if the parties could not agree a new price for the coal. One argument raised by the defendant was that any arbitrated figure would approximate the market price and thus the plaintiff would not experience any loss after the next arbitration. The appeal court rejected this argument, indicating that the arbitration would reflect the fact that the coal seams were very close to the plaintiff's business and would likely produce a lesser figure than if the plaintiff was required to enter the market. Arbitration would also mean that another variable was introduced to set the contract price over which the parties had little control.[56] On appeal, the

---

55   [1909] A.C. 293 (P.C.).
56   See *Dominion Iron Steel Co.* v. *Dominion Coal Co.* (1908), 43 N.S.R. 77–44 at 143, Russell J. (C.A.).

Privy Council affirmed the lower courts on the interpretation of the contract but confined the plaintiff to damages. In the opinion of the Privy Council, this was not a contract where, on present authority, a court of equity would decree specific performance. No authority was given in support, and the cases cited by counsel raised the issue of difficulty in supervision rather than inadequacy of damages.[57]

The position taken in *Dominion Steel* can be contrasted with the cases dealing with interlocutory injunctions, and the use of injunctions to enforce negative stipulations. With respect to interlocutory injunctions, the courts are more willing to engage in supervisory problems and to balance the litigants' competing interests. Obviously, the effect of the order is limited in duration, which may justify a greater interventionist approach. With respect to injunctions to enforce negative stipulations (discussed below) we will see that the courts have been more willing to give specific performance, but in a roundabout fashion[58] — by diminishing the importance of proof that damages are an inadequate remedy, and not having a requirement to engage in complex acts of supervision where the decree is framed in negative rather than affirmative language.

The position in *Dominion Steel* can also be contrasted with the experience in the United States under U.C.C. § 2-716. The official commentary of the Code states:

> Output and requirements contracts involving a particular or peculiarly available source or market present today the typical commercial specific performance situation, as contrasted with contracts for the sale of heirlooms or priceless works of art which were usually involved in the older cases. However, uniqueness is not the sole basis of the remedy under this section for the relief may also be granted "in other proper circumstances" and inability to cover is strong evidence of "other proper circumstances."

---

57   See *Blackett v. Bates* (1865), L.R. 1 Ch. 117; and *Powell Duffryn Steam Coal Co. v. Taff Vale Rly Co.* (1874), L.R. 9 Ch. 331. Jones & Goodhart, above note 37 at 148 suggest that from these cases "it may be inferred that the Privy Council concluded that, since the coal supplied had to be reasonably suitable for the steel company's purposes, the contract required the court's constant supervision and hence was not specifically enforceable." It is interesting to note that the Nova Scotia appellate court was quite able to identify objective criteria, namely the percentage of sulphur and impurities that were permissible in the coal for the production of steel, upon which to base a decree of specific performance. The level of court supervision would have been quite minimal.

58   See, for example, *Sky Petroleum*, above note 19 and accompanying text.

Numerous long-term supply agreements have been enforced under this provision.[59] It is also interesting to note that in the United States the most contested argument has been adequacy of damages and whether cover can be secured on similar grounds as the contract, rather than concerns over difficulties with supervision, which is rarely raised. It would appear that the litigants' relationships are sufficiently strong that once a court resolution is made to grant specific performance, the parties move to work out an harmonious implementation plan. This fact has lead one commentator to argue for a judicial power to adjust long-term contracts where through an unanticipated disruption large losses are made by one of the parties.[60] It is probably also fair to say that in many of these contracts the defendant is not being required to perform a losing contract, but merely to forego larger profits that could be made if allowed to escape the current output or requirement contract. As a consequence, the motivation and incentive to escape the contract is lessened.

In some situations the dispute is not over price fluctuations but is about protecting the supply of an item integral to the plaintiff's business.[61] The protection of the buyer's goodwill or other business interests warrants *in specie* relief because damages will not adequately compensate the plaintiff. However, all these cases would appear to have been argued either as interlocutory or mandatory injunction cases.[62]

No doubt it is easier to assess damages that flow from breach of a long-term agreement today than it was at the turn of the nineteenth

---

59   See H. Greenberg, "Specific Performance Under Section 2-716 of the Uniform Commercial Code: 'A More Liberal Attitude' in the "Grand Style' (1982) 17 New Eng. L. Rev. 321, particularly at 347.

60   See R.A. Hillman, "Court Adjustment of Long-Term Contracts: An Analysis Under Modern Contract Law" [1987] Duke L.J. 1.

61   See Sharpe, above note 11 at § 8.480.

62   For example, *Baxter Motors Ltd.* v. *American Motors (Canada) Ltd.* (1973), 40 D.L.R. (3d) 450 (B.C.S.C.), interlocutory injunction awarded preventing the defendant from terminating a car franchise which had been in existence for 49 years: "a 'dealer franchise agreement' is not a mere contract for the sale of goods. It possesses many unique factors and creates goodwill which is effectively destroyed by termination of the agreement. Damages for breach of this agreement would be extremely difficult to ascertain and would not afford adequate compensation. The damages would not be limited to mere loss of profits on the anticipated sale of new units and parts": Anderson J. at 457. See also *Oceans Seafoods Ltd.* v. *Ichiboshi L.P.C. Ltd.* (1995), 163 N.B.R. (2d) 266 (Q. B. T.D.), interlocutory injunction granted requiring the defendant to stop selling her snow crab catch to anyone else other than the plaintiff. The plaintiff could show that without the defendant's supply the plaintiff's operating costs and overall long-term financial security could be imperiled.

century. The ability to model future predictive market behaviour has come a long way and some of the factors raised in *Dominion Steel*, such as discount rates, have since been standardized. Nevertheless, if the plaintiff wishes to take on the burden of proving that damages are inadequate, (normally where the market is either non-existent or inactive), there seems to be no real justification to arbitrarily denying specific performance.

D. CONTRACTS FOR THE SALE OF SHARES

Unlike sale of chattel contracts, courts have been more willing to grant specific performance of contracts for the sale of shares. A number of earlier authorities granted specific performance of these contracts, despite the clear inference that the shares were being acquired for investment purposes.[63] However, a distinction was soon drawn between shares freely available on the stock market, and where specific performance was declined, and those that were not, where the remedy was granted[64]. The modern-day rule now reflects similar concerns to sale of goods contracts: where the shares are commonly traded on the stock market and an alternative can be readily acquired, specific performance will be refused.[65] However, where the plaintiff can establish that she cannot purchase the shares on the market,[66] or that particular circumstances make the purchase unique, then specific performance will be awarded. For example, if the share purchase means that the plaintiff will obtain a controlling interest in the company,[67] or, if a plaintiff's share acquisition presents an opportunity to sell at a market premium that would be difficult to quantify, then specific performance will be decreed.[68] That a plaintiff may simply be purchasing shares for investment purposes, or is likely to quickly sell once a controlling interest has been acquired, does not appear to be determinative of the issue.[69]

---

63   See *Paine* v. *Hutchinson* (1868), 3 Ch. App. 388.

64   See *Duncuft* v. *Albrecht* (1841), 12 Sim. 189, 59 E.R. 1104 (Ch.).

65   See *Asamera Oil Corp.* v. *Sea Oil & General Corp.* (1978), [1979] 1 S.C.R. 633 at 644, Estey J. [*Asamera*].

66   See *Connor* v. *MacCulloch* (1974), 18 N.S.R. (2d) 404 (S.C. T.D.); and *Payne* v. *Memex Software Inc.*, [1998] B.C.J. No. 111 (S.C.).

67   See *Dobell* v. *Cowichan Copper Co.* (1967), 65 D.L.R. (2d) 440 (B.C.S.C.); and *First Finance Finders Ltd.* v. *Ewachniuk*, [1986] B.C.J. No. 821 (S.C.).

68   See *Asamera*, above note 65.

69   See *A.N.Z. Executors and Trustees Ltd.* v. *Humes Ltd.* (1989), [1990] V.R. 615 (S.C.).

The decision of the Supreme Court in *Semelhago* v. *Paramadevan*[70] is likely to have repercussions in this area, restricting specific performance when the purchaser is only acquiring the shares for investment purposes. This approach would strengthen the argument made by Sharpe, that only where market valuation is difficult should specific performance be awarded.[71] Paradoxically, vendors of shares have also been successful at getting specific performance, presumably on the basis of affirmative mutuality, although such awards are rare and may be explained on the peculiar facts presented. Many of these cases involve situations where calls remained to be paid on the shares and the vendor was attempting to establish who was responsible for meeting the call.[72]

E. AGREEMENTS FOR THE PAYMENT OF MONEY

Where the essence of a contract is the payment of money, and the breach lies in failure to pay, one naturally concludes that damages should be an adequate remedy and that specific performance is therefore not available. Indeed, this is the dominant principle in this area.[73] However, increasingly frequent we see cases where the surrounding circumstances make damages inappropriate and where specific performance has been ordered.

The dominant principle has been articulated by the Privy Council in *Loan Investment Corporation of Australasia* v. *Bonner*.[74] In that case the plaintiff had purported to purchase two properties from the defendant for £13,300, provided that on settlement the defendant would deposit with the plaintiff's loan and investment company the sum of £11,000 for a period of ten years at 7.5 percent. In this way the purchaser was requesting the vendor to finance the purchase, although rather than taking a mortgage back over the property the vendor would become an unsecured creditor of the purchaser's company. Prior to completion the defendant rescinded the agreement and the plaintiff

---

70   [1996] 2 S.C.R. 415.

71   See Sharpe, above note 11 at § 8.520–8.560.

72   See *New Brunswick & Canada Rly & Land Co.* v. *Muggeridge* (1859), 4 Drew. 686, 62 E.R. 263 (V.C.).

73   *Gray* v. *Cameron*, [1950] S.C.R. 401 [*Gray*].

74   [1970] N.Z.L.R. 724 (P.C.) [*Bonner*]. See also *South African Territories* v. *Wallington*, [1898] A.C. 309 (H.L.).

brought suit for specific performance and, alternatively, damages. The sole question before the Privy Council was the issue of appropriate remedy. The majority of the Privy Council characterized the agreement as being a composite of two distinct transactions; one, the sale of land, and two, an unsecured loan of money. While specific performance is routinely available in the former, it is not for the latter. The reason why it is not available is that

> [i]t would have a one-sided operation, creating a position of inequality. The borrower obtains immediately the whole advantage of the contract to him, namely the loan itself .... The lender on the other hand has to wait and hope for the payment of interest from time to time and for the eventual repayment of the capital. The court has means of compelling a party to pay a sum of money if he is able to do so. But no writ of attachment or sequestration or other equitable process can compel the borrower to repay the loan ....[75]

In this case, because it was predominantly of a commercial nature and the loan was a principal rather than merely ancillary transaction, specific performance was refused and the plaintiff confined to damages. However, in a strong dissenting judgment, Barwick C.J. rejected the characterization of the contract as being anything other than a sale of land. Even if the contract was simply the loan of money, it was not a principle of equity that inequality, outside hardship, or difficulty in making the borrower repay the loan should justify denial of specific performance of an agreement to loan money. Rather, it was the simple fact that damages were generally equally as beneficial to the plaintiff as specific performance. But this assumption was not always accurate and "must yield in any case when in fact in the particular circumstances damages would not do justice between the parties."[76]

The wisdom of Barwick C.J.'s approach seems to have been borne out in *Wight v. Haberdan Pty. Ltd.*[77] The plaintiff had entered into an agreement to purchase property that he intended to subdivide and develop, and had been encouraged to expand his proposal by assurances from the defendant that financing would be forthcoming. The plaintiff went ahead with his plans, incurring significant expenses along the way. When the deal was about to close, the defendant indicated that it would not provide financing. The plaintiff was being pressured by the vendor to close and commenced proceedings against the

---

75   *Bonner*, above note 74 at 735, Lord Pearson.
76   *Ibid.* at 742.
77   [1984] 2 N.S.W.L.R. 280 (S.C.).

defendant for specific performance of the financing agreement. The court granted the decree on the basis that the plaintiff did not have the time to arrange alternative financing and the scheme was such that the involvement of the defendant on other aspects of the property would make it unattractive to a new investor. Finally, the plaintiff would face difficulties in quantifying damages that would make it "extremely difficult, if not virtually impossible, to assess with reasonable accuracy."[78]

The decision in *Wight* seems to be correct.[79] It focuses attention on the application of the inadequacy of damages criteria rather than creating a special category of cases for money loans. However, a court will need to carefully scrutinize a claim of inadequacy so that the risk to the financier is not increased above what was envisaged in the initial contract.

Another area where there has been enforcement of agreements for the payment of money has been the specific performance of annuity contracts. These have been ordered on the basis that the decree avoids the plaintiff having to commence a multiplicity of suits as each annuity falls due.[80] Of course, the dynamic of the marketplace would now allow for the assessment of damages being the costs involved in purchasing an alternative annuity on the same terms from another life assurance carrier.

A monetary benefit to be paid to a third party presents a unique challenge for the law. The suit of the promisee may only support nominal damages in common law because the benefit is to be enjoyed by the third party. The third party does not enjoy an independent suit against the promisor because he lacks privity of contract, having provided no consideration for the promise. In the rare facts of *Beswick* v. *Beswick*,[81] the third party beneficiary also happened to be the administratrix of her late husband's estate and therefore enjoyed the advantage of being able to sue for enforcement of the annuity contract made between the defendant nephew and her deceased husband. The House of Lords granted specific performance in these circumstances, on the basis that damages would be an inadequate remedy as well as to avoid a

---

78   *Ibid.* at 290.

79   But compare with *Central Guaranty Mortgage Corp.* v. *Eastland Development Ltd.* (1991), 109 N.S.R. (2d) 200 (S.C. T.D.). On a summary judgment application Kelly J. doubted whether a contract to loan money for the purchase of property was not specifically enforceable.

80   See *Beswick* v. *Beswick* (1967), [1968] A.C. 58 at 97, Lord Upjohn (H.L.).

81   *Ibid.*

multiplicity of suits if the plaintiff was confined to damages.[82] The wider issue is the extent to which the law will allow a third party an independent right to enforce a contract made for her benefit. Both the Supreme Court of Canada[83] and the High Court of Australia[84] have demonstrated a willingness to circumvent the requirement of consideration where the justice of the situation dictates.

FURTHER READINGS

BRIDGE, M.G., *The Sale of Goods* (Oxford: Clarendon Press, 1997) at 531

ONTARIO LAW REFORM COMMISSION, *Report on Sale of Goods*, vol. 2 (Ottawa: Ministry of the Attorney General, 1979) at 436.

TREITEL, G.H., "Specific Performance in the Sale of Goods" [1966] J. Bus. Law 211

---

82   See also *Gray*, above note 73. The parties had entered into an agreement in which Gray agreed to assume the obligation to indemnify a company's indebtedness to the Royal Bank owed by Cameron and to relieve Cameron of his guarantee. In an action by Cameron to enforce this agreement the majority of the Supreme Court of Canada affirmed the lower court's order which awarded specific performance. The only way to comply with such a decree would appear to be to pay the debt guaranteed by Cameron to the bank. As the minority in dissent pointed out, this violated a long-standing practice not to grant specific performance of money contracts or contracts to pay money to a third party.

83   See *London Drugs Ltd.* v. *Kuehne & Nagel International Ltd.*, [1992] 3 S.C.R. 299; and *Fraser River Pile & Dredge Ltd.* v. *Can-Dive Services Ltd.*, [1999] 3 S.C.R. 108.

84   See *Trident General Insurance Co.* v. *McNiece Bros. Pty. Ltd.* (1988), 165 C.L.R. 107 (Austl. H.C.).

CHAPTER 14

SPECIFIC PERFORMANCE: CONTRACTS OF PERSONAL SERVICE

A. INTRODUCTION

The enforcement of contracts of personal service raises particular concerns for courts. The contract itself is unlike others in that it is heavily imbued with complex social and political overtones, as for most people their livelihood is a central part of their well-being. As well, employment law has undergone dramatic legislative change, often as a result of substantive principles and judicial practices being out of step with contemporary conditions and attitudes. Legislation creating specialty administrative tribunals for both unionized and non-unionized workers has removed from courts much jurisdiction over employment contracts. It has also transformed the issues, which are no longer adjudicated under the principles of private contract law but are now under the rubric of judicial review of administrative action.

The traditional rule in this area has been that courts would not order specific performance of a contract of personal service. However, even when this rule was being formulated, the use of an injunction to restrain breach of a negative stipulation often appeared to grant specific performance indirectly. While reverence is still paid to the traditional principle it does not accurately reflect the position today. Courts are now more willing to grant specific performance or an injunction restraining breach of a personal service contract, although the frequency of requests would appear to remain low.

B. TRADITIONAL APPROACH

The traditional rule, that specific performance would not be granted of a contract for personal service,[1] was underpinned by essentially four concerns:

- a lack of mutuality in that one party could not compel the other to actually perform the service promised,
- difficulty with court supervision of the decree,
- the perception that enforcement of a personal service decree was tantamount to involuntary servitude, and
- resistance to forcing parties back into a relationship where trust and confidence had been lost.[2]

Lack of mutuality has already been discussed in chapter 10, section E, "Mutuality." There it was seen that the objective behind mutuality is simply to give the defendant adequate assurance that any executory obligations owed to her will be carried out if she is ordered to specifically perform the contract. In a personal service contract, the employer's usual obligations will be to pay wages and provide work. On the employee's side, it will be to perform the assigned work. Where specific performance is sought for an employee's breach it would seem that the risk of lack of mutuality is easily met, all that has to be enforced is the employer's obligation to pay wages, a quantifiable monetary amount. Where specific performance is requested by an employee, lack of mutuality experienced by the employer raises concerns with how to ensure that the employee carries out the work in a diligent manner. The specific performance decree should not emerge as a license for idleness. However, since most contracts of employment contain "termination on reasonable notice" clauses, and the specific performance decree will not affect the ability to dismiss for cause, the employer's risk is marginal. Lack of mutuality should not be considered a serious impediment today.

Difficulties with supervision generally have also been discussed, in chapter 10, section D, "Problems with Supervision." There it was seen that the law is becoming more liberal in granting specific performance,

---

1   Historically, some contracts of personal service were often enforced by criminal proceedings: see D. Cohen, "The Relationship of Contractual Remedies to Political and Social Status: A Preliminary Inquiry" (1982) 32 U.T.L.J. 31.

2   See G.H. Jones & W. Goodhart, *Specific Performance*, 2d ed. (London: Butterworths, 1996) at 169.

as evidenced in cases like *Giles & Co. v. Morris*[3] and *Posner v. Scott-Lewis.*[4] In other respects there has been a hardening in demarcation between specific performance of an "activity" as against a "result," as evidented in *Co-operative Insurance Society Ltd. v. Argyll Stores Ltd.*,[5] (although it should be noted that this case did not concern a personal service contract, and the decision may not be followed in Canada). Not all personal service contracts are alike. Specific performance requiring an artist to perform in a movie or stage show can be described as much as effecting an "activity" as a "result." Similarly, requiring an employer to continue employing an employee in a position that he has performed well for a considerable period seems to pose little risk (apart from concerns about confidence and trust, discussed below). There is no uncertainty about what is required under the contract, and what the employee actually performs. Any productivity indicators used by the employer in the past will provide some objective criteria to evaluate an employee's compliance in the future.

The perception that enforcing a contract of personal service amounts to involuntary servitude arises from the fact that disobeying a specific performance decree is a contempt of court and can result in the imposition of fines or imprisonment. In the context of organized labour frequent resort is made to these heavy-handed remedies in an effort to punish the withholding of labour in an illegal strike. Obviously this is a one-sided argument. If an employee is able to bring an application for specific performance, he has discounted this perception, his service cannot be described as "involuntary." If the employer brings the application, the perception may be more real. However, it would be wrong to characterize the modern contract of employment as anything akin to servitude, as that term was understood in its historical context. Again, the right to terminate on reasonable notice held by both parties undermines any characterization of involuntary servitude.

The last concern, that courts are reluctant to force parties back together when their initial breakdown has demonstrated a loss of confidence and trust, is perhaps the strongest argument against more readily resorting to specific performance of personal service contracts. It would seem futile to require both parties to resume a relationship that required a high level of co-operation and communication if litigation is now the only means to attain that result. But we should not conclude that every contract of personal service demands this co-operation. The

---

3   [1972] 1 W.L.R. 307 (Ch.).
4   (1986), [1987] 1 Ch. 25.
5   [1998] 1 A.C. 1 (H.L.).

need for confidence and trust is clearly diminished where an employee is merely required to perform routine tasks of an impersonal nature, or where he works in a environment that has fairly well-defined objective productivity measures (such as sales targets, or production quotas). It should be noted that this is a distinctly one-sided argument, used by employers against being forced to take back a dismissed employee. In contrast, where the employee is required to personally advise or work closely with the employer, confidence and trust is probably a key characteristic of the relationship.

C. MODERN APPROACH

The modern approach to personal service contracts recognizes the inconsistencies of the traditional barriers to specific performance, and attempts to transcend the rhetoric that supports them by analyzing the true nature of the dispute and the litigants' interests. The decision of the English Court of Appeal in *Hill* v. *C.A. Parsons & Co.*[6] is widely held up as embodying this new approach. The plaintiff and others brought an interlocutory injunction application requiring their employer to re-employ them. The employer had dismissed the plaintiff as a result of a labour dispute, not because of any complaint over work performance. The employer had entered into a collective agreement with a trade union, which included a "closed shop" provision that precluded the employer from employing anybody other than a union member. The plaintiff had refused to join the trade union, and the employer had dismissed him. At trial, the injunction had been refused on the basis that to make the order would be tantamount to ordering specific performance of a contract for personal service. A majority in the Court of Appeal overruled the lower court. The real dispute was between the plaintiff and the trade union, over the issue of compulsory unionism and the propriety of a closed shop. Trade union legislation was about to be proclaimed that would restrict the union's right to bargain for a closed shop provision. Damages would be an inadequate remedy, because it would not reflect the fact that the plaintiff's rights were about to be "increased" as a result of the legislative changes. To the majority, the traditional approach was not an inflexible rule.

---

6   (1971), [1972] Ch. 305 (C.A.).

It would be wrong to take *Hill* v. *Parsons* too far.[7] Several important limitationing factors were addressed by the majority. First, the fact that the employer was not reluctant to continue employing the employee was noted. Second, the employer was still left with the ability to terminate employment after reasonable notice was given. In the facts of this case, within that time period the impending industrial legislation would be proclaimed. Third, even where the order was granted it did not require the company to offer the plaintiff actual work. Thus, as long as the employee remained ready and willing to work, the court would simply require the employer to continue to pay wages to the employee.[8] However, it is also interesting to note that the exception to the traditional approach largely advanced the employer's interest at the expense of organized labour.

The approach adopted in *Hill* v. *Parsons* has been termed the "sufficiency of confidence" test.[9] The test looks at a number of factors to determine whether the relationship is one that requires a high level of confidence, where specific performance will be refused, or whether there is a low level of confidence, possibly resulting in specific performance being granted, if the other discretionary grounds for granting relief are met. The factors reviewed in the test are: the nature of the work, the people with whom the plaintiff has to work, and the likely effect on the employer and her operation if forced to continue employing the plaintiff.[10]

Because the employer can always choose to terminate employment by giving the employee reasonable notice, it has been difficult for courts to escape the conclusion that at some point damages are an adequate remedy for breach of a contract for personal service. This has lead to the position that specific performance, and more often an interlocutory injunction tantamount to *in specie* relief, will only be awarded where "special circumstances" are present.[11] Special circumstances are

---

7   The case was described as "unusual" in *Chappell* v. *Times Newspapers Ltd.*, [1975] 1 W.L.R. 482 at 503, Stephenson L.J. (C.A.).

8   The last point has been varied in Canada, where it has been said that an employment contract can still be in good standing even though the plaintiff is no longer ready and willing to perform, as long as he or she has been clearly told by the other party that his or her services will not be required to be performed: see *Philp* v. *Expo 86 Corp.* (1987), 45 D.L.R. (4th) 449 at 461, Lambert J.A (B.C.C.A.) [*Philp*].

9   See Jones & Goodhart, above note 2 at 174.

10 See *Powell* v. *London Borough of Brent*, [1987] I.R.L.R. 466 (C.A.); and see R.J. Sharpe, *Injunctions and Specific Performance*, looseleaf (Aurora, Ont.: Canada Law Book, 1998) § 7.600.

11 See *Francis* v. *Kuala Lumpur Municipal Councillers*, [1962] 1 W.L.R. 1411 at 1418, Lord Morris (P.C.).

often found to exist where an employer has failed to observe certain procedural requirements in dismissing an employee,[12] or to preserve a peculiar pension or benefit entitlement.[13]

In Canada both the "sufficiency of confidence"[14] and the "special circumstances"[15] tests have found their way into law. Many of these cases cross over into administrative law, and involve suits for judicial review based on a right to due process before dismissal. Thus in *McCaw v. United Church of Canada*,[16] the defendant was ordered to reinstate the plaintiff to the church rolls of ordained ministers after it had failed to invoke the church's proper process for the disciplining or dismissal of ministers. And in *Shephard v. Colchester Regional Hospital Commission*[17] an interlocutory injunction was issued ordering the defendant to reinstate hospital privileges to a physician. The defendant had terminated the privileges because the plaintiff had failed to take a competency test, but under the contract the defendant had no right to impose such a test as a condition of conferring hospital privileges.

The cases involving office-holders are more complicated.[18] Because an office-holder normally holds his position at the pleasure of the appointing officer, and therefore determinable without notice or cause, there has traditionally been no right to reinstatement. However, the Supreme Court of Canada has held that an office-holder must be

---

12   See *Irani v. Suthampton and South West Hampshire Health Authority*, [1985] I.R.L.R. 203 (Ch.) (failure to carry out certain dispute procedures before dismissal); *Jones v. Lee* (1979), [1980] I.R.L.R. 67 (C.A.) (no hearing granted a headmaster before being dismissed); and *Vine v. National Dock Labour Board* (1956), [1957] A.C. 488 (H.L.) (lack of jurisdiction by disciplinary board which had dismissed a registered dock worker constituted an *ultra vires* act).

13   See the example given by Lord Denning in *Hill v. Parsons*, above note 6 at 314.

14   In *Red Deer College v. Michaels* (1975), [1976] 2 S.C.R. 324 at 344, Laskin C.J. cited with approval *Hill v. Parsons* and distinguished it from the case at hand on the very point that confidence between employer and employee had been maintained in *Hill v. Parsons* whereas it had been lost in the case before the Court.

15   See *Philp*, above note 8; and *Stevenson v. Air Canada* (1982), 35 O.R. (2d) 68 (Div. Ct.).

16   (1991), 4 O.R. (3d) 481 (C.A.). See also *Frogley v. Ottawa Presbytery of the United Church of Canada* (1995), 16 C.C.E.L. (2d) 249 (Ont. Gen. Div.).

17   (1991), 103 N.S.R. (2d) 361 (S.C. T.D.).

18   A distinction may also be made on the basis that office holders appointed under some statutory provision have traditionally not been regarded as employees subject to the law of master and servant. See also the discussion in *Simpson v. Blacks Harbour (Municipality of)* (1995), 160 N.B.R. (2d) 375 (Q.B. T.D.); and in *Hallyburton v. Markham (Town of)* (1988), 63 O.R. (2d) 449 (Ont. C.A.), particularly the dissent of Findlayson J.A.

accorded procedural fairness when being dismissed,[19] and thus judicial review will arise bringing with it the possibility of reinstatement. The right to procedural fairness has also been regarded as a contractual term that gives rise to the possibility of specific performance for its enforcement.[20]

While courts have started to relax the traditional rule on the availability of specific performance for personal service contracts, few if any have granted the remedy in areas which could not be described as presenting unique and unusual circumstances.

D. RE-EVALUATION OF THE NEED FOR SPECIFIC PERFORMANCE

Reinstatement as a remedy for wrongful dismissal is far more common in unionized settings. Geoffrey England has suggested that the presence of a union to police a reinstatement order ensures its success.[21] In contrast, reinstatement is not resorted to as frequently in non-unionized settings, despite its provision in various labour codes[22] — labour adjudicators are reluctant to require reinstatement in the face of opposition from an employer in the belief that this will engender hostility in the workplace.[23] It is ironic that the remedy is denied largely based upon the actions of the wrongdoer, thus belying the law's traditional reluctance to allow a wrongdoer to profit from his own wrong. England states that this approach can be contrasted with the prevailing attitude

---

19 *Knight v. Indian Head School Division No. 19*, [1990] 1 S.C.R. 653.

20 See *Kopij v. Metropolitan Toronto (Municipality of)* (1997), 29 O.R. (3d) 752 (Gen. Div.), overruled on the basis that the facts did support a finding that the plaintiff had been accorded procedural fairness (1998), 41 O.R. (3d) 96 (C.A.).

21 See G. England, "Section 240 of the *Canada Labour Code*: What are the Current Pitfalls?" in *Current Developments in Administrative and Employment Law: Some Things Old, Many Things New* (Ottawa: Canadians Bar Association, 1998) at 15.

22 See *Canada Labour Code*, R.S.C. 1985, c. L-2, s. 240.

23 In *Atomic Energy of Canada Ltd. v. Sheikholeslami*, [1998] 3 F.C. 349 (C.A.), the Federal Court of Appeal confirmed that under the *Canada Labour Code*, arbitrators had a right to reinstate and that this was meant to alter the common law position. However, difficulties with supervision and the problem of confidence still remained issues to be considered in the discretion to grant reinstatement. In this case the employee had lied to the arbitrator and this was the reason that he had declined to award reinstatement because it justified a lack of confidence by the employer in wanting to continue the relationship with the employee. The Court affirmed the decision of the arbitrator.

adopted by human rights tribunals, where reinstatement is routinely required and the employer further ordered to restore the workplace relationship.[24] Similarly, in some *Charter* cases where an employee has raised a challenge to mandatory retirement provisions, courts have been disposed to granting interlocutory relief requiring the employer to reinstate the employee pending a disposition of the case.[25] Thus, in both human rights cases and unionized settings, courts and specialty administrative tribunals are willing to scrutinize an employer's claim that the relationship is one based on confidence.

The Supreme Court of Canada's emerging approach to employment law places a high value on the role of employment in society, and recognizes how the role of work is fundamental to a person's well-being in ways that transcend mere economic benefit. Employment is a central way in which individuals define and identify themselves within the community, and the law must strike a reasonable balance between employer demands for efficiency and employee rights to dignity. Advancing specific performance as a remedy available to employees seems in keeping with this direction, because it is best able to protect the intangible interests now recognized as being associated with work. An obvious parallel with the protection of "consumer surplus" can be made. Making specific performance more readily available would not constitute a radical change. The award (and most likely an interlocutory injunction action), will simply protect the employee during a reasonable notice period if the employer is determined to terminate the employment. But, as any personnel relations consultant will advise, it is easier to secure alternative employment while employed than when unemployed.

A plea for specific performance will still necessitate that the plaintiff show that damages are inadequate, although this may be quickly assumed in light of the recognition given to work. The focus will then turn to evidence from the employer that there is a real concern about confidence and workability if the employer is required to take the employee back; this is perhaps the most significant change being suggested. The likelihood that an employer will seek specific performance is remote — the financial disincentives are just too great to make it a

---

24   See England, above note 21. See also R. Brown, "Contract Remedies in a Planned Economy: Labour Arbitration Leads the Way" in B.J. Reiter & J. Swan, eds., *Studies in Contract Law* (Toronto: Butterworths, 1980) 93.

25   See, for example, *Vancouver General Hospital v. Stoffman* (1985), 23 D.L.R. (4th) 146 at 153 (B.C.C.A.), where the hospital was required to reinstate the plaintiffs physicians' admitting privileges after they had been terminated because the plaintiffs' were over the age of sixty-five.

practical option against an employee who has terminated her employment without reasonable notice.

E. THE *LUMLEY* V. *WAGNER* INJUNCTION

Despite the traditional reluctance to award specific performance of the positive obligations contained in a contract for personal service, courts have been more willing to restrain a defendant from breaching her contract by enforcing negative obligations, either expressed or implied in the contract. When considering enforcement of personal service contracts it is important to remember that any clause in restraint of trade must first survive the substantive contract doctrine, which states that for these clauses to be enforceable they must be both reasonable and not against the public interest. Only when the clauses survive this scrutiny do we move onto the remedial considerations of whether they should be specifically enforced, either directly or indirectly.

The classic case expressing this doctrine is known as *Lumley* v. *Wagner*.[26] Wagner undertook to sing for Lumley at his theatre, two nights a week for a period of three months. She further agreed not to perform for anyone else during that period without Lumley's express consent. Wagner later contracted to sing for Gye at his theatre in Covent Garden. Lumley brought an action to restrain Wagner from singing for Gye. Lord St. Leonards V.C. held that while specific performance could not be given of the obligation to perform for Lumley, an injunction enjoining Wagner from singing for Gye could be granted. The granting of the injunction was not dependent upon finding an express negative stipulation, and one implied was sufficient. To do otherwise would be to "have broken the spirit and true meaning of the contract."[27] Lord St. Leonards V.C. was also conscious of the fact that the injunction may well have the effect of encouraging Wagner to fulfill her engagement.[28]

Lumley v. *Wagner* was further discussed in *Warner Brothers Pictures Inc.* v. *Nelson*.[29] Bette Davis, an American actress, had contracted to act when and where required by the plaintiffs for a period of one year, subject to further renewals by the plaintiff for a period of eight years. Concerned that the plaintiff would not give her appropriate roles now that

---

26 (1852), 1 De G.M. & G. 604, 42 E.R. 687 (Ch.).

27 *Ibid.* at 693.

28 Lumley later went on to sue Gye and in doing so established the tort of inducing breach of contract: see *Lumley* v. *Gye* (1853) 2 El. & Bl. 216, 118 E.R. 749 (Q.B.).

29 (1936), [1937] 1 K.B. 209.

she had achieved a certain celebrity status, Davis entered into another contract to perform for a third party in the United Kingdom. The plaintiffs quickly moved to enforce their contract by seeking an injunction to restrain the defendant from performing for anyone else. Branson J. granted the injunction, and stated:

> The conclusion to be drawn from the authorities is that, where a contract of personal service contains negative covenants the enforcement of which will not amount either to a decree of specific performance of the positive covenants of the contract or to the giving of a decree under which the defendant must either remain idle or perform those positive covenants, the Court will enforce those negative covenants ....[30]

The justification for granting an injunction in these cases is based upon the distinction between ordering a person to work for the plaintiff, as against ordering the person not to work for anyone else. However, enforcing the latter must not be tantamount to the former. Thus, much turns on the extent to which a defendant has alternative ways of earning a living other than being effectively compelled into performing for the plaintiff, and, the extent to which any alternative is similar in nature to the work to be performed under contract to the plaintiff. The level of compulsion set by Branson J. was low, and was satisfied if the defendant could find any form of employment even if it was totally unrelated to her chosen location. He had found Bette Davis to be

> a person of intelligence, capacity and means, and no evidence was adduced to show that, if enjoined from doing the specified acts otherwise than for the plaintiffs, she will not be able to employ herself both usefully and remuneratively in other spheres of activity, though not as remuneratively as in her special line.[31]

However, in *Warren v. Mendy*[32] the English Court of Appeal thought that Branson J. may have gone too far in favouring the employer by pitching the level of compulsion at such a low level. The court rephrased the test as follows:

> Compulsion is a question to be decided on the facts of each case, with a realistic regard for the probable reaction of an injunction on the

---

30   *Ibid.* at 217.
31   *Ibid.* at 219.
32   [1989] 1 W.L.R. 853 (C.A.).

psychological and material, and sometimes the physical, need of the servant to maintain the skill or talent. The longer the term for which an injunction is sought, the more readily will compulsion be inferred. Compulsion may be inferred where the injunction is sought not against the servant but against a third party if either the third party is the only other available master or if it is likely that the master will seek relief against anyone who attempts to replace him.[33]

In that case the plaintiff, a professional boxing manager and promoter, had sought an injunction against a rival promoter, who had induced a promising boxer originally under exclusive contract to the plaintiff. The injunction was intended to prevent the rival from acting for the boxer. The trial judge had refused to grant one, partially on the basis that because the plaintiff was likely to move against anyone seeking to supplant him as the boxer's sole manager, the effect of any injunction would be to compel the boxer back to the plaintiff. Since the boxer had lost confidence in the plaintiff, the order was not granted. The Court of Appeal affirmed the trial judge's exercise of discretion.

In one recent Australian case the level of compulsion is extremely low and only requires the defendant to have an alternative that will keep her from becoming destitute.[34] Australian courts have also varied the extent of the restraint imposed under the injunction to reflect the employment prospects of the defendant enjoined. Thus, in one case a professional football player, who also enjoyed a second career as a dental technician, was enjoined from playing football for any other club because he had the option of pursuing his dental technician's career.[35] Whereas, in a similar case involving the same football club, the defendant football player was only restrained from playing for any team against which the plaintiff club would compete, but was allowed to play in other football leagues because that was the only skill he had.[36]

---

33   *Ibid.* at 867, Nourse L.J., citing with approval the judgment of Stamp J. in *Page One Records Ltd.* v. *Britton (trading as The Troggs)* (1967), [1968] 1 W.L.R. 157 (Ch.) [*Page One Records*].

34   See *Curro* v. *Beyond Productions Pty. Ltd.* (1993), 30 N.S.W.L.R. 337 at 348 (C.A.) [*Curro*]. The decision is tempered by the fact that the court accepted that the *Lumley* v. *Wagner* injunction was only available in contracts for "special services."

35   See *Hawthorn Football Club Ltd.* v. *Harding*, [1988] V.R. 49 (S.C.).

36   See *Buckenara* v. *Hawthorn Football Club Ltd.* [1988] V.R. 39 (S.C.). See also discussion on this point in B. Kercher & M. Noone, *Remedies*, 2d ed. (Sydney: Law Book Company, 1990) at 203.

In Canada both *Lumley* v. *Wagner*[37] and *Warner Brothers*[38] have been referred to favourably, although there are few cases in which a Canadian court has been asked to enforce a negative stipulation contained within a contract of personal service. The case constantly cited in this regard is *Detroit Football Co.* v. *Dublinski*.[39] The plaintiff brought an interlocutory injunction application to restrain the defendant, a football player, from breaching his contract of employment that obligated him to play exclusively for the plaintiff's team. At the time, the defendant had accepted a position with a rival team in different football league. Wells J. declined to grant the injunction citing with approval Branson J.'s judgment in *Warner Brothers*. Two facts were highlighted in Wells J.'s judgment: one, the uncontroverted evidence of Dublinski that he would be unable to earn a living if prevented from playing football; and two, the inability of the plaintiff to show irreparable harm other than the loss of money spent on training the defendant and the inconvenience in securing a replacement. Dublinski did not possesses unique skills or ability.

When *Dublinski* came on for substantive hearing, McRuer C.J.H.C. devoted most of his judgment to whether the exclusive player clause was subject to the restraint of trade doctrine, and concluded that it was. However, he also held that before a plaintiff could get an injunction to enforce a negative stipulation, he would have to show some interest in restraining the defendant, other than merely seeking to coerce the defendant to honour the contract. Such an interest could be found if the defendant was proposing to join a competitor's organization in direct competition with the plaintiff. But in this case, all that the defendant had done was to join a team in a different league, not in direct competition with the plaintiff. Under this approach, both *Lumley* v. *Wagner* and *Warner Brothers* can be explained on the basis that the injunctions were necessary to prevent competitors from gaining the star appeal of the respective performers at the expense of the respective plaintiffs.[40] However, this does not appear to have been part of the decision in the cases of the same vintage as *Lumley* v. *Wagner*, and it seems to be very reminiscent of the requirement to establish a proprietary interest in order to enforce a restraint of trade clause.

---

37   See *I.L.A., Local 273* v. *Maritime Employers' Assn.* (1978), [1979] 1 S.C.R. 120.

38   See *Detroit Football Co.* v. *Dublinski*, [1955] O.W.N. 805 (H.C.) (interlocutory proceeding), varied [1956] O.R. 744 (H.C.), rev'd on a different issue [1957] O.R. 58 (C.A.).

39   *Ibid.* (H.C.).

40   But note that Sharpe, above note 10 at § 9.300, indicates that not all the cases can be reconciled on this argument.

In *Capitol Records – EMI of Canada Ltd.* v. *Gosewich*[41] the plaintiff sought an interlocutory injunction preventing its senior manager from taking employment with a competitor. The contract contained a clause preventing the defendant from inducing any of the plaintiff's artists from giving up their employment with the plaintiff. Lerner J. declined to give the injunction on the basis that the plaintiff had provided no evidence that the defendant had actually breached the clause, and because the effect of the injunction, if granted, would be to "probably cause him [the defendant] to remain idle for the balance of the term of his contract" and to prevent the defendant from being employed in a specific area in which he was most knowledgeable.[42] Interestingly, the plaintiff had offered to pay the full salary of the defendant during the remainder of the term of his contract and not require him to come to work, thus effectively sidelining him. This was rejected by Lerner J. and was used as an argument to support the suggestion that if the defendant was left to remain idle, even on full pay, he would still suffer irreparable loss.

It is difficult to summarize the current state of the law in this area. Clearly, there is a resistance to granting injunction if it will lead directly to the specific performance of the positive obligations in a personal service contract. This is particularly evident where the contract entails a relationship of confidence.[43] Beyond this, each case will turn on its particular circumstances. Some courts have purported to restrict the ambit of the injunction approach, confining it to cases of "special services" which have included artists, sports stars, and some senior managers.[44] Courts will scrutinize what choices the defendant will be left with if the injunction is granted. Courts are more likely to grant an injunction whose duration will be short, even if the defendant will be restricted from taking any alternative employment. A short period of idleness, presuming that the defendant is not persuaded to return to perform for the plaintiff, can be tolerated. However, if for longer periods the defendant will be prevented from pursuing her vocation, or cannot reasonably find alternative employment in another field, the injunction will be refused and the plaintiff confined to damages. Alternatively, an injunction will be framed so that it will only protect the plaintiff's interest over and above the plaintiff's desire for the defendant to return to her service.

---

41 (1977), 17 O.R. (2d) 501 (H.C.).

42 *Ibid.* at 504.

43 See *Page One Records*, above note 33; and *T-W Insurance Brokers Inc.* v. *Manitoba Public Insurance Corp.* (1997), 115 Man. R. (2d) 305 (C.A.).

44 See *Curro*, above note 34.

FURTHER READINGS

BALL, S.R., *Canadian Employment Law*, looseleaf (Aurora, Ont.: Canada Law Book, 1999) § 22.70

BRODIE, D., "Specific Performance and Employment Contracts" (1998) 27 Indust. L.J. 37

EWING, K.D., "Remedies for Breach of the Contract of Employment" (1993) 52 Cambridge L.J. 405

MCCUTCHEON, J.P., "Negative Enforcement of Employment Contracts in the Sports Industries" (1997) 17 Legal Stud. 65

CHAPTER 15

ENFORCEMENT OF CONTRACTS BY INJUNCTIONS

A. INTRODUCTION

We have already seen how injunctions can be used to enforce contractual terms; both in the preceding chapter, and in discussion of interlocutory injunctions in chapter two. In this chapter we focus on the use of injunctions to enforce negative stipulations contained within contracts outside the area of employment law.

A contract is normally considered to be an expression of positive conduct obligating the parties to perform the specific promises undertaken. One express promise could be the promise not to undertake a particular activity — an agreement not to open up in competition with the promisee, for example. However, an express promise can also infer a promise to undertake a particular task to the exclusion of all other tasks, (such as purchasing exclusively from the other contracting party). In both situations, courts have shown a willingness to grant injunctive relief. From early on courts have accepted that it was easier to restrain them from doing something than to order a person to carry out a particular act, and thus injunctions were routinely granted. However, courts would not allow injunctions to become a roundabout way to effect specific performance. Courts today are still mindful of this restriction, but are more willing to grant an injunction, preferring to focus on the substance of the dispute and on whether awarding an injunction will really violate some other discretionary concern.

B. TRADITIONAL APPROACH

The traditional approach has been articulated by the still often-cited judgment of Lord Cairns in *Doherty v. Allman (for Allen)*.[1] In that case the tenant of a property subject to a 999-year lease wished to make internal structural changes to the building so as to turn it from a storehouse into dwelling-houses. The holder of the reversion objected, and sought an injunction to restrain the lessee from making any changes. The court found that the contract did not contain any negative covenant preventing improvements to the property. Had it contained such a covenant, then:

> ...I apprehend, according to well-settled practice, a Court of Equity would have had no discretion to exercise. If parties, for valuable consideration, with their eyes open, contract that a particular thing shall not be done, all that a Court of Equity has to do is to say, by way of injunction, that which the parties have already said by way of covenant, that the thing shall not be done; and in such case the injunction does nothing more than give the sanction of the process of the Court to that which already is the contract between the parties. It is not then a question of the balance of convenience or inconvenience, or of the amount of damage or of injury — it is the specific performance, by the Court, of that negative bargain which the parties have made, with their eyes open, between themselves.[2]

The court then went on to determine whether similar considerations applied to affirmative covenants; in this case, the court could order specific performance, but the grant of relief was subject to the court's discretion, and particularly, whether damages would be an adequate remedy. In *Doherty*, damages would prove to be adequate if suffered at all. In addition, the lessee would be put to great inconvenience if not allowed to place the premises in a condition that would allow them to be rented, and therefore, the injunction was denied.

Doherty has been followed on numerous occasions, although the strict notion that a court has no discretion but to grant the injunction to enforce a negative stipulation has not been applied. Rather, later courts have characterized the question as one of discretion, seeing the rule as

---

1   (1878), 3 App. Cas. 709 (H.L.).
2   *Ibid.* at 719–20.

neither "rigid nor inflexible."[3] However, the position of readily enforcing negative covenants ahead of positive obligations has been followed. The justifications for this flow from the practical arguments that a court will not be engaged in complex issues of supervision of the injunction, and because the defendant's personal autonomy is not threatened as much as in specific performance. There is also the additional argument that damages are likely to be more difficult to calculate when the obligation is to restrain from doing some act as opposed to actually undertaking the act.[4] Sharpe has suggested[5] that damages will be "presumed" to be inadequate concerning the enforcement of negative covenants.[6]

Different considerations apply to interlocutory injunction applications. A plaintiff is still required to prove that damages are inadequate, and that irreparable harm will be suffered without the injunction. However, if the breach is plain and uncontested, or, in the case of a restraint of trade clause, the clause is reasonable, then the interlocutory injunction will be readily granted.[7]

C. MODERN APPROACH

One of the difficulties with *Doherty* is that by distinguishing between negative and positive covenants it invites a plaintiff to frame an otherwise positive obligation in negative form, so as to be able to gain greater access to injunctive relief where traditionally specific performance would not be available. It has been accepted that the principle in *Doherty* is not restricted to express negative covenants but has been

---

3   See *McDonald's Restaurants of Canada Ltd. v. West Edmonton Mall Ltd.* (1994), 159 A.R. 120 (Q.B.) [*McDonald*]; and *Servicemaster Industries Inc. v. Servicemaster of Victoria Ltd.* (1979), 101 D.L.R. (3d) 376 (B.C.S.C.).

4   See *A.G. v. Barker*, [1990] 3 All E.R. 257 (C.A.), where the defendant was restrained from breaching his contract, which included a confidentiality clause, and thus from disclosing information he had learned while in the employment of the royal household as a servant. The court suggests that in such a case damages would be difficult to calculate.

5   R.J. Sharpe, *Injunctions and Specific Performance,* looseleaf (Aurora, Ont.: Canada Law Book, 1998) at § 7.240.

6   Followed in *McDonald's*, above note 3. See also *Hampstead & Suburban Properties Ltd. v. Diomedous* (1968), [1969] 1 Ch. 248 at 259, Megarry J. [*Hampstead*].

7   See *Hampstead*, above note 6, followed in *Hardee Farms International Ltd. v. Cam & Crank Grinding Ltd.*, [1973] 2 O.R. 170 (H.C.); and *Miller v. Toews* (1990), [1991] 2 W.W.R. 604 (Man. C.A.).

applied where the negative covenant is merely implied.[8] It has been recognized for some time that enforcing a negative stipulation, either express or implied, by injunction can be tantamount to specific performance in a roundabout fashion.[9] For this reason, courts have said that they will not grant an injunction if the contract was incapable of specific performance. In a leading case on this point, *Fothergill v. Rowland*,[10] the plaintiff sought an injunction to prevent the defendant from entering into another contract to sell any of the coal from his colliery, which he had contracted to sell to the plaintiff for a period of five years. In declining orders for both specific performance and injunction, because the plaintiff could be adequately protected by a damage remedy for what amounted to breach of contract to supply ordinary goods, Jessel M.R. opined:

> I cannot find any distinct line laid down, or any distinct limit which I could seize upon and define as being the line dividing the two classes of cases — that is, the class of cases in which the Court, feeling that it has not the power to compel specific performance, grants an injunction to restrain the breach by the contracting party of one or more of the stipulations of the contract, and the class of cases in which it refuses to interfere.[11]

However, in spite of the reluctance to grant an injunction if that would be tantamount to granting specific performance, the *Doherty* approach has often found favour in enforcing long-term supply agreements, requiring the defendant to purchase exclusively from the plaintiff. In *Thomas Borthwick & Sons (Australasia) Ltd. v. South Otago Freezing Co.*[12] the New Zealand Court of Appeal granted an injunction requiring the defendant to honour its contractual commitment to buy, kill, and process stock exclusively for the plaintiff. The obligation had a further ten years to run. Cooke J. readily conceded that the injunction would effect specific performance in a roundabout way. He also noted that the advantage of the express negative covenant was that it "enables the court readily to define what the defendant may be

---

8   See *Metropolitan Electric Supply Co. v. Ginder*, [1901] 2 Ch. 799; and *Bower v. Bantam Investments Ltd.*, [1972] 1 W.W.R. 1120 (Ch.).

9   See *Wolverhampton & Walsall Railway Co. v. London & North Western Railway Co.* (1873), L.R. 16 Eq. 433; and *Whitwood Chemical Co. v. Hardman*, [1891] 2 Ch. 416 (C.A.).

10   (1873), L.R. 17 Eq. 132.

11   *Ibid.* at 141.

12   [1978] 1 N.Z.L.R. 538 (C.A.).

enjoined from doing," and, by emphasizing what the defendant had "unequivocally accepted," made it more difficult for the defendant to then set up hardship.[13] Similar cases exist in Canada, although they tend to be situations where the exclusive purchase requirement is linked to mortgage financing or to some other land purchase.[14]

Arguably, a distinction can be made in these cases. Enforcement of a negative stipulation leaves the defendant with a choice either to return to the strict terms of the contract, (in *Borthwick*, to continue purchasing from the plaintiff), or to comply with the injunction, if granted, by not purchasing from anyone else. Specific performance would allow only the former as a legitimate course of action. However, the practical effect of the order is to grant specific performance in a roundabout fashion. Few defendants are able or willing to make such a sacrifice as to forego any economic benefits of the contract. More commonly, what the defendant is losing is the opportunity to make additional gains above that expected from being forced to deal with the plaintiff.

The better view would be to reconcile the anomaly of *Doherty* with the contemporary position towards the availability of specific performance. If grounds exist to refuse specific relief — due to difficulties in supervision, or because the order smacks of imposing involuntary servitude — the order should be refused, regardless of whether it is framed as an injunction or an order for specific performance. However, if these concerns can be met then the order should be granted. In this sense, an injunction may be preferable to specific performance because the actual framing of the order may be more restrictive in ambit and thus readily capable of court supervision. Arguably, the anomalous position of *Doherty* may not be as great as suggested here. The recognition that its principles are subject to judicial discretion, and the fact that interlocutory applications (which includes restraint of trade covenants, confidentiality clauses, and the vast majority of these cases), already adhere to different criteria, tends to minimize any real differences in application.

---

13 *Ibid.* at 547.
14 See *Cities Service Oil Co.* v. *Pauley*, [1931] O.R. 685 (H.C.); and cases assembled in Sharpe, above note 5 at § 9.140.

D. INJUNCTIONS TO RESTRAIN AN INTERFERENCE WITH CONTRACT

The common law recognizes the tort of wrongful interference with contract, commonly called inducing breach of contract. The essence of the tort is the intentional interference by a tortfeasor in the contractual relationship of the plaintiff with another. The "intentional" requirement means that actual knowledge of the existence of a contract is an essential element of the tort.[15] Perhaps not surprisingly, equity[16] has developed a similar response in making injunctive relief available to prevent a person from interfering with the contract of another.

The initial expression of equity's development came in *De Mattos* v. *Gibson*.[17] The owner of a ship chartered it to the plaintiff for a voyage between Tyne and Suez. The owner then mortgaged the ship to the defendant, who had actual knowledge of the plaintiff's charterparty. The defendant was subsequently owed money for repairs he paid for on the ship and ordered it back to Newcastle. The plaintiff then sought an order for specific performance against the owner and an injunction against the defendant to restrain him from interfering with the charterparty. The orders were initially refused in interlocutory proceedings but granted on appeal. Knight Bruce L.J. summarized the legal principle:

> Reason and justice seem to prescribe that, at least as a general rule, where a man, by gift or purchase, acquires property from another, with knowledge of a previous contract, lawfully and for valuable consideration made by him with a third person, to use and employ the property for a particular purpose in a specified manner, the acquirer shall not, to the material damage of the third person, in opposition to the contract and inconsistently with it, use and employ the property in a manner not allowable to the giver or seller.[18]

In applying this rule the court granted an interlocutory injunction restraining the defendant from interfering with the plaintiff's charter voyage, although it was eventually lifted at trial as there was no evidence of interference with the charterparty.

---

15   See L.N. Klar, *Tort Law*, 2d ed. (Scarborough, Ont.: Carswell, 1996) at 498 ff.

16   The origin of this tort action derives from the case *Lumley v. Gye* (1853), 2 El. & Bl. 216, 118 E.R. 749 (Q.B.), the sequel to *Lumley v. Wagner* (1852), 1 De G.M. & G. 604, 42 E.R. 687 (Ch.).

17   (1858), 4 De G. & J. 276, 45 E.R. 108 (Ch.).

18   *Ibid.* at 110.

M.H. Ogilvie[19] has pointed out that the *De Mattos* rule was formulated before the doctrine of privity of contract had developed, and in the area of real property it was later superceded by the doctrine of *Tulk* v. *Moxhay*,[20] dealing with the enforcement of restrictive covenants over land. While the principle in *De Mattos* is clearly inconsistent with the privity of contract doctrine, that only a person who is a party to a contract can be subject to its liabilities, it has been subsequently applied in a few cases[21] although it has also received criticism in others.[22]

The difficulty with *De Mattos* is that it appears to grant a right exercisable over others without the need to establish a prior equitable interest. It is an accepted principle of equity that where a party can satisfy the requirements of a specific performance decree, they acquire an equitable interest in the subject matter of the contract.[23] This interest will only be defeated by any legal interest and by a *bona fide* purchaser for value without notice. The most recent formulation of the *De Mattos* principle given by Browne-Wilkinson L.J. suggests that a mere contractual interest alone will support an injunction against third parties:

1) The principle stated by Knight Bruce L.J. in *De Mattos* v. *Gibson* ... is good law and represents the counterpart in equity of the tort of knowing interference with contractual rights.

2) A person proposing to deal with property in such a way as to cause a breach of contract affecting that property will be restrained by injunction from so doing if when he acquired that property he had actual knowledge of that contract.

3) A plaintiff is entitled to such an injunction even if he has no proprietary interest in the property: his right to have his contract performed is a sufficient interest.

---

19   See M.H. Ogilvie, "Privity of Contract and the Third Party Purchaser," (1987–88) 13 C.B.L.J. 402 at 418.

20   (1848), 2 Ph. 774, 41 E.R. 1143 (Ch.).

21   See *Lord Strathcona Steamship Co.* v. *Dominion Coal Co.*, (1925) [1926] A.C. 108 (P.C.); and *Swiss Bank Corp.* v. *Lloyd's Bank Ltd.*, [1979] Ch. 548, rev'd on other grounds (1980), [1982] A.C. 584 (C.A.) [*Swiss Banks*]. In the context of a ship charter the *De Mattos* principle has been referred to with approval in *Banco Do Brasil S.A.* v. *Alexandros G. Tsavliris (The)*, [1992] 3 F.C. 735 at 749 (C.A.) citing Brandon J. in *The Myrto*, [1977] 2 Lloyd's Rep. 243 at 253 (Q.B.).

22   See *Port Line Ltd.* v. *Ben Line Steamers Ltd.*, [1958] 2 Q.B. 146.

23   Where property is sold under a contract the purchaser is said to acquire an equitable interest from the time the contract is entered. This principle is known as "conversion" and derives from the equitable maxim, "equity looks on that as done which ought to be done": see G.H. Jones & W. Goodhart, *Specific Performance*, 2d ed. (London: Butterworths, 1996) at 17–19, 22–23.

4) There is no case in which such an injunction has been granted against a defendant who acquired the property with only constructive, as opposed to actual, notice of the contract. In my judgment constructive notice is not sufficient, since actual knowledge of the contract is a requisite element in the tort.[24]

To the commercial lawyer, *De Mattos* is obviously a threat to certainty in commercial transactions — the principle reintroduces notice without registration of a prior contractual right as sufficient to affect a later purchaser's rights over chattels. However, where other parties are not adversely affected, there seems no reason to deny an injunction and good reason to support one in these circumstances. If a subsequent purchaser with actual knowledge of a prior equitable interest is bound by that interest, it is not too far to accept that a prior contractual right should also bind. The competing equities are the same.[25] Such an approach is also consistent with the growing tendency to erode the function of privity of contract where that doctrine merely protects the unmeritorious.[26]

FURTHER READINGS

COHEN-GRABELSKY, N., "Interference with Contractual Relations and Equitable Doctrines" (1982) 45 Mod. L. Rev. 241

OGILVIE, M.H. "Privity of Contract and the Third Party Purchaser" (1987-88) 13 C.B.L.J. 402

---

24   *Swiss Bank*, above note 21 at 575.

25   But see G.H.L. Fridman, *The Law of Contract in Canada*, 3d ed. (Scarborough, Ont.: Carswell, 1994) at 201 ff for a criticism of this development.

26   An example where the *De Mattos* principle could have application is in the sale of unascertained goods. While the original purchaser will not be entitled to a specific performance decree and cannot claim to have established any proprietary or equitable interest in the goods, they may, nevertheless, on the principle of *De Mattos* claim an injunction against any subsequent purchaser of the goods with knowledge of the plaintiff's contract.

CHAPTER 16

ENFORCEMENT OF EQUITABLE COURT ORDERS

A. INTRODUCTION

Equitable court orders of injunction and specific performance are principally enforced through contempt of court proceedings. Enforcement through the use of the courts' most coercive powers has been one of the distinguishing features of equitable relief. All superior courts of record have as an aspect of their respective inherent jurisdictions the power to exercise contempt of court powers. This power can be conferred by statute on other inferior bodies, but it cannot be removed from superior courts unless by constitutional amendment.[1]

B. CIVIL AND CRIMINAL CONTEMPT

The contempt of court power serves two distinct functions. One is to ensure that the court's order is obeyed as between the parties — this is often termed civil contempt. The other function is to maintain respect and integrity of the rule of law, and the public's support for judicial authority — this has often been termed criminal contempt. This distinction remains important but is often blurred by the courts.

---

1   See *MacMillan Bloedel Ltd.* v. *Simpson*, [1995] 4 S.C.R. 725 [*Simpson*].

1) Civil Contempt

The object behind civil contempt is to ensure compliance with the court's order. On occasion it has been called "private" contempt.[2] The aim of the court's intervention is to punish the contemnor for the violation or the harm committed to the complainant, rather than to the public or anyone else. The punishment is designed to coerce compliance and to compensate for the harm done, rather than to effect general deterrence or exact retribution.[3]

In a civil contempt the complainant must establish beyond a reasonable doubt all the elements of the complaint.[4] Those elements include actual knowledge of the order and evidence of its infringement.

2) Criminal Contempt

The object behind criminal contempt is to both punish and deter others from disobeying a court order. Deterrence has been described as the primary objective behind criminal contempt.[5] It is the "element of public defiance of the court's process in a way calculated to lessen societal respect for the courts" that transforms civil into criminal contempt.[6] The Supreme Court of Canada wrote:

> The gravamen of the offence is not actual or threatened injury to persons or property; other offences deal with those evils. The gravamen of the offence is rather the open, continuous and flagrant violation of a court order without regard for the effect that may have on the respect accorded to edicts of the court.[7]

---

2   See *Apotex Fermentation Inc.* v. *Novopharm Ltd.* (1998), 162 D.L.R. (4th) 111 (Man. C.A.).

3   See *Ibid.* at 191; *MacMillan Bloedel Ltd.* v. *Brown*, [1994], 7 W.W.R. 259 at 282–83, at 190 (B.C.C.A.); and *Lambert J.A.* v. *Bridges* (1990), 78 D.L.R. (4th) 529 at 532–33, McEachern C.J.B.C (B.C.C.A.).

4   See *Bhatnager* v. *Canada (Minister of Employment and Immigration)*, [1990] 2 S.C.R. 217 [*Bhatnager*].

5   *Ontario (A.G.)* v. *Clark*, [1966], 2 O.R. 547 at 580, Gale C.J. (H.C.) aff'd (1966), [1967] 1 O.R. 609n (C.A.), leave to appeal to S.C.C. refused [1966] S.C.R. vii [*Clark*].

6   *United Nurses of Alberta* v. *Alberta (A.G.)*, [1992] 1 S.C.R. 901 at 931, McLachlin J. [*United Nurses of Alberta*].

7   *Ibid.* at 932. See also *Poje* v. *British Columbia (A.G.)*, [1953] 1 S.C.R. 516 at 522, Kellock J.

Criminal contempt is a criminal offence, albeit one at common law, and all the element of the offence must be proved. McLachlin J. explained those elements as follows:

> To establish criminal contempt the Crown must prove that the accused defied or disobeyed a court order in a public way (the *actus reus*), with intent, knowledge or recklessness as to the fact that the public disobedience will tend to depreciate the authority of the court (the *mens rea*). The Crown must prove these elements beyond a reasonable doubt. As in other criminal offences, however, the necessary *mens rea* may be inferred from the circumstances. An open and public defiance of a court order will tend to depreciate the authority of the court. Therefore when it is clear the accused must have known his or her act of defiance will be public, it may be inferred that he or she was at least reckless as to whether the authority of the court would be brought into contempt. On the other hand, if the circumstances leave a reasonable doubt as to whether the breach was or should be expected to have this public quality, then the necessary *mens rea* would not be present and the accused would be acquitted, even if the matter in fact became public. While publicity is required for the offence, a civil contempt is not converted to a criminal contempt merely because it attracts publicity ... but rather because it constitutes a public act of defiance of the court in circumstances where the accused knew, intended or was reckless as to the fact that the act would publicly bring the court into contempt.[8]

There is no clear division between civil and criminal contempt and simply because a matter has started as a civil contempt does not prevent it being converted into a criminal contempt; although in the latter case, it is usual for the attorney general to bring forward the prosecution.[9]

---

8   *United Nurses of Alberta*, above note 6 at 933.
9   See *MacMillan Bloedel Ltd. v. British Columbia (A.G.)* (1996), 22 B.C.L.R. (3d) 137 (C.A.).

C. ELEMENTS OF A CONTEMPT CITATION[10]

1) The Order

It is perhaps axiomatic to say that there must be a court order before a person can be found in contempt. The order must be clear and unambiguous.[11] An order that is wrong, in that it is unconstitutional, under appeal, or simply incorrect, must still be obeyed until it is set aside. The appropriate response is to appeal the order, not disobey it.[12] An order of an inferior board or tribunal can be entered as a court order if the legislation creating the tribunal so provides. The court can then punish disobedience in the same way as it would for its own orders.

In extraordinary circumstances where the contempt is said to be *in facie* (in the face of the court) it is possible to have contempt proceedings without there having been a court order. This type of contempt proceeding is designed to cover matters where there is urgency, where it is imperative that the court act, and where all the circumstances of the alleged contempt are within the personal knowledge of the court such that the judge can act summarily.[13] For example, such contempt proceedings have been used where a witness has made verbal outbursts and refused to participate,[14] and where court staff involved in a labour dispute picketed outside the courthouse.[15]

2) Whom Does the Order Bind?

A court order will bind those to whom it is addressed. In addition, non-parties can be bound after they have received notice or been apprised of the order.[16] Commonly, a court order will be addressed to officers, members, and servants, to ensure that third parties do not aid and abet in the breaching of a court order.[17] These parties will themselves be in

---

10   See generally the material accepted by Teitelbaum J. as setting out the current position on the law of contempt in Canada, in *Tele-Direct (Publications) Inc. v. Canadian Business Online Inc.* (1998), 151 F.T.R. 271 (T.D.).

11   See *Skybound Developments Ltd. v. Hughes Properties Ltd.*, [1988], 5 W.W.R. 355 (B.C.C.A.).

12   See *Canada (Human Rights Commission) v. Canadian Liberty Net*, [1998] 1 S.C.R. 626.

13   See *R. v. Kopyto* (1987), 62 O.R. (2d) 449 (C.A.).

14   See *R. v. Bunn*, [1994] 10 W.W.R. 153 (Man. C.A.).

15   See *B.C.G.E.U. v. British Columbia (A.G.)*, [1988] 2 S.C.R. 214 [*B.C.G.E.U.*].

16   See *Simpson*, above note 1. See also discussion above in chapter 2, s.H, "John and Jane Doe Orders."

17   See *Z Ltd. v. A-Z and AA-LL*, [1982] Q.B. 558 (C.A.).

contempt where they have actual knowledge of the court order. Under special circumstances, knowledge can be inferred — it is possible that where a person's solicitor is made aware of the court order, the solicitor's knowledge will be enough to infer it to the actual client.[18]

The question of vicarious liability has not been settled in Canada. In *Bhatnager* v. *Canada (Minister of Employment and Immigration)*[19] the Supreme Court held that because contempt was largely a criminal offence the doctrine of vicarious liability had no role to play. There are a couple of exceptions: one is in the case of corporate liability, where there is no actual person to have the necessary *mens rea*; here, the theory of identification provides for the corporation to be held liable for the actions of a person who can be identified as its directing mind or will. Another exception is the principle of delegation, which only applies where the delegator is acting under a specific statutory duty that has been broken by the delegate. Even in the latter case, Sopinka J. held doubts as to its correctness in criminal law.[20] In this case the Minister for Employment and Immigration was not held either personally liable or vicariously liable for contempt when he failed to deliver a file by a certain date as requested by the court. There was no evidence that the Minister had been personally served or had knowledge of the court's order.

The position in *Bhatnager* can be contrasted with the result in *Beloit Canada Ltée/Ltd.* v. *Valmet Oy*.[21] In that case the Federal Court of Appeal (leave to appeal refused by the Supreme Court of Canada) indicated that a corporation could be held vicariously liable in contempt for actions by its agents and servants, or a third company established to circumvent the court order and under the control of the contemnor.[22] This is also the position adopted in the United Kingdom.[23]

The position in *Bhatnager* may have less relevance with respect to civil contempt where the goal is simply to ensure compliance.[24]

---

18 See *Bhatnager*, above note 4.
19 Above note 4.
20 *Ibid.* at 230.
21 (1988), 82 N.R. 235 (F.C.A.), leave to appeal to S.C.C. refused (1988), 21 C.P.R. (3d) v.
22 See also *Apple Computer, Inc.* v. *Minitronics of Canada Ltd.*, [1988] 2 F.C. 265 (T.D.).
23 See *Heatons Transport (St. Helens) Ltd.* v. *Transport & General Workers' Union* (1972), [1973] A.C. 15 (H.L.).
24 See R.J. Sharpe, *Injunctions and Specific Performance*, looseleaf (Aurora, Ont.: Canada Law Book, 1998) § 6.240.

3) What Constitutes Breach?

The *actus reus* of the contempt offence is the disobeying of the court order. A party must exercise every diligence to observe both the strict letter of the order and the spirit of the order.[25] For criminal contempt, the Crown must also prove that the contemnor defied the court order in a public way.[26]

The *mens rea* for civil contempt does not require the applicant to show that the contemnor intended to disobey the order. It is sufficient to prove that the contemnor had knowledge of the court order and in fact disobeyed it. For criminal contempt the test laid out by McLachlin J. must be met; the crown must prove beyond a reasonable doubt that the accused defied or disobeyed a court order in a public way with intent, knowledge, or recklessness as to the fact that the public disobedience will tend to depreciate the authority of the court.[27]

The intent of the contemnor and the presence of good faith can play a mitigating role when an appropriate sanction is being considered.[28] Casual, accidental, or unintentional acts of disobedience do not usually amount to contempt.[29]

4) Procedure

The procedure for bringing a contempt citation is determined under the respective codes of civil procedure.[30] For criminal contempt, it is usual for the Attorney General to bring the action, which can be done either pursuant to the Criminal Code[31] (section 127) or by simple motion. The court itself may also initiate proceedings.[32]

---

25 See *Canada Metal Co.* v. *Canadian Broadcasting Corp.* (No. 2) (1974), 4 O.R. (2d) 585 (H.C.), aff'd (1975), 11 O.R. (2d) 167 (C.A.).

26 See *United Nurses of Alberta,* above note 6. But note Cory J.'s dissent on this point at 913. Transforming civil contempt to criminal contempt should not turn on the simple issue of whether the contemnor has acted in public. Criminal contempt should turn on the issue whether there has been a real threat to the rule of law. Such an example would be where there is a real threat of violence or actions by large groups that could lead to a serious breakdown in social order.

27 See *United Nurses of Alberta, ibid.*

28 See *Baxter Travenol Laboratories of Canada Ltd.* v. *Cutter (Canada) Ltd.,* [1983] 2 S.C.R. 388.

29 See *Browne* v. *Britnell & Co.* (1924), 27 O.W.N. 232 (H.C.).

30 See for example, Ontario *Rules of Civil Procedure,* R.R.O. 1990, Reg. 194, r. 60.11.

31 R.S.C. 1985, c. C-46.

32 See *B.C.G.E.U.,* above note 15. (Injunction issued by Chief Justice enjoining picketing around courthouse).

D. SANCTIONS

The sanctions imposed for civil contempt tend to be modest. The normal practice is to suspend the penalty, to give the contemnor a chance to comply with the court order. However, even after complying, the contemnor may still be liable to criminal contempt so as to punish and deter others.[33] To ensure compliance the court can sanction a person to successive lengths of imprisonment, which will be discharged once the person has complied with the order. The court may also impose a fine, which is paid to the state rather than to the complainant — in the case of corporate contemnors a fine is the usual practice. The court can also order the sequestration of property until the contemnor has purged its contempt.

In the case of criminal contempt indefinite sentences are not appropriate. In the opinion of the Ontario Court of Appeal a sentence of over five years imprisonment for contempt of court could not now be supported.[34]

In determining the appropriate length of imprisonment, or fine, courts will be guided by similar principles applicable to criminal law sentencing. The court will look at

- the gravity of the offence,
- whether the action was deliberately planned, or an impulsive act,
- the possibility of reformation, and
- other mitigating factors; Has an apology been given? Has the contemnor admitted guilt? Was the protest non-violent.[35]

Sentences typically involve imprisonment of a few days or months,[36] fines for corporate contemnors lie in the thousand and hundred-thousand dollar range.[37]

---

33 See *Re Ajax & Pickering General Hospital* (1982), 35 O.R. (2d) 293 (C.A.).
34 See *R. v. Cohn* (1984), 48 O.R. (2d) 65 (C.A.).
35 See *Clark*, above note 5.
36 See *Simpson*, above note 1, approving of prison terms of thirty days and fines of $1000 and $1500 for violation of a prohibitory injunction issued to prevent logging protests.
37 See, for example, *R. v. B.E.S.T. Plating Shoppe Ltd.*, (1987), 59 O.R. (2d) 145 (C.A.), approving a fine of $100,000 against a corporate defendant, and six months imprisonment against the sole shareholder for continually flouting a prohibition order.

E. SPECIFIC PERFORMANCE

In addition to proceeding for contempt of court, a plaintiff in a specific performance suit can enforce judgment against a recalcitrant defendant by requesting the court to appoint a party to execute the court's order for specific performance. The disobedient party can also be ordered to pay the costs of the party appointed to execute the court's order.[38] Alternatively, the court may make a vesting order that conveys the property to the plaintiff.[39]

FURTHER READINGS

MILLER, J., *The Law of Contempt in Canada* (Scarborough, Ont.: Carswell, 1997)

---

38 See, for example, British Columbia *Law and Equity Act*, R.S.B.C. 1996, c. 253, s. 38; and *Federal Court Rules, 1998*, S.O.R./98–106, rule 431.

39 See, for example, Ontario *Courts of Justice Act*, R.S.O. 1990, c. C.43, s. 100.

CHAPTER 17

EQUITABLE DAMAGES

A. INTRODUCTION

In this chapter we explore the extent to which chancery courts can award equitable damages. Historically, chancery always exercised a jurisdiction to award monetary awards, either as equitable compensation (see below) or as an account of profits. However, the jurisdiction to grant damages was doubtful. By 1858 it was felt necessary in England to pass the *Chancery Amendment Act*,[1] better known as *Lord Cairns' Act*, so as to empower chancery courts with jurisdiction to award damages in claims for injunctions and specific performance.[2] Although the legislation was subsequently repealed, its sentiments have been retained, principally in legislation that describes the composition, procedure and jurisdiction of superior courts. In Ontario, section 99 of the *Courts of Justice Act*[3] reads as follows:

---

1   *An Act to amend the Course of Procedure in the High Court of Chancery, the Court of Chancery in Ireland, and the Court of Chancery of the Country Palatine of Lancaster, 1858* (U.K.), 21 & 22 Vict., c. 27.
2   For an excellent history of the development of this jurisdiction, see P. McDermott, *Equitable Damages* (Sydney: Butterworths, 1994)
3   R.S.O. 1990, c. C.43.

A court that has jurisdiction to grant an injunction or order specific performance may award damages in addition to, or in substitution for, the injunction or specific performance.

Similar provisions can be found in most other provinces,[4] although in some others the jurisdiction is derived from the express preservation of general equitable jurisdiction.[5]

It may appear paradoxical to award damages in lieu of an equitable remedy that is itself conditional on proving that damages is an inadequate remedy. But as we shall see, there are two situations where equitable damages come in to their own: where there is no common law remedy at all, or where the defendant has raised sufficient arguments against the awarding of specific performance or injunction so that the court is left with no alternative but to award damages.

Of late, the continued vitality of equitable damages as a distinctive form of redress has been undermined by developments in the availability of common law damages and equitable compensation. However, there are still important areas of difference. These will be the focus of this chapter.

B. JURISDICTION

The legislative jurisdiction for equitable damages states that they can be awarded in addition to or in substitution for an injunction or specific performance. Thus, if a court has jurisdiction to grant either an injunction or specific relief, it also has jurisdiction to grant equitable damages. In the past much debate was generated over whether barriers to specific performance and injunctions went to jurisdiction or merely discretion. If the barrier went to jurisdiction, then no damages could be awarded in lieu of the equitable relief. However, if the barrier was merely a discretionary impediment, the denial of equitable relief did not equally deprive the plaintiff of an award of equitable damages.

The jurisdictional issue was raised before the Supreme Court of Canada in *Dobson* v. *Winton & Robins Ltd.*[6] The plaintiff, a vendor, origi-

---

4   See Alberta *Judicature Act*, R.S.A. 1980, c. J-1, s. 20; Manitoba *The Court of Queen's Bench Act*, S.M. 1988-89, c. 4, s. 36; Saskatchewan *The Queen's Bench Act*, 1998, S.S. 1998, c. Q-1.01, s. 66(1); and Prince Edward Island *Supreme Court Act*, R.S.P.E.I. 1988, c. S-10, s. 32.

5   See Nova Scotia *Judicature Act*, R.S.N.S. 1989, c. 240, s. 41; British Columbia *Law and Equity Act*, R.S.B.C. 1996, c. 253, ss. 2, 4 & 5. In Newfoundland there appears to be something of a lacuna, where the adoption of English law took place before the enactment of *Lord Cairn's Act* and where no similar provision has since been enacted.

6   [1959] S.C.R. 775.

nally sought specific performance of a contract for the sale of land, but by the time the action was heard, he had sold the land and simply wanted to recover damages. One of the questions litigated was whether the plaintiff could amend his pleadings to allow for the claim for damages. Both lower courts had held that the plaintiff could not recover damages in lieu of specific performance, and the plaintiff's actions in selling the property now prevented such remedy. Without being able to grant specific performance the court had no jurisdiction to grant equitable damages in lieu. The Supreme Court affirmed this position but then approved of pleadings expressed in the alternative that kept alive the plaintiff's election to claim for common law damages. Although the decision leaves jurisdictional arguments unresolved, it is perhaps important to note that the court framed the problem as one of pleadings.

Of course, there are many circumstances where specific performance will not be granted. In previous chapters we have seen that difficulties with supervision, lack of mutuality, and adequacy of damages have all been given as reasons to deny specific performance. If these were perceived as always going to jurisdiction it would greatly diminish the ambit of equitable damages and would have serious repercussions on how one could adequately advise on their availability. While earlier judgments adopt this approach,[7] later decisions have tended towards conceiving these same matters as going only to discretion rather than jurisdiction.[8] (But see discussion below in section C, 4.)

Jurisdiction to award either an injunction or specific relief must have existed at the commencement of proceedings.[9] However, a plaintiff may also seek equitable damages after the commencement of proceedings if by the time of the hearing a right to have either specific performance or an injunction had accrued.[10] An award of equitable damages can also be made after equitable relief has been decreed.[11]

---

7   See, for example, *Lavery v. Pursell* (1888), 39 Ch. D. 508; and *Carter v. Irving Oil Co.*; [1952] 4 D.L.R. 128 (N.S.S.C.) [*Carter*].

8   See in particular the comments of Goff L.J. in *Price v. Strange*, [1978] Ch. 337 at 356, and Buckley L.J. at 370 (C.A.). See also G.H. Jones & W. Goodhart, *Specific Performance*, 2d ed. (London: Butterworths, 1996) at 278; McDermott, above note 1 at 54; and I.C.F. Spry, *The Principles of Equitable Remedies: Specific Performance, Injunctions, Rectification and Equitable Damages*, 5th ed. (Sydney: LBC Information Services, 1997) at 625 ff.

9   See *Brockington v. Palmer* (1871), 18 Gr. 488 (Ont. H.C.).

10 See *Roberto v. Bumb*, [1943] O.R. 299 (C.A.).

11 See *Johnson v. Agnew*, (1979), [1980] A.C. 367 (H.L.).

C. EXCLUSIVE CLAIMS TO EQUITABLE DAMAGES

There are a number of areas where in the absence of either specific performance or an injunction the plaintiff will have no right to common law damages. In these circumstances the only damages available are equitable damages.

1) Equitable Damages in Substitution For an Injunction Having Prospective Effect — *Quia Timet* Injunctions

Because there can be no violation of any common law right when a court is considering granting a *quia timet* injunction the plaintiff will have no right to damages at common law. In these situations the courts have been prepared to substitute equitable damages for the injunction, which are given for all future losses.[12] At the same time damages can be given for past losses in addition to the injunction. Where an injunction has already been issued, damages in substitution cannot be granted for the period covered by the injunction. However, if the injunction is later lifted damages can then be substituted.[13]

In the case of future trespass or nuisance cases the accepted test by which courts determine whether equitable damages should be substituted is that provided by A.L. Smith L.J. in *Shelfer* v. *City of London Electric Lighting Co.*:[14]

> [I]t may be stated as a good working rule that —
> 1) If the injury to the plaintiff's legal rights is small,
> 2) And is one which is capable of being estimated in money,
> 3) And is one which can be adequately compensated by a small money payment,
> 4) And the case is one in which it would be oppressive to the defendant to grant an injunction: —
> then damages in substitution for an injunction may be given.[15]

When the court will apply these criteria has already been discussed in chapter 7. One of the difficulties in this area is that once damages are

---

12   See *Leeds Industrial Co-operative Society Ltd.* v. *Slack*, [1924] A.C. 851 at 857, Viscount Finlay (H.L.).

13   See *St. Anne Nackawic Pulp & Paper Co. Ltd.* v. *C.P.U. Local 219*, [1986] 1 S.C.R. 704 at 727–28.

14   (1894), [1895] 1 Ch. 287 (C.A.) [*Shelfer*]. Applied in *Clark* v. *McKenzie* (1930), 42 B.C.R. 71 (S.C.), aff'd (1930), 42 B.C.R. 449 (C.A.) [*McKenzie*]; and *Mayo* v. *Hefferton* (1972), 3 Nfld. & P.E.I.R. 236 Nfld. S.C. (T.D.) [*Mayo*].

15   *Shelfer*, above note 14 at 322–23.

awarded for a prospective loss, there should be some way to prevent subsequent purchasers of the property from raising the continuing trespass or nuisance and requesting either an injunction or damages. At present there seems to be no way to encumber the land with such an order.[16]

2)   Equitable Damages for Breach of a Restrictive Covenant Affecting Land

Only in equity is a restrictive covenant enforceable against an assignee of the covenantor, and so only equitable remedies are available for enforcement.[17] While the usual remedy is an injunction there are occasions where equitable damages have been awarded in substitution of either a mandatory or prohibitory injunction. In *Wrotham Park Estate Co. v. Parkside Homes Ltd.*[18] the defendant had constructed a road and fourteen houses in breach of a restrictive covenant contained in a building scheme. Under the building scheme the defendant was required to obtain the permission of the plaintiff prior to any development, but had been poorly advised about the binding nature of the restrictive covenant. Brightman J. declined to order a mandatory injunction which would have necessitated the destruction of the homes. The homes had been occupied and the integrity of the overall building development had not been jeopardized. The plaintiff had not actually experienced any monetary decline in the value of his property and thus, arguably had not suffered any loss. Nevertheless, Brightman J. thought that to deny granting damages would be unjust in that the defendant would be benefiting from wrongdoing. He granted equitable damages, calculated on the basis of what a willing seller would have been prepared to accept to relinquish the right to enforce the restrictive covenant.[19]

Wrotham Park Estate has been affirmed in *Jaggard v. Sawyer*[20] and has been followed in Canada.[21] In *Arbutus Park Estates Ltd. v. Fuller*[22] the

---

16   See discussion by S.M. Waddams, *The Law of Damages*, 3d ed. (Aurora, Ont.: Canada Law Book, 1997) at § 13.540. In one United States case the land was encumbered with a servitude: see *Boomer v. Atlantic Cement Co.*, 257 N.E.2d 870 (N.Y. 1970).

17   See generally the discussion in the Ontario Law Reform Commission, *Report on Covenants Affecting Freehold Land* (Toronto: Ministry of the Attorney General, 1989) at 47–49.

18   [1974] 1 W.L.R. 798 (Ch.) [*Wrotham Park Estate*].

19   See Waddams, above note 16 at § 9.80.

20   [1995] 1 W.L.R. 269 (C.A.) [*Jaggard*].

21   See *Trawick v. Mastromonaco* (1983), 45 A.R. 276 (Q.B.); and *Arbutus Park Estates Ltd. v. Fuller* (1976), 74 D.L.R. (3d) 257 (B.C.S.C.) [*Arbutus Parks Estates*].

22   Above note 21.

defendant failed to build a garage in accordance with a building scheme. The court declined an injunction, largely because the restrictive covenant was vague as to what types of garages were permissible and thus it was difficult to determine the extent to which the defendant's garage violated the covenant. Although damages were not awarded, Toy J. indicated that the plaintiff could amend its pleadings, so that damages would be assessed as the savings the defendant had made in not retaining an architect to design an "aesthetically appropriate plan" for the garage.

3) Equitable Damages Based Upon a Right to Enforce a Contract through the Doctrine of Part Performance

Where a contract is unenforceable in law because it violates the *Statute of Frauds*, we have seen that the equitable doctrine of part performance may be called into assistance and the contract enforced in equity. No action for common law damages can exist because of the statutory impediment; however, equitable damages can be awarded in lieu of specific performance after the plaintiff has successfully raised the doctrine of part performance. This has also been recognized in Canada.[23]

---

23 See *Pfeifer* v. *Pfeifer* (1950), [1951] 1 D.L.R. 1227 (Sask. C.A.); and *Carter*, above note 7. But compare with the *obiter dicta* of Orsborn J. in *James* v. *Alcock* (1996), 143 Nfld. & P.E.I.R. 106 Nfld. (S.C. (T.D.)). See also the discussion by J.M. MacIntyre, "Equity — Damages in Place of Specific Performance — More Confusion About Fusion" (1969) 47 Can. Bar Rev. 644; and M.G. Bridge, "The Statute of Frauds and Sale of Land Contracts" (1986) 64 Can. Bar Rev. 58 at 87. One of the most glaring examples of this doctrine is given in the unreported New Zealand case of *Ward* v. *Metcalfe* (11 April 1990), Hamilton A 176/84 (H.C.), and discussed by R.O. Mulholland, "Part Performance and Common Law Damages" [1991] N.Z.L.J. 211. In that case the plaintiff had agreed to swap her existing unit in a condominium complex for a different one. The defendants never executed a formal transfer of title, although they had assisted the plaintiff to move and never objected to her possession of the new unit. The defendants sought to remove the plaintiff and she commenced proceedings to enforce her oral contract. By the time of trial the plaintiff's unit had been sold under a mortgagee sale, and she had been forced to move into a pensioner apartment. Fisher J. found that a contract existed through the intervention of specific performance. He then gave equitable damages in spite of the fact that it was impossible for him to award specific performance at the time of trial. What would be the position if the right to specific performance had been lost prior to the commencement of proceedings?

4) Equitable Damages for Rights Accruing in Equity's Exclusive Jurisdiction

Numerous rights traditionally arose only within equity's exclusive jurisdiction. Trust law is clearly recognized as being one such body of rights. However, in Canada it is often difficult to distinguish whether the court is articulating a right born from equity's exclusive jurisdiction or from common law development. Canadian courts tend to eschew debates about the fusion of law and equity and we increasingly tend to conceptualize our common civil law in one *corpus juris*. This development blurs what may previously have been clearly delineated approaches to remedies. For example, in the past it would have been readily accepted that the principles of damage assessment for common law damages and equitable damages were different and distinct — while differences remain, it could not now be said that the principles are distinct.

Equally blurred are the principles of assessment for equitable compensation (discussed below), equitable damages, and common law damages. In some situations, the breach of an exclusive equitable right will give rise to equitable compensation and in others, the right will give rise to equitable damages. There is no clear demarcation between these areas. Equitable compensation flows as an inherent remedy for breach of a substantive equitable right. Equitable damages flow from either adding to or substituting for an equitable remedy. Within this heading we can say that if the exclusive equitable right is normally protected by an injunction remedy then equitable damages can be awarded. However, often the pedigree of the substantive right in these cases is not attributed, and thus it is not clear whether the eventual damages remedy adopted by the court stems from common law damages or equitable damages.

For the equity purist, the jurisdictional underpinning of a particular substantive claim will be important because of differences in assessment principles applicable to equitable compensation, equitable damages, and common law damages. In the case of equitable damages, the necessary precondition must exist; that is, an entitlement to either specific performance or injunction.

To adherents of the fusion of common law and equity, jurisdictional differences are merely archaic anachronisms. The choice of remedy should depend upon the particular function (compensation, disgorgement, or punishment) to be fulfilled, and a balance of the equities involved. This approach still recognizes differences in assessment principles, but seeks to match those principles to the remedial goal being pursued rather than to the underlying historical jurisdiction for the cause of action.

From the most recent statements of the Supreme Court of Canada, the latter view prevails in Canada. In *Cadbury Schweppes Inc.* v. *FBI Foods Ltd.*,[24] a company called Duffy-Mott had licensed another company called Caesar Canning to produce Clamato juice. As part of this contract, Duffy-Mott had communicated confidential information about its product to Caesar Canning. Caesar Canning had in turn subcontracted with FBI Foods to produce the Clamato juice. Subsequently, Caesar Canning went bankrupt and FBI Foods purchased all its assets including the right to produce Clamato juice. Duffy-Mott was itself purchased by the Cadbury Schweppes Inc., the respondents. After purchasing Duffy-Mott, the respondents terminated the licensing agreement with FBI Foods. Under the original licensing contract, upon termination the appellants were forbidden from using the marketing term "Clamato," and from producing any combination of clam and tomato juice for a period of five years. Following termination, the appellants had been able to reproduce the respondent's juice without using clam juice and had marketed this product under the brand name Caesar Cocktail. The appellants had wrongfully utilized the confidential information communicated to it. The trial judge had found that the appellants would have been able to successfully launch a competitive product within twelve months of the termination of the licensing agreement; however, the use of the confidential information had given them a springboard. The trial judge awarded damages in the amount of what a consultant would have charged to assist in developing a new product. The trial judge declined a permanent injunction because of the prolonged period of delay by the respondents and because much of the confidential information was in the public domain or of little consequence. The Court of Appeal granted an injunction and ordered damages assessed on the profit that the respondents would have made in the twelve months following termination of the licensing agreement. This assessment assumed that the respondents would have sold the same amount of Clamato juice as Caesar Cocktail was sold in that period.

The Supreme Court was thus confronted with determining the appropriate remedy for a breach of confidence. The parties had argued that different remedial outcomes turned on the precise jurisdictional and doctrinal parameters of the right to confidence. The Supreme Court, Binnie J. giving the decision of the court, clearly saw the protection of confidences as originating in equity. However, the equitable doctrine could coincide with other causes of action lying in contract,

---

24   [1999] 1 S.C.R. 142 [*Cadbury Schweppes*].

tort, and property law. In this sense the jurisdiction of the law of confidence could be said to be *sui generis*.[25] Binnie J. then stressed the need to match the equities of the claim with an appropriate remedy: "In short, whether a breach of confidence in a particular case has a contractual, tortious, proprietary or trust flavour goes to the *appropriateness* of a particular equitable remedy but does not limit the court's *jurisdiction* to grant it."[26]

In determining an appropriate remedy, the court took into account a variety of factors. There was an absence of a fiduciary relationship or duty, there being no aspect of surrendering self-interest or vulnerability. The contract between the original parties did not negate any obligation of confidence owed between the parties. An analogy to patent protection was not favoured because the necessary bargain underlying that protection did not adequately describe the relationship before the court. Nor had the respondent traded patent protection in return for public disclosure of its trade secrets. All these factors militated against the use of a proprietary remedy. What the respondents had lost was the opportunity to market their Clamato juice free of any competition from the appellants for a period of twelve months following termination of the licensing agreement. This lost opportunity should provide the measure for damages. However, it should not be assumed that all sales of Caesar Cocktail made in the first twelve months were at the expense of Clamato juice. The "account of profits" measure was not favoured because the court could not conclude with any certainty that, "but for" the breach, the appellant would not have been able to compete in some legitimate way for the respondent's business. The respondent should be put to the task of actually proving its own lost profits.

Turning to the issue of equitable damages, Binnie J. noted that strict reliance upon the statutory principles of *Lord Cairns' Act* may prove unhelpful. The Act would not allow damages for any loss incurred prior to the application for the injunction.[27] The fact that the trial judge was disinclined to grant an injunction would open the jurisdiction to grant equitable damages up to challenge — had the judge declined to grant an injunction based on exercise of his discretion, or

---

25   *Ibid.* at 158, recalling the judgment of Sopinka J. in *LAC Minerals Ltd.* v. *International Corona Resources Ltd.*, [1989] 2 S.C.R. 574 at 615.

26   *Cadbury Schweppes*, above note 24 at 161.

27   This reason for limiting *Lord Cairns' Act* seems to be at odds with the intent of the legislation, in that it was partially designed to minimize the inconvenience on a litigant from having to move back into a common law court for a damage assessment.

because he believed there was no jurisdiction to grant an injunction at all? Finally, there may be a jurisdictional problem in cases where there is nothing to enjoin against the appellants. However, the narrowness of equitable damages under *Lord Cairns' Act* was offset by the expansive jurisdiction possessed to grant equitable compensation. Binnie J. stated:

> In my view, therefore, having regard to the evolution of equitable principles apparent in the case law, we should clearly affirm that, in this country, the authority to award financial compensation for breach of confidence is inherent in the exercise of general equitable jurisdiction and does not depend on the niceties of *Lord Cairns' Act* or its statutory successors.[28]

The approach taken by the Supreme Court presents a paradox. On the one hand, the comments on equitable damages appear to harden the jurisdictional boundaries issue, and thus run counter to the tendency to see these matters as going to discretion. However, on the other hand, the decision to award equitable compensation suggests that there is a broad-based inherent jurisdiction to award financial compensation for breach of any equitable right. The effect this has on the right to equitable damages under the previous three headings is not known but the direction of this judgment leads to the inevitable conclusion that for breach of an exclusively equitable right there is monetary compensation apart from equitable damages.

5) Equitable Damages and Injunctions Upholding Public Rights

One area where courts appear to have refused to grant damages in lieu of an injunction is where the court declines to grant an injunction to enforce a public right, unless it creates a private civil cause of action. Courts in New Zealand[29] and Australia[30] have refused to grant damages in such circumstances. One of the principle objections is that the wrong is suffered by the public at large rather than the individual. However, if the plaintiff has overcome the standing issue (discussed above in chapter 9), and the only reason the court is denying the injunction is on some equitable discretionary ground, there seems no reason why damages should not be substituted, even if the amount is

---

28   *Cadbury Schweppes*, above note 24 at 179.
29   See *A.G. v. Birkenhead Borough*, [1968] N.Z.L.R. 383 (S.C.).
30   See *Wentworth v. Woollahra Municipal Council (No. 2)*, (1982), 149 C.L.R. 672 (Austl. H.C.).

nominal. The substitution of damages here is similar to the tortious action for breach of statutory duty,[31] if that was allowed in Canada.[32]

D. NON-EXCLUSIVE CLAIMS TO EQUITABLE DAMAGES

In the vast majority of situations where a plaintiff seeks equitable relief, there is also a common law cause of action. An injunction is sought as part of equity's auxiliary jurisdiction. There is no barrier to granting equitable damages in lieu of specific performance or an injunction in these cases. In the past, often an equitable remedy was chosen because it was felt that procedural advantages would accrue in the damage assessment process. For example, it was often thought that the assessment date for equitable damages was different than for common law damages for breach of contract — the former being at the date of judgment, and the latter at the date of breach. The assessment principles are largely similar now, and if a plaintiff is denied equitable relief, there is no harm done by confining her to common law damages. The single biggest difference remaining is the fact that equitable damages can be given for prospective losses whereas common law damages are only awarded for actual losses. This brings an added advantage in that equitable damages can be awarded to avoid a multiplicity of suits, which would be the inevitable consequence of confining a plaintiff to common law damages for a continuing wrong.

It is possible to conceive of situations where damages at law prove inadequate, specific performance is declined, and equitable damages substituted. One example is the problem of the enforcement of a contractual benefit to a third party. The promisee's measure of damages is small because he has experienced no actual loss.[33] Specific performance has been favoured in similar situations in the past, but there is

---

31 See the discussion by P.D. Finn, "A Road Not Taken: The Boyce Plaintiff and *Lord Cairns' Act*" (1983) 57 Aust. L. J. 493 & 571; Spry, above note 8 at 437; and McDermott, above note 1 at 147 ff.

32 In Canada there is no independent tort of breach of statutory duty. The statute can be used to set a standard of care for an action in some other common law tort, such as negligence.

33 See Waddams, above note 6 at § 5.180, where he argues that common law damages could also be measured as the value of performance on the basis that by breaching the obligation the promisor has deprived the promisee the benefit of negotiating a release from performance of the obligation.

no theoretical problem with granting the promisee equitable damages in lieu of the specific performance decree. The damages should substitute for the value of the decree.

E. THE DISCRETION TO AWARD EQUITABLE DAMAGES

Unlike common law damages, which are awarded as of right, equitable damages remain discretionary.[34] The discretionary grounds that govern the awarding of specific performance or an injunction also play a role in determining equitable damages. However, the discretionary denial of the former does not preclude the awarding of the latter. In addition to factors such as delay and hardship, the court will also consider the criteria previously discussed in *Shelfer* v. *City of London Electric Lighting Co.*[35] The awarding of equitable damages allows for greater flexibility to balance the competing interests of the parties. If the awarding of equitable relief would cause the defendant hardship that is out of all proportion to the benefit obtained by the plaintiff, then damages will generally be favoured. An added advantage of equitable damages is that, although they are granted in lieu of an injunction, the plaintiff's interest is still being vindicated by the court through the use of a coercive rather than substitutionary remedy.

F. ASSESSMENT PRINCIPLES

1) Equitable Damages in Substitution for Specific Performance[36]

Equitable damages usually serve to provide compensation to the plaintiff. If the award is in substitution of a specific performance decree then the usual measure of equitable damages is similar to contract damages, and aims to put the plaintiff in the position she expected to be in through entering the contract. It was once thought that the assessment principles for equitable damages and common law damages differed,

---

34 See *McKenzie* v. *Hiscock*, [1967] S.C.R. 781; and *Elsley Estate* v. *J.G. Collins Insurance Agencies Ltd.*, [1978] 2 S.C.R. 916 at 935, Dickson J.

35 Above note 14.

36 For damages in addition to specific performance, see the section on specific performance and abatement chapter 12, S.C.

but the House of Lords in *Johnson v. Agnew*[37] held that they were the same. The plaintiff vendors of a property had entered into a contract to sell it to the defendant purchaser. The purchaser defaulted, and the vendor commenced proceedings to seek enforcement of the contract. An order for specific performance was granted; however, the purchaser continued to resist compliance. Some months later the mortgagee of the property exercised its power of sale and sold the property to a third party. From that point in time the vendor could no longer give specific performance and sought to claim damages for breach of contract. The disputed issue before the House of Lords was the appropriate measure of damages. Was the vendor to be confined to damages assessed at the original date of breach, or in substitution for specific performance when first ordered, or when the mortgagee exercised its power of sale, or at the date of judgment?

Lord Wilberforce stated a number of assessment principles that he termed uncontroversial. These principles confirm the right of the plaintiff to plead in the alternative for both damages and specific performance, leaving his election until trial. If the plaintiff accepts the defendant's repudiation of the contract, then the contract is brought to an end, and the plaintiff cannot at a later date revert to specific performance. Where the plaintiff pursues specific performance, the contract remains in effect. The plaintiff can seek to enforce the specific performance decree through contempt of court proceedings, or he may apply to dissolve the order and ask the court to bring the contract to an end. Where the plaintiff seeks the latter, the court can award damages for breach of contract. The damages will be assessed as at the date where, without his own default, the contract was lost. In *Johnson v. Agnew* that date was when the mortgagee exercised its power of sale and thus made specific performance an impossibility. Lord Wilberforce also indicated that in a situation where both common law damages and equitable damages were available the assessment principles did not differ, and equity followed the law.

Johnson v. Agnew was approved by the Supreme Court of Canada in *Semelhago v. Paramadevan*,[38] subject to what has already been said about the need for the plaintiff to establish a reasonable justification for pursuing specific performance. Both courts have affirmed the fact that the date of damage assessment is flexible both for common law and equitable damages. Equitable damages are to be awarded as a true substitute for

---

37   Above note 11.
38   [1996] 2 S.C.R. 415 [*Semelhago*].

specific performance, this means substituting damages when the decree is lost either because the plaintiff elects at a later time to accept the continuing repudiation of the contract by the defendant, or because the actions of a third party have made specific performance an impossibility.

Moving to a date of trial[39] for assessment purposes, on the basis that the specific performance decree is then lost, can have a dramatic effect on the quantification of damages particularly where there has been a significant market increase. For example in *Wroth* v. *Tyler*[40] the plaintiff purchaser had entered into a contract to purchase the defendant's property for a contract price of £6000. The vendor failed to close because his wife had lodged a caveat on the title to protect her matrimonial property interest. The plaintiff brought an action for specific performance. Megarry J. declined to award specific performance but gave equitable damages in substitution. At the date fixed for completion, which was the date of breach, the house was worth £7500. At the date of the hearing the property was worth £11,500. Megarry J. awarded damages calculated on the difference between contract price and the value of the property at the date of the hearing. Only this measure of damages would provide a true substitute in lieu of specific performance. Neither the House of Lords nor the Supreme Court of Canada disagreed with Megarry J.'s approach, although such a result could now be attained in common law. One issue left open is whether a plaintiff purchaser should be required to bring into account as a deduction in damages any savings realized in not having to carry finance charges between the date of completion and the date of trial. In *306793 Ontario Ltd.* v. *Rimes*[41] the Ontario Court of Appeal declined to make any such deductions. However, in *Semelhago* the same court approved deductions for both the savings on carrying charges for finance which would have been borrowed, as well as for interest actually earned on the money the purchaser had in hand to complete the purchase. In the Supreme Court of Canada this issue was not appealed although the Court did express doubt on how the Ontario Court of Appeal had distinguished its earlier ruling in *Rimes*. If there is to be a deduction for these carrying costs between completion and trial it seems only fair

---

39   The date should be the date of judgment, on the basis that it is from that point the court would usually make a decree for specific performance, which is being substituted by damages. However, the evidential foundation is usually provided based on damages proved at the date of trial, the date of judgment being beyond the control of the litigants. See *Semelhago, ibid.* at 425.

40   (1973), [1974] Ch. 30 [*Wroth*].

41   (1979), 25 O.R. (2d) 79 (C.A.).

that the vendor be made to account for any profits or savings realized through maintaining occupancy of the property.[42]

One further point from *Johnson* v. *Agnew* is whether the plaintiff must seek the court's intervention to dissolve the specific performance decree before seeking damages. This aspect of the judgment has been criticized,[43] although the court's supervisory role has recently been reaffirmed by the Ontario Court of Appeal.[44] (See discussion above chapter 11 section F, "Election").

2) Equitable Damages in Addition to or Substitution for an Injunction

In the case of equitable damages in addition to or in substitution for an injunction, equity will again usually follow the law. The usual measure of damages is to place the plaintiff in a position as if the wrong had not occurred. Thus in trespass, nuisance, and cases dealing with restrictive covenants the courts have substituted an injunction with damages measured as the loss suffered by the plaintiff.[45] However, this is not always the case, and the courts have been flexible in fashioning an appropriate response in damages. Part of the problem is that there are no common law principles for either continuing wrongs or prospective losses. In the case of damages in lieu of a *quia timet* injunction, the courts have been willing to measure the damages as the cost of undertaking remedial work to prevent the prospective injury from arising. In *Hooper* v. *Rogers*[46] the defendant had created a track below the plaintiff's farm house. In creating the track the defendant had removed soil such that there was a real fear that in time the plaintiff's house would be undermined. The court awarded the plaintiff damages in lieu of a *quia timet* injunction measured as the cost to the plaintiff of restoring and consolidating the soil to its original slope. On other occasions courts have turned to restitutionary principles and have awarded the

---

42 See Waddams, above note 16 at § 1.1230, makes the point that if no deduction is made from the damages reflecting the purchaser's carrying charges, then the purchaser ends up with the equivalent of the increase in market value of the property as a measure of damages, without having in any way been required to incur the cost of making that capital accretion.

43 See M. Hetherington, "Keeping the Plaintiff Out of His Contractual Remedies: The Heresies that Survive *Johnson* v. *Agnew*" (1980) 96 L.Q. Rev. 403 at 409–10.

44 See *Lubben* v. *Veltri & Sons Corp.* (1997), 32 O.R. (3d) 65 (C.A.).

45 See *Jaggard*, above note 20; *McKenzie*, above note 14; and *Mayo*, above note 14.

46 (1974), [1975] Ch. 43 (C.A.).

plaintiff equitable damages based on the benefits derived from the prospective infringement,[47] or on a judicial price set at what a willing seller would have accepted to relinquish the right to enforce an injunction.[48]

3) Limiting Principles

Whether the limiting principles of causation, remoteness, and mitigation differ for equitable damages has not been definitively determined. With respect to mitigation, the issue will be linked to whether the plaintiff had a reasonable justification for pursuing equitable relief. However, once she has exercised her election and reverted to common law damages the usual rules on mitigation apply. With respect to causation and remoteness, and to the extent that equity follows the law, similar common law principles should apply.[49] However, because equitable damages are always subject to traditional equitable discretionary defences, (i.e., clean hands, delay, and hardship), it may be that these concepts would have a different outcome when compared to the straight application of common law principles. For example, a plaintiff's conduct or delay may disentitle her to specific performance but the court may nevertheless still award damages in lieu which will equally reflect those equitable considerations. In comparison, there are no common law equivalents. The closest principles will be statutory limitation periods, contributory negligence, and the proposition that a person cannot benefit from their own wrong.[50]

By endorsing the approach adopted in *Johnson* v. *Agnew*, the Supreme Court of Canada has confirmed the position that common law damage assessment principles should always govern equitable damages. These principles include concepts relating to remoteness, causation, and mitigation. However, on other occasions the Supreme Court appears to have likened equitable damages to equitable compensation,[51] where the limiting principles are quite distinct from common law principles. (These are discussed in chapter 18.)

When considering the relationship of equitable damages to common law it is perhaps appropriate to be reminded of the observation made by Dickson J. in *Elsley Estate* v. *J.G. Collins Insurance Agencies Ltd.*

---

47   See *Arbutus Park Estates*, above note 21.
48   See *Wrotham Park Estate*, above note 18.
49   This would appear to be the approach adopted by Megarry J. in *Wroth*, above note 40.
50   See Spry, above note 8 at 646.
51   *Cadbury Schweppes*, above note 24.

How then should the measure of such damages be determined? It will generally be appropriate to adopt in equity rules similar to those applicable at law ... This is so not because the Court is obliged to apply analogous legal criteria, but because the amount of compensation which would satisfy the loss suffered, and which the Court considers it just and equitable be paid, usually happens to be equivalent to the amount of legal damages which would be appropriate. The award is still governed, however, by general equitable considerations which would not apply if the plaintiff were seeking damages at law rather than in equity. These considerations might serve, for example, to reduce the amount, due to such factors as delay or acquiescence.[52]

Where a case gives rise to concurrent claims for equitable and common law damages, it is sound policy to reach similar measures of damages. However, we should not rush to conclude from these cases that it would be better to completely subsume equitable damages into common law damages. There are particular areas where apart from equitable damages no monetary award can presently be granted. There are also distinctive concerns born from equity's procedures and methods which it is better to preserve than to extinguish.

FURTHER READINGS

JOLOWICZ, J.A., "Damages in Equity — A Study of *Lord Cairns' Act*" [1975] Cambridge L.J. 224

MCDERMOTT, P.M., *Equitable Damages* (Sydney: Butterworths, 1994)

TILBURY, M., "Equitable Compensation" in P. Parkinson, ed., *The Principles of Equity* (Sydney: LBC Information Services, 1996) c. 22

---

52   Above note 34 at 935.

CHAPTER 18

EQUITABLE COMPENSATION

A. INTRODUCTION

Equitable compensation is a remedy derived from equity's inherent jurisdiction.[1] In this sense it is quite distinct from equitable damages under *Lord Cairns' Act*.[2] It is perhaps surprising to speak of a compensatory remedy giving damages in equity. As we have seen, much of equity's remedial jurisdiction only flows following a finding that common law damages are inadequate: where damages are adequate, equity follows the law. Why then the development of equitable compensation? The chief reason is to provide remedies for the infringement of purely equitable rights. Where the common law would not recognize a given equitable right it was left to equity to create its own compensatory regime. Other equitable remedies award monetary relief; namely, specific performance with abatement, monetary adjustments accompanying rescission, and orders for an account. However, the goal of these remedies is usually restitution. The goal of equitable compensation is to compensate a plaintiff's actual provable losses.

---

1   See *Cadbury Schweppes Inc. v. FBI Foods Ltd.*, [*Cadbury Schweppes*], [1999] 1 S.C.R. 142; and I.E. Davidson, "The Equitable Remedy of Compensation" (1981–82) 13 Melb. U. L. Rev. 349.

2   *An Act to amend the Course of Procedure in the High Court of Chancery, the Court of Chancery in Ireland, and the Court of Chancery of the Country Palatine of Lancaster, 1858* (U.K.), 21 & 21 Vict., c. 27.

Recently in Canada, attention has been focused upon equitable compensation as part of the expansion of equitable rights, particularly fiduciary duties. There are now numerous situations where a relationship can be described as being fiduciary in nature yet the essential elements of a trust, (i.e., trust property), do not exist. In these situations the appropriate remedy for an infringement is often difficult to find. The type of breach committed by the fiduciary may not offend either the "profit" or "conflict" rules[3] which define the fiduciary relationships. The abusive and predatory sexual assault cases in *Norberg v. Weinrib*[4] and *M.(K.) v. M.(H.)*,[5] for example, do not immediately lend themselves to such classification.

As such, equitable compensation stands to become the remedy of choice at the confluence of three developments in the law relating to fiduciaries. First, where fiduciary relationships extend into new areas.[6] For example, it is possible to routinely find fiduciary relationships in commercial transactions, where one party undertakes to act in the interests of the other party with respect to a particular matter,[7] even where the parties stand at arms length. Another area has been in regard to fundamental human and personal relationships.[8] Second, as McCamus has identified, within the fiduciary relationship the recognition that the wrong can be other than an infringement of the profit and conflict rules has created a claim "essentially for failure to take proper care

---

3   These rules define the essential characteristics of a fiduciary as a person who does not profit from being entrusted with the beneficiary's property, and who does not allow her own self-interest to conflict with their duty owed to the beneficiary.

4   [1992] 2 S.C.R. 226 [*Norberg*]. A doctor breached his fiduciary duty when he took advantage of his patient's addiction to narcotics which he prescribed in exchange for sexual favours.

5   [1992] 3 S.C.R. 6. [*M.(K.)*] A father breaches his fiduciary duty owed to his child when he engaged in an incestuous relationship with his daughter.

6   See the articles by A. Mason, B.M. McLachlin & R. Cooke in section one, "The Place of Equity and Equitable Doctrines in the Contemporary Common Law World" in D.W.M. Waters, ed., *Equity, Fiduciaries and Trusts* (Scarborough, Ont.: Carswell, 1993).

7   See *LAC Minerals Ltd. v. International Corona Resources Ltd.*, [1989] 2 S.C.R. 574; and *Hodgkinson v. Simms*, [1994] 3 S.C.R. 377 [*Hodgkinson*].

8   See *Guerin v. Canada*, [1984] 2 S.C.R. 335 [*Guerin*]; *Norberg*, above note 4; and *M.(K.)*, above note 5.

in carrying out the task that has been assigned to the fiduciary."[9] Third, again from McCamus, recognition is now given to non-economic losses or interests being protected as part of the fiduciary's duties. New situations where equitable compensation is awarded are opening up all the time. It has recently been awarded as the appropriate remedy for breach of confidence in the absence of any fiduciary relationship.[10]

The similarity between these types of actions and traditional common law actions based on negligence or breach of contract where a duty of care is owed to the other contracting party, has raised the issue of what damage assessment principles will be applied, and whether the principles differ from common law principles.

B. ASSESSMENT PRINCIPLES

1) Historical Basis For Assessment

Because equitable compensation grew out of providing relief for breach of fiduciary duty the initial concepts of assessment drew heavily from trust law. The decision of the House of Lords in *Nocton* v. *Lord Ashburton*[11] is taken as confirming a general chancery jurisdiction to confer equitable compensation. In that case Lord Ashburton, acting on advice of Nocton, his solicitor, had been induced to advance £65,000 on mortgage. At a later time Nocton had advised Lord Ashburton to release some of the mortgage security. It was alleged by Lord Ashburton that in so doing Nocton had advanced his own security interest in the property and had rendered Lord Ashburton's security insufficient. Lord Ashburton subsequently lost both the principal and accrued interest and sued Nocton for breach of fiduciary duty. The House of Lords confirmed that such an action could be brought. The appropriate remedy was to indemnify the plaintiff, that is, to make restitution for the losses incurred, rather than award damages.

---

9   J.D. McCamus, "Equitable Compensation and Restitutionary Remedies: Recent Developments" (1995) Spec. Lect. L.S.U.C. 295 at 319–20. McCamus describes, at 304, the type of wrong in *Guerin*, above note 8, as "a failure to follow [the principal's] instructions [in negotiating a deal]"; and in *Canson Enterprises Ltd.* v. *Boughton & Co.*, [1991] 3 S.C.R. 354 [*Canson Enterprises*], as "failure to disclose information that would have been material to the principal's decision to enter into a transaction with someone other than the fiduciary and with respect to which the fiduciary had no personal interest."

10 See *Cadbury Schweppes*, above note 1.

11 [1914] A.C. 932 [*Nocton*].

The notion of restitution in *Nocton* is used in the sense of restoring the plaintiff to his position before the fiduciary's infringement. Another manifestation of this notion of restitution is provided in the influential decision of Street J. in *Re Dawson (dec'd): Union Fidelity Trustee Co. v. Perpetual Trustee Co*[12] A trustee improperly paid out £4700 in trust monies (New Zealand pounds). The funds were lost to the trust estate. The trustee was under a duty to restore the trust funds. At the time of the loss the New Zealand pound had parity with the Australian pound, but by the time of the action the Australian pound had lost parity and the trustee would be required to pay £5829 in Australian pounds. Street J., held that the trustee must effect complete restitution and pay the full amount regardless of the currency exchange fluctuations. For Street J., "[c]onsiderations of causation, foreseeability and remoteness do not readily enter into the matter."[13] However, it is significant to note that in *Dawson* equitable compensation is being ordered to restore trust property.

The notions of restoration from *Nocton* and *Re Dawson* can be contrasted with restitution proper, where the object of the relief is to make the fiduciary disgorge any unauthorized profits that she may have made from the breach of fiduciary duty. The rationale for the disgorgement approach is to keep the fiduciary "up to the mark." This remedy is pursued so stringently that it is often said to have a prophylactic effect, so that even where a principal could not have made the profit in his own right, the fiduciary is still required to disgorge the profit.[14]

Confusingly, the principles of equitable compensation assessment have been drawn from common law principles, fiduciary duty, and equity. Because restitution in the *Nocton* sense can closely resemble common law damage assessments for negligence, common law principles have been utilized. Because we are dealing with fiduciaries, the desire to effect some prophylactic or punitive response has been pursued. And, because we are dealing with equity and good conscience, there is a perception that the remedial schema should profess equity's with regard to damage-limiting principles.

---

12 [1966] 2 N.S.W.L.R. 211 (S.C.) [*Re Dawson*].
13 *Ibid.* at 215.
14 See P. Birks, *An Introduction to the Law of Restitution* (Oxford: Clarendon University Press, 1989) at 332.

2) Modern Canadian Developments[15]

Canadian jurists articulate two distinct positions on the relationship of equitable compensation to common law damages. The McLachlin J. position, which is subscribed to by Australian and English courts,[16] views equitable compensation as being quite distinct in its methods of assessment and quantification, extrapolating from trust principles, although sometimes drawing analogus support from the common law. LaForest J.'s position sees much less division between equitable compensation and the common law and indeed will only part from the latter where there are demonstrable reasons to do so. At the heart of this debate is the extent to which particular approaches to remedies should be used to reflect the more stringent standards of conduct expected of fiduciaries.

The McLachlin J. and LaForest J. positions come from their judgments in *Canson Enterprises Ltd.* v. *Boughton & Co.*[17] and *Hodgkinson* v. *Simms.*[18] In *Canson* the plaintiffs (Canson) had agreed to purchase a property on which they were intending to build a warehouse. The defendant, solicitor for Canson, was aware that the property had been "flipped" and that a secret profit was being made by an intermediary. The defendant did not profit from this "flip" or disclose the information to Canson. Following the purchase, Canson contracted with engineers to design and build a warehouse. Due to the negligence of the engineers, the warehouse began to sink. In an action against the engineers for negligence, the engineers were unable to pay all the damages, leaving Canson with a shortfall of $801,920. Based on the breach of fiduciary duty, Canson commenced an action against the defendant for the outstanding amount. In the course of the trial, Canson gave evidence that they would not have proceeded with the purchase of the property if they had been informed of the "flipping" and secret profit by the vendors.

---

15   Much of this material is taken from J. Berryman, "Equitable Compensation for Breach of Fact-Based Fiduciaries: Tentative Thoughts on Clarifying Remedial Goals" (1999) 37 Alta. L. Rev. 95.

16   See the endorsement given by the House of Lords in *Target Holdings Ltd.* v. *Redferns*, [1995] 3 W.L.R. 352 (H.L.) [*Target Holdings*], 785, and similar sentiments expressed by the Full Court of the Federal Court of Australia in *Commonwealth Bank of Australia* v. *Smith* (1991), 102 A.L.R. 453 (F.C. Austl.); and *Hill* v. *Rose*, [1990] V.R. 129 (S.C.).

17   Above note 9. See also P.M. Perrell, "Compensation and the Scope of Equity's Remedial and Restitutionary Generosity" (1999) 37 Alta. L. Rev. 114.

18   Above note 7.

McLachlin J. endorsed Street J.'s judgment in *Re Dawson*,[19] to the effect that full restoration had to be made, but quickly added a limitation stating that while the assessment should be made with the full benefit of hindsight, it is "essential that the losses made good are only those which, on a common sense view of causation, were caused by the breach."[20] Applied in *Canson* there was no link between the breach of fiduciary duty and the particular loss: "The solicitor's duty had come to an end and the plaintiffs had reassumed control of the property." LaForest J., speaking for the majority in *Canson* held that, where the measure of the duty is substantially the same as a common law duty, then, *in the absence of different policy considerations*, the result obtained in either common law or equity should be the same. Thus, common law doctrines of foreseeability, remoteness, and causation can be drawn by analogy into the quantification of equitable compensation.

In *Hodgkinson* the plaintiff was a person who had recently experienced a miraculous growth in personal salary and wished to shelter as much of it as possible from tax liability. The defendant was an accountant experienced in minimizing tax, particularly through the use of multi-unit residential buildings (MURBs), where the investor becomes a partner in a property development scheme. At the time the plaintiff approached the defendant for financial planning advice, the defendant was acting for Olma Brothers, a company that specialized in developing MURBs. The defendant was, in fact, instructing Olma on how to maximize the tax deductibility of the MURB schemes and had an arrangement that he would receive "extra billings" for any investors he referred to Olma. In the course of advising the plaintiff, the defendant suggested that he should invest in four of Olma's MURB schemes. The defendant did not disclose his relationship with Olma to the plaintiff. While the advice was quite sound with respect to minimizing the plaintiff's tax liability, it proved disastrous as an investment. Owing to a decline in the residential property market in Vancouver the plaintiff lost most of his investment. In a suit against the defendant, the plaintiff was successful in recovering the full value of his investment less the accrued tax advantage.[21]

LaForest J., speaking for the majority, held the accountant liable for breach of fiduciary duty. He applied a "but for" test: "But for" the

---

19 Above note 12.

20 *Canson Enterprises*, above note 9 at 556.

21 See also *Burns* v. *Kelly Peters & Associates Ltd.* (1987), 41 D.L.R. (4th) 577 (B.C.C.A.) (investment consultant held to a fiduciary duty to disclose conflict of interest and profit it was making on recommending the sale of certain Hawaiian condominiums as part of a balanced investment portfolio).

accountant's failure to disclose his personal dealings with the company, the plaintiff would not have purchased the investment, and would not have lost the value of it, even though that loss came as a result of the downturn in the Vancouver housing market. The defendant, not unnaturally, raised the causation issue from *Canson*. In particular, he argued that even if disclosure had been made, the plaintiff would still have invested in the real-estate tax shelters. This submission squarely confronted the *Brickenden* rule, taken from the Privy Council's decision in *Brickenden* v. *London Loan & Savings Co.*,[22] which states that where a plaintiff has made out a case of non-disclosure and has provided evidence of loss, the onus is upon the defendant to prove that the innocent party would have suffered the same loss regardless of the breach. This issue was dismissed by LaForest J. on the basis that the defendant had provided no evidence to rebut the plaintiff's assertion that it would not have made the investment had it know the true facts.

A second causation issue raised by the defendant in *Hodgkinson* was whether the failure to disclose was the proximate cause of the loss, an argument that had been successful in *Canson*. LaForest J. distinguished *Canson Enterprises*. In particular, in that case there "was no particular nexus between the wrong complained of and the fiduciary relationship," the loss was caused by the act of a third party unrelated to the breach of fiduciary duty, and the fiduciary solicitor did not "exercise any control over the risks that eventually materialized into a loss for the plaintiff."[23] In *Hodgkinson* the loss was directly related to the service the defendant had been retained to advise on, namely, suitable investments. The fact that a fiduciary relationship was found to exist was partially established by the fact that the defendant did exercise control over the plaintiff with respect to the types of investments and the commensurate risk he was exposed to. LaForest J. added that he did not see *Canson* as being a retreat from the principle of full restitution. Rather, it was at one end of the spectrum at which the fiduciary had been essentially innocent, as against the other end where a fiduciary is deceitful. LaForest J. commented:

> Put another way, equity is not so rigid as to be susceptible to being used as a vehicle for punishing defendants with harsh damage awards out of all proportion to their actual behaviour. On the contrary, where the common law has developed a measured and just principle

22   [1934] 3 D.L.R. 465 (P.C.) [*Brickenden*].
23   *Hodgkinson*, above note 7 at 445.

in response to a particular kind of wrong, equity is flexible enough to borrow from the common law.[24]

The defendant was held liable to make good all the losses on the investment, including those attributable to the decline in market value because of an economic downturn. As LaForest J. pointed out, without such a remedy, persons in the position of financial adviser would not be deterred from the very conduct undertaken. In the language of *Canson Enterprises*, there was now a sound policy justification — the recognition of the special duties held by financial advisers — necessitating a higher level of compensation than what was available at common law.

McLachlin and Sopinka JJ., who dissented on finding a fiduciary relationship, simply assessed the damages based on breach of contract. Under this assessment, no damages would be awarded for the shares' loss in value, for three reasons. Firstly, because a simple "but for" causation test was not utilised for either equitable or common law claims. Secondly, because the losses were not caused by the defendant's breach with respect to the inadequacy of the advice, but were brought about by forces beyond his control, and were thus not within the first rule of *Hadley* v. *Baxendale*.[25] And, thirdly, the losses caused by a downturn in the market were not within the reasonable contemplation of the parties as likely to arise from the defendant's failure to disclose, and therefore, not within the second rule of *Hadley* v. *Baxendale*.[26]

The Supreme Court of Canada has returned yet again to the assessment principles of equitable compensation in *Cadbury Schweppes Inc.* v. *FBI Foods Ltd.*,[27] the facts of which have been outlined in the previous chapter. For the court, the choice of appropriate remedy turned on matching the "remedy to underlying policy objectives,"[28] and they had four possible approaches to choose from.

One option was to confer a proprietary remedy of constructive trust, or equivalent equitable compensation, of the profits made by the defendant as if its sales were treated as assets that had been pirated

---

24   *Ibid.* at 444.

25   (1854), 9 Ex. 341, 156 E.R. 145.

26   LaForest J. does suggest that the assessment of common law damages for breach of contract in this case would result in a similar award to equitable compensation. This is based on the breach being a failure to provide independent advice rather than merely an obligation to disclose. This is somewhat difficult to maintain as the defendant had provided perfectly sound tax sheltering advice. See *Hodgkinson*, above note 7 at 454.

27   Above note 1.

28   *Ibid.* at 161.

from the plaintiff. This approach would have been favoured if a fiduciary relationship existed, but the court could find none.

A second approach was based on the notion that confidential information could be regarded as property and thus an analogy with the governing principles of damages assessment in regard to conversion of property could be made. The confidential information could be likened to intellectual property, again favouring a proprietary remedy. However, the court noted the controversy surrounding the idea that confidential information was "property." The information lacked the "bargain aspect" of intellectual property, where the patentee is given a monopoly in return for complete disclosure. Also significant from an intellectual property perspective was the fact that at trial the plaintiff had waived any right to claim either disgorgement or an accounting of profits.

A third approach was to award damages in substitution for an injunction. This has been discussed in the previous chapter.

A fourth option was to draw an analogy with tort damages. The plaintiff ran into difficulties here because of the trial judge's finding that the information was of little value and that the plaintiff had experienced no financial loss. The court admitted that different principles may apply to the assessment of common law damages when compared to equitable compensation. However, in this case the assessment under either approach would produce the same result. This conclusion turned on the finding that the basis of compensation was not the intrinsic value of the information itself — rather, it was the plaintiff's lost opportunity in not being able to market their product without the defendant's unfair competition for a year following the termination of the licensing agreement. How was this interest to be calculated? The trial judge had given the plaintiff the equivalent of what a consultant would have charged the defendant to assist in developing their competing product. The court did not favour this assessment, because the plaintiff was never in the business of selling its secrets or consulting. In the Court of Appeal the plaintiff had been given compensation based upon the profit the plaintiff would have made in selling its own product to the same levels achieved by the defendant in the year following termination of the licensing agreement. The Supreme Court accepted this, except that it required the plaintiff to prove its actual decline in sales rather than assume that all the defendant's sales would have gone to the plaintiff in absence of any competition.

After the decision in *Cadbury Schweppes* we are left with a situation where the Supreme Court has expressly endorsed McLachlin J.'s approach to equitable compensation assessment, yet has spent much of its time animating the policy differences, if any, that would justify a departure from common law principles of assessment. However, what is clear is that at some point there are distinct differences between the assessment of equitable compensation and those applied to common law damages.

3) Points of Difference Between Common Law Damages and Equitable Compensation

With respect to damage quantification the recognisable differences between common law and equity are:

- the role of causation and remoteness,
- whether contributory negligence or apportionment principles are applied,
- the effect of limitation periods,
- the heads of damages recoverable,
- the date of damage assessment,
- issues of mitigation, and
- the continued role of equitable presumptions.

a) Causation

The issue of causation has already been touched upon above. McLachlin J.'s approach confirms that the normal common law principles of causation, remoteness, and foreseeability do not apply to equitable compensation. In their place is the more amorphous concept of a "common-sense view of causation."[29] LaForest J.'s approach is similar to the tort of deceit in that it applies a "but for" test to establish "cause in fact." This is distinct from "cause in law" where LaForest J. calls into consideration other policy factors that may justify making the defendant the absolute insurer of the plaintiff's losses. An important policy factor will be the need to keep fiduciaries "up to the mark." In this sense, compensatory damages also serve an explicit punitive and deterrence function.

b) Contributory Negligence and Apportionment Principles

In *Canson Enterprises* the majority clearly adopted the judgment of Cooke P. in *Day* v. *Mead*[30] to the effect that equity would adopt, by reference, common law principles on apportionment and contribution.

---

29 See also the remarks of Lord Browne-Wilkinson in *Target Holdings*, above note 16 at 358–59, where he adopts McLachlin J.'s approach to assessment.

30 [1987] 2 N.Z.L.R. 443 (C.A.).

c) Limitation Periods

Where a claim lies in equity's exclusive jurisdiction, such as breach of fiduciary duty, there are no statutory limitation periods outside those relating to trusts and trustees found in the Limitation Acts.[31] However, such a claim will be subject to equity's analogous limitation rules centred around delay, laches and acquiescence. (See discussion in Chapter 7 D.1).

There is no doubt that many fiduciary claims in Canada have been advanced to gain advantage of equity's favourable limitation period.[32] However, this advantage may have been effectively eliminated by the adoption in tort law of the discoverability test for determining the point at which limitation periods commence to run.[33]

d) Heads of Damages Recoverable

Canadian courts have allowed both punitive and non-pecuniary damages to accompany claims for equitable compensation. In M.(K.) v. M.(H.)[34] the majority indicated that compensation for the sexual assault would be the same as that for the breach of fiduciary duty, where the underlying policy objectives animating the calculation of the damages were the same. McLachlin J. proffered a different opinion, suggesting that the respective actions may lead to differing results. In a number of sexual abuse cases, plaintiffs have argued that there are two distinct losses; one arising from the actual assault, often leading to a claim for non-pecuniary damages, and the other, from the breach of fiduciary duty. In subsequent cases, some courts have readily acceded to the majority's opinion that only one compensatory award should be made whether it is for breach of fiduciary duty or assault.[35] However, other courts appear to have granted compensatory damages under both causes of action[36] without any discussion on the possibility of double recovery.

---

31 See for example, in Ontario the Limitation Act R.S.O. 1990, c. L.15 ss. 42–44, and
    G. Mew, *The Law of Limitations* (Toronto: Butterworths, 1991) at 22 and 199.

32 See M.(K.), above note 5. In fact the same advantage was probably the reason
    fiduciary duty was advanced in *Nocton*, above note 11 after the plaintiff's claim in
    contract was statute barred: see *McCamus*, above note 9 at 301.

33 See *Kamloops (City of)* v. *Neilsen*, [1984] 2 S.C.R. 2; and *Central Trust Co.* v. *Rafuse*,
    [1986] 2 S.C.R. 147.

34 Above note 5. See also *Mustaji* v. *Tjin* (1996), 25 B.C.L.R. 220 (C.A.).

35 See, for example, *J. (L.A.)* v. *J.(H.)* (1993), 13 O.R. (3d) 306 (Gen. Div.).

36 In *C.(S.L.)* v. *M.(M.J.)* (1996), 179 A.R. 200 (Q.B.), Sullivan J. awarded both
    $100,000 as general damages for non-pecuniary loss as well as $75,000 damages
    for breach of fiduciary duty to each of the plaintiffs, daughters of the defendant
    who he had sexually assaulted over much of their respective childhoods. In *B.(P.)*
    v. *B.(W.)* (1992), 11 O.R. (3d) 161 (Gen. Div.), Cunningham J. awarded $100,000
    non-pecuniary damages and an additional $75,000 aggravated damages for breach
    of trust against a father who had sexually assaulted his daughter.

One novel suggestion is that equitable compensation may provide an opportunity to add damages for non-pecuniary losses, and aggravated and punitive damages, in more traditional scenarios of breach of trust or fiduciary duties. Where such a breach is accompanied by mental distress or anguish there seems no reason why such losses should not be recovered in order to achieve full compensation.[37]

e) Date of Damage Assessment and Mitigation

Assessment date and mitigation are inextricably intertwined. It is commonly said that the date for damage assessment in equity is the date of judgment or when the restoration of the trust property should have taken place.[38] But this is not a universal rule. It must be tempered by an obligation to mitigate — otherwise, the person to whom the fiduciary obligation is owed could speculate at the fiduciary's expense. In *Canson Enterprises,* McLachlin J. suggested that the requirements of mitigation may have to be relaxed when considering equitable compensation for breach of fiduciary duty. The requirement on a plaintiff to mitigate loss is part of the law's general incentive to an individual to safeguard their own self-interest. In a breach of fiduciary duty, the fiduciary has assumed a responsibility to act in the plaintiff's best interest; it would be somewhat inconsistent to require plaintiffs who have ceded control to the fiduciary to remain eternally vigilant of their own self-interest. While at some stage the plaintiffs may be expected to reassume the primary function of safeguarding their own interest, McLachlin J. indicates that this point will only arise when a plaintiff, "after due notice and opportunity, fails to take the most obvious steps to alleviate his or her losses," at which time we may conclude that the plaintiff is now the "author of his own misfortune."

f) Equitable Presumptions

There is an equitable presumption that the plaintiff is entitled to have compensation assessed as if she would have made the most favourable use of the property. In *Guerin v. Canada,*[39] the plaintiff was entitled to recover damages based on the value of the lost opportunity to develop the land at its most profitable use. The plaintiff did not have to prove that he would have, in fact, undertaken that development had the

---

37 See McCamus, above note 9 at 325.

38 See *Re Dawson*, above note 2; and *Target Holdings*, above note 6.

39 Above note 8.

Crown not breached its fiduciary duties. There is obviously some evidential advantage in this presumption although it did not alleviate the plaintiff's burden actually proving the damages.

Another equitable presumption is that enshrined in the *Brickenden* rule. It was cast by the Privy Council in the following manner:

> When a party, holding a fiduciary relationship, commits a breach of his duty by non-disclosure of material facts, which his constituent is entitled to know in connection with the transaction, he cannot be heard to maintain that disclosure would not have altered the decision to proceed with the transaction....[40]

As originally conceived, the rule operated as an absolute barrier to the defendant introducting evidence to prove that a plaintiff would have proceeded with the transaction even if disclosure had been made. The strict rule still has currency in Australia where it has recently been upheld by the High Court.[41] However, in Canada the rule now only survives as a presumption that shifts the onus upon the defendant to prove that the plaintiff would have proceeded with the impugned transaction regardless of the non-disclosure.[42]

C. CONCLUSION

The principles of equitable compensation remain in a state of flux in Canada. However, because Canadian law is at the forefront of developing fiduciary relationships (particularly in non-trust settings), and other equitable rights, the importance of the remedy is not to be underestimated. It will be problematic it the principles of equitable compensation provide higher levels of compensation than common law principles in cases which are open to concurrent actions in equity and common law. Some critics have already voiced concern over the creation of a form of equitable tort regime and the distortion of law of fiduciaries[43] that advancing equitable compensation may cause.

---

40   Above note 22 at 469.

41   See *Maguire* v. *Makaronis* (1997), 188 C.L.R. 449 (Austl. H.C.).

42   See discussion in Berryman, above note 15.

43   See J.D. McCamus, "Prometheus Unbound: Fiduciary Obligation in the Supreme Court of Canada" (1997), 28 C.B.L.J. 107; and P. Finn, "The Fiduciary Principle" in T.G. Youdan, ed., *Equity, Fiduciaries and Trusts* (Toronto: Carswell, 1989) 1.

FURTHER READINGS

BERRYMAN, J., "Equitable Compensation for Breach of Fact-Based Fiduciaries: Tentative Thoughts on Clarifying Goals" (1999) 37 Alta. L. Rev. 95

DAVIDSON, I.E., "The Equitable Remedy of Compensation" (1981-82) 13 Melb. U. L. Rev. 349

DAVIES, J., "Equitable Compensation: 'Causation, Foreseeability, and Remoteness'" in D.W.M. Waters, ed., *Equity, Fiduciaries and Trusts, 1993* (Agincourt, Ont.: Carswell, 1993) 297

MCCAMUS, J.D., "Equitable Compensation and Restitutionary Remedies: Recent Developments" [1995] Spec. Lect. L.S.U.C. 295

MCCAMUS, J.D., "Prometheus Unbound: Fiduciary Obligation in the Supreme Court of Canada" (1997) 28 C.B.L.J. 107

PERRELL, P.M., "Compensation and the Scope of Equity's Remedial and Restitutionary Generosity" (1999) 37 Atla. L. Rev. 114

RICKETTS C. & T. GARDNER, "Compensating for Loss in Equity: The Evolution of a Remedy" (1994) 24 Vict. U. Well. L. Rev. 19

RECTIFICATION

A. INTRODUCTION

The equitable remedy of rectification is one of great antiquity: it provides for the correction of documents that, until corrected, inaccurately record the intention of the parties. Although it is common to find the remedy included with the law of mistake, rectification only corrects errors in recording the intentions of the parties. It does not correct or provide relief for mistakes in subject matter or terms of a contract. Where the parties agree that they have inaccurately recorded their agreement, you would expect that they would agree to voluntarily correct the document. But because one party has a vested interest in resisting such a correction, these cases are continually litigated. The party pleading rectification may be trying to escape a bargain made improvident through a change of circumstances and will argue that the document does not record the parties' agreement. The opposing party will argue that it does, and that the other party is labouring under mistake.

Adding further confusion is the fact that Canadian courts have been opposed to allowing parol evidence to either alter, vary, or contradict a written contract.[1] A plea of rectification provides an exception to the parol evidence rule. Even if the plea is unsuccessful the probative value of the now admitted evidence may have a bearing on the

---

1   See *Hawrish v. Bank of Montreal*, [1969] S.C.R. 515.

other alleged causes of action. Thus, there is an incentive to argue rectification if only to surmount the parol evidence rule.

Rectification of a contract must also be kept distinct from *construction* of a contract. The former will look at how the subjective intentions of the parties have been recorded, whereas the latter will look at objective intentions as manifest by the contract. It is for this reason that particular attention is paid to the standard of proof required of a plaintiff in pleading rectification.

B. ELEMENTS

1) Instrument

Although rectification of contracts is the most common form of action, it is not restricted to contractual disputes. It is possible to have rectification of most instruments, including voluntary settlements, cheques, and leases.[2]

2) Continuing Intention

The basis of rectification is that the parties had a prior agreed intention, that has continued to the point at which the document was created, but which has been inaccurately recorded in the document, and this is what the plaintiff must show. While it was once said that the agreed intention had to have concluded in an antecedent oral contract, that is no longer required. It is sufficient to have a continuing intention on the disputed point even if the contract is only formally concluded when the document is created.[3]

The continuing agreed intention must have been clearly manifested by the parties in words or conduct. An undisclosed intention will not be sufficient. Similarly, the plaintiff must be able to prove the content of the agreed intention. It is not sufficient merely to show that the document is not an accurate record of the parties' intention. Because the court is imposing an obligation on the parties, the court must be assured as to the content of what was agreed to.

---

2   See the collection of instruments in I.C.P. Spry, *The Principles of Equitable Remedies: Specific Performance, Injunctions, Rectification and Equitable Damages*, 5th ed. (Sydney: LBC Information Services, 1997) at 609; and P. Parkinson, ed., *The Principles of Equity* (Sydney: LBC Information Services, 1996) c. 27 at¶ 2704.

3   See *Peter Pan Drive-In Ltd.* v. *Flambro Realty Ltd.* (1978), 22 O.R. (2d) 291 (H.C.), aff'd (1980), 26 O.R. (2d) 746 (C.A.), leave to appeal to S.C.C. refused (1980), 32 N.R. 538 [*Peter Pan Drive-In*]; and *Joscelyne* v. *Nissen*, [1970] 2 Q.B. 86 (C.A.).

3) Evidence

The court is entitled to hear parol evidence to establish the plea for rectification. The courts have insisted upon a high level of proof. It is still unclear what is the exact level — some courts have referred to the criminal standard of "beyond all reasonable doubt,"[4] others have adopted a lower standard of "convincing proof" or "irrefragable" proof.[5] The evidential burden is higher because the plaintiff is required to confront the natural inference that the existing written contract was an accurate reflection of the parties' agreement.

4) Mutual Mistake

The plaintiff must establish that the mistake in recording intentions was mutual. Where the mistake is merely one of inadvertently failing to record an agreed intention, or including a term that was not meant to form part of the document, rectification will be ordered. Where the mistake is not so much as to the inclusion or exclusion of a particular term, but is to the meaning and effect of those terms, rectification is more difficult. However, it has been said by one judge that rectification is "available where the words of the document were purposely used but it was mistakenly considered that they bore a different meaning from their correct meaning as a matter of true construction."[6]

5) Unilateral Mistake

Where the mistake in recording intentions is made by one party alone, and it is shown that the other party intended that result, it is difficult to argue that rectification has any place. There are situations where the court has ordered rectification flowing from a unilateral mistake; however, something more than mere unilateral mistake is required. The plaintiff must be able to show that the defendant knew of the plaintiff's unilateral mistake such that it would be tantamount to fraud or sharp practice to now take advantage of the plaintiff's mistake. This position has since been further ameliorated. In *Downtown King West Development Corp.* v. *Massey Ferguson Industries Ltd.*[7] Robins J.A. for the court said:

---

4   See *Brisebois v. Chamberland* (1990), 1 O.R. (3d) 417 (C.A.).

5   See *Peter Pan Drive-In*, above note 3.

6   *In re Butlin's Settlement Trusts*, [1976] Ch. 251 at 260, Brightman J. But compare *Rose (Frederick) (London) Ltd.* v. *William H. Pim Jr. & Co.*, [1953] 2 Q.B. 450 (C.A.).

7   (1996), 28 O.R. (3d) 327 (C.A.), leave to appeal to S.C.C. refused [1996] S.C.C.A. No. 258.

More recently, these limits on the availability of an remedy have been relaxed so that where one party is mistaken as to the terms of the agreement, and the other knows of the mistake and does not draw it to the attention of the mistaken party, it suffices that it would be inequitable to allow the non-mistaken party to insist on the binding force of the document, either because this would benefit him or because it would be detrimental to the mistaken party.[8]

And later in the judgment:

Equity and fair dealing in modern commercial transactions require that this form of relief be available in situations where one party may not actually have known of the other's mistake but the mistake was of such a character and accompanied by such circumstances that the party had good reason to know of it and to know what was intended.[9]

This would appear to be a fairly loose standard. In other courts the notion of inequitable conduct has been used to describe circumstances where the defendant has misrepresented or made false statements, or has done something else to contribute to the plaintiff's unilateral mistake.[10] To accept less may work an injustice on the defendant. As Waddams has pointed out, it is one thing to have the contract rescinded because of the unilateral mistake by one party — it is something else to force the mistaken party's understanding of the contractual terms onto the other party. Waddams suggests that this is why some courts have accorded the non-mistaken party the option of submitting to either rescission or rectification.[11]

---

8   *Ibid.* at 336.

9   *Ibid.* at 338.

10   See the discussion in *Commissioner for the New Towns v. Cooper (Great Britain) Ltd.*, [1995] Ch. 259 (C.A.).

11   S.M. Waddams, *The Law of Contracts*, 4th ed. (Aurora, Ont.: Canada Law Book, 1999) at § 343. The notion of an option for the non-mistaken party to either submit to rectification or rescission is supported by *Paget v. Marshall* (1884), 28 Ch. D. 255; and *Devald v. Zigeuner* (1958), 16 D.L.R. (2d) 285 (Ont. H.C.), although it has since been rejected in the United Kingdom: see *Riverlate Properties Ltd. v. Paul* (1974), [1975] Ch. 133 (C.A.).

6) Defences

As an equitable remedy, rectification is discretionary, and all the usual equitable defences apply. However, because there is no alternative to rectification it is rare that if a case is made out for rectification it will be refused on discretionary grounds. A right to rectification creates a "mere equity" so that it will not affect a third party interest.[12]

FURTHER READINGS

DAVIS, C., "A Restrictive Approach to Rectification?" [1992] Conv. & Prop. Law 293

FRIDMAN, G.H.L., *The Law of Contract in Canadian* 4th ed. (Scarborough: Carswell, 1999) 867 ff.

SPRY, I.C.F., *The Principle of Equitable Remedies: Specific Performance, Injunctions, Rectification and Equitable Damages*, 5th ed. (Sydney: LBC Information Services, 1997).

WADDAMS, S.M., *The Law of Contracts*, 4th ed. (Aurora, Ont.: Canada Law Book, 1999) § 336 ff.

---

12   See *Dominion Bank v. Marshall* (1922), 63 S.C.R. 352.

GLOSSARY

Anton Piller **order:** *Anton Piller* order takes its name from a decision of the English Court of Appeal in *Anton Piller K.G.* v. *Manufacturing Processes Ltd.* [1976] Ch. 55 (C.A.). The appellant, Anton Piller, was a German manufacturer of motors and electric generators used in the computing industry. The respondent was the appellant's agent in the United Kingdom. As agents the respondents had received confidential information surrounding the appellant's business. The Appellants found out that the respondents had been in secret communication with other German companies called Ferrostaal and Lechmotoren with a view to giving those companies detailed plans and drawings of the appellant's products so that they could be copied. The appellants were about to launch a new product and feared that details of it might get into the hands of competitors if the respondents were forewarned that the appellants were aware of the respondents breaches of confidence. Anton Piller commenced *ex parte* proceedings seeking an injunction to restrain copyright infringement as well as a court order to permit entry to the respondent's premises to search and remove all confidential information owned by the appellants. The injunction was granted but the order for inspection and removal was refused. The appellants appealed the denial of the latter order. In the Court of Appeal the order was granted. From this initial order has grown the jurisprudence on *Anton Piller* orders, commonly known as civil search warrants. (See chapter 5.)

Black: An expression used in trade union circles to indicate that a union has placed a restriction on a particular employer so that other trade union members will not have any dealings with the employer while they are engaged in an industrial dispute.

Clean hands: An equitable doctrine that purports to limit the availability of equitable relief where the applicant has been guilty of fraud or some other sharp practice in relation to the specific claim made against the defendant.

Consumer surplus: A measure of the personal idiosyncratic value that a person places on having possession of a particular chattel or realty. Consumer surplus is a measure of the price that an individual is prepared to pay, over and above the market value, for a particular commodity or service. There is a real fear that consumer surplus will be under-compensated when assessing damages for breach of contract or tort because it is based on idiosyncratic and subjective values and is therefore difficult to measure.

CISG – United Nations Convention on Contracts for the International Sale of Goods: This convention is the culmination of the work by the United Nations Commission on International Trade Law (UNCTRAL). The convention was approved at a Diplomatic Conference in 1980. Since that time the convention has been adopted and ratified in over 53 states including the majority of trading nations. The convention has been adopted and ratified in Canada and the respective Provinces. The convention applies to all contracts of sale of goods between parties whose places of business are in different states. However, the Convention excludes goods bought for personal, family or household use. The convention also provides for individual parties to contract out or vary the functioning of the Convention.

Certiorari: An administrative law remedy ordering an inferior court or tribunal to "deliver up" a case record (evidence, submissions and decision) for review by a superior court, and if appropriate, to set aside the lower decision.

Deponent: A person who makes an affidavit or gives evidence.

Enjoin: A court order, often an injunction, which instructs a party to refrain from continuing or starting a particular course or conduct.

Exigible: Subject to execution. Thus, assets that are exigible are those that the plaintiff is able to seize and to sell.

Ex relator: Taken from the term *ex relatione* used to describe an action commenced by the government on information filed by a citizen called the relator. It now refers to a person who is allowed to bring an action in the name of the attorney general. It is commonly used to allow an individual to bring an action to abate a public nuisance in the name of the attorney general.

Gravamen: The essence or fundamental issue in a dispute.

Hadley v. Baxendale: A decision of the English Court of Exchequer that established the rules on remoteness of damages ((1854), 9 Exch. 341, 156 ER 145). The plaintiff was a miller. His mill had stopped because of a breakage of the mill's crankshaft. The plaintiff had contracted with the defendant, a common carrier, to take his broken crankshaft to a manufacturer to be used as a template to cast a new crankshaft. The defendant had delayed in shipping the crankshaft. As a result the plaintiff had lost profits caused by the delay in having his mill made operational. The defendant argued that the plaintiff's losses were too remote in that at the time of entering the contract the lost profits could not have been contemplated by the parties. The court held that the damages were too remote. In doing so the court established two rules for the determination of remoteness of damages in contract:

[1] A defendant will be liable for damages that may reasonably be supposed to have been in the contemplation of the parties arising in the normal course of events.

[2] Where special circumstances are communicated, a defendant will be liable for damages that may have been reasonably contemplated by the parties acquainted with that special knowledge.

These principles are widely known throughout the common law world. For an excellent article explaining the history and consequences of this case see, F. Faust, "*Hadley* v. *Baxendale* – an Understandable Miscarriage of Justice", (1994), 15 *J. of Legal History* 41.

In camera: A proceeding that takes place either in a judge's chamber or a courtroom where all but the parties have been excluded so as to preserve confidentiality an privacy.

In personam: An *in personam* claim only determines the rights between the respective parties to the action and does not affect the rights of any other third party. Thus a right *in personam* can only be asserted against a party to the dispute. It is to be contrasted with an *in rem* claim.

In rem: An *in rem* claim determines the rights of all parties regardless of whether they were part of the dispute. A right *in rem* can be asserted against all the world and everyone must respect the claimant's right.

In specie: In kind. The specific thing itself.

Irrefragable: Unanswerable. Irrefragable proof is evidence that cannot be contradicted.

Lis pendens: A pending lawsuit. The term is commonly used to describe a notice to a third party who is interested in acquiring real property that a prior claim has been made to the property and is pending the resolution of a lawsuit.

Mandamus: An administrative law remedy of a superior court that orders an inferior court or tribunal to exercise its jurisdiction, or for a public official to do his duty.

Mareva **injunction**: *Mareva* injunction takes its name from a decision of the English Court of Appeal in *Mareva Compania Naviera S.A.* v. *International Bulkcarriers S.A.* [1975] 2 Ll. Rep. 509 (C.A.). It is a particular type of injunction that allows a plaintiff to restrain a defendant from disposing or otherwise remove assets away from the court's jurisdiction pending the final resolution of the plaintiff's action. See Chapter 4.

Mutuality: Mutuality of remedy, is a doctrine of equity that requires the court to consider the availability of appropriate equitable relief to a defendant before granting the plaintiff the equitable relief that he has proved that he is otherwise entitled to. See discussion Chapter 10.

Parens patriae: Literally means the father of the country. It refers to the right of the crown to exercise a form of guardianship over the state and persons in need. It is commonly used to indicate the right of the crown to enforce public rights and to represent the public interest.

Parol: Oral. Parol evidence is oral evidence. A parol contract is usually though of as being a purely oral contract. In some circumstances a parol contract is any contract that is not made under seal.

Pretium affectionis: Similar to consumer surplus. It is the subjective value that a person puts on a thing because of her personal attachment to the item.

Prior restraint: Censorship before publication. It commonly refers to attempts to restrain publication of material prior to a court adjudicating on whether the publication would give rise to any civil action such as defamation or breach of confidence.

Quia timet: Literally means, "because he fears." It refers to an action for either an injunction or damages prior to the plaintiff having suffered any actual loss but because such harm is threatened.

Replevin: An ancient common law action that allowed a person to bring a summary action to recover personal property unlawfully taken. It is now a form of summary action that allows the plaintiff to take custody of personal property in which the ownership is disputed. See Chapter 13.

Rescission: An equitable remedy that annuls or avoids a contract. Rescission is a remedy granted to a plaintiff in the case of fraud, innocent misrepresentation, or because of some other action on the defendant's behalf that amounts to undue influence, unconscionability or makes the bargain questionable on some other equitable grounds. Rescission in equity operates to roll the contract back to the position the parties were in prior to contracting. This is referred to as rescission *ab initio*, or "from the beginning." It is to be distinguished from rescission *de futuro*, or "for the future." The latter terminology is unwisely used to describe the position of a plaintiff who is entitled to terminate a contract for breach. As an equitable remedy rescission is subject to a number of discretionary barriers including delay and affirmation. It is also important for the plaintiff to be able to effect *restitutio in integrium*. That requires both parties to be restored to their pre-contractual positions. The degree of complete restoration will vary depending on the particular underlying cause of action. In the case of fraud a court will be less particular with giving complete restoration, whereas for an innocent misrepresentation, anything less that complete restoration will bar rescission.

Riparian: pertaining to water or shoreline. Riparian rights refer to the rights of landowners who abut a lake, river, or shoreline to have access and use of the water.

Stare decisis: The legal doctrine that obligates a lower court to follow and apply the decisions and precedents of a higher and superior court in the same judicial hierarchy.

Trace, tracing: The right of a party to follow property into the hands of a defendant and other third parties. It is common to find tracing as a remedy for breach of trust or other breach of fiduciary.

UCC – Uniform Commercial Code: This is the principal legal statute covering all aspects of the sale of goods and secured transactions in the United States. The code originated in the work of the National Conference of Commissioners on Uniform State Laws and the American Law Institute who were charged with creating a uniform sales law for all states to adopt. Since the first edition, published between 1942 and 1952, the code has undergone subsequent revisions, the most recent being in 1990, and has been adopted in all the states of the United States.

Ultra vires: Literally means, "beyond the powers." A person who acts *ultra vires*, acts outside the scope of her authority.

Undertaking: An assurance. It is commonly used to describe a promise made by either a party or his lawyer to the court to perform a particular task. A party seeking an interlocutory injunction will normally be required to give an undertaking to pay any damages the defendant may incur as a result of the injunction having been wrongfully obtained by the plaintiff.

Use: Benefit. The beneficial ownership of property. Thus, a person entitled to the beneficial ownership of property subject to a trust is known as a *cestui que use*.

TABLE OF CASES

INDEX

ABOUT THE AUTHOR

Jeff Berryman. LL.B., M.Jur., LL.M., is Professor of Law at the Faculty of Law, University of Windsor, where he teaches remedies and contract law. He is a member of both the Law Society of Upper Canada and a barrister and solicitor of the High Court of New Zealand. He is a contributing author to the only Canadian casebook on remedies, *Remedies: Cases and Materials* (Emond Montgomery, 1977), now in its third edition, and has written extensively on remedies both in Canada and internationally.